SKETCHES
OF CURIOUS EVENTS AND PRACTICES
in the Lives of the Intriguing People
Who Inhabited Early America.

SKETCHES
OF
CURIOUS EVENTS
AND PRACTICES
IN THE LIVES OF THE
INTRIGUING PEOPLE
WHO INHABITED EARLY AMERICA.

BY
FRANK E. KURON

TOLEDO, OHIO
KURON PUBLISHING
2024

Kuron Publishing
Copyright © 2024 by Frank E. Kuron

All rights reserved, including the right of reproduction
in whole or in part in any form.

Designed by Frank E. Kuron

Manufactured in the United States of America

ISBN 979-8-218-36571-4

For Those Who Love to Ponder

CONTENTS.

ILLUSTRATIONS		viii
PREFACE		ix
ACKNOWLEDGEMENTS		xiii
SKETCH I	From Where to Eternity	1
SKETCH II	Temper, Temper Mr. McGary	27
SKETCH III	Watchdogs of the Wilderness	63
SKETCH IV	The Winds of Change	95
SKETCH V	No More Squabbling	163
SKETCH VI	I Spy…	187
SKETCH VII	The Lore of Loramie Creek	229
SKETCH VIII	One for the Road	267
SKETCH IX	Fightin' and Hangin' Around the Firelands	293
SKETCH X	The Stars Behind the Star Spangled Banner	325
HMMM…	26, 61, 94, 161, 184-185, 227, 265, 292, 323,	353
SKETCH NOTES		354
INDEX		367

ILLUSTRATIONS.

Heart of the Monster 5	Martha 183
Creation Turtle 12	1700s Dress 185
Hopewell 17	Arthur St. Clair 191
The Sillibaboo 22	Josiah Harmar 194
Harrod's Town 31	Washington's War Map 201
Battle of Blue Licks Map 40	Piominko 204
Rachel (Donelson) Jackson 57	Richard Sparks 204
Andrew Jackson 57	William Wells 219
William Whitley 66	Roche de Bouef 227
Fort Logan 69	Ohio Rivers Map 230
Canebrake 70	Celeron Plate 237
Wilderness Road Map 75	Celeron Ceremony 242
Whitley House 1934 76	Loramie Creek Map 251
Whitley House 2008 77	John Johnston 260
Whitley House Brickwork 77	Mesopotamian Cylinder Seal 269
Whitley House Staircase 78	Medicine Advertisement 1799 272
Sportsman's Hill 87	Old Stone Tavern 281
Simon Kenton 102	Treber Inn 284
Boonesborough 109	Firelands Map 299
Bryan Station 114	Cleveland Public Square 302
Dorchester Heights Map 119	Lorenzo Carter 307
Battle of Long Island Map 124	Joshua R. Giddings 314
Washington Crossing 131	Marblehead Map 317
Battle of Stony Point Map 134	Marblehead Memorial 322
Race to the Dan Map 139	Francis Scott Key 327
Battle of the Chesapeake 146	Star Spangled Banner 330
Battle of Lake Erie 155	Fort McHenry Map 337
Passenger Pigeon 165	Indian Queen Hotel 342
Shooting Pigeons 168	Mary Scott Pickersgill 347
Netting Pigeons 173	George Armistead 347
Junius B. Booth Jr. 180	

PREFACE.

This is the third history book I've written. It is the second one to be created in a format of "sketches" rather than "chapters." The reason for this is that these are stand-alone stories; not necessarily a sequence of events. This template is purposefully used in an attempt to mimic the style of some of the books written in the early American era. Many historians of that day wrote in a form that mixed biography with story-telling. This book, like my previous work, attempts to be a similar blend of personal profile and literature.

One may have noticed that the title of this book like its predecessor is quite lengthy. This too is intentional, as many books of the 1700s and 1800s had very long headings. Paperback books with colorful covers are a relatively recent development. Books from early America were mostly hard-bound. If they had an imprint, it was minimally made on the cloth-covered binding. The first paper page of these books was usually the title page, and it was congested with the heading and pertinent attributions. My cover designs are an attempt to transform that title page format of old into a contemporary outside cover.

Several of the stories in this book are sketches of the broader beliefs, conditions, and occurrences in the lives of people who dwelled in North America before our time. For this reason the title is somewhat inverted from that of the first book, *Sketches of Intriguing People and the Curious Events They Suffered While Living in the Wilderness of the Northwest Territory*, to, *Sketches of Curious Events and Practices in the Lives of the Intriguing People Who Inhabited Early America*. As one will see, the sketches in this book are not exclusive to events in the Northwest Territory, hence the further change in its title.

The purpose behind writing these books is to present the facts of history, not opinions. The reader may find that I have gone to the brink of offering opinion in some of these sketches, but I sincerely hope that I have successfully avoided stepping over that precipice. My purpose is to make one honestly consider the past as they evaluate the present.

In many ways the people of early America were different from the people of today, but in many more ways they were identical. Some were good, some were bad. Some good people on occasion did bad things; and some bad people occasionally did good things. As found throughout time, all had a sense of right and wrong. Living conditions may have been very different from what is experienced today, but basic emotions and moral standards were generally similar. The reader is entitled to evaluate any given person or situation of history and come to their own conclusions about their character or the appropriateness of an event or practice. That can only be done fairly by knowing the context of those times.

Although an author can sway an audience toward a particular perspective by the information he or she decides to include or exclude; I have made every effort to present a balanced story. It is not my purpose to espouse any agenda, political view, or prejudice toward anyone or anything in America's early history. My goal is to trigger the reader to simply think a little longer and deeper about the situations experienced, and the lives lived, before ours. Perhaps this will generate a clearer perspective on the some of the challenges being faced today.

The old adage of wanting to hear something "directly from the horse's mouth" applies in my approach to these sketches. The use of longer than usual quotes, and many of them, is deliberate. It is my hope that in so doing the reader will get a glimpse of the personality of the individuals cited, as well as their unadulterated, first-hand comments. This being said, I have placed myself in the position of compiling pertinent background information so that the true context of these remarks and observations can be discerned. I have endeavored to write all the sketches in an easy to understand and entertaining style, much like a short story, in the hope that through them one can momentarily step back in time.

On a grammar note, the use of various punctuation symbols needs a short explanation. Every effort has been made to reproduce any and all quotes in the exact form in which they were found by the author. Sometimes documents were discovered in poor condition with parts of their original content missing or illegible. Because of this, the use of an ellipsis (...) is used to fill the gap of indiscernible, missing, or purposefully omitted words. If parentheses, ( ), or underlines (_), or *italics* appeared in the original documents, they have been left unchanged. Anything found in brackets [ ] is the author's addition; inserted to clarify or make the passage more readable.

Throughout the regular text, parentheses appear for any extraneous notations deemed necessary by the author.

Regardless of whether any of the individuals or occurrences recounted in this book are familiar to you, it is my hope that you will now discover, or re-discover, them. The people of early America, with their experiences and approaches to life, are worth knowing because they are a part of our foundation. These souls were far more complex than the sometimes romanticized caricatures which some of them have since been turned into. They had goals and setbacks, they prayed and backslid, they worried and laughed, they were single and married, some raised families and some raised hell!

My hope is that their words and experiences might generate a spark of appreciation for a time gone by. And, perhaps my re-telling of their stories will fan that spark of interest into a flaming desire to learn even more about them and history in general – which is so much more intriguing than anything one can make up. ♦

THE AUTHOR

ACKNOWLEDGEMENTS.

While researching my first book, I discovered a good deal of historical material that was truly fascinating; however, not relevant to my topic at hand. Therefore, I decided to write a second book, by which means I could tell the stories of those people and events that I had found earlier. Through that writing process, even more curious tales were uncovered, but they were too numerous to fit into one book. This third effort presents that additional material, and more, which I felt was just too intriguing not to be told.

This time around, as before, many people were very helpful in many ways. First, I sincerely thank Jesus, for giving me the desire and ability to write. (Thanks, also, for keeping me alive to see this work to its completion!) Ever since I began my writing adventures nearly twenty years ago, the support of my wife Debra has never waned. Her gentle nudges of reassurance always turned me away from occasional feelings of frustration. She, along with my son, Major Matthew Kuron, have served as my editors and proofreaders — two crucial responsibilities. The moral support I received in the past from the rest of my immediate family and close friends, has continued as well. Special thanks go to my daughter, Sara, and son-in-law, Doug Wegrzyn.

I have to admit that the research on this book came somewhat easier than it had for my first two works. That is due to the magic of the worldwide web. Previously, a large amount of time and money was required for travel to libraries, museums, and historical societies in order to track down the old records that make up much of the content of my books. However, because many of those organizations have been digitally scanning their antiquated documents and making them available online, I was able to surf rather than drive to these sources of information. Please take a bow, academia!

Still, several institutions which provided materials and insights were visited in person or electronically and their staffs need to be thanked. These include: The Library of Congress, the Toledo Lucas County Public Library, the Allen County Public Library, the OhioLINK Library System, the Ohio History Connection, the University of Toledo Carlson Library, the Bowling Green State University Jerome Library, and the William L. Clements Library at the University of Michigan,

A few individuals made the stories herein more accurate by contributing their expert knowledge. A special "thank you" goes to Dr. Edwin Barnhart, Director of the Maya Exploration Center, for his insights on the ancient Indian cultures of South and North America. And, while working on an archaeological dig of the recently discovered Fort Loramie, Ken Sowards and Mark Schulze, historians of the Piqua, Ohio region, graciously took an extended amount of time to share their long-studied understanding of the site and the events that transpired there.

Further appreciation is due to Jerome P. Brubaker, Curator of the Old Fort Niagara Association; Adam Rubin, librarian at the Buffalo History Museum Research Library; Susan G. Pearl, Historian at the Prince George's County Historical Society; Linda Huber of the Ottawa County Museum; and Emily Brown, Librarian at the Naval History and Heritage Command.

I would like to conclude by thanking the many historians, history enthusiasts, historical site employees, re-enactors, and numerous other individuals who shared their personal knowledge, as well as stories of their own ancestors and events, of early America. I have been blessed to have made the acquaintance of so many people with a deep interest in our heritage.◆

I.
FROM WHERE TO ETERNITY.

> In fourteen hundred ninety-two,
> Columbus sailed the ocean blue...

Remember that verse? If you were schooled in the twentieth century you most likely do, as it was widely read in classrooms across the country as a means of making 1492 one of the most remembered dates in history. Later lines in the poem added,

> ..."Indians! Indians!" Columbus cried;
> His heart was filled with joyful pride.
> But "India" the land was not;
> It was the Bahamas, and it was hot. [1]

Along with untold volumes of history books, this light-hearted poem solidified the fact that, at least when he first landed, Columbus thought he had arrived at his intended destination – the East Indies. Today this includes the islands of Malaysia, the Philippines, New Guinea and others situated in the eastern region of the Indian ocean. Hence, Columbus named the people he found living where he landed "Indians." In actuality, he had landed in the Bahama Islands and then Cuba and other islands of the Caribbean.

In the minds of fifteenth century Spaniards, it was generally believed that only three continents made up the world: Africa, Asia, and Europe. And interestingly, Jerusalem was geographically at the center of that known world, which adds a spiritual dimension to their understanding. European minds were quite settled on this point. Therefore, some historians suppose that Columbus wouldn't have been able to fathom the idea that a new, unknown continent could have possibly stood in his way of reaching the East. They suggest that the only concern on Columbus's mind was the distance from Spain to the East coast of the Asian kingdoms and his ability to endure the trip. As noted, he probably truly believed he had arrived in the East Indies; but some historians come away with a different point of view. After studying Columbus's own writings, they interpret them to be proof that he knew full-well that he had discovered a new continent; however he wanted this knowledge, and the treasures found there, to be kept his and Spain's little secret. We'll leave that argument to those who have thoroughly studied the records.

A bigger question surrounds the people that Columbus met on those islands situated just off the coast of the new continent. How did those "Indians" come to be living there in the first place? Just as historians have differing opinions regarding where they think Columbus believed he had landed; to this day they likewise continue to disagree about the origins of the people he made contact with. The term "indigenous" is very often used when referring to those he met. But that is a tricky word. It can mean people originating, from scratch so-to-speak, in a particular region or country. But, it can also take a subtle turn to mean the earliest people to inhabit a region or country. The latter leaves the door open to the idea that although the inhabitants are the first to be somewhere, they might not have been created there. Instead, they may have been the first to have gotten there — from somewhere else. This is a key point as we'll soon see.

The origin of the Native Americans is at least a curiosity to most people; and in academic and scientific circles it is being studied with more and more fervor. The descendents of cultures based in Europe, Africa, and Asia have ready access to records of their history that go back millennia. Such is not the case for the people of the Americas.

The North, and to a lesser degree the South, American histories seem to start with the days of Columbus, or there about. Only in relatively recent years has progress been made in trying to unearth what transpired earlier. New archaeological discoveries are being made on a regular basis, and the information gathered from them has finally begun to lay the groundwork for learning the true history of the American continents before Columbus, and before Christ.

Attempts to discern the authentic ancestry of today's Native

Americans gets complicated. Well-intentioned and well-studied historians, archaeologists, anthropologists, and the like, have come to sometimes very different conclusions about the origins of people in the Americas. Their interpretations, and sometimes assumptions over the facts, lead to hypotheses, and then to theories, that can be at odds with each other. The diverse opinions, however, shouldn't dissuade us from trying to find the truth. Instead they should encourage us to reason through them even deeper. After all, every theory has some truth in it in order to validate its being offered for consideration in the first place. That is until something disproves it. So let's analyze the most credible, and some of the more intriguing, suppositions whilst keeping a wary eye toward inconsistencies.

The most logical place to begin seems to be with the Native Americans themselves. What did they have to say about their origins?

Well, except for only a few records of the earliest known communities in Central and South America, little was ever written down by the North American cultures. There is no library of ancient documents to review. In the scheme of things, it has been only recently that members of tribes have documented any of their traditional narratives in print.

The life of ancestors, moral lessons, and even whimsy were embedded into stories that were handed down from one generation to the next orally. This doesn't mean that these stories should be dismissed on the chance that their content may have changed with each repetition over centuries. Quite the opposite is true. Because everything was on a verbal basis, with constant repetition everyone grew to know the stories by heart. No other versions of the stories existed. If anyone doing the telling wavered from the script, as it were, they would have immediately been corrected and probably chastised for doing so.

As of this writing, there are 574 recognized Native American tribes in the US. Some of these are splinter groups from clans that had existed in the early American era; and even more groups still exist which are as yet not officially recognized by the government. Add to this the over 800 tribes inhabiting South and Central America, and another 60 or more in Canada and Mexico each, and one can see that discerning the origin of the culture or cultures which led to today's Native Americans is one grand puzzle.

Due to conflict and disease, the populations of these tribes have swelled and diminished over the centuries, but most historians agree that many millions had inhabited both continents at the time of Columbus's arrival; a couple million in the islands alone.

Some tribes shared a language, but most had their own. Not only were they identified by their speech, but each had original stories that were repeated for generations to their members. Such diversification of tribes across the two continents was extraordinary.

In the cerebral library of each tribe was shelved at least one book on creation, and often several. These tales were unique to each individual band. While the details of the stories varied, several general themes were held in common across the land.

Some accounts speak to the particulars involved in the creation of an individual tribe, others to the world as a whole, and still others to a combination of both. The words myth or folklore are often used to describe them today because of their imaginative nature. One can find talking animals, the sudden appearance of deities, and improbable actions by people, nature, and gods throughout. Many creation stories also show some relationship to the geographical environment in which the tribe lived. The bottom line is that the people gained an understanding of how their world began through allegorical stories that used all kinds of creatures and situations that were familiar to them in the days they lived.

Though creation stories abound, migration stories are few and far between. It seems that the vast majority of Native Americans believed that they were indeed created on the North or South American continent just as their ancient stories had told them. If their ancestry could only be traced back to a certain point in time, which is often the case, said persons previous to that period were often referred to as the "ancients" of their tribe. Little detail about the ancients' origin or possible migration routes were known to them. Of the few stories that mention travel, most only document movements across the two continents. And so it has been, and still is, the work of archaeologists and historians to put forth theory after theory of how the populations of all these tribes came to be. And their analysis cannot ignore the stories of each tribe.

A look at the Nez Perce, or Nimiipuu, provides an example of a Native American story of creation from the western region of the current United States. This tribe has a physical landmark, pertinent to the

The Heart of the Monster.
The venerated site referred to in the creation story of the Nez Perce people.
Located in the Nez Perce National Historical Park in Idaho.

tale, that is still visitable in today's city of Kamiah, Idaho. It's known as the "Heart of the Monster;" a mound large enough to be called a hill, but surrounded by level ground. As the tale goes, a great monster had once attacked and swallowed all the animals of the region. Coyote (Iceye'ye) came to their rescue. His confrontation with the monster resulted in the creation of the Nez Perce of today, as well as the beginning of numerous other tribes.

Several versions of this lengthy story exist. Here is a portion of one of them that is easier than some to follow. It shows how detailed, clever, and amusing some creation stories can be.

... Coyote was tearing down the waterfall at Celilo [Falls, Oregon] and building a fish ladder, so that salmon could go upstream for the people to catch. He was very busy at this, when someone shouted to him, "Why are you doing that? All the people are gone now because the Monster has eaten them."

"Well," said Coyote to himself, "then I'll stop doing this because I was doing it for the people, and they are gone. Now I'll go along too."

From there, he went upstream, by the way of Salmon River country. As he was walking along, he stepped on the leg of Meadowlark and broke it. Meadowlark got mad and shouted, "Lima, lima, lima! What chance do you have of finding people walking along like this?"

Coyote said, "My Aunt! Please tell me what is happening, and I will make for you a new leg from the wood of a chokecherry tree."

So the Meadowlark told him, "Already all the people have been swallowed by the Monster."

Coyote replied, "Well, that is where I, too, am going." Then he fixed Meadowlark's leg with a chokecherry branch. From there, he traveled on. Along the way he took a good bath, saying to himself, "I will make myself tasty to the Monster." Then he dressed himself all up, saying, "This is so he won't vomit me up." Coyote tied himself with rawhide rope to three great mountains, Tuhm-lo-yeets-mekhs (Pilot Knob), Se-sak-khey-me-khs (Seven Devil's Mountain), and Ta-ya-mekhs (Cottonwood Butte). After the people came, these same mountains were used by young men and women as special places to seek the wey-a-kin, or spirit, who helped guide them through life.

From there, Coyote went along the mountains and over ridges. Suddenly, he saw a great head. He quickly hid himself in the grass and gazed at it. Never before in his life had he seen anything like it. The head was huge, and sweating off somewhere in the distance was its big body. Then Coyote shouted to him, "Oh Monster, let us inhale each other!" The big eyes of the monster looked all around for Coyote, but did not find him, because Coyote's body was painted with clay and was the same color as the grass. Then Coyote shouted again, "Oh Monster, let us inhale each other!" Coyote shook the grass back and forth where he sat.

Suddenly Monster saw the swaying grass and said, "Oh you Coyote, you inhale first. You swallow me first." So Coyote tried. Powerfully and noisily he drew in his breath, the great Monster only swayed and shook.

Then Coyote said, "Now you inhale me. You have already swallowed all the people, so you should swallow me too, so I won't be lonely." The Monster did not know that the Coyote had a pack strapped to his back with five flintstone knives, a flint fire-making set, and some pure pitch in it.

Now the Monster inhaled like a mighty wind. He carried Coyote right towards him, but as Coyote went, he left along the way great keh-mes (Camas bulbs) and great serviceberry fields, saying, "Here the people will find and will be glad, for only a short time away is the coming of the , 8." Coyote almost got caught on one of the ropes, but he cut it with his knife. Thus he dashed right into the Monster's mouth.

Coyote looked around and walked down the throat of the Monster. Along the way he saw bones scattered about, and he thought to himself, "I can see that many people have been dying." As he went along he saw some boys and he said to them, "Where is the Monster's heart? Come, show me." As they were heading that way, Grizzly Bear rushed at them, roaring. Coyote said, "So! You make yourself scary to me," and he kicked Bear on the nose. Thus, the bear today has only a short nose.

As they went on, Rattlesnake rattled at them in fury. "So, only towards me you are vicious. We are nothing but dung to you." Then he stomped on Rattlesnake's head, and flattened it out. It is still that way.

Coyote then met Brown Bear who said, "I see the Monster has kept you for last. Hah! I'd like to see you try to save your people!"

But then, all along the way, people began to greet Coyote and talk to him. His close friend, Fox, greeted him from the side and said, "The Monster is so dangerous. What are you going to do to him?"

Coyote told him, "You and the boys go find some wood or anything that will burn."

About this time, Coyote had arrived at the heart of the Monster. He cut off slabs of fat from the great heart and threw them to the people. "It's too bad you are hungry. Here, eat this." Coyote now started a fire with his flint, and smoke drifted up through the Monster's eyes, nose, ears, and anus.

The Monster said, "Oh, you Coyote! That's why I didn't trust you. Let me cast you out."

Coyote said, "If you do, people will later say, 'He who was cast out is giving salmon to the people.'" "Well, then, go out through the nose," the Monster said.

"But then they will say the same thing."

"Well, then, go out through the ears," the Monster said.

"If I do," answered Coyote, "they will say, "There is old ear-wax, giving food to the people.'"

"Hn, hn, hn. Oh you Coyote! This is why I didn't trust you. Then, go out through the anus."

And Coyote replied, "Then people will say, 'Old feces is giving food to the people.'"

The fire was now burning near the Monster's heart, and he began to feel the pain. Coyote began cutting away on the heart, but then broke one of his stone knives. Right away he took another knife and kept cutting, but soon that one broke, too. Coyote then said to the people, "Now gather up all the bones around here and carry them to the eyes, ears, mouth, and anus of the Monster. Pile them up, and when he falls dead, kick them out the openings." With the third knife he began cutting away at the heart. The third knife broke, and then the fourth, leaving only one more. He told the people, "All right, get yourselves ready because as soon as he falls dead, each one of you must go out through the opening that is closest to you. Take the old women and old men close to the openings so that they may get out easily."

Now the heart hung by only a small piece of muscle and Coyote was cutting away on it, using his last stone knife. The Monster's heart was barely hanging when Coyote's last knife broke. Coyote then threw himself on the heart, just barely tearing it loose with his hands. Then the Monster died and opened up all the openings of his body. The people kicked the bones out and then went out themselves. Coyote went out, too.

The Monster fell dead and the anus began closing, but the Muskrat was still inside. Just as the anus closed he squeezed out, barely getting his body out, but his tail was caught. He pulled and pulled and all the hair got pulled right off. Coyote scolded him, "Now what were you doing? You probably thought of something to do at the last minute. You're always behind in everything."

Then Coyote told the people, "Gather up all the bones and arrange them well." They did this. Then Coyote said, "Now we are going to cut up the Monster." Coyote smeared blood on his hands and sprinkled this blood on the bones. Suddenly there came to life again all those who had died while inside the Monster. Everyone carved up the great Monster and Coyote began dealing out parts of the body to different areas of the country all over the land, towards the sunrise, toward the sunset, towards the North, towards the South. Where each part landed, he named a tribe and described what their appearance would be.

The Cayuse were formed and became small and hot tempered. The Flatheads got a flat headed appearance. The Blackfeet became tall, slender, and war-like. The Coeur d'Alene and their neighbors to north became skillful gamblers. The Yakima became short and stocky and were fishermen.

He used up the entire body of the Monster in this way. Then Fox came up to Coyote and said, "What is the meaning of this Coyote? You have used up the body of the Monster and given away lands, but have given yourself nothing for this area."

"Well," snorted Coyote, "Why didn't you tell me this before? I was so busy that I didn't think of it." Then he turned to the people and said, "Bring me some water with which to wash my hands." He washed his hands and made the water bloody. Then with this bloody water, he threw drops over the land around him and said, "You may be little people, but you will be powerful. You will be little because I did not give you enough of the Monster's body, but you will be very brave and intelligent and will work hard. In only a short time, the La-te-tel-wit (Human Beings) are coming. And you will be known as the Nu-me-poo (later referred to as Nez Perce), or Tsoop-nit-pa-lu (People Crossing over into the Divide). Thus the Nu-me-poo Nation was born. [2]

Another creation story comes from a band of the Lakota tribe (part of the Sioux confederation) who also lived in the northwestern region of the US. It's one of several tales describing how their nation came into existence and it too, is rich in metaphor with ties to numerous other tribal stories.

There was another world before this one. But the people of that world did not behave themselves. Displeased, the Great Spirit set out to make a new world. He sang several songs to bring rain, which poured stronger with each song.

As he sang the fourth song, the earth split apart and water gushed up through the many cracks, causing a flood. By the time the rain stopped, all of the people and nearly all of the animals had drowned. Only Kangi - *the crow* - survived.

Kangi pleaded with the Great Spirit to make him a new place to rest.

So, the Great Spirit decided the time had come to make his new world. From his huge pipe bag, which contained all types of animals and birds, the Great Spirit selected four animals known for their ability to remain under water for a long time.

He sent each in turn to retrieve a lump of mud from beneath the flood waters.

First the loon dove deep into the dark waters, but it was unable to reach the bottom. Ptan, the otter, even with its strong webbed feet also failed. Next, the cápa (beaver) used its large flat tail to propel itself deep under the water, but it too brought nothing back. Finally, the Great Spirit took the kéya (turtle) from his pipe bag and urged it to bring back some mud.

Turtle stayed under the water for so long that everyone was sure it had drowned.

Then, with a splash, the turtle broke the water's surface! Mud filled its feet and claws and the cracks between its upper and lower shells.

Singing, the Great Spirit shaped the mud in his hands and spread it on the water, where it was just big enough for himself and the crow. He then shook two long eagle wing feathers over the mud until earth spread wide and varied, overcoming the waters.

Feeling sadness for the dry land, the Great Spirit cried tears that became oceans, streams and lakes. He named the new land "Turtle Continent" in honor of the turtle, which provided the mud that formed the land.

The Great Spirit then took many animals and birds from his great pipe bag and spread them across the earth.

From red, white, black and yellow earth, he made men and women. The Great Spirit gave the people his sacred pipe and told them to live by it. He warned them about the fate of the people who came before them.

He promised all would be well if all living things learned to live in harmony. But, the world would be destroyed again if they made it bad and ugly.³

In the Midwest and eastern regions of the US, as seen in this Lakota tradition, tribal creation stories often include a scene of various animals diving deep into a world of water and bringing up mud to create land. Here is an abbreviated story of creation from the Wyandot/Huron tribe of the Great Lakes region.

In the beginning there was only one water and the water animals that lived in it.

Then a woman fell from a torn place in the sky. She was a divine woman, full of power. Two loons lying over the water saw her falling. They flew under her, close together, making a pillow for her to sit on.

The loons held her up and cried for help. They could be heard for a long way as they called for other animals to come.

The snapping turtle called all the other animals to aid in saving the divine woman's life.

The animals decided the woman needed earth to live on.

Turtle said, "Dive down in the water and bring up some earth."

So they did that, those animals. A beaver went down. A muskrat went down. Others stayed down too long, and they died.

Each time, Turtle looked inside their mouths when they came up, but there was no earth to be found.

Toad went under the water. He stayed too long, and he nearly died. But when Turtle looked inside Toad's mouth, he found a little earth. The woman took it and put it all around on Turtle's shell. That was the start of the earth.

Dry land grew until it formed a country, then another country, and all the earth. To this day, Turtle holds up the earth.

Time passed, and the divine woman had twin boys. They were opposites, her sons. One was good, and one was bad. One was born as children are usually born, in a normal way. But the other one broke out of his mother's side, and she died.

When the divine woman was buried, all of the plants needed for life on earth sprang from the ground above her. From her head came the pumpkin vine. Maize came from her chest. Pole beans grew from her legs.

The divine woman's sons grew up. The evil one was Tawis-karong. The good one was Tijuskaha. They were to prepare the earth so that humans could live on it. But they found they could not live together. And so they separated, with each one taking his own portion of the earth to prepare.

The bad brother, Tawis-karong, made monstrous animals, fierce and terrifying. He made wolves and bears, and snakes of giant size. He made mosquitoes huge, the size of wild turkeys. And he made an enormous toad. It drank up the fresh water that was on the earth. All of it.

The good brother, Tijus-kaha, made proper animals that were of use to human beings. He made the dove, and the mockingbird, and the partridge. And one day, the partridge flew toward the land of Tawis-karong.

"Why do you go there?" Tijus-kaha asked the partridge.

"I go because there is no water. And I hear there is some in your brother's land," said the partridge.

Tijus-kaha didn't believe the bird. So he followed, and finally he came to his evil brother's land. He saw all of the outlandish, giant animals his brother had made. Tijus-kaha didn't beat them down.

And then he saw the giant toad. He cut it open. Out came the earth's fresh water. Tijus-kaha didn't kill any [more] of his brother's creations. But he made them smaller, of normal size so that human beings could be leaders over them.

His mother's spirit came to Tijus-kaha in a dream. She warned him about his evil brother. And sure enough, one day, the two brothers had to come face to face. They decided they could not share the earth. They would have a duel to see who would be master of the world.

Each had to overcome the other with a single weapon. Tijus-kaha, the good, could only be killed if beaten to death with a bag full of corn or beans. The evil brother could be killed only by using the horn of a deer or other wild animal. Then the brothers fixed the fighting ground where the battle would begin.

The first turn went to the evil brother, Tawis-karong. He pounded his

The Creation stories told by numerous Native American tribes often include the idea of the world being supported on the back of a turtle.

brother with a bag of beans. He beat him until Tijus-kaha was nearly dead. But not quite. He got his strength back, and he chased Tawiskarong. Now it was his turn.

He beat his evil brother with a deer horn. Finally, Tijus-kaha took his brother's life away. But still the evil brother wasn't completely destroyed. "I have gone to the far west," he said. "All the races of men will follow me to the west when they die."

It is the belief of the Hurons to this day. When they die, their spirits go to the far west, where they will dwell forever. [4]

A good number of themes are common in tribal accounts. One is the idea of a world composed of nothing but water. This is an often repeated scene that sometimes includes the occurrence of a great flood. Further, animals of all kinds often dive to find and bring up mud from the bottom of the abyss with which land is eventually formed. The animals involved change from tribe to tribe, but the script reads the same.

Another premise is that of a female being falling from the sky. Sometimes this is a human, other times a deity. The plunge may be accidental, voluntary, or a malicious act of another. Descents from the sky may be made by other entities as well. It could be humans, or gods, or even planets who may then transform something or someone into a different something or someone; or they themselves are changed.

Just as frequently people or creatures rise up and out of deep waters or caves below the earth's surface. For example, the Hopi, Navajo, and other tribes of the southwest US have comparable narratives of their people coming out of caves in the beginning of the world. In fact, many espouse that there were four worlds: one above ground and three layered below the ground. Though different in their particulars, the essence of their creation stories hold that the first people and/or other animals and spirits, escaped the overcrowding in the caverns below by growing a plant in the deepest one. This was usually a cane or reed that rose through the other caves until it reached the outer surface. Along this trellis, all people were able to climb up and into the new, open world above them. Shades of the childhood fairy tale "Jack and the Beanstalk" come to mind. And, ironically since scholars have dated a form of the beanstalk story back to an Indo-European culture of some 5,000 years ago, perhaps their is some worldwide ancient truth to the idea of a plant growing so tall that it provided an escape from one world and into another.

Good versus evil is another very popular theme that is found across numerous tribal stories. It plays out differently in each tale by pitting animals, deities, humans, or even personified natural objects against each other in multiple combinations. Sibling and other familial rivalries are common. The Wyandot's Tijus-kaha versus Tawis-karong provides a good example of how this clash metaphorically plays out. Sometimes there is no conflict at all; men, creatures, or deities just exist without an explanation of their origin.

From this brief sampling it is impossible to ignore that these Native American stories have some fundamental similarities to both ancient biblical and mythological stories that many of us are familiar with. How this connection may have occurred, and what it implies, is what makes this puzzle so engaging.

Although we are focussed on the Native Americans of North America, the stories of Central and South American tribes are just as diversified, yet in some ways similar. As an example, here is a simplified version of the creation story of the Canari people who populated part of modern-day Ecuador from AD 600 to the 1500s.

> A long time ago, in the time before, the Pachamama [goddess] inundated the land with rain. It rained so hard that people found it impossible to escape the floods that poured from the mountains. Two brothers,

Cusicayo (and) Ataorupagui, climbed the side of Wakayñan, the tallest mountain around. The higher they climbed, the higher the water rose until they found themselves at the tippy top. Still they feared for their lives. Finally, the rain subsided and the brothers found themselves alone, the only survivors of the great flood.

As the waters slowly began to recede, the brothers started a new life. None of their friends and family had survived. They were alone. First, they built a small house on the mountainside. They survived by eating roots and the few greens they could find. But nothing really satisfied them. They missed the food made by their mothers and their sisters.

One day, while foraging for something better than meager roots and greens, they found a cave. They stepped inside to explore. To their surprise, inside the cave they found food and chicha [a corn-based beer]. They ate until their stomachs were full and drank until their thirst was more than satisfied. And only then did they begin to wonder from where the food came.

No one had survived the flood so how could the food have just appeared? Yet appear it did, day after day until the brothers had regained their strength.

One morning, they approached the cave and saw two Guayacamayas soaring in the sky. They circled the brothers, then landed, flapping their colorful wings. The brothers could see that these beautiful and brightly colored macaws were actually two women. They had prepared the meals and the chicha and placed them in the cave. The two young men quickly fell in love.

With the sun and the moon and the stars bearing witness, the brothers soon married the Guacamayas and together they walked down into the fertile valley left by the receding floodwaters. The Guacamayas gave birth to many children who in turn gave birth to more. They are the fore bearers of the modern Cañari. [5]

Once you get passed the metaphors and symbolism in all these stories you are left with one root principle. Almost all of them suggest that each tribe originated, indisputably, on either the North or South American continent. Many Native Americans still hold to this belief, as do a few archaeologists. However, with scientific evidence being found and evaluated at an ever increasing pace, most scholars dismiss this belief as fanciful thinking. They agree that the natives were indigenous, but only in the sense of being the first to inhabit the Americas, not necessarily as being created there. They suggest that these tribes originated on other continents and migrated to the western hemisphere.

What keeps the discussion lively in the anthropology, archaeology, and history communities is that every new discovery affects all pre-existing theories regarding how, when, and from where the Native Americans arrived. It is only in our very recent history through the discovery of more artifacts, the improved science of dating them, and certainly the breakthroughs in DNA studies, that we have been enabled to discern more confidently where and when migrations may have occurred. Still, it's best that we speak in generalities and in trends of theories, as the science is ever-evolving. It remains a precarious leap for today's scholars to make any definitive claims.

When viewing the Native American time line, we see that so far we have only discussed the tribes of the, so-to-speak, recent past; those who occupied North and South America from approximately AD 1500, when the Spanish arrived, to the present. With that in mind, a look at the cultures that preceded this time period is in order. However, every step we take backwards has less detail in it, which allows for more speculation to come into play.

The immediate predecessors to the Native American tribes are referred to as the moundbuilders for the obvious reason that they left mounds across the continents which we wonder at to this day. Based on the existing evidence, most scientists will agree that there seems to have been three successive waves of moundbuilder societies, and each wave consisted of several sub-groups co-existing in different regions. Working our way back from AD 1500 we first meet the Mississippians; before them the Hopewell, and before them the Adena.

The Mississippians lived in expansive societies along the Ohio and Mississippi River valleys as well as across broad regions of the southern US. The height of their civilization was generally reached between AD 500 and the 1500s. Each group is believed to have consisted of skilled farmers and artisans who traded with each other. Presumably, wars and disease, not to mention deforestation, wildlife depletion, and over-population, all contributed to their demise; or to their dissemination into some of today's tribes. The Osage, Chickasaw, and Peoria nations claim an affiliation with this era's population. Even more specifically, some attach themselves with the people of Cahokia who were the first to build a very large populace on the continent of North America.

Cahokia seems to have begun as far back as 800 BC as a seasonal location for hunter/gatherer groups. It's located just east of present-day St. Louis. Over many centuries the populations developed more and more sophisticated farming methods which allowed them to eventually settle permanently in this location. By the eleventh century the community stretched over five square miles and grew to 20,000 in number. It's centerpiece is Monk's Mound, so-named because it was later occupied, in the 1800s, by French monks. It's an earthen, stepped pyramid that spans slightly more acreage than the Great Pyramid of Egypt and rises ten stories. Cahokia was the grand center of trade with other Mississippian cultures that had risen across the continent.

With another step backwards in time from this Mississippian period, we find the Hopewell nation which survived for over seven centuries – from 200 BC through AD 500. Their communities stretched from present New York State region to the upper Midwest. They too were skilled in agriculture and were creative, as evidenced by the many decorative tools discovered and dated to their era. Because these artifacts are often made of raw materials not native to where they were found, it's assumed that they were involved in trade with their distant groups just as the Mississippians had been with theirs. In fact, scientists have named and categorized nearly two dozen Hopewell era regions throughout the expanse of land between the Appalachians and the Mississippi River. The Ohio Valley Hopewell group gets the most attention because of its proliferation of mounds, especially the unique Serpent Mound.

This curvaceous man-made structure winds its way along a creek in southern Ohio. Completely formed from the earth, its meandering body measures well over four hundred yards in length, is up to eight yards wide, and stands over a yard tall. Though very impressive to this day, its original purpose is still debated.

Interestingly, the Serpent Mound presents us with evidence that cultures may have overlapped and intermingled more than we had previously understood. Here's how. The dating of some of the materials at the site show that this snake-like structure was worked on by a group known as the Fort Ancient culture who inhabited the region between

Mounds and enclosure walls at the Hopewell Culture National Historical Park in Chillicothe, Ohio. Surviving earthworks like these provide a glimpse into the lives of some of the earliest inhabitants of the continent.

AD 1000 and 1700. Some scholars believe the Shawnee and possibly other tribes descended from these Fort Ancient people. Complicating the matter, scientists disagree as to whether the Fort Ancient society was actually part of the broader Mississippian civilizations of that day or whether it was a sister culture that had a different heritage. Regardless of their relationship to each other, people of this Mississippian era were definitely hands-on with the Serpent Mound. But wait, that's not all.

Some other materials found in this mound date back to an even earlier period of time, 1,000 through 200 BC, when a culture known as the Adena lived in this same area. They are the predecessors to the Hopewell and Fort Ancient peoples. Scientists now agree that it was the Adena people who first created the serpentine earthwork and it was the Fort Ancient society who added to it.

These early Adena people were less sophisticated than the Hopewell and Mississippians who came after them. They did not farm; but instead depended on hunting, gathering, and fishing. Tools and weapons have been discovered, however; showing their skilled craftsmanship and artistic talents, especially in pottery works.

All three cultures; the Mississippians, Hopewell (and Fort Ancient), and Adena, built mounds. Some were circular, usually for graves; some rectangular as living spaces; some stepped into a pyramid form presumably as a site for spiritual worship; and even some that resembled animals as is the case of the Great Serpent Mound. Still debated is whether these cultures were independent of each other and ceased to exist due to untold circumstances; or whether they evolved into each other over time. The latter suggests that at least some were the ancestors of modern tribes. However it happened, the building of mounds and those who constructed them, seems to have ended about the time Columbus had landed.

Often overlooked, is that the great cultures of Central and South America were active over this very same stretch of time. The Mayans of Central America had the longest existence beginning around 2000 BC and lasting until the Spanish conquered them in the 1500s. It was the Aztecs who lived as a northern neighbor to the Mayans for three of those latter centuries, until the Spanish took them out as well. And the Incas, who dwelled along a lengthy stretch of South America's western coast, lasted over a century beginning in AD 1400 until they too were vanquished by those same Spanish forces.

Keeping in mind that our understanding of all these civilizations changes with every new discovery, a few more questions might still be asked. Could trade have been going on between the moundbuilders of North America and the major cultures to the south? Did any members of the moundbuilder societies ever venture south and influence the development of the Maya, Aztecs, Incas, or others? Or was it the other way around, with some of the early South American people moving to the north and evolving into the moundbuilders?

The next artifact to be discovered just might create a brand new theory regarding migration patterns here-to-fore unexpected. Already we can observe the fact that pyramid style constructions are prolific in all these groups. The major difference in these structures is that the southern ones, like those of the Mayans, were built of stone because that was the raw material in abundance; while the northern pyramids were made of earth and wood because that was what they had in ready supply. The northern mounds and pyramids are less recognizable today only because their construction materials have naturally worn away over time.

Now that we've established that moundbuilders of various types inhabited both continents from roughly 2000 BC through AD 1500, how do we learn who preceded them to the western hemisphere? This is an even more difficult challenge.

Tales of creation, like those of more recent Native Americans, are hard to be found among older civilizations. The Incas are one of the exceptions as they provide several versions of their creation which have some themes that we're now familiar with.

One tells of the first Inca people coming out of a cave while another relates how an original man and woman birthed the Inca nation. The most noted story talks of a creator god, Viracocha, who curiously came across the Pacific Ocean and rested at Lake Titicaca on the present border of Peru and Bolivia. There he created the sun, a goddess named Into. The Inca were brought up from under the ground by Into.

This latter story hints at migration, at least of the creator, across the expansive waters west of South America. It's interesting to note that the most strongly held theories of today's scholars involve migration, in some fashion, from the West. It's primarily a question of which region of the West they came from, and by what means, that fosters so many divergent theories. Adding a further twist to this study are the handful of scholars who make a reasonable case for the original settlers to have come from the East, across the Atlantic Ocean, at various points in time.

The preponderance of today's scientific evidence points to a migration beginning anywhere from 12,000 to 15,000 years ago. This is the timeframe presented as a result of the testing of all human remains which have been found to date. It must be kept in mind that though testing methods are generally trusted, some scientists have admitted that there is some potential for skewed results. Additionally, it must be remembered that the next human remains to be found could change the established time line yet again.

That said, today's most accepted theory is that northern Asian people living around 10,000 BC crossed over a land or ice bridge between Siberia and Alaska and moved down and across North America. The crossing region of that time is referred to as Beringa. It was then that the ocean waters were much lower because the receding glaciers of North America were just beginning to melt. Dry land, or perhaps solid ice, had presumably connected the two continents over which people and animals might have migrated on foot. Once the glaciers melted, ocean water levels rose and submerged the "bridge."

The theories only begin here. More variations to this basic idea are readily suggested by other scholars. For instance, some agree that it was people from northern Asia who first made the trip, but they believe it was by boat. Perhaps their excursion began in the same Bering Sea region, they say, but their vessels skirted the coastlines of Beringa to the shores of North America and perhaps continued all the way down to South America.

Here are just some of the additional questions that complicate the theories even further. Did some members of the migration settle along the way in North America while others continued on to the south and east? Was the migration a one time event or were there waves of migrants over thousands of years coming across Beringa? If so, how many and how often? Did they travel back and forth? Were they all from one general region of northern Asia, say today's Siberia, or could groups from Japan and the deeper interior of today's Russia or China have also made the trip?

A lesser accepted theory says that it was the people of southern Asia, the Polynesian region, from which a migration took place around AD 1200 and perhaps even earlier. It points to the fact that another culture may have at least visited South America with some of them perhaps settling amongst the peoples already living there, several centuries before the Spanish arrived.

A little closer look at this theory reveals that the Polynesians were master sailors. They constructed double-hulled outrigger canoes whose design prevented them from being capsized. It is accepted as fact that they were the first to settle the Hawaiian Islands around AD 400. That was over a 2,000 mile jaunt across the Pacific Ocean. With South America situated due east of the Polynesian Islands, and admittedly having a more formidable 5,000 miles of water between them, it is still not out of the question that they made the trek.

In fact, the Polynesians seem to have understood much more about sailing than we might have expected. Their routes were charted in the movements of the stars and they studied the action of waves in relation to the winds and water currents. They observed the trade winds finding them steady, predictable, and accommodating to navigation. And, as the name given to this ocean implies, the waters were generally docile, or pacific.

One real life example of the Polynesians' ability to travel great distances comes from the records of Commodore Perry in 1853. (No, not Oliver, the hero of the Battle of Lake Erie, but his younger brother, Matthew.) Commodore Matthew Perry was on assignment in the Pacific to open trade between the United States and Japan. In his journals, while commanding the *Southhampton*, is recorded a chance encounter with a small boat of natives as they were sailing in the waters near the Philippines. An excerpt reads:

> ... a boat was discovered to windward. The ship was to hove to, and presently succeeded in getting on board, the boat and its contents. When hoisted in and measured, the craft was found to be twelve feet long, four wide, and seventeen inches deep. On board of the boat, when the ship thus picked her up, were six males, four of whom were adults, and two were boys, the one about ten and the other fourteen years of age. They were all of healthy appearance, of medium stature, of a dark color, the hair cut close, not tattooed, and did not appear to be much exhausted. Captain Boyle supposed, from their appearance, that they might have been adrift some two or three days. They had in the boat about two or three dozen ears of Indian corn (maize), a few sweet potatoes, some prepared betel nuts, a cask, two gongs, a fishing net, an axe, a small piece of grass cloth as a sail, and a colored piece supposed to be a flag. Of water they had none; but from the frequent showers encountered by the ship, Captain Boyle concluded they had not suffered much from want of it.
>
> To what nation or people these poor creatures belonged no one could tell, as nobody on board could understand their language. It was observed, however, that the word most frequently on their lips was Sil-li-ba-boo...

The Americans, in good faith, tried to get these men, whom they thus named the Sil-li-ba-boo, back to their homeland, but with no understanding of the language it was truly a hit and miss effort. They hoped someone at the closest port would recognize their speech. The nearest land to the ship was over a hundred miles westward. However, because the wind was from the east the Americans guessed that heading the one hundred and eighty miles in that direction, to the Babuan islands, might prove to be the area they came from.

> ...When the ship came near and passed through the group of islands just named, the commander watched closely to observe if they showed

An image of the Sillibaboo people who were assisted by Commodore Mathew Perry's crew during his expedition to Japan in 1853.

any mark of recognition. Their attention was called to them by signs, and they seemed to understand the panomimic inquiry, for they invariably shook their heads as if to imply that their home was not there, and pointing towards the eastward, said, "Sil-li-ba-boo…"

The Americans next sailed to the China port of Com-sing-moon and escorted the six men along the docks from one vessel to another in the hope that someone would recognize their language.

…At length they uttered some words when on the deck of the English ship Bombay, which Captain Jamieson, the commander, thought he recognized as belonging to the language of the natives of the Bentinck Isles. On perceiving that their words were attracting notice, they made their usual salaam, and uttering Sil-li-ba-boo, afterwards held their peace…

There was an island by that name, but it was twelve to fifteen hundred miles from where they had been picked up. It seemed unfathomable to all that they could have travelled such a distance in such a tiny craft.

…With imperfect means of knowledge, the best Captain Jamieson could gather from them was, that they did come from Sil-li-ba-boo, distant as it was; that they left the land in their boat with some articles of food for a vessel in the offing, met a fresh breeze which carried them out to sea, and, by its continuance, prevented their return to land, and that they had been in the boat fifteen days when the Southhampton picked them up...[6]

So, as of 1853, we have evidence that people of the Near East could withstand long-term travel over a great distance. Add to this the successful excursions of Thor Heyerdahl who in 1947 sailed his Kon-Tiki raft from Peru to the islands, and one can see that the trans-pacific migration theory has sea legs in both directions.

One other bit of evidence of contact between these two civilizations is the appearance of the humble sweet potato in Polynesia. Though it is known to have originated in South America, it has been a staple Polynesian crop since roughly AD 1200. How did it get there? The debate rages on as to whether the Polynesians sailed to South America and brought the potato, and maybe even some of the people, back to the islands, or whether it was the South American civilization of that time which cruised to Polynesia. Still others think the seeds were simply carried by the winds or the waters to their new island homes. Though one might think that recent DNA studies would clarify the situation, the interpretations of the results vary and fuel even more controversy. This simple question of whether Polynesians and South Americans made contact provides an exquisite example of how hard it is to prove any theory.

Let's now cross the globe and take a peek at the proposals stating that there was a migration across the Atlantic Ocean to the Americas, before Columbus's adventure.

The predominant theory centers on the ancient civilization of the Phoenicians who existed from 2500 BC until they were conquered by Rome in 64 BC. Today's Lebanon was the home to most of the Phoenicians' permanent population. Over time it established city-states throughout the Mediterranean, especially along the lower Mediterranean coastline. Their largest was Carthage. The Phoenicians, like the Polynesians, were known to be expert mariners. Their industry was trade, and it was carried out with the utmost competence across much of their region for centuries.

They were known to exchange their own goods such as purple textiles, glassware, and cedar with others for what they needed; but they also acted as a delivery driver of goods between other nations — the UPS (United Phoenician Service) of their day. Besides the many ports of the Mediterranean Sea, they sailed beyond the Straits of Gibralter and into the Atlantic Ocean both to the north and south. Down the western coast of Africa they traded for ivory, and all the way northward to ancient Britain they exchanged goods for tin. Since they are proven to have gone this far into the Atlantic, some of today's scholars theorize that they could have crossed it as well. Such trans-Atlantic travel, circa 600 BC, was proven possible when in 2019, Philip Beale successfully sailed his replica ship, Phoenicia, from Carthage, Tunisia to Santo Domingo, Dominican Republic.

The idea of Phoenicians coming to the Americas two thousand years before Columbus is alluring because it has been proven possible; but tangible evidence that it really happened is scarce. Suppositions have been made regarding some of the artifacts found in the Americas which date to the Phoenician era, however the connection is a loose one so far. Proponents of this theory cite the fact that several ancient historians have written to the fact that the Carthaginians spoke of a large island situated a long way out in the Atlantic ocean that had mountain ranges and numerous rivers. They speculate that these Carthaginians were referring to North America and that perhaps they never settled, only visited. They were traders, after all, who gained their fortune by selling their finds while keeping their sources secret.

It is well documented that Leif Erikson of Viking fame came to the Newfoundland region of North America in AD 1,000. A site known as L'Anse aux Meadows is tangible proof to this day that Norsemen lived in that area for at least a short time. Very little evidence exists, as yet, that they continued to colonize the continent.

On a similar note, there is an ancient tale told amongst some of the Cherokee about a certain moon-eyed people who they encountered centuries ago. According to some versions of the legend, these people were pale in appearance, with large blue eyes, red hair, and a sensitivity to the sun; hence they usually came out at night. Details beyond this description vary and are romanticized in much the same way we've seen it done with other Native American creation stories. There is a lot of skepticism about this myth; but, if these characteristics are accurate, a practical and scientific eye might see these moon-eyed people, who were peculiar to the Cherokee, as displaying some of the physical characteristics of a Celtic people.

Bolstering this idea is the fact that a certain prince of Wales by the name of Madoc sailed across the Atlantic more than a hundred years after Leif Erikson's arrival and is believed to have landed on the shores of present-day Alabama. With his ship full of adventurous Welsh citizens they supposedly traveled up the Alabama River and into the Tennessee Valley, never to be heard from again. The Cherokee resided in that region and their legend goes on to say that the Creeks eventually drove the moon-eyed people out, forcing them westward. It's totally unprovable, but some claim that the Welsh people associated with Prince Madoc may have interbred with various natives over a few centuries and thus evolved into a Native American tribe of their own.

We can see from all of this, and all of this is just scratching the surface of information and theories about the origin of the Native Americans, that there are three broad schools of thought.

The first belief is the one retained by the Native Americans themselves and a few scholars. It asserts that they were created right where their ancient stories say they were; on the North or South American continents.

The second view is the one held by the majority of scholars at the time of this writing, It states that they are exclusively descendents of northern Asian peoples who crossed over or sailed along the Bering Strait region and proceeded into and along North and South America beginning around 10,000 BC.

The third theory has a lot of loose ends, but it holds enough evidence to not be dismissed. It espouses that periodically, over thousands of years, people from several diverse cultures and several continents came to settle these two "new" land masses.

No matter which general theory is confirmed to be correct in the future, if indeed any one of them can ever be absolutely proven; the ancestors of today's Native Americans have certainly had a long and colorful past. What an intriguing study it is of these "Indians" who Columbus discovered and whose beginnings we are just beginning to understand. ♦

HMMM...

The Twenty-one Precepts or Moral Commandments of the Ottawa and Chippewa Indians, by which they were governed in their primitive state, before they came in contact with white races in their country...

1st. Thou shalt fear the Great Creator, who is the over ruler of all things.

2d. Thou shalt not commit any crime, either by night or by day, or in a covered place: for the Great Spirit is looking upon thee always, and thy crime shall be manifested in time, thou knowest not when, which shall be to thy disgrace and shame.

3d. Look up to the skies often, by day and by night, and see the sun, moon and stars which shineth in the firmament, and think that the Great Spirit is looking upon thee continually.

4th. Thou shalt not mimic or mock the thunders of the cloud, for they were specially created to water the earth and to keep down all the evil monsters that are under the earth, which would eat up and devour the inhabitants of the earth if they were set at liberty.

5th. Thou shalt not mimic or mock any mountains or rivers, or any prominent formation of the earth, for it is the habitation of some deity or spirit of the earth, and thy life shall be continually in hazard if thou shouldst provoke the anger of these deities.

6th. Honor thy father and thy mother, that thy days may be long upon the land.

7th. Honor the gray-head persons, that thy head may also be like unto theirs.

8th. Thou shalt not mimic or ridicule the cripple, the lame, or deformed, for thou shall be crippled thyself like unto them if thou shouldst provoke the Great Spirit.

9th. Hold thy peace, and answer not back, when thy father or thy mother or any aged person should chastise thee for thy wrong.

10th. Thou shalt never tell a falsehood to thy parents, nor to thy neighbors, but be always upright in thy words and in thy dealings with thy neighbors.

11th. Thou shalt not steal anything from thy neighbor, nor covet anything that is his.

12th. Thou shalt always feed the hungry and the stranger.

13th. Thou shalt keep away from licentiousness and all other lascivious habits, nor utter indecent language before thy neighbor and the stranger.

14th. Thou shalt not commit murder while thou art in dispute with thy neighbor, unless it be whilst on the warpath.

15th. Thou shalt chastise thy children with the rod whilst they are in thy power.

In the Centinel of the North-Western Territory, August 1, 1795[7]

II.
TEMPER, TEMPER MR. McGARY.

Most of the exploits of Daniel Boone are common knowledge to those who study American history. He is truly legendary. However, what a number of people tend to overlook is the fact that Boone rarely acted alone. Sure, he had his solitary moments of note, but, most often he had friends, family, and associates with whom he shared his many accomplishments and alongside whom he experienced his unbelievable adventures. One of these lesser-known, occasional companions was an intriguing man by the name of Hugh McGary, who himself had a life brimming with very compelling exploits.

Born in Ireland, McGary arrived in the colonies with his parents at the tender age of six. Their passage over the Atlantic Ocean to the British colonies was not without cost. They came as indentured servants. The year was 1750, and under the long-established, and common British practice of servitude, a would-be immigrant could contract with a Colonial to provide labor for them over a set period of time. Usually this amounted to four or five years. In return for the work, the indentured party was given free initial transport to the colonies, as well as food, shelter, and clothing for the full term of service agreed to. However, there were no wages beyond these necessities.

McGary, had likely begun working in some capacity for his keep with the rest of his family before he reached his fifteenth birthday; but it was at this age that he and his brother Edward were already documented landowners in Augusta County, Virginia. The property had been awarded to them for service to their colony. For some period of time during the French and Indian War, which lasted from

1754 through 1763, it is supposed that the then teenage McGary and his brother were either driving cattle or wagons of supplies alongside British troops on at least one of their military campaigns.

In 1766, at age twenty-two, he married Mary Buntin Ray, a widow with three children. The following year the family moved from Virginia to North Carolina. There they established themselves along the Yadkin River in the general vicinity of the Daniel Boone's home. For an unspecified length of time, McGary was the Sheriff in his new homeland of Wilkes County. However, it wouldn't be long before his restless spirit would have him moving on to new adventures.

When the war with France had ended in 1763, thus transferring the lands that would become Kentucky and Tennessee from French to British control; a yearning to see them gripped the colonists. The most adventurous ones began to check it out. This influx quickly resulted in King George the Third making a Royal Proclamation prohibiting the colonists from venturing into the West. The Indians still occupying the lands didn't care much for the new visitors, and made their voices heard. The King's edict was supposed to appease the western Indians and contain the colonists. However, it proved to be merely an unenforceable platitude, generally ignored by those along the coast who were prone to exploration. By 1768, just five years later, the signing of the Treaty of Fort Stanwix between the Iroquois nation and the British authorities declared the territory south of the Ohio River to be open to settlement by the colonists. This inevitably prompted more and more parties, some led by Boone, to head west where they canvassed the lands and staked their claims.

During the winter of 1772-1773, Boone made one of these treks in the company of five other North Carolina men. One of them was Hugh McGary. It would be McGary's first trip into the Indian lands. So completely was he smitten with them, that he determined to make this wilderness his family's permanent home.

In August of 1775, Boone led an even larger group of pioneers back into the region. This time, besides a number of adventurous single men, all of the immediate members of Boone's, McGary's, and two other families were included as well. They were headed to lands they had previously determined to be best suited to their needs. The whole company of settlers made their way along the trail that Boone had blazed just six months previous at the behest, and while he was under the employ, of Richard Henderson.

Henderson was a man of many interests, but at this moment in time he was laser-focused on his wilderness land holdings. He had just negotiated a treaty with the Cherokee for a huge swath of land that encompassed half of what would become Kentucky and a smaller portion of Tennessee. He named it Transylvania and soon would solicit the newly formed Continental Congress to turn his great expanse into the fourteenth colony. The effort was more of a business venture than simple colonization, with Henderson and others profiting from the sales of lots to would-be settlers. Within a year or two, his scheme would be rejected by both Virginia and North Carolina legislatures who did not recognize his right to negotiate with the Cherokee as an individual, nor as a business, for the purchase of British lands. That was solely King George's prerogative.

Nearing the last leg of their journey, the Boone/McGary party paused along the Dix River, near today's town of Brodhead, Kentucky. From here, the group would split up. It would be another forty miles or so to each of their destinations, but in different directions. Boone's family, and some of the others, headed north to the cabins he had already built at the site that would bear his name — Boonesborough (or Boonesboro). There, Henderson impatiently awaited him, having just negotiated the land treaty with the Cherokee. Meanwhile, McGary with his wife, three step-children, and a baby that was the first of four to be born to the couple, along with several other pioneers in the group, headed to the northwest where James Harrod had founded a site a year earlier. In that year of 1774, by order of Lord Dunsmore, the British Governor of Virginia, Harrod had been commissioned to find suitable land to be awarded to veteran officers of the recent French and Indian war. He did so, and in the process laid out property of his own which became known as Harrod's Town, or Harrodstown, and today as Harrodsburg, Kentucky.

The main path that Boone had cleared led to Boonesborough. It was soon to become known as the Wilderness Road. From where the full group had separated, McGary's party had to follow a much more obscure route to Harrodstown which caused them to temporarily lose their way. Eventually, both groups made it safely to there desired destinations.

An old settler who was among the first to come to the region once noted that

> there were but four women in Ky., and they were at Hdsbgh [Harrodsburg]: Mrs. Denton, Mrs. McGary, Mrs. Ashley? [Hogan] and Mrs. Harrod. There were just enough for 2 four handed reels: and part of the men would guard at one time, and part at another, while the rest alternately danced. [1]

The "reel" referred to here was the Virginia reel; a popular folk dance of the day akin to modern square dancing. It provided a much needed respite from the perpetual workload and chronic fear of Indian attacks.

As he settled into the frontier life, Hugh McGary began to build quite a reputation for himself. In fact, it was one that encompassed the term often used to describe people of his heritage: "Fighting Irish." The history books are replete with some rather damning adjectives to describe his personality. They include: impetuous, fiery, ferocious, rash, foolish, vain, seditious, and headstrong — just to name a few. At first reading of those attributes, one might dismiss Hugh as a real "bad egg," so to speak. He was definitely plagued with a quick and sometimes violent temper. And when it erupted it usually triggered some sort of dire consequence for others, himself, or both parties; which inevitably overshadowed what may have been his well-intentioned purposes at the outset. With an objective and scrutinizing eye of some of the noteworthy episodes in his life, as well as the day-to-day responsibilities he had on his shoulders, the reasons for McGary's abrasive behavior might be revealed. And, just perhaps, one may be able to dispense a small dose of absolution in his direction.

As the first families from the east coast began to take root in the wilderness; like a weed, adversity planted its own seeds among them. The Indians around and about Kentucky were none-too-happy with the colonists making permanent homes in the lands that they had hunted and lived upon for centuries. They would not ignore the evolving situation. Small parties of warriors made frequent, random attacks on the

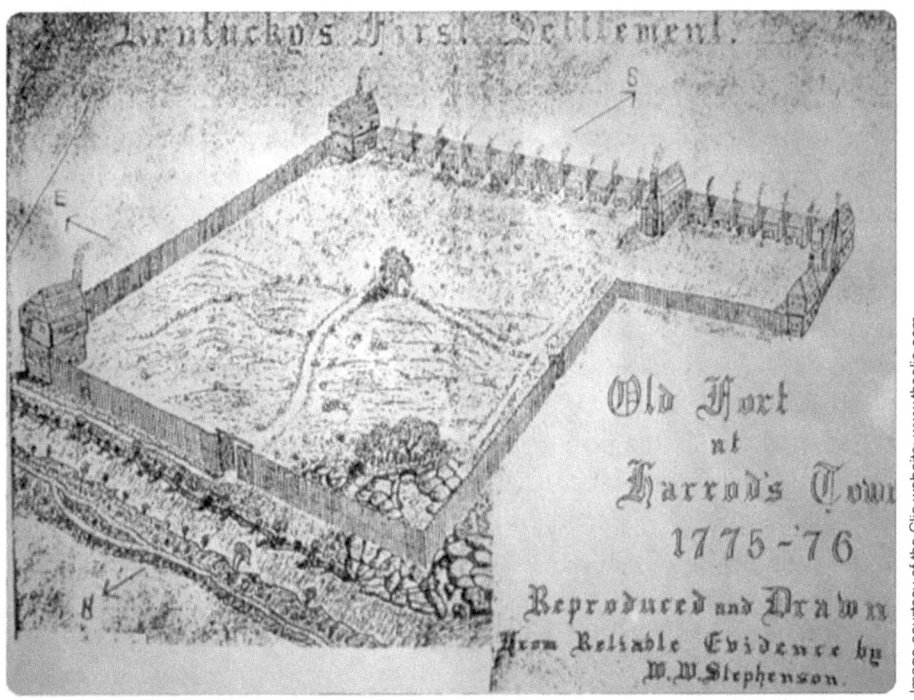

Sketch of Harrod's Town circa 1775 - 1776.

intruders. They would often seek out the flatboats moving along the Ohio River, or the travelers following paths through the woods, and even the individuals who strayed from their cabins to tend to their livestock, crops, or other affairs. One had to keep a constant, wary eye on their surroundings.

In December of 1776, the Virginia General Assembly re-organized its land holdings. The wilderness which had stretched from the Appalachians westward to the Mississippi River as an extension of Virginia was christened as the county of Kentucky; just sixteen years before it would become the state of the same name. It encompassed Harrodstown, Boonesboro, Logan's Fort and the numerous other stations being erected ever so rapidly by enterprising colonists. The plight of these frontiersmen initially took a back seat to affairs along the coast as the Revolution had just begun in the colonies. It wasn't long, however, before the war poured over the mountains. The British soon took a more aggressive approach on the frontier. They began to encourage the Indians to disturb the peace of the new inhabitants of Kentucky. And, they supplied them with the weaponry they needed to do so. The scattered settlers were in a precarious position. They eagerly sought a military presence for their safety. As the distinguished chairman of the newly formed committee of Kentucky County, it was Hugh McGary who would officially seek the protection they all wanted.

A formal petition to the Virginia delegation, which had recently declared its independence from Britain and established itself as a commonwealth, was drafted by McGary in February of 1777. The document detailed several of the deadly attacks that they had recently endured. McGary implored the Governor for aid by pointing out that the war was no longer confined to the east coast. On behalf of all the residents of Kentucky, McGary stated that

> it is with reluctance they [the petitioners] at this time trespass upon the time of the Honourable Governor & Council, but they hope that their unsettled state, their great distance from the source of power and relief, added their extremely hazardous situation, will sufficiently plead their excuse…
>
> … We are surrounded with enemies on every side; every day increases their numbers. To retreat from the place where our all is centered would be little preferable to death. Our Fort is already filled with widows and orphans; their necessities call upon daily for supplies. Yet all this would be tolerable could we but see the dawn of peace; but a continuance of our woes threaten us: A rueful war presents itself before us.
>
> The apprehension of an invasion on the ensuing spring fills our minds with a thousand fears. The brave despise danger, even death, upon their own accounts; it is the state of weak infancy and helpless widowhood that set heavy on us. Forced by these considerations, and encouraged by favors already received from the commonwealth, we most humbly present this our most dutiful Petition praying that the Hon.'ble Governor and Council would take into serious consideration our distressed state and devise some method to guard against the attacks of our merciless enemy, till our country, strengthened by new adventurers, shall be in a capacity to defend itself, and your petitioners in duty bound shall pray. [2]

As feared by the residents, more organized Indian attacks were realized across the county through 1777; justifying the year becoming known as the "bloody sevens." The Revolution had come to the frontier, but the coastal colonies didn't seem as concerned about them as they were their own communities. Shortly after McGary delivered his petition to Virginia, he was sent to Fort Pitt in Pennsylvania, by the order of General George Rogers Clark. He carried with him a letter seeking their help in recovering horses that were stolen by Indians in Kentucky. In a separate letter, this one to the Virginia delegation, Clark reported the purpose and justified the expense of sending McGary on this trip to Pittsburgh.

> Hugh McGary humbly sheweth, That in the months of March and April last the northern Indians invaded the County of Kentucky, killed many of the inhabitants; destroyed part of their stock & took off upwards of two Hundred horses. News arriving that Government had ordered an Expedition against the Towns of the enemy Indians from Pittsburg The Commanding officer at Kentucky sent your petitioner thither as Express with a List of Horses lost & their descriptive marks in order that they might be recovered to the Owners... [3]

These particular correspondences did not result in the recovery of the stolen horses, nor any progress toward peace; but it does show that McGary was a trusted leader and emissary for high level commanders. In addition to these responsibilities, McGary had been serving as a Justice in the county and an officer in the militia.

Still, while many considered McGary to be a blustering man; one should not confuse that trait to mean that he was a cowardly one as well; because he certainly was not. It's likely that McGary had his fair share of physical confrontations with fellow settlers. One of them occurred at Harrod's Station between Captain Abraham Chaplin and himself. It's not known what triggered the fight, but the story goes that

> McGary was very Insolent in his disposition[,] quarrelsome when he dared[,] and took ocation [occasion] to insult A. Chaplin who was as Brave as Brave could be[.] he cautioned Mc[Gary] to behave himself better[,] but that only made the matter wors so the Captain challenged him to single Combat and they striped of to the skin and went at it in good earnist - the good wishes of the Women, men Boys & Girls all for the Captain and the fortune of War dec'd in favor of the Captain and he gave him a real good Beating to the real satisfaction of all the fort. [4]

Early in this same year of 1777, McGary had begun work on a station of his own. It was only a few miles northeast of Harrodsburg at what is still known as Shawnee Springs, Kentucky. One day in March, while helping out at Harrodsburg, McGary sent two of his teenage step-sons, William and James Ray, along with an old friend of his, to a woods of Maple trees near the station he was still building. It was the time of the sugar run and the boys went there to tap into the flow. With no warning, just a week after McGary's petition for help against attacks was sent to Virginia legislators, an assault was made on the threesome of maple syrup gatherers by a band of marauding Indians. An early pioneer of that day, Jacob Stevens, explained that

> Wm. Ray, [James Ray,] and an old irishman, living at McGary's, were out in the fields [maple tree grove] ... at work, when the indians killed Wm. Ray. Jas. made his escape to the fort at Harrodsburgh, and the irishman hid behind a log where the party found him, sound and secure, when they came from the fort. Next day Harrodsburgh was attacked. McGary killed an indian: that he found had his step-son's [William's] shirt on, and cut him up and fed him to the dogs. [5]

Yes, you read that correctly. By this event, it is easy to see how McGary had begun to create his alarming reputation! This vicious act certainly casts a nasty light on the man, but there is a bit more to the story which rarely gets told. Lyman Draper, historian of the mid 1800s, who interviewed the pioneer Stevens for this story, made a comment in the margin of his own notes stating:

> He [the Indian who killed William] indeed cut him [William] up in pieces and stuck him on the bushes. McGary's wife and his [William's] mother, took sick, and didn't live long after that. This was what made him [McGary] so fierce against the indians. [6]

Vengeance for the horrific dismemberment of his step-son's body by this Indian was the reason for McGary's similarly gruesome act. McGary was at Harrodstown when James escaped the attackers and brought news of it back to him. He immediately solicited Harrod to round up the men to go in pursuit. Harrod refused, not wanting to leave Harrodstown vulnerable to attack with all the men gone. The two friends engaged in a heated and escalating argument that peaked with each man threatening the other with guns in hand. Only an intervention by Mary, McGary's wife, kept the incident from becoming a fatal one. McGary arrived at the scene of the Indian's attack with about thirty men. Whether William's mother, Mary, saw the spectacle of her son's body parts skewered on numerous branches of bushes is unknown. However, she did grow deathly ill from the time of this event and passed away a year later at the young age of thirty-nine. She had borne Hugh four additional children.

A few months after Mary's death, McGary married again. It would be to Catherine (Caty) Yokum; a girl he had already been familiar with during Mary's decline. Hugh and Caty spent the next twenty-three years living out the prime of their lives together. Eight more children would result from their union.

Attacks between the frontiersmen and the British-backed Indians continued to escalate through the latter 1770s. In November of 1777, the peace-seeking Shawnee Chief Cornstalk was killed by some errant militiamen while he was on a mission of friendship to Fort Randolph, built on the site of the American's earlier victory of Point Pleasant. Cornstalk's murder triggered more trouble. Daniel Boone was kidnapped by the Shawnee in January of 1778 while he was gathering salt near the Licking River. He managed to escape from his captors and in the fall of that same year successfully lead the defense of Boonesborough when a major Indian attack was made upon it.

In other parts of the frontier, regular military troops as well as frontier militia began to fight back on a larger scale. In 1778, George Rogers Clark and John Bowman were key figures leading forces to victories at Kaskaskia and Cahokia in the Illinois country. In 1779, Vincennes had to be re-taken and further attacks were made on the Indian villages just north of the Ohio River. McGary participated in both of these later efforts.

The aggressions continued. By March of 1782 a new series of attacks were made by the Indians on more of the forts west of the Kentucky River. One of these assaults came against James Estill, a pioneer who had established a station of his own a few miles southeast of today's Richmond, Kentucky, only fifteen miles from Boonesborough. While the men of his fort were all out scouting the area for what they had suspected was a large force of Indians on the prowl, a smaller contingent of warriors appeared outside his settlement. The women and children were alone and essentially defenseless. The attackers had captured a young girl of this community. They purposefully brought her in full view of the shuddering women peering over the walls of the fort and dramatically murdered and scalped her. A runner alerted the absent men of the atrocity and they immediately turned back in pursuit of the band of Indians. A skirmish ensued and ended with several deaths in both parties. This was the beginning of a string of assaults in the vicinity.

Through the summer of that same year, the Indians had amassed a significant force of over five hundred men. The notorious traitors Simon Girty and Alexander McKee, who had renounced their allegiance to the Americans and their rebellion, joined forces with the British Ranger William Caldwell who spearheaded the Indian operations in service to the Crown. There was little secret that the British were blatantly and more heavily supplying weapons and strategic direction to the Indian army at this time.

About fifty miles to the north of Estill's was another station which was built by the Bryan brothers. It was the next target in the enemy's sights. On the evening of August 15, 1782, Indians were spotted hiding in the woods surrounding the fort. The inhabitants discreetly restrained themselves from reacting in haste against the would-be attackers, except for secreting two men out into the darkness in order to secure reinforcements from nearby Fort Lexington. From there, runners were sent to Boonesborough, Harrodstown, and lastly the most-distant fort of Logan's. A siege ensued the next day, but was lifted when word from Indian scouts reached the attackers that a substantial militia was indeed on the way. Hugh McGary was among the men heading to their aid from Harrodsburg.

On August 18, two days after the attack and subsequent withdrawal of the Indians, the reinforcements came riding in from the various settlements. They were a bit late to help at Bryan's, but luckily the casualties were light and all was now quiet. However, the force determined that the Indians had to still be within range and trackable. The militia now numbered upwards of two hundred men, all on horseback. Many of these men were farmers and laborers who were not necessarily skilled in the art of warfare, especially against the Indians' techniques. A decision loomed. Should this body immediately go in pursuit of the known enemy or should they wait for Colonel Benjamin Logan to arrive with an additional force of nearly three hundred men? Afterall, Logan had the highest credentials of all of the men present, and through numerous previous confrontations, had become quite adept at fighting the Indians. A conference was held by the leaders.

Daniel Boone and John Todd were colonels in charge of the men from Boonesborough and Lexington, respectively. Colonel Stephen Trigg and, at that time with the rank of Major, Hugh McGary, led the militias from Lexington and Harrodstown. Pros and cons were exchanged and a vote was taken. It was not unanimous. Oddly enough, it was the usually impetuous McGary who was reticent to move on without the support of Logan's leadership and force. Todd, who had the most experience and highest authority, chastised McGary as being timid. That accusation may have played a significant part in what transpired soon thereafter.

With McGary being out numbered, the united militia left in pursuit of the supposed forty or so Indians who had attacked them at Bryan's Station. Little did they know that they would be facing a much larger Indian force once they had tracked them down at the Blue Licks site on the banks of the Licking River.

From this point forward, some confusion creeps into the analysis of what part McGary had played in triggering the now famous confrontation. It is certain that the Americans suffered a devastatingly embarrassing defeat on the morning of August 19 in what has become known as the Battle of Blue Licks; but the specifics of what led to it are muddled by accusatory, contradictory, and speculative commentaries. That said, nearly, but not all, of the historians who have written about this battle, cite Hugh McGary as the villain. Although there are numerous testimonies to support this conclusion, most of them have been given by participants, or friends and relatives of participants, several decades after the fact. That is not to say that they are by any means invalid, but memories do get distorted over such a stretch of time. And, a deeper analysis of the accounts reveals some interesting twists and turns.

Along the forty mile stretch from Bryan's station to these salt licks, the tracking instincts of Boone had been heightened. It's said that he had become troubled by the signs left by the Indians because they were much too numerous and obvious. Smoldering campfires, broken branches, and such, led him to believe that the militia were being baited into a trap. If they proceeded directly across the river, Boone felt that they would find themselves in an ambush; and one executed by a much larger force than they had anticipated. He voiced his concerns in another conference held between the officers as they approached the Blue Licks site.

It was Humphrey Marshall who was the first to write a definitive history of how the lands of Kentucky were settled. In his *History of Kentucky* he presented the public with the first telling of the Battle of the Blue Licks in print. He included quotes attributed to McGary during this event, but neglected to cite any sources for them. Further, his book was published in 1812, some thirty years after the battle. Marshall states that it was as the officers were in the midst of their conference at the Licks, weighing Boone's options of how to proceed, that

> Major M'Gary, ardent, and impatient of delay, rushed his horse forward to the water's edge, then raising the war-whoop, and crying out with a loud voice, 'Those who are not cowards will follow me, I will shew them where the Indians are,' spurred his horse into the water. One followed, and another followed, in quick succession; the council was broken up, the officers, who might have been otherwise inclined, were forced along in the crowd and tumult – no authority was observed – no command was given; they crossed the river; they pursued the road, as the leading guide; on either side of which parties flanked out, as the unevenness, and irregularity of the ground would permit; all moving forward, with the utmost disorder... [7]

In this case, an old adage to the effect that, "Once something is written as fact, it becomes so," seems to apply. Many of the testimonies given by participants and cited in histories written since this one given by Marshall in 1812 seem to use very similar phraseology. This can be taken to either confirm the truth of the quotes and actions of McGary, or it could suggest that they had read Marshall's work in the intervening years and it eventually became mixed into their own recollections. A few of the other testimonies of what McGary shouted out include examples that bear this out. One says, "Delay is dastardly; let all who are not cowards follow me, and I will show them where the Indians are." [8] Another reports that he said, "All who are not d____d cowards follow me, and I'll soon show you the Indians." [9] And yet another states, "We have force enough to whip all the indians we will find." [10]

It is further suggested that McGary had acted this way in direct disobedience to orders of the three superior officers at hand: Colonels Trigg, Todd, and Boone. All this conjecture is significant because by supposedly rearing up his horse with a war whoop and dashing into the river toward the Indians, McGary is forever blamed in the history books for bringing on the slaughter of over seventy of his fellow men.

Some, like this account from a militia spy, were slightly different from Marshall's. Jacob Stevens states that he and four of his companions had been some distance ahead of the main body when they spotted Indians on a ridge, and many more in the distance lying behind timbers that had fallen. They then

> stopped till the main army came up; where a council of war was immediately called.
> The army marched in three columns, headed up by Hugh McGary, Col. John Todd, and Steven Trigg... In the council McGary, only a ... private [actually a Major], wanted to know by Godly (as he wo'd say when he was in earnest) what we came here for? They said, to fight the indians. By godly said he, then why not fight them. "Then let's fight them. They that aint cowards follow me." [11]

What is noteworthy is the fact that the lead officers who had survived the conflict all made official reports to their superiors within a couple weeks, if not a few days, of the battle. Not one of them implicated McGary in any fashion. In fact, McGary's name, if mentioned at all, was used only in reference to his physical location in the field. In no letter was McGary ever described as charging recklessly into the river. This is odd and contrary to the decades-old testimonies of others.

The first of these official reports was made, unsolicited, by a private named Andrew Steele just a week after the battle. He told Governor Benjamin Harrison of Virginia in part that

> The Seventeenth, we were Reinforced from Lincoln [county], with one hundred & fifty Horse men, Commanded by Lieut: Col: Stephen Trigg & Joined by a few of the Fayette Commanded by Colo. Jno.

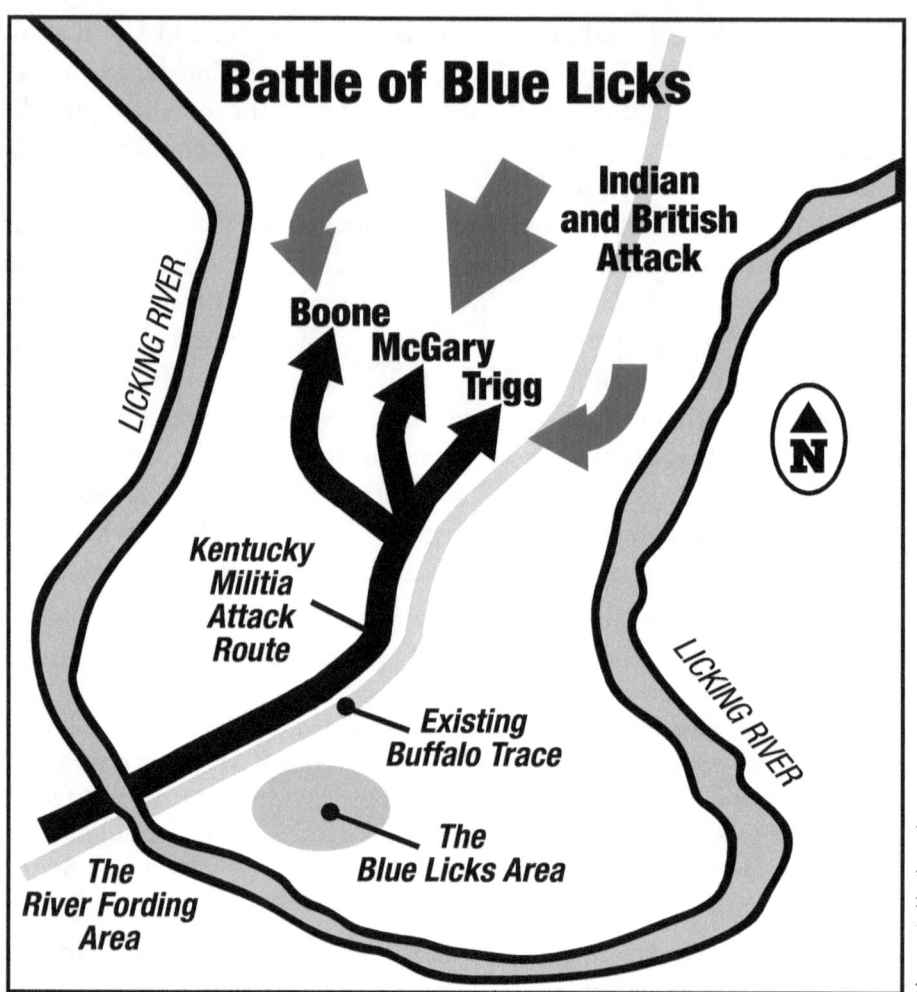

Todd, who compos'd an Army of one Hundred & Eighty Two. We followed them to the Lower Blue Licks, where Ended the Direfull Catastrophy – in short we were defeated – with the loss of seventy-five men – among whom fell our two Commanders [Todd and Trigg] with many other officers & soldiers of Distinguished Bravery... [12]

Eleven days out, Colonel Daniel Boone wrote the governor. He stated that when the attack on Bryan's Station had ended and the enemy had left the area, it was with the help that had arrived from the neighboring stations that

we Imediately collected 181 Horsemen commanded by Colo. Jno.

Todd: Including some of the Lincoln County Militia Commanded by Colo. Trigg, and having pursued about 40 miles, on the 19th Instant we Discovered the Enemy Lying in wait for us, on Discovery of which we formed our Column into one Single Line and march'd up in their front within about forty yards before there was a gun fired: Col: Trigg on the right, my Self on the Left, Major McGary in the centre, Major Harlin with the advance party in the front – and from the manner wee had form'd, it fell to my lot to bring on the attack, which was done with a very heavy [fire?] on both Sides: and extended back the lines to Colo. Trigg, where the Enemy was so strong that the[y] Rushed up and Broke the right wing at the first fire. So the Enemy was immediately on our Backs, so we were obliged to Retreat with the loss of 77 of our men and 12 wounded... [13]

Notice that Boone clearly states that, "it fell to my lot to bring on the attack."

Colonel Benjamin Logan addressed Governor Harrison a day after Boone had written him. Because Logan had only arrived shortly after the battle had ended, he had no eye-witness account of it. He did include a diagram of the battleground, however, with some description of what transpired; presumably based on what he learned from the survivors.

The indians kept the path from Bryants to the licks, and when Colo. Todd arrived at the Top of the hill on this side of the river, the enemy made a shew of ab't 30 in the bend. Our men marched over upon the Hill. The indians had a very strong line in front which extended from one point of the river to the other. They had flankers and also a party in the rear in order to prevent a retreat. As the river was very deep only at the licks and the clifts so steep that a passage was impracticable only where they first marched in – thus circumstanced the Savages, sure of victory rushed immediately up and threw our men into confusion. What escaped returned mostly by way of the Lick – many were killed after they were made prisoners, as they were seen tied.

From Bryant's Station to the Blue Licks ab't 40 miles & from thence to the Ohia ab't 20 or 25. The Bent of the river was generally ab't 1/2 mile over & from the top of the ridge each way made down small dreans – in these places lay many indians undiscovered until the attack begun.

It appears near all the warriors' on this side of De Troit were on this expedition; some allow 600 or more... [14]

Shortly after the battle, Colonel Levi Todd, brother to Colonel John Todd who was the leading commander killed in the fight, wrote to his other brother, Captain Robert Todd. He passed on the sad news of John's death in the midst of a fuller report of how the battle played out.

> On the morning of the 18th we collected 182 men all on Horseback, and pursued the Enemy till 8 o'clock in the morning of the 19th, when we got sight of them forming in a Ridge in a Loop of the River, about three Quarters of a Mile North of the lower blue Lick and over the Licking [River]. We had then pursued about 40 miles. We rode up within 60 yards, dismounted, gave & sustained a heavy and general Fire. The ground was equally favorable to both Parties and the Timber good. The left wing rushed on & gained near 100 yards of ground. But the Right gave way, and the Enemy soon flanked us on that side, upon which the center gave way & shifted behind the left Wing. And immediately the whole broke in Confusion after the Action had lasted about five minutes. Our men suffered much in the Retreat, many Indians having mounted our men's Horses, haveing open woods to pass through to the River, and several were killed in the River. Several efforts were made to rally, but al in Vain. He that could remount a horse was well off, and he that could not saw no time for delay. Our Brother received a Ball in his left Breast, and was on Horseback when the men broke. He took a course I thought Dangerous, and as I never saw him afterwards, I suppose he never got over the River... [15]

A couple weeks later, the same Levi Todd wrote his own report to Governor Harrison, and again did not mention anything of McGary.

Because Trigg and Todd were both killed, their version of what transpired can never be known. However, as we've just seen, in all the reports of the surviving officers, nary a one says a bad word about McGary. Well, that's not exactly true. There were two more letters written within weeks of the battle, but not to Governor Harrison. And, they are a little distinctive in their own right.

One was penned by Arthur Campbell which is second only to the narrative of Marshall in his *History of Kentucky*, as the most often cited document used by historians to make McGary the scapegoat. This is part of Campbell's letter, written to his friend and Commander of the 1st Virginia Regiment, Colonel William Davies.

Sir

From Col. Christian and other accounts sent by Major Netherland, the Executive may be fully informed of the State of the War in the Kentucky Country. What if it should be the policy of the British Ministry to drive in from the other side of the Apalacian mountain before the signing the preliminaries of peace.

At any rate they are uniting the Savage Tribes and endeavoring to sow the seeds of deep laid animosity, which will lengthen the Indian war to a longer period than most imagine. Nothing now will put an end to it, but a decided blow to the enemies country, and a peace given them in the hour of their panic and misfortune, afterwards conducted by a proper Superintendency, or that Canada becomes ours, or our Allies.

The method of arming and arraying our militia ought to be varied. The Bayonet and Seymeter [razor] must be introduced to enable us now to face the Indians. And Evolutions suited to the woods should be learned both by Foot and Horse. All our late defeats have been occasioned thro' neglect of these and a want of a proper authority and capacity in the Commanding Officers. Never was the lives of so many valuable men lost more shamefully than in the late action of the 19th of August, and that not a little thro' the vain and seditious expressions of a Major McGeary. How much more harm than good can one fool do. Todd & Trigg had capacity but wanted experience. Boone, Harlin and Lindsay had experience, but were defective in capacity. Good however would it have been, had their advice been followed. Logan is a dull, narrow body from whom nothing clever need be expected. What a figure he exhibited at the head of near 500 men to reach the field of action six days afterwards, and hardly wait to bury the dead, and when it was plain, part of the Indians were still in the Country. Genl. Clarke is in that country, but he has lost the confidence of the people, and it is said become a Sot; perhaps something worse. [16]

Campbell, the author of this letter, was a noteworthy leader in the political and military circles of Virginia. After spending three of his teenage years as an Indian captive, he rose to prominence as a commander during the Revolution and a delegate to the Virginia legislature. As the frontier population grew through the early 1780s, and the Revolution's end seemed near, there were any number of power plays being made by the state and federal governments regarding how new states would soon be carved out of the western lands. Campbell, with ambition resembling that of Richard Henderson of Transylvania fame, was deeply involved. He wanted to declare a broad stretch of frontier land stretching across parts of Alabama, Virginia, Georgia, Tennessee, and Kentucky, as a new state he would call Frankland. In fact, it did come into existence, but only encompassing what today are the eastern counties of Tennessee. The name was altered to Franklin and it existed for a few years after the Revolution. But, at its outset, this endeavor of Campbell's caused much wrangling among the frontiersmen. The Kentuckians generally wanted no part of it. This fueled Campbell's consternation.

Three months before the Blue Licks disaster took place, with Frankland still just an idea, Campbell had solicited other movers and shakers interested in his concept to attend a planning meeting at Harrodsburg. The gathering was well attended and the next steps toward statehood were being discussed until the Kentucky militia showed up and dispersed the crowd. The commander of these policing Kentuckians was Hugh McGary.

In fact, McGary was not alone in his opposition to Campbell. Harrod, Logan, Clark and others were all against his scheme. This might explain the antagonistic and demeaning sentiments in Campbell's letter toward McGary and the otherwise highly respected Logan and Clark. Though cited extensively by historians, often with the misconception that Campbell was actually in attendance at the Licks (which he was not), few historians have pursued the underlying relationship of Campbell with McGary and these other acclaimed Kentuckians.

The second letter of note was written just nine days after the battle. Though it is rarely cited in historian's accounts of this event, it was sent by McGary himself to Colonel Logan. It includes these sentiments:

> Sir I understand I am much sensured for incouraging the men to fight the Indians when we came up with them[.] I should have informed you of a grand scheam that was planed when I saw you only I thought perhaps it would cause a Riot and you may Judge the Matter yourself[,] only it is hard to Judge dead men [.] you saw Trigg did not wright to you until he was shure you could not come up with us, and Todd took Captns Craigs word for the Number of Indians so we

> Marched in order to gain great applause with our men as it was well known that you would have had the Command[.] as almost all the men was of our County and their scheam met with a sad misfortune which I am sorry for[.] So I suppose you have heard of my bad conduct perhaps by some person that was conserned in the scheam and if you think I am faulty I should be fond to have a hearing in the Matter[.] [17]

What? Did McGary just suggest that the other officers wanted the glory of a victorious battle for themselves and not for Logan, who would have had rightful command if he had shown up in time? He sure did. Perhaps he was laying down a conjecture as a preemptive excuse for his actions; but perhaps the officers' egos were more involved in their decision making than they should have been. We'll never know. In the least, aside from this intriguing insight, McGary did admit to some sort of maneuver that was frowned upon. And, he went even further to ask Logan to hold a formal inquiry into his actions if he felt it was warranted. There is no record that any sort of official investigation was ever made into this event.

Another perception of the officers' temperaments just before the engagement states that the commanders were somewhat perplexed on how to proceed. It comes in an account from Major Madison who states that

> the principal officers appeared to be confused in their council[.] Each afraid to speak Candidly for fear of being Suspected of Timerity [timidity]; but the whole Moved forward apparently without order... [18]

Speaking of timidity, that topic seemed to be a particularly hot one during this event. At this time in our history, in this wild country an accusation of this nature was the greatest insult a frontiersman could bear as it bordered on a charge of cowardice. It has been reported that Colonel Todd had accused McGary of timidity when they were engaged in the first officers' conference at Bryan's Station because McGary was the only one to opt for waiting for Logan before beginning the pursuit of the Indians – which ironically goes against all that has been attested to about McGary's temperament. Because of Todd's taunt, McGary did a "one-eighty" in his attitude when they reached the Blue Licks and held their second council.

McGary supposedly went so far as to challenge Boone's courage during this second meeting. Rebecca Boone Grant, a grand-niece of Daniel Boone, reported the memories that her uncle William, who was at the battle, had often told her father. Accordingly, after leaving Bryan's Station

> They reached the ford of North Licking [River] without opposition, and halted to consider. From Uncles [Boone's] knowledge of the Geography of the country and of Indian warfare, he feared they were encamped on the hill sides which commanded a deep ravine just opposite the ford, and proposed crossing the river either above or below the ford and decoy the Indians into open battle. But Col McGary a brave yet imprudent man and the Same officer rashly declared that, "no man but a coward would refuse to fight." My brother Wm who was standing by Uncle at the time, has often told me, that this unjust and cutting taunt so deeply affected Uncle Daniel that he actually burst into tears and after answering that no man before had even dared to call him a coward, commanded his men to follow him, saying, "come on we are all slaughtered men"! No sooner had they entered ... than the enemy opposed their fire upon them from the clifts and cut them down by scores, or, as some have remarked "shot them down like pigeons." [19]

Lo, the power of words to set men of honor into action!

Though McGary is implied by most accounts to be a lone wolf calling all to fight, Peter Houston, one of the earliest settlers at Boones Station, says that there was at least one other who was eager to engage the enemy. In a biography of Boone he wrote in the 1840s, Houston details the conference among the leaders and concludes that Boone wanted to wait for Logan; but, "so impetuous were the feeling of Major McGary and Harlan that Boone's counsel was not heeded." [20] Major Silas Harlan, a co-founder of Harrodstown and of whom George Rogers Clark once said, "he was one of the bravest and most accomplished soldiers that ever fought by my side," seems to have been in strong agreement with McGary that action should not be delayed.

The account of Houston continues to confirm Harlan's feelings and brings up a potential attitude problem in Colonel Todd.

> After hearing Boone, Todd was decidedly in favor of awaiting the arrival of Col. Logan who was much more experienced in indian warfare than he or any other officer in his command. But McGary and

Harlan became impatient at the detention by Boones Council, and seeing that Todd was Swayed by Boone, McGary flourished his hand in the air, wheeled his horse for the ford and cried out "all that aren't cowards follow me." And the enthusiastic young men followed him. Boone appealed to Todd, who was commander in chief to assert his authority and stop the procedure, but he replied, "let them go, and we will remain in the rear, and if they are surprised by the Indians, the blame will be on McGary and he will have the brunt to bear." [21]

It seems that Houston may have read Marshall's History as he includes the supposed quotes of McGary that Marshall cited thirty years previous. However, much more importantly, he points out that if McGary had in truth led the charge, Todd could have stopped it, but didn't. Further, Todd had predetermined to set any blame on McGary before the events had even unfolded.

With so many reports to consider, coming to a definitive conclusion of what, if any, actions and words are legitimately attributable to Hugh McGary seems impossible. However, based on his own letter to Col. Logan, it would seem safe to assume he made some sort of comment or took some impulsive action. There is evidence that perhaps his comments were made strictly in the counsel of the officers and not necessarily in earshot of the regulars. Furthermore, he wasn't seemingly alone in his wanting to fight without waiting for reinforcements. And, any of his actions could have been spurred on by his having been accused of cowardice by Todd the day before. As Boone's nephew attests, cowardice was the ultimate insult a man could throw at another man on the frontier. As in most tragic events, it is human nature to make someone the scapegoat, and in this one, McGary's temperament made him the best candidate.

In spite of all the controversy surrounding his part in the battle at the Blue Licks, the worst defeat the Kentuckians had ever suffered through the Revolution, any censure of McGary was extremely short-lived. Just two months later, in November of 1782, he was again serving under George Rogers Clark in a retaliatory strike against the Shawnee villages north of the Ohio River. He even rescued a man who was still being held prisoner by the Indians for four years after he had been captured along with Boone back in 1777.

McGary continued to do his part as conflicts arose through 1783. There is record that McGary had run into a bit of trouble in May of 1783 when he was judged to be an infamous gambler. At a time when the state of Virginia was under an "Act to Suppress Excessive Gambling," his bet on a race won him a mare valued at twelve pounds. That translates to about three hundred dollars in 2024, apparently an inordinate amount of winnings in that day. His penalty was to be prohibited from serving in any form of public office for one year. It seems his sentence was only a reprimand as a mere four months later he was again sitting on the county bench as judge.

The American Revolution had officially ended in September of 1783. As a result, as far as everyone except the Indians were concerned, the lands between the Appalachians and the Mississippi River were now owned by the new United States. Two years into its existance, the young country's representatives approached some of the tribes living in the Ohio Valley with a document. It was presented to them at Fort McIntosh, just a short stretch of distance from Pittsburgh. The so-called treaty was actually more of a coerced acknowledgement that the United States were now the owners of the former British and Indian lands. Specifically it focussed on the area north and west of the Ohio River. By signing this authorization, the Delaware, Ottawa, Wyandot, and Chippewa tribes agreed not to contest its control. Though some reports suggest that these papers were incomprehensible to these Indians on many levels, they did sign the document.

A year later, in January of 1786, the Shawnee, who had not attended the Fort McIntosh meeting and who still heavily occupied much of the land in question, were approached to discuss the terms of the treaty. This time the meeting would be held at Fort Finney, near present-day Cincinnati. The Delaware and Wyandot again participated, but the Shawnee were very reluctant to attend. When they finally arrived, later than requested, it was with obvious chips on their shoulders.

The discussions began on an inflammatory note. As at Fort McIntosh, the purpose of the gathering was to point out to the Indians in no uncertain terms that the US owned the lands of the Ohio Valley and at their discretion the Indians could use parts of them. Again, this was received with incredulity and indignation. With a firm warning, the US promised to continue to attack the Indian villages if they did not remove themselves voluntarily from defined regions. As tensions grew, a highly respected chief came forward. His name was Moluntha, an elderly and much respected leader of the Shawnee. He addressed the assembly with a little more discretion than the others before him had shown. Still, after expressing his views, he saw little recourse. He and the Shawnee war chiefs who were present ended up signing the so-called Treaty of Fort Finney. However, the majority of the Shawnee warriors vehemently disagreed and remained steadfast in their determination to defend their lands.

By October of that same year, tensions had peaked. The better part of the Shawnee were continuing to resist the American's claim to ownership of their lands. Small retaliatory raids were led by both sides against one another throughout the Ohio Valley, resulting in destruction of property, theft of horses, and deaths. Colonel Logan was ordered to lead a large force of regulars and militia into what were known as the Macacheek towns of the Shawnee; situated along the Mad, Great, and Little Miami Rivers of southwest Ohio (generally in the present-day region of Bellefontaine and Piqua).

When he arrived, Logan discovered that the Indian villages he had targeted were for the most part absent of warriors. The majority of the Indian fighters had left the area for the villages situated along the Wabash River of the Indiana territory; which they went to defend after learning that they were going to be attacked by George Rogers Clark. Only a few men were left behind to guard the women and children. None-the-less, Logan's troops destroyed the villages' structures, their crops, and took many of the residents captive. One of the villages in this mix was known as Moluntha's town. Here the distinguished, aged chief lived with the sister of the former renowned chief known as Cornstalk.

The movements and actions of Logan and the Indians is recounted by the infamous Simon Girty who was stationed in Upper Sandusky at this time, approximately fifty miles northeast of the villages. Just a few days after the raid, in a letter to Alexander McKee, another of the British Indian agents who had a home amongst the Shawnee, Girty relates:

I inform you that on the 8th Inst. there arrived an Express from the

Shawanese Towns, to Upper Sandusky, that the American Army had arrived at the Shawanese Towns and I receiving this news made no delay, but immediately sent two runners to said Towns to know the certainty thereof and this day the Runners are arrived to me again, and give you an account that the American Army came into the Town at 12 o'clock in the day; and some time before the Army had arrived in Town, there came a Deserter, who told the Indians that the Yankee Army was coming, but the Indians would not believe the Deserter, that they were coming when the Army appeared in sight. Shortly after the Indians of the Maycockey Town, on seeing them[,] rose their Yankee colours to receive them, but their hoisting their colours was to no purpose, the Army immediately destroy'd the Town, then proceeded to Wakitumikie Town, and destroy'd that likewise; then proceeded from thence to Your House and destroy'd that, immediately from thence proceed'd to Blue Jackets and brought that immediately to the ground; and then they returned instantly back to Wakitumikis and there encamped and remain'd on the ground that night, and next day made a Retreat back again. Whether they have made a total Retreat or not I cannot tell as yet, but this is the word at present, in short I will be able to acquaint you farther.

The number of Indians that were killed I do not know, but in the Town where Capt Eliot lived there were 10 Indians found lying in the Town dead, and among them was the Chief of the Town... [22]

The first point of interest in this letter is the admission that it was only when the troops were actually seen approaching them, that the Indians raised the US flag over their village. It's understandable that they would sue for peace by flying the colors, but it was an obvious smoke screen, else the flag would have been up beforehand. Afterall, the treaty of Fort Finney had supposedly confirmed the Shawnee acknowledgement of US ownership of the land.

It is likely that the chief, noted by Girty as being found dead in the town, was Moluntha. The stories of how and under what circumstances he was killed vary only slightly in the numerous tellings; but as at the Blue Licks, it was Hugh McGary who was at the core of this major incident. This time there is no doubt that the now Lieutenent-Colonel McGary was the one who killed the respected Shawnee chief in a brutal fashion. There were simply too many witnesses.

One account of Moluntha's death comes from Henry Hall, an American who was nearby when the assault took place.

> Moluntha's Town was about a mile from Mackacheek, at the head of the prairie. There was Moluntha, & his queen & several others - some 15 or 20 prisoners, one or two of whom were white girls - one of these was badly cut by one of the Colonels mistaking her for an Indian. After the prisoners had been an hour, McGry went up to Moluntha, who had about his person a good many silver trinkets & jewelry, and asked - "Do you remember the Blue Licks Defeat?" "Yah, I do," replied Moluntha - upon which McGary cursed him, and snatched a squaw hatchet from the queen & with two blows killed Moluntha. Don't recollect about McGary cutting the queen's fingers off. McGary was much blamed - it was strictly ordered, that no prisoners, after having surrendered, should be injured. No recollection of McGary justifying himself for the act. [23]

As with the numerous Blue Licks accounts, the killing of Moluntha stories are mostly given decades afterwards. The above from Hall came fifty-eight years post mortem.

Another was given by William Lytle, a member of Logan's troops, who would later go on to be a member of President Andrew Jackson's so-called "kitchen cabinet" (a collection of close friends who advised Jackson while his official cabinet was in chronic disarray). The account is again given many years after the fact. It begins with his description of the approach to the village.

> As we came up with the flying savages, I was disappointed, discovering that we should have little to do. I heard but one savage, with the exception of the chief, cry for quarter. They fought with desperation, as long as they could raise knife, gun or tomahawk, after they found they could not screen themselves. We dispatched all the warriors we overtook, and sent women and children prisoners to the rear. We pushed ahead, still hoping to overtake a larger body, where we might have something like a general engagement. I was mounted on a very fleet gray horse. Fifty of my companions followed me. I had not advanced more than a mile, before I discovered some of the enemy, running along the edge of a thicket of hazel and plum bushes. I made signs to the men in my rear to come on. At the same time pointing to the flying enemy... When I arrived within fifty yards of them I dismounted and raised my gun. I discovered at this moment, some men on the right wing coming up on the left. The warrior I was about to shoot held up his hand in a token of surrender, and I heard him order the other Indians to stop. By this time the men behind had arrived,

and were in the act of firing upon the Indians. I called to them not to fire, for the enemy had surrendered. The warrior that had surrendered to me came walking towards me, calling his women and children to follow him. I advanced to meet him, with my right hand extended; but before I could reach him the men of the right wing of our force had surrounded him. I rushed in among their horses. While he was giving me his hand, several of our men wished to tomahawk him. I informed them they would have to tomahawk me first. We led him back to the place where his flag had been. We had taken thirteen prisoners. Among them were the chief, his three wives — one of them a young and handsome woman, another of them the famous grenadier squaw, upwards of six feet high — and two or three young lads. The rest were children. One of these lads was a remarkably interesting youth, about my own age and size. He clung closely to me, and appeared keenly to notice everything that was going on.

When we arrived at the town a crowd of our men pressed around to see the chief. I stepped aside to fasten my horse, and my prisoner lad clung close to my side… Colonel McGary, the same man who had caused the disaster at the Blue Licks, some years before, coming up, General Logan's eye caught that of McGary. "Colonel McGary," said he, "you must not molest these prisoners." "I will see to that," said McGary in reply. I forced my way through the crowd to the chief with my young charge by the hand. McGary ordered the crowd to open and let him in. He came up to the chief, and the first salutation was in the question, "Were you at the defeat of the Blue Licks?" The Indian, not knowing the meaning of the words, or not understanding the purport of the question, answered, "Yes." McGary instantly seized an axe from the hands of the grenadier squaw, and raised it to make a blow at the chief. I threw up my arm to ward off the blow. The hand of the axe struck me across the left wrist and came near breaking it.

The axe sunk in the head of the chief to the eyes, and he fell dead at my feet. Provoked beyond measure at this wanton barbarity, I drew my knife, for the purpose of avenging his cruelty by dispatching him. My arm was arrested by one of our men, which prevented me inflicting the thrust. McGary escaped from the crowd…

… The name of the Indian chief killed by McGary was Moluntha, the great sachem of the Shawnees. The grenadier squaw was the sister to Cornstalk, who fell (basely murdered) at Point Pleasant. [24]

Lytle, the author of this account, seems to stress his utmost determination to not harm, or let anyone else harm, a prisoner of war.

Though this sentiment is extremely admirable, Lytle's going to the extreme of attempting to kill rather than discipline McGary, the offender of this policy, seems contradictory and extreme. In fact, the language of Logan's order regarding the treatment of prisoners, and whether he even gave it or modified it, has been questioned. In her exhaustive research of Hugh McGary, biographer Mary Powell Hammersmith notes that

> Logan had originally told his men that if any person attempted to come to the army they were to be received in a friendly manner. This was thought to have been because there were white prisoners in the Indian camps. By October 6, however, Logan was concerned that his order might cause his men to avoid fighting as they really needed to, so he told his soldiers they should save white people but could treat Indians any way they wanted to. [25]

According to the records of the state of Virginia, within six months of this event, a general court martial was held against McGary.

> PROCEEDINGS OF A GENERAL COURT MARTIAL, Held by order of the Council for the trial of Colonel Hugh McGary, of Mercer county, who was charged with murdering with a tomahawk or small ax one of the Cheifs or King of the Shawanese Indians, named Malunthy, after the said Cheif had surrendered himself a Prisoner of war, and was received as such and brought back to the Town of Macocheek.
> Secondly, With acting in disobedience of orders, which was to spare all prisoners, which orders were never countermanded.
> Thirdly, With behaving in a disorderly manner in insulting and abusing Lieutenant-Colo. Trotter, of Fayette County, for taking measures to prevent the Prisoners being murdered, and swore, by God, he would chop him down, or any other man who should attempt to hinder him from killing them at any time.
> Fourthly, With abusing several Field Officers in a public manner, but who were absent at Limestone on the return of the Expedition; And his Conduct in general was unbecoming the character of a Gentleman and an Officer.

Surprisingly, McGary had counter charges of his own which were presented against two of the other officers in charge. The records continue:

> Also, for the trial of Colonel Robert Patterson and Lieutenant-Colonel

James Trotter, of Fayette county, on complaint made by Colo. Hugh McGary, That they had impressed one Barrel of Rum at Limestone, where the Troops crossed the Ohio River, and by so doing, and drinking part of the same, and putting the Remainder on the public Horses, and having twenty Beeves [cows] shot down without orders from the Commanding Officer, or making application to the Commissary for provisions, and he present, was the means of delaying the army more than one day. He further complained that Colonel Trotter gave his men positive orders to shoot down any man that killed an Indian after he was captured, and said orders given in time of action, and not known what might be the consequence the engagement.

And the verdicts were:

The Court, on maturely considering the Evidence, together with the circumstances of the case, are of the opinion that Colo. Hugh McGary is guilty of the first charge, viz: of murdering Molunthy, the Indian King, after he had surrendered himself a prisoner. Not guilty of the second charge, viz.: Disobedience of Orders.

Guilty of the third charge, viz.: of abusing Col. Trotter, &c. In part guilty of the fourth charge, viz.: That his conduct in general was unbecoming the character of an officer and a Gentleman: And Sentence him to be suspended for one year.

The court then proceeded, pursuant to adjournment, to consider the charges McGary had brought against Col. Robt. Patterson. Having considered the Charges and Evidence, are of the opinion that the impressment of the Rum does not come under their notice, and that the legality or illegality of it ought to be determined by a civil Court. They are of opinion that the application of the Rum impressed by Col. Patterson was, in some measure, irregular. He was guilty of disobedience of Orders in not making application to the Commissary, and in proceeding to have the Beef killed without his participation. They are of the opinion that the army was not delayed by the irregularity of killing Beeves, but that some waste was incurred thereby, and sentenced him to be severely Reprimanded by Colonel Levi Todd, of Fayette County, at the head of his Regiment. There appearing no evidence against Col. Trotter, he was released and restored to his Command. [26]

The order of Colonel Logan regarding the treatment of Indian prisoners grew to be a key factor in the charges against McGary. Because this happened in an atmosphere of war, the question became whether the killing of Moluntha was an acceptable act in the course of a battle or was it murder in defiance of a superior's order? As it happened,

> Benjamin Logan, his [McGary's] commanding officer, testified at the trial and said he had changed his orders; in other words, he had said during this change of orders that soldiers could kill Indians who might come to the Kentucky lines before the fighting had ended. During the trial, evidence was presented that some of the fighting had taken place after Moluntha was killed, so, strictly speaking, what McGary did was not in violation of Logan's order. [27]

Many further examples of how this event transpired are available; but all cite similar wording and comparable wielding of a tomahawk to the head of Moluntha. One last account, however, is contrary to most by claiming that Moluntha had clearly understood McGary's question; as evidenced by his more explicit response. If true, it doesn't acquit McGary, but it does provide a little more reason for his action.

> Moluntha surrendered — was smoking the pipe & passing it to others — a crowd around him smoking. McGary, in another part of the many, hearing that he was there, came up. Moluntha held out his hand & McGary took it, asked him if he was at the Blue Lick defeat? Moluntha answered that he commanded the warriors of his town. Then McGary in a rage, exclaimed "G_d d_m you, I'll give you Blue Lick play", and sunk his tomahawk into the old chief's head. [28]

After serving his suspension of one year from the military, McGary remained active in local government as a member of his county courts. Among other responsibilities, he was often the arbiter of land purchase disputes. This, as one might expect, left half the people in the county admiring him and the other half disparaging him, depending on his rulings.

In 1793, another high-profile case was heard in Mercer County. This one was a suit for divorce. Though divorce is common today, in McGary's day, extremely good cause had to be shown for a separation to be granted. No, it wasn't McGary's marriage that was in trouble, but he was called as a key witness; and three decades later his testimony in this case would be used to influence a presidential election.

It was in September of 1793 when Lewis Robards filed for divorce from his wife Rachel (Donelson) Robards on the grounds that she had committed adultery. At the time, it was merely good, local gossip that Rachel had run off to New Orleans with another man whom she married at that place while still legally married to Lewis. Because divorce was a tough suit to be filed on the 1790s frontier, a special act was created to handle Lewis Robard's charge. In fact it was titled, "An Act Concerning the Marriage of Lewis Robards." Though filed on December 20, 1790, this case came at a time when the preponderance of legal attention was focussed on Kentucky becoming the fifteenth state in the union. As a result, the actual trial was delayed nearly three years.

The adultery in this case was alleged to have occurred between Rachel and Andrew Jackson during the summer of 1790. Yes, it was that Andrew Jackson. So famous was the story that acclaimed author Irving Stone wrote a novel about it in 1951 and it soon became a movie starring Susan Hayward and Charlton Heston. Rachel had earlier separated from Lewis. It is said that she had travelled down what became known as the Natchez Trace; leaving from Nashville to the town of Natchez in the soon to become the state of Mississippi. There she met up with Jackson. In a short time they were married.

Lewis Robards was granted his divorce in September of 1793, in no small part due to the testimony of Hugh McGary. One of the most critical elements in the case was whether Rachel had her adulterous affair before December of 1790, when the special Act for Lewis's suit was issued, or whether it was afterwards, in 1791, which would have made Lewis's claim invalid. The issue came to light nationally only when Jackson decided to run for president. Accusations of adultery against the couple, who were married for nearly four decades by the 1828 campaign, flooded the newspapers and the streets on signs carried by Anti-Jackson (pro-John Quincy Adams) crowds.

McGary provided testimony in court in 1793 stating that he had led the group that Andrew and Rachel were a part of along the Natchez Trace in 1790, not 1791. One resident of Mercer County stated that Lewis, "got a full Devorce through the influence of Conl. hugh McGeary as he seen them beding together in the Wilderness as

Portrait of Rachel (Donelson) Jackson by Ralph Eleazer Whiteside Earl, circa 1825.

Portrait of Andrew Jackson by James Barton Longacre, circa 1829.

man and Wife." [29] As a result of all the controversy surrounding the case, the first marriage between Andrew and Rachel was finally considered an act of bigamy. Therefore, the couple was compelled to marry again, which they did in 1794.

Counter claims flew during Jackson's campaign that the long-since dead McGary had had a serious disdain for Jackson and so naturally had provided a false testimony against him all those years ago. The only basis for this conjecture came from Jackson's close lifetime business associate, John Overton. During the presidential campaign, Overton alluded to arguments between the two men while on the cited trip along the Natchez Trace. The disagreements were regarding a possible attack by Indians. Knowing the temperaments of both men to be volatile and commanding, it's not unlikely that disputes could have risen between them. The unsolvable question is whether in fact the quarrels occurred, and if so, whether they had triggered such hatred between the two men that McGary would perjure himself. For all that McGary was, good and bad, a liar under oath didn't seem to be one of his traits. It is interesting to note that he was called to swear to the behavior of a man who possessed much the same disposition as himself.

Jackson won the election by a landslide on December 3, 1828, inspite of the marital controversy; but shortly thereafter suffered an overwhelming loss. The vile personal attacks on Rachel were forever considered by Andrew as the cause of her death by a heart attack less than three weeks afterwards. It seems that mudslinging was as ruthless a political weapon two hundred years ago, just as it is today.

By 1795 McGary had opened a tavern in Harrodsburg which he ran for a couple years. His residences thereafter are sketchy because of varied reports and the loss of some court records. It seems likely that around 1798 he moved for a short time to the area of today's Bowling Green, Kentucky. It was there that his daughter and her husband had recently moved from Shawnee Run after hearing of the "goodly" quality of the land and the abundant wildlife. By 1800 or so, he is known to have been operating another inn and tavern. This time it was in Red Banks, today's Henderson, Kentucky. While living here, yet another negative incident further colored the reputation of McGary. This one tarnished his honesty which had never before been in dispute.

The story goes that a farmer living along the Little Miami River in the Ohio country was in desperate need of money and so personally loaded a massive amount of produce from his land onto a flatboat and headed down the Ohio River to the markets of New Orleans. It was worth the trip. He scored two thousand dollars for his effort. However traveling back, either up the river or by land, was a very dangerous task with both routes known to be constantly watched by thieves and Indians seeking their prey. The farmer cunningly scratched a specific mark on each piece of gold he carried, so they could be identified if lost or stolen. He then boarded a boat for his return with a large group of travelers; safety in numbers was his thinking. However, he soon became seriously ill and was forced to disembark some distance below Red Banks. When he recovered sufficiently, he rode his horse northward over the land route. He made it to Red Banks, but his sickness returned even worse than before. He was taken in at McGary's inn.

McGary tended to him and even sought out a physician. Because of McGary's generous care, the farmer confided to him that he had a small treasure in his saddlebags. McGary promised to keep it protected under lock and key, which he did. After a longer than expected stay, the man finally headed home again. Three days later, when he delved into his bags, he discovered worn horseshoes and pewter instead of his gold. He hadn't suspected any foul play earlier because the weight of the bags when he saddled up at McGary's seemed right.

McGary became the man's prime suspect, and having devised a sly plot, he returned to the Red Banks and waited. He had singled out a local resident to secretly watch McGary's transactions; perchance to catch him using his marked gold for a purchase. It took three months, but it finally happened. McGary bought a horse from the very man the farmer had solicited. The local fellow got word up to the farmer in Red Banks who returned with officials and a warrant for McGary's arrest. The gentleman farmer then

> privately offered McGary if he would refund him the money he would not appear on trial against him. Gladly did McGary avail himself of this his only chance to secure himself from conviction; but he had already used for his own purposes, seven hundred dollars of the money; to replace this he sold his house and lots — the man with his money left for the valley of the Little Miami. The good people of the Red Banks somehow got wind of the transaction, and not relishing their neighbor, told him plainly that he must leave the place, that he sh'd have so many days to do it in, and if he remained beyond that period, they would strenuously urge to prosecution of the trial against him. Thus circumstances, covered with guilt though probably not with shame, he packed upp his wearables and went down the river to Shawneetown on the Illinois shore of the Ohio. It was at that day a fit place for such a character as McGary; but he did not live sufficiently long to reap many new laurels among his new acquaintences! [30]

As it happened, McGary's wife, Caty, passed in 1800, sometime before this incident occurred. There would be one more marriage for Hugh in 1801 to Mary Ann Jones Howell. McGary had two more children by her and made one final move to the Indiana Territory in 1803 – likely due to the edict from the people of Henderson to move out of their town. There they built a home in what grew to be Princeton, Indiana. Three years later, in 1806, Hugh McGary found peace with his maker. Just as controversy had surrounded the tales of his life, his burial site is still in dispute to this day; though it is likely to be near his last home in Princeton.

To decide that Hugh McGary was a good man or a bad man is not the appropriate task. He was a man, like all men, who acted both wisely and foolishly on any given occasion. He possessed many of the traits common to most of the men inhabiting Kentucky. All of them had to be rugged, bold, and fearless or they would not have ventured into the wilderness in the first place.

The thing that made McGary different was his inability to control his emotions; especially anger toward his enemies. "An eye for an eye," was the philosophy seemingly always in his heart. Many of his actions were extremely rash and inexcusable. However, some of them may not have occurred exactly as the history books say they had. In fact, the history books only allude to the dishonorable facets of his life; presumably because the provocative events draw the most interest.

To be fair, McGary had to of been held in at least some esteem by his neighbors, else he wouldn't have been chosen to serve in highly responsible positions throughout his life. He had risen to the military rank of Lieutenent-Colonel, always serving faithfully and repeatedly. He was trusted to communicate with some of the highest government authorities at the behest of the people living with him on the frontier. He had been appointed to be a judge and held other civic positions. He was a family man as well. Through three marriages he fathered fourteen children and three more who were adopted through his first wife.

Hugh McGary should have been held accountable for his misdeeds, and by most accounts, he was. However, his memory does not need to be exclusively focussed on them. He also deserves to be noted for the cloak of passion he wore for his freedom, family, and friends; even if it was hiding under his gruff exterior. ♦

HMMM...

While based with his northwestern army at Upper Piqua in September of 1812, General William H. Harrison received a disturbing letter from one of his scouts alerting him that Fort Wayne was under attack...

...upon reading it [he] immediately assembled his men, and addressing them said; "If there is a man under my command who lacks the patriotism to rush to the rescue, he, by paying back the money received from the government, shall receive a discharge, as I do not wish to command such."

A man named Miller, of the Kentucky militia, responded to the proposition.

The narrator says that he received his discharge on the morning of Sept. 6; his comrades, not willing to let him go without some special manifestation of their appreciation of his course, put him on a rail, carried him around the lines to the music of the "Rogues March" and down to the Miami, where they took him off the rail, led him into the water, and baptised him in the name of King George, Aaron Burr, and the Devil. As he came up out of the river the men formed in two lines, making him run the gauntlet, each man throwing a handful of mud on him as he passed, and then let him go.

In John A. Raynor's, The First Century of Piqua, Ohio, 1916 [31]

III.
WATCHDOGS OF THE WILDERNESS.

Though we hope that they never come, it's the hardships and overwhelming challenges in life that force us to dig deeper into our souls for strength and answers. Many of us finally develop a relationship with our Creator when we are at our most vulnerable point. If not brought low, and called upon to act beyond our self-imposed limitations, so many of us might never have discovered who we were meant to be. Such was the case with most of the people who dared to venture into the wilderness lands west of the Appalachians in the second half of the eighteenth century.

These were not a naive bunch. Before they began their travels, they were well aware that they were bound to face many physical and emotional hardships; not to mention potential trouble with the Indians who had laid claim centuries earlier to the lands they were settling upon. However, when things did get real, well, it made some of the best of then stagger a bit. Most regained their balance and came to realize that they were more resilient than they had expected. They also discovered that as independent as they desired to be, they truly needed each other. Communities emerged.

The men who had fought to gain the West through the French and Indian War felt entitled to venture into it when the fighting ended in 1763. The British government saw things differently, but their restrictions on the colonists' movements proved unenforceable. A few defiantly crossed the mountains; at first it was to hunt, soon thereafter it was to settle. The terrain proved to be just too magnificent.

Details about these earliest adventurers are hard to track down unless they were the ones to establish homesteads that grew into the larger communities which bore their names. There were the Harrods, the Boones, and the Logan's, among others. As well, more is known of those personalities who rose to prominence because of their government or military affiliations. Their deeds were recorded as a matter of law. Isaac Shelby, the state's first governor, and George Rogers Clark, the head of the frontier military during the Revolution come to mind.

Often overlooked, however; are the other hundreds, then thousands of people who faced the same, unimaginable challenges as these more recognized personalities. All of them, rich or poor, young or old, had quickly learned to look out for each other no matter what it took, lest they all perish in the wilderness. All became more than they thought they were. One of the names of this era that should be as prominent as those most often cited, but who's story seems to have faded over the years, is "Whitley."

To be specific, we're speaking of William Chapman Whitley and his wife Esther. It wasn't long after their arrival on the frontier that this couple experienced one of those reality checks that life forces upon everyone sooner or later. They took a few hits, but would quickly rebound and rise to moral heights that were both appreciated and admired by everyone they encountered. The couple left their mark on their fellow settlers and thus on history because their sincere faith, hope, and charity coalesced into unavoidable integrity.

William and Esther's parents had all emigrated to the colonies from the Ulster region of Ireland. They were referred to as Scots-Irish because at that time members of those two cultures had blended in northern Ireland. By the 1730s, their Presbyterian beliefs were being threatened by the established Anglican church. As well, the poor economy had taken a toll. They decided to flee, and they weren't alone. The ocean voyage they embarked on was one of many taken by tens of thousands of others who decided to leave Ulster behind.

Unfortunately for the Whitleys, the Scots-Irish were often held in low esteem by the established colonists who saw them as merely poor farmers who drank too much, were argumentative, and wanted as much land as they could acquire. Because of their poverty, these families sometimes had to squat upon the lands they found, rather than purchase them. A rumored saying of their day attests to the existing colonial's attitude toward the new immigrants: "a Scotch-Irishman is one who keeps the Commandments – and every other thing he can get his hands on!" In general, they lived in tight-knit groups, built their own schools and churches, and were steadfast in their Presbyterian faith. They were also fruitful and multiplying.

William was born in 1749; Esther (Fullen) six years later. They grew up where their families had settled in the Shenandoah Valley of northwestern Virginia. By the time the two had married in 1770, the better lots of farmland had already been taken. The poor soil that the newlyweds were left to till required an extraordinary amount of work to make it viable for a good harvest. Every afternoon, the mountains to the west cast their shadow over the Whitley's home. He ventured over their heights a few times to hunt game for his family. Usually he was accompanied by George Clark, a cousin of George Rogers Clark and more importantly the husband of William's sister. They admired the wilderness lands as they tracked their prey. By 1775, William was tiring of the extraordinary amount of work it took to produce a reasonable return on investment from his Virginia land. He thought it might be time to make a bold change.

> ... he said to his wife, he heard a fine report of Kentucky, and he thought they could get their living there with less hard work. "Then, Billy, if I was you I would go and see," was the reply. [1]

With Esther's blessing, Whitley and his brother-in-law were on their way back over the mountains just two days after mentioning it to his wife. They went deeper into the cane lands than they had ever gone before. They wanted to see for themselves what some of their neighbors, who had already ventured further west, had been so colorfully talking up. This time they weren't out hunting for a meal, but for the perfect setting in which to establish a homestead. Eventually they came upon a region that they found to be more beautiful than they could have ever imagined. It was around a branch of the Kentucky River already known as Dick's River. Though they were amongst the earliest Virginians to explore this region, they were not the very first. A few years earlier a band of long hunters which included several

Portrait of William Whitley circa 1830-1850. Artist unknown.

brothers in the Skaggs family, were in this vicinity when they met a party of Cherokee Indians. Learning they were hunting for meat, the head or chief Indian, Capt. Dick (who was pleased at being recognized by several of the party who had seen him at the lead mines on the waters of Holston), told them to go up that creek [now Skaggs Creek] to the head, and cross the Brushy ridge, and they would come upon his — ever since called Dick's — river, where they would find meat plenty; "to kill it, and go home." Deer and bear were plenty. [2]

Today it is known as the Dix River. Confident about their choice, Whitley and Clark returned to their families and all agreed that they would leave the Virginia farm behind and head to the bountiful country that the two men had set their sights on. In the autumn of that same year, 1775, they gathered all of their children, their horses, and whatever belongings they thought they could manage to transport. With a lingering glance back at their relatives and friends, they moved out toward the land they would dwell upon for the rest of their lives.

It seems insufficient to say the trip was treacherous. It was potentially deadly. This was proven too many times by those who lost their lives on similar journeys. Whitley himself said that while Esther was astride her horse, he had to strap his three-year-old daughter, Elizabeth, behind her while she held their one-year-old, Isabella, in her lap. He went on to explain that:

> Many times in our travels we had to unpack & at times leave the family to find out a way to go on, at times my wife would fall, horse & all & at other times, she and her children all in a file tied together for where one went all must go in that situation. We were 33 days in the wilderness in this unkind season of the year, had rain hail & snow with the disadvantages of large cane brakes to wade through, we then landed at [what became] Whitley's Old Station.[3]

As noted, sometimes the train of horses, that had been laden with the goods and supplies of the families, had to be unloaded before progress could be made. The struggle to maneuver along the rugged terrain could be just too foreboding at times for the animals to attempt moving on with equipment or people on their backs. Freezing rains, snows, and ice often coated the rock-strewn mountain paths, making them even more dangerous than they were in good weather. Parts of the route were nothing more than narrow ledges with sheer drops. As such, the unburdened horses and mules would still have to be led across these types of difficult stretches of the trail. Whitley and Clark had to risk their own safety as well by making repeated trips to bring the off-loaded goods forward again to be re-strapped to the backs of the animals.

Some time after they had made it through the Cumberland Gap, the party discovered that they were not alone on the path that they had chosen. They were caught up to and passed by an even larger group of forty new settlers. It was the Henderson party which included Daniel Boone and Hugh McGary among others. Some of them were on their way to Harrod's new settlement, others to Boonesborough. As it happened, sometime after they had been passed, gunshots echoed through the woods. Whitley's group supposed that an Indian attack may have been made on Henderson's party. They braced for trouble. To their surprise, and relief, a short time later a runner appeared from ahead carrying something over his shoulder. It was a large cut of fresh bear meat; a gift, and an explanation of what the gunfire was all about. The Henderson group considered that the Whitley party might be fearing the worst, so they sent back a portion of their good fortune. Looking out for each other was just what these people did, always.

Late in 1775, the Whitley's had arrived at their destination. It was along a tributary of Dix River known as Cedar Creek. The picturesque area was covered in walnut trees and nearby was an orchard of crabapples. In a short time, a village would grow around that orchard and take the setting for its name, Crab Orchard. Another seven or eight miles up the barely discernible trail from where the Whitleys had stopped was Benjamin Logan's newly built station. He called it St. Asaph because the day they settled upon the spot was May 1, the said saint's feast day. It would grow into today's Stanford, Kentucky. The very first settlement in this region was made a year earlier by James Harrod about fifteen miles further to the northwest of Logan's. So although the Whitleys were isolated near Crab Orchard, with these two other settlements within a short ride, they were not truly alone in this stretch of wilderness.

The Indians were not pleased to see colonists from the east begin to make permanent residences in their traditional hunting grounds. Though things were generally quiet through the first several months of Whitley's presence; conflict was inevitable. In the spring of 1776, about forty miles from the Whitleys, Jemima Boone, daughter of Daniel, and two of her friends, the Callaway sisters, were kidnapped by Indians near Boonesborough. Their story and rescue became legendary through James Fennimore Cooper's *Last of the Mohicans* novel. Throughout the rest of that year, several men from the surrounding stations were also captured or killed in random attacks. Fear was festering in the guts of the frontier people. By the fall of the year, word came that a declaration of their independence had been proclaimed back in the colonies and that a war with Britain was officially at hand. They decided to seek safety in numbers.

The Whitleys suspended any further building of their homestead at Walnut Flat and moved to the St. Asaph community where an effort was underway to build a true fortress. It was planned to cover an area of fifty by thirty yards. However, when they arrived it was not yet sufficiently built to provide protection. William sent Esther, who was now pregnant, and his two children further north to Fort Harrod. Logan did the same with his wife and kids, as a team of men

Interior of the re-created Fort Asaph / Fort Logan in Stanford, Kentucky.

remained with him to build Fort Logan.

In February of 1777, the Whitley's welcomed Levissa into the world, their third child. It would be through Levissa, years later, that we came to hear the thoughts of William himself, for she had saved a memoir of sorts that her father had dictated to his son-in-law, Peter Soublett.

Soon after her birth, Levissa and family moved back to St. Asaph with the others as the finishing touches were being put on Logan's new fort. The inhabitants numbered only about thirty people; fifteen men and five women with a few children. As it happened, near the end of May, a band of nearly sixty Indians began making assaults on the new fortress. This would be the Whitleys' first considerable and sustained engagement with the Indians. The fighting was sporadic but constant over nearly two weeks. A few men were lost, but it could have been much worse. The families, some now missing a husband or father, carried on; albeit cautious of even further attacks. The Whitleys' had played their part in achieving the generally successful outcome of the assault.

All the women had worked at making ammunition by melting pewter dinnerware into musket balls; but the fearless Mrs. Whitley went even further. She is said to have on occasion donned a man's frock and hat in order to deceive the enemy as she took her turn on patrol

Cane such as this was common across Kentucky during the settlement days of the 1700s. Although this picture is of a canebrake in Louisiana, it shows the height and density they could reach.

along the walls. Several of the attacking Indians were kept at bay by her expert marksmanship.

In the latter days of this episode of fighting, when it seemed the siege might be over, a handful of men proposed that the women leave the fort to milk the cows that were still roaming nearby. They all could use the nourishment, especially the children. Only Mrs. Logan, a black woman she owned, and Esther, took up the challenge of venturing out to get what milk they could. The four men who had suggested the endeavour joined the ladies as their guards. It wasn't long, however, before shots rang out and the women were on the run back to the gate. Three of the men were severely wounded, one died where he was shot. The women made it safely inside, but not before Esther had to seemingly prove her defiance of the enemy. On her sprint back, her hat, a favorite of hers and a family heirloom, had blown off. Instead of leaving it to be retrieved later, in the midst of the gunfire she nonchalantly stopped, went back to pick it up, and then resumed her escape to the fort.

It was in this same event that William's keen skills of observation had saved one of those four guard's lives. It was assumed that two of the men were killed where they had fallen until, as Whitley tells it:

> I discovered that Burr Harrison was not dead for I saw him move his

head, I gave the alarm & Cpt. Ben Logan spoke to him & told him if he was in his senses to Move his foot, he did so, Logan reply'd Lay still, don't be discouraged, I will have you in at the risk of my life. Logan took a bag of wool & moved it before him Until he got to Harrison[,] took Harrison in his arms & ran in the fort...[4]

Unfortunately, Mr. Harrison passed away from his wounds a week later, but the reputation of Ben Logan had been enhanced, and Whitley's had begun.

Skirmishes and assaults continued on and off over the next few years as the Revolution had arrived on the frontier. Playing off of the already festering anger of the Indians against the settlers, the British promised support to many of the Indian tribes. Their causes aligned. Both wanted the American encroachment into the wilderness to stop. However, the British promise to preserve the land for the Indians alone was deceitful. All-along they viewed it as the King's property, and the Indians were simply their front-line weapon in its defense.

In June, when the attack at St. Asaph had waned, Logan returned to the Holston Valley of Virginia to get desperately needed supplies and extra manpower. He soon returned with some goods, but it wasn't until September that tangible reinforcements had finally come. It turned out to be a meager count of six men. They were from a company led by Isaac Ruddell, who would soon build his own family station in the region. As the men neared Logan's fort they were attacked by Indians. Five of them escaped, but one was killed. A note was left on his dead body. It's placement there by an Indian was a less than discreet way of demonstrating the alliance between themselves and the British. The paper read as a proclamation from the scorned British leader on the frontier, Colonel Henry Hamilton. It was Hamilton, known as "the hairbuyer," who had incentivized the warriors to kill Americans by offering them a monetary reward for each scalp brought to him at his Fort Detroit headquarters. According to Whitley the letter explained:

> ...that all those who would come off with their arms & use them in defence of his British Majesty should be humanly dealt with, Virtually [with victuals/food] & Lodg'd and those who bore commissions should bear the same under his Britannic Majesty[.] he promised that at the

Expiration of the War should Constitute 200 acres & several others of like Magnitude." [5]

There is no record that any of the residents of St. Asaph took Hamilton up on his offer.

In the summer of 1778, Whitley voluntarily joined the militia forces aiding George Rogers Clark on a mission to capture British forts in the Illinois country. The Americans met with little resistance at these locations because many French residents were still inhabiting the sites in a loose alliance with the British. The French were much more sympathetic to the American revolutionaries than to the country that had recently defeated them in the French and Indian War. As a result, the posts of Kaskaskia, Cahokia, and later Vincennes soon had an American flag flying over them. Whitley returned to Logan's fort after this three-month campaign. With perilous incidents seeming to be on the decline, in January of 1779 he decided to return with Esther and the kids to his own property. It was time to once again take up the construction of his own homestead.

The first station that he had begun building, before opting for the safety of the established settlements, was a little west of Cedar Creek at a spot known as Walnut Flat. Over the three years that he and the family were at Harrod's and Logan's forts, it is believed that the Indians had destroyed his original cabin or cabins. In 1777, it is certain that they had stolen his horses, because he talks about it in his narrative.

> Shortly after Logan's return from Virginia I started out with John Carpenter in order to hunt my horses[.] in the course of the day I found great Quantity of Indian Signs near to Whitleys Old Station[.] I found they had got all my horses beside many others[;] at least I saw where they had camp'd the night before & had tied 19 horses[,] their fire still Burning,[.] We made towards the Station not following any path for Roads, We had none as yet. On my return, I heard a bell I was acquainted with – being sometime in the night we made our way to the horses; I came within 10 feet of a Beast of Logan's tied in a pound with Blankets lying a cross the beast[.] This was one of the times [I] felt for the Bullets but found none[.] We made our escape & the balance of the Horses follow'd us to the Station. [6]

Luckily, the horses knew their true owner and followed him away from their captors without a shot being fired.

The term "station" was attributed to most of the settlements in the wilderness during these early days because beyond being the owners' homes, the dwellings generally served as rest stops for travelers. The Whitleys ended up building three such stations over time. Somewhere near the first home, which was dismantled by the Indians, they built a new one. The specifics of its expanse are sketchy, but it's likely that it consisted of at least a few wooden structures. This assumption makes sense because that year, 1779, William's parents came from Virginia to live with him; and his family had already consisted of a wife and three kids with one more on the way. Their first child, a girl, was named after William's mother, Elizabeth. Soon after the elderly Whitleys had moved in, William presented his father, Solomon, with the gift of naming his first son after him. Certainly, this many Whitleys needed some space. As William's wealth grew through the acquisition of significant amounts of property, and the profits he gained from the sale of the crops and livestock he had grown upon those lands, it is supposed that he could afford to build whatever he needed. In due time he proved that to be the case.

However, while Whitley was increasing his station in size and stature, the British had re-captured the fort at Vincennes; the one he had helped Clark secure the previous year. This was a serious threat to the safety of the frontier settlements, so in March of 1779, George Rogers Clark led a new force, without Whitley, and successfully repossessed the former English fortress. Nearly thirty British soldiers were taken prisoner. Under an American guard of nearly the same number of men, the POWs began an incredible march of over four hundred miles back to the Holston region of Virginia and eventually on to Williamsburg for legal proceedings. From Vincennes (Indiana) the entourage first stopped briefly at Harrod's and then Logan's forts. The next and last station they would visit was the Whitley's. Here they

> bought a small ox, three bags of corn and some dried meat to serve as food for the fourteen days they estimated it would take to pass through the wilderness to the settlements on the Holston. [7]

One of the men being led away was a surprise captive. It was none other than the infamous "hair buyer" himself. Whitley had to of been thrilled to see Colonel Hamilton under these circumstances, but; with only an internal smile, he remained cordial to his enemy as he provided provisions for the whole contingent of guards and prisoners alike.

Over the next few years, the route used by Whitley and his neighbors to move between settlements, and from the Appalachians to their homes, saw many more travelers. The once vague path became worn into a noticeable trail. Soon it could be called a road. Appropriately, it became known as the "Wilderness Road," and the Whitleys were regarded as its guardians because of the hospitality and generosity they showed toward the travellers upon it. The path that Boone had blazed back in 1775 led to Boonesborough. It turned northward at a point near present-day Brodhead, Kentucky. This was the original Wilderness Road. But at Brodhead, there was a fork that headed to the northwest. A few years previous to Boonesborough being established, the Skaggs, and soon thereafter the Harrods, the Logans, and the Whitleys all had proceeded on this less obvious path that would eventually end when it reached the falls of the Ohio River at Louisville, Kentucky. Though at first less travelled, this route was generally regarded as an arm of the Wilderness Road and the main path into the heart of Kentucky. Once established, William and Esther's home was the first one any travellers would see after they had taken the western fork at Brodhead. Likewise, it would be the last home they could visit when they were heading back to Virginia. The couple were always accommodating no matter which direction the parties were moving.

There was safety in numbers for such travellers, so every few weeks to months notices were placed in the *Kentucky Gazette* newspaper that groups were forming for a trip back to the states. The people would meet at Crab Orchard where the Whitleys lived. One typical announcement appeared on December 26, 1789, and spotlights the fact that the government had not yet provided adequate military protection along the route. It simply read:

> A large company will start at the Crab Orchard, the 1st day of January for the Eastern settlements; all to go well armed. [8]

The second Whitley Station served them and others well through

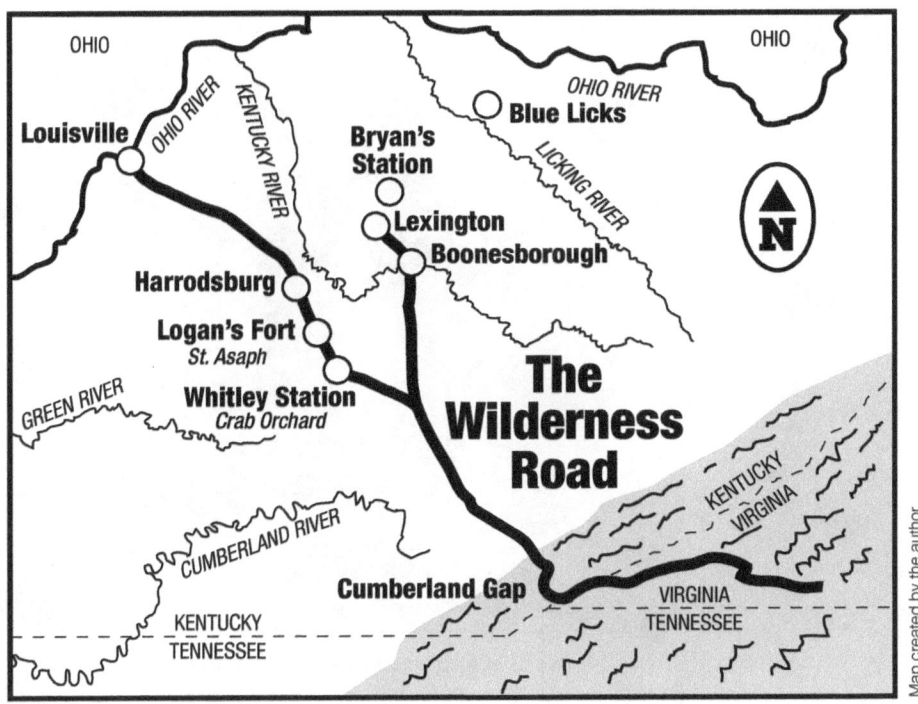

the early 1780s, but William had higher aspirations for his homestead. Sometime in the middle of the decade, he began to build the first brick home to be seen in the wilderness of Kentucky. It would be on the eastern side of Cedar Creek, just south of the crabapple orchard. When completed, the ostentatious dwelling he had erected caused the settlers and Indians alike to view it in awe. It would take several years to complete the mansion and it was so well constructed that it still stands today as a salute to Whitley and the builders he solicited to construct it. The actual date of its occupation by the family is disputed by historians, but most believe it was by the end of the 1780s; some think as late as 1794.

The details of the structure are worth noting because of the cleverness and patriotism that they reveal about the Whitleys. The overall brickwork pattern is known as Flemish bond. It was a style used at this time period for the construction of more refined colonial buildings; especially in Virginia where Whitley would have certainly noticed it. The bricks were laid in an alternating pattern of a stretcher (the

William Whitley House as it appeared in some disrepair in 1934.

long face) followed by a header (the short end). Each such row would be staggered over the one below it. The technique required skilled masons. Though this design was traditionally used only on the front of buildings, Whitley used it throughout. Many of the headers were glazed to a light-gray appearance which contrasted with the regular red-toned bricks. They were all used to create a decorative diamond pattern on the sides of the house and a checkered look on the front and back. As if to autograph his structure, Whitley had glazed headers positioned in the form of his initials, WW, over the front door. And, not to be discounted, Esther's EW was embedded over the back door. Whitley's house was unquestionably upscale for its day.

A few other features of the structure are quite intriguing. The walls were thick – nearly two feet. Nothing but cannonballs could possibly penetrate them. All the bricks were made on-site and the masons were regularly treated to whiskey as a bonus payment for their daily efforts. It's been rumored that some extra alcohol strategically made its way into the mortar as a presumed protection against freeze damage during the harsh Kentucky winters.

The windows of the first floor were set higher than normal, their

The refurbished William Whitley House as it appeared in 2008. Note William's initials in the brickwork over the front door. An "EW" for Esther Whitley is found over the back door.

The Flemish Bond brickwork pattern used on all sides of the house.

base at about six feet above the ground. This was done in order to prevent any Indian afoot from having a clear view, let alone a clear shot, into the dwelling.

The interior had plenty of surprises and never-before-seen designs as well. One was a partial wall, or partition, that covered a section of the windows from ceiling to floor in order to provide added protection from incoming rifle shots. It was so designed that it created a slot through which the Whitleys could poke their rifles and fire at their attackers while being somewhat shielded. It was this need of defense against Indian aggression that motivated the entire plan of this fortress, disguised as a house. The doors were twice normal thickness. A secret, narrow stairway supplemented the obvious one that rose between the first and second floors. It gave access to a concealed two-foot high crawl space that ran below half of the second level's floor-

William Whitley House staircase as it appeared in 1933.

ing. When viewed from below, its base was the first level's ceiling. It was an ingenious hiding place should any enemies gain entrance to the home. A smaller secret compartment in another part of the house was large enough to discreetly hide a couple children, as well. Beyond all these built-in defenses, the three-story house provided plenty of space and functionality to support the ever-growing family. After all, the Whitleys parented eleven children.

William's patriotism and artistic flair is also evident in some of the interior's decorative designs. For instance, though their meaning is not exactly clear, thirteen s-shaped carvings, similar to dollar signs, decorate the mantle of the main fireplace. It's believed they somehow reference the thirteen original states and their growing wealth. As well, before it was part of building codes, Whitley had put thirteen steps into the main stairway; each with a carved eagle holding an olive branch in its beak. The handrail is supported by spindles and begins with a thick bowed post at the base step. When viewed from a short distance it presents the illusion of being a grandiose harp.

Several other structures were built around the main house. They served as additional dwellings, storage barns, stables, etc. All in all, this was a very prominent station. Though it was so much more elaborate than the previous ones, it served the same two major purposes. It was a home to the Whitley family and a respite for travelers moving through the wilderness. Besides being the meeting point for large parties heading in either direction, many individuals or small groups of sojourners would stop to rest, enjoy a meal, or get a good nights sleep before carrying on. They were always welcomed and provided for by the Whitleys. One might say it was a bed and breakfast of its day; but at no charge.

A further example of Whitley's wealth, and his generous dispersal of it, came in 1792 when the Wilderness Road itself was in need of a little enhancement. Impediments of ruts, fallen trees, stumps, etc., slowed parties down between Crab Orchard and the Cumberland Gap. Kentucky had just become a state in the summer of that year, but there were no government monies yet available for fixing the trail. Ranking citizens of the region took matters into their own hands because they saw the value such an upgrade would have on encouraging an even larger influx of people to the new state. They decided to donate their own money to the cost of the repairs. Rather than just throw cash at this first endeavor to make such improvements, Whitley knew how to gain the hearts of the workers as well. He promised to fuel the men with bacon over what proved to be a three-week project. No wonder he was such a popular fellow.

A few years later, the state would find the money to make the route a legitimate, thirty-foot wide road. That three-year project caused the stretch from Virginia toward the Whitleys and beyond to officially be deemed the Wilderness Road. Though both forks of the routes had been referred to by this name for some time, as the settlement of Boonesborough faded over the next decade, so did the use of the fork leading to it.

Conflicts with Indians of the region continued for most of Whitley's life. He became famous for his persistent readiness to help, protect, and fight for his family and neighbors. Accounts of the numbers vary, but it is reasonable to say that William was engaged in at least twenty-five significant encounters with the British or Indians over his sixty-five years; possibly twice that number. The organized military affairs he participated in would gain him several promotions; culminating with his highest rank of lieutenant-colonel in 1791. This official service to his country was sporadic. He was somewhat "on call" for government actions with the Kentucky militia in reaction to any events as they happened over the years. However, just as many if not more heroics were performed by Whitley as an individual. So many of Whitley's friends and neighbors were helped in some way by him taking the initiative to act or react on their behalf. He had wilderness "road smarts," if you will.

Thefts of horses and goods, destruction of homes and property, random violent Indian raids on individuals, as well as major attacks like the one made on nearby Boonesborough in 1777, all made Whitley one of the most vigilant men on the frontier.

Horse stealing was a big deal at this time. You can imagine the importance of the horse for transportation of people and goods. We still get quite upset today if our automobiles are stolen. These people had no buses, taxis, bicycles, subways, trains, or airplanes to fall back on to get around; only their own two feet. Besides, though some say they love their cars, the horses were majestic, living beings that garnered a more tangible affection. Whitley would participate in, and usually lead, numerous raids to recapture horses. Occasionally, those recovery efforts might include the addition of a few steeds that didn't originally belong to any of the settlers. This was viewed as payment due for previous unrecovered thefts and as vengeance for the murders of friends and neighbors. The tit for tat became a perpetual practice by both sides in the fights.

Whitley wasn't always successful in his attempts to help his neighbors, but he never shied away from the effort. One fight of note had him acting as a scout for Colonel John Bowman, George Rogers Clark's second in command, during the summer of 1779. The attack was planned upon the Shawnee living north of the Ohio River at Chillicothe. It would be retaliation for the most conspicuous event of the "bloody sevens"; Blackfish's lengthy attack on Boonesborough. Whitley had already made several raids on this Indian village over the years to recover stolen horses and so he was chosen to scout the area before Bowman's forces drew near. Whitley says

> I raised a company & also Capt. Logan another. We joined Bowman at the mouth of the Licking [River]. I think we had bout 300 men. I was then appointed pilot and my men joined Logan. We went on to the towns without ever being discovered. We surrounded the towns and in going round there was an Indian in the fields. I suppose to keep out the stock, and discovered us. As he made to the houses he was shot by Hugh Ross and killed. He gave several screams which the warriors

came out and the whites fired on them which commenced the action on both sides. We fired on both sides all night by intervals until daylight, then the firing became general from all quarters. We soon got possession of one half of the town and an old Negro woman came out and informed Col. Bowman that Simon Girty was within a few miles with 500 warriors. Upon the information Bowman ordered a retreat. We lost 9 men and 2 wounded… We burned half the town, took a great quantity of plunder & about 300 horses. There was nine Indians killed, amongst whom was the commander The Blackfish. That same day we were attacked by savages again & we killed one within 7 or 8 miles of the towns. [9]

This was a significant battle, and was followed up a year later by another one led by Clark. Whitley would again serve as a scout, or pilot, in the campaign. In 1782, Whitley arrived at the Blue Licks disaster with Logan's company. They were the much needed reinforcements, but had arrived too late to fight in what turned out to be a rout of the Americans. Whitley and the rest of his company could only bury their dead friends.

Though military contests like these involved hundreds of men, many more confrontations were had between only a handful of individuals or even one-on-one. To gain some perspective, from Whitley's own papers we learn that numerous attacks were made on the locals just over the course of two years; 1780 and 1781. One of the incidents was an Indian ambush during May of 1780 on a party of fourteen travelers along the Wilderness Road near the Cumberland Gap. All were killed except a small girl who was scalped and left to die, which she sadly did. Two men from Logan's Fort were likewise attacked in the same area in the fall of the year; one was killed and the other captured. Just a mile from Whitley's Station, two teenage boys were bathing in Cedar Creek when one was suddenly killed by a shot through his thigh and the other was tomahawked to death. Trappers across the area were being randomly shot at and often killed while on their hunts.

Solomon Clark, a nephew of William, relates one of these many types of incidents that William was involved in. It was an attack on the home of Samuel Daviess who

> lived at Gilmore's Lick, about three miles from Whitley's Station.

Old Sam'l Daviess got up early in the morning, started, in his shirt only, to go to the Lick & kill a deer & crossed a hemp patch, a short distance. The Indians in the hemp, seeing him pass, went to the house – & Daviess saw them going in, when he ran off to Whitley's for aid. All in the [Daviess] house were in bed & the Indians ordered them up, & when dressed Mrs. Daviess endeavored to detain the Indians by showing them her dresses, quilts [etc.], to attract their attention – thinking Mr. Daviess had probably gone for aid. The Indians asked Mrs. Daviess how far it was to the nearest house; Mrs. Daviess perceiving the Indians expected whites to come, quieted their fears by holding up both hands, thumbs and fingers – indicating ten miles. The Indians had got into the knobs [small wooded hills], on the borders of which Mr. Daviess lived – when Mrs. Daviess was being led off a prisoner with her family – her oldest son James was carrying his little sister Polly, an infant; & Jack a bright, pert boy of some 6 or 8 years, seeing Whitley's party coming, exclaimed "Come on, Capt. Whitley, here's Indians a plenty!" – when the Indians seized the infant & knocked its head against a tree, breaking its skull, & threw it down, – & knocked James down & scalped him – & having time for no further mischief, darted off – & among the knobs, they had a fine chance to escape, which they easily effected…[10]

In another instance, a neighbor of Whitley suddenly turned feint of heart when called upon to rescue his own wife and kids. He refused to join a group of his neighbors, organized by Whitley, intent on tracking down the Indians who had attacked and captured his family. It became known as McClure's Defeat and clearly highlights Whitley's bravery, determination, and scorn of cowardice. The McClure family was traveling along the Wilderness Road

> when attacked, Mr. McClure ran off & left his family. At first when the Indians fired, Mrs. McClure got off in a kind of sink hole, with her three children – & to prevent the Indians from hearing the youngest cry, put her hand on its mouth. At length the Indians found her & her children, & they at once killed the three children, & put her upon a wild horse who treed her – then they tied her on, & the horse ran through brush and trees, till he got worn down. They finally stopped to camp & Mrs. McClure was engaged in cooking, while the scalps of her three children hung up on a tree beside the fire – & the Indians engaged in dancing, & others swapping clothes of people they had killed & plundered on the wilderness road – When Col. Whitley with a party fired upon & probably killed some of them & dispersed

the rest – & recovered Mrs. McClure, & a large quantity of plunder. Col. Whitley could not prevail upon Mr. McClure to join his party, & Whitley advised Mrs. McClure not to live with such a cowardly man. But she did. [11]

The love William had for children is evidenced by the bountiful number of them he had with Esther. However, in yet another tragic story, his love of other's children and his high standard for personal integrity is made crystal clear. As well, Esther's sound reasoning is on display. The story goes that

> on the Wilderness road, the Indians defeated a camp, & a man & woman named Drake ran off & left their little Betsy, some eight years old, who was made prisoner. She was often left alone at the Indian camp, when the Indians went probably to watch & way-lay the wilderness road to entrap unwary travelers, – there was a white man with the Indians acting as one of them. Betsy recollected something about the Crab Orchard, & concluded she could find it. – Started & unfortunately took the wrong end of the trail. After the defeat, Whitley raised a party & pursued – found the child's tracks, & Whitley knew of a deep stream ahead, & was afraid the child would drown in attempting to cross it, & pushed on rapidly – the men saying, "You'll make us all kill our horses by such rapid pursuit." "I will kill mine or recover the child," replied Whitley, & did overtake her. Col. Whitley resolved on keeping & raising the little girl as his own, & when Mrs. Drake sent for her daughter, Whitley sent her word, that she had deserted her child, and let it fall into the hands of the Indians – & he thought he could do as good a part by it as the Indians. Mrs. Drake at length came herself, but Whitley would not part with the little girl, & finally Mrs. Drake from grief for the loss of her child was taken with fits, when by Mrs. Whitley's interference, Colonel Whitley gave the girl to her mother. [12]

One more true story further exemplifies Whitley's fortitude and relentless efforts to help his neighbors.

> At another time, the Indians defeated a party on the Wilderness road – & two little girls got scattered off. One had been riding behind her father, who was shot off – she kept on & rode off, & the little dog followed her. She kept on, & when weary, she would get off, tie the horse, & go to sleep. Finally she was tracked & found by Col. Wm Whitley & a party, who found her asleep & her horse nearby, & her little dog watching beside her. – He found the other little girl alone – she had

wandered off – particulars not recollected. Col. Whitley overtook & defeated the Indians & recovered the plunder. The relatives of the little girls got them subsequently from Col. Whitley, who had taken them to his own house. Col. Whitley always restored recovered plunder to the owners or friends. [13]

These are just a few of the utterly tragic episodes that Whitley was involved in. He was the go-to guy who would willingly take the initiative to get any situation resolved, usually putting his own life at risk for his friends and neighbors. One can only imagine the toll that these horrors had taken on his psyche; but he was loathe to show it. He saw the victims who suffered the loss of loved ones and possessions and the effect it had on them. Rather than lament these situations, William chose a different path. To offset the pains incurred by others and upon himself, he tapped into a gift that was God-given – his joyful spirit.

Whitley was a robust fellow. He loved to tell stories and jokes. He made up poems and sometimes wove them into whimsical songs. Quite often he and Esther would invite the neighbors and friends to their house and party like it was 1799. Guests would gather on the third floor of the house, which was one, large open room covering the full expanse of the house. Most days it served as a quiet place for Esther to spin wool, mend clothes, or work her loom. Likely the younger kids often ran around playing while the older girls helped mom. Neighbor ladies were known to come over for day long sewing bees. In the early years, the third floor was occasionally used for official business as a county courtroom. However, it was the festive occasions that most of the residents remembered; when the spinning wheels were pushed aside and the open space was transformed into a dance floor. The local fiddler would set everyone in motion with lively tunes. William and Esther would join in on all the whirling and twirling of the Virginia Reel. With few diversions from their daily worries, these get-togethers that the Whitleys hosted were not only welcomed, but they were likely mentally life-saving to the residents along the Wilderness Road.

One physical example of William's poetic efforts remains to this day etched into the horn that held the powder for his gun. It reads:

> Wm. Whitley I am your horn
> The truth I love, A lie I scorn

> Fill me with the best of powder
> Ile make your rifle crack the louder
> See how the dread terrifick ball
> Make Indians bleed and Tories fall
> You with powder Ile supply
> For to defend your Liberty [Li-ber-tie]

On August 20, 1794, Whitley strapped on that powder horn as he geared up to lead a company of Kentucky militia southward into another fight with Indians. That same morning General "Mad" Anthony Wayne was over three hundred miles to the north in the Maumee River Valley of today's northwest Ohio where he was famously defeating the Indian alliance led by Little Turtle and Blue Jacket. Wayne's fight became known as the Battle of Fallen Timbers; a pivotal victory that opened three-quarters of the soon to be state of Ohio to settlement. A number of Kentucky militia had voluntarily fought alongside Wayne and his legion while Whitley was rounding up and leading another company of Kentuckians to the Tennessee lands. Whitley's endeavor would become known as the Nickajack Expedition.

The frequency of attacks on individuals and all parties along the Wilderness Road was once again on the increase in the early 1790s. Whitley was certain that it was the Chickamauga who were responsible. They were a band that splintered away from the Cherokee and had always supported the British through the Revolution. At this time, they continued to assault any anglo-European settlers that they could find. Their home villages were clustered near the Tennessee River; one of them was known as Nickajack. Whitley, long fed-up with these Indian assaults, initiated an effort to attack them where they lived. He sought permission to do so from his old friend, then Governor, Isaac Shelby. Authorization was granted and an additional force led by John Montgomery of the Southwest Territory joined his at Nashville. The joint companies moved out and soon gave the Americans a complete victory over the Chickamauga. It was one worth celebrating.

Some two hundred men had been under Whitley's command at Nickajack. As a well-deserved "thank you," to these neighbors who had volunteered to risk their lives in the effort, Whitley threw what was arguably the largest party to date in that region. Under the shade of the trees that graced the front of his house, the buffet table held an array of foods that was said to stretch over one hundred feet. Banquets like this were extraordinary on the frontier. Of course there were foods still loved by most people today such as lamb, salmon, beef, and pork. However, other foods served would be quite exotic to modern tastes, such as baked o'possum with sweet potatoes, broiled squirrel, and bear leg. Add in dozens of side dishes, desserts, and of course various wines and whiskeys, and you had a celebration to remember.

The highlight of the affair yet again displayed Williams sense of humor.

> The table was well supplied with viands [choice foods], vegetables & fruits, & what called out roars of convulsive laughter, were the two well-roasted shoats [young hogs], with an Irish potato in each of their mouths, & a sweet potato under their tails. Some were so full of laughter that they rolled off their seats upon the grass and tumbled over & over… [14]

That whimsy is again evident in a short poem attributed to William which was apparently written in the midst of one of his precarious expeditions.

> If on this campaign I am lucky
> I'll kiss the first white girl I meet in Old Ky
> Should she refuse me I will leave her to her Will
> And kiss my Esther Dear, who lives at Sportsmans Hill [15]

Sportsman's Hill? Yes. Many referred to the couple's estate as Whitley Station, but others called it Sportsman's Hill. This is because by 1788, William had transformed a natural knob hill, which was a stone's throw from his house, into the first half-mile, oval, horse racing track in Kentucky. It was simply a place on William's property where friends could challenge each other astride their favorite steeds and maybe enjoy the revelry with some friendly wagering on the outcomes.

Whitley was one of those guys who although he came to rub shoulders with men of similar wealth and influence, never allowed those friendships to supersede the ones he had with his long-time neighbors of lesser means. He sincerely valued relationships over prestige.

Sportsman's Hill as seen from the front of the Whitley House in 2008.

That said, they all came to race at Sportsman's Hill and some were the movers and shakers of their day. Governor Isaac Shelby, George Rogers Clark, Daniel Boone, Ben Logan, James Harrod and more watched and raced. It was all about fun – a necessity on the perpetually dangerous frontier. It is fascinating to note that it was Whitley, who was so American, and so anti-British, that he was the first one to insist that his friends race counter-clockwise around his knob hill. This was a deliberate thumb-of-the-nose to the English who had always run their horses clockwise, and still do. The practice stuck. To this day, horses, and automobiles, that race on oval tracks in the United States circle counter to the direction that England's racers run. Adding a little further distinction to the American way, Whitley purposefully ran his horses on a clay track rather than the turf used in England. The course at Sportsman's Hill continued to see action until the mid 1800s when the Civil War broke out. It was at its height of popularity just as the War of 1812 was declared. In fact, on the Fourth of July of that memorable year, over one thousand people gathered atop and around his knob hill to watch and wager on the ponies while enjoying a feast comparable to the one Esther and he gave the heroes of the Nickajack expedition eighteen years earlier.

It was obvious that Whitley loved horses. He rode, recovered, and raced them all his life. What he developed at Sportsman's Hill was a destination for horse enthusiasts across the growing frontier of Kentucky. The fact that it attracted crowds soon after it was built can be attested to by the fact that the courts of Lincoln County ordered the building of a more direct road between "Whitley's Race Path" and the courthouse. High profile horse racers of the day came to Whitley's track from the coastal states as well. The history of horse racing in Kentucky tends to overlook what William Whitley did at Crab Orchard. Though straight line horse races were taking place a few years previous in Lexington, he should be regarded as one of the founding fathers, if not the founding father, of that state's honored oval-track horse racing tradition which still garners so much esteem today.

Whitley traded for premier horse breeds with anyone who was willing to deal. Sometimes his bartering was with various Indian tribes who likewise had a genuine appreciation for fine horses. Most often he dealt with the Cherokee. Perhaps this sounds surprising after all of the attacks between the two cultures over so many years. However, the adversarial attitude of the frontiersmen was not necessarily a blanket hatred of all Indians. Nor did all Indian tribes on the whole despise the whitemen. The contempt of the settlers was for the tribes proliferating violence on innocent people. Many tribes were peacefully aligned with the settlers for the sake of trade and general cooperation. William had many such friendships amongst the Cherokee and a few other tribes. He even opened his home to certain Indian buddies who sometimes spent the night in his home. On one such occassion a treaty was signed. At another time, his Cherokee pals had challenged William to a friendly shooting contest. According to William's nephew,

> It was Mrs. Col. Wm. Whitley, not any of her daughters who shot at a mark with the Cherokees in Ky & beat them. A large company of them had come to visit Col. Whitley, looking upon him as a sort of governor of the country – a big captain & he had them to entertain for many days together. Bantering the Colonel to shoot at a mark – & Mrs. Whitley was a better shot at a mark than the colonel – so there was policy in his getting her to shoot with them. When beaten, the Indians, astonished, inquired, how she, a squaw, had learned to shoot so well. She replied, she had learned on purpose in order to kill them should occasion ever make it necessary.[16]

And thus we learn that Esther had the same bold yet whimsical bluntness as her husband. And, that she was indeed a great shot. Other stories tell of her many displays of marksmanship. One of a more serious nature occurred at her home.

> During an attack at the Whitley House an Indian climbed the tree opposite the third floor window so that he could shoot at any who might be seen from it. Esther shot and killed the savage from the window just above the "man-hole," – the hiding place of the women and children in case there was an attack. [17]

Verifiable accounts like these prove that Esther was as smart and tough as any man when it was called for. There is one other recorded occasion when Esther showed her astute character by taking the initiative to help after nine people were ambushed and killed while traveling along the Wilderness Road. A nephew of William's relates that

> once when news came in of some Indian mischief, & Whitley was absent, Mrs. Whitley rallied together twenty men & had them all in readiness by the time he returned; & Whitley said his wife had collected by the time he got home twenty as good riflemen as ever fired a gun. [18]

One can imagine the singular challenges of raising eleven children in such a dangerous environment, let alone having your husband so often away on life-threatening missions helping others or engaging in military battles. Yet, it seems that the two had a loving understanding of their roles, even if they sometimes overlapped. Esther was a kind and devoted mother, friend, and wife who was astute enough to understand her environment and skilled enough to protect all those she loved.

The dangers were ever-present, but as the years went by the settlers carried on with their daily lives. William continued to prosper as a farmer and speculator. He took a temporary respite from his enterprises when in 1797, just five years into Kentucky's statehood, he gave politics a try. He was elected to the state's legislature as a congressman. It didn't take long for him to realize that he was more suited to physical, rather than legal, wranglings. After one, two-year term he resumed his main occupations of raising crops, grooming horses, and of course defending his neighbors.

Through the late 1790s, life on the frontier had taken on a semblance of normalcy as the population continued to grow and Indian attacks diminished. That peace lasted for a time but then tensions rose again. This time, however, it was not on the frontier. Uneasiness began to spread across Europe as the 1700s rolled into the 1800s. Soon the Napoleonic Wars were initiated and as a result embargoes, tariffs, and other hostile actions were taken toward the United States. Limits on trade were causing serious hardships. Things came to a head for the Americans in June of 1812 when war was again declared against England.

The call went out across the country for militia to reinforce the regular military. In Kentucky, Colonel Richard M. Johnson, a future vice-president under Martin Van Buren, organized a regiment of mounted militia who would head north to the Great Lakes region where the fighting was most intense. At sixty-five years of age, and still in robust health, Whitley enlisted. Though he had attained the rank of colonel years previous, he signed on as a private and refused any compensation. The fires in his patriotic heart had been rekindled and he could not sit home while those around him engaged in the fight.

It was in May of 1813 when Fort Meigs, an American fortress overlooking the Maumee River in the vicinity of Wayne's Fallen Timbers victory almost twenty years earlier, was attacked by a British and Indian alliance. English forces under General Henry Proctor along with a confederation of Indian tribes led by Tecumseh had made the assault. After two weeks of bombardment, General William H. Harrison, head of the Northwest Army, had withstood the siege and the enemy retreated. Johnson's men had arrived at Fort Meigs shortly after this successful standoff.

The Kentucky regiment was temporarily sub-divided for multiple duties. Some went up to the Raisin River, at today's Monroe, Michigan, to bury fellow Kentuckians who were killed there nearly six months earlier. Others stayed at Fort Meigs and some went elsewhere to serve in various capacities as several more engagements would be had between the Americans and the British/Indian alliance throughout the summer and fall of that year.

In mid-July, Proctor and Tecumseh returned to give an assault on Fort Meigs a second try. Again, it failed. Knowing that there was a smaller fort named Stephenson, just twenty miles away in today's Fremont, Ohio, the enemy alliance headed there for an anticipated quick and easy capitulation. Such would not be the case. On August 2, the tandem forces had to retreat once again across Lake Erie to the British garrison known as Fort Malden, a bit south of today's Windsor, Ontario. From there, on September 10, they could hear bombs exploding from across Lake Erie. The ships of British General Robert Barclay and US Commodore Oliver Perry were engaged in a decisive fight near the islands of the lake. Perry won the day, giving control of the waters to the Americans. Through all these actions, Whitley was with the troops, but in what capacity is unknown. It is certain that he was with Johnson's full regiment which circled the western end of Lake Erie in their pursuit of the enemy who was retreating after Perry's victory.

With that defeat of the British fleet, Proctor and Tecumseh knew that General Harrison would now have his army and Johnson's mounted regiment of Kentucky militia on the move to Canada. The two leaders argued over whether to stay put and fight the Americans from Fort Malden or to retreat to Lake Ontario where they could gain reinforcements. Proctor won the debate and a full-scale retreat began along the Thames River which runs parallel with the north coast of Lake Erie. Over the first few days of October, the Americans continued to gain ground on their enemy. Finally, on October 5, 1813 they caught up to them and the Battle of the Thames, near today's Chatham, Ontario, took place.

It was here that the esteemed Shawnee leader, Tecumseh, was killed. By whom, and by what means, he was taken down in this battle is still a historical mystery. The history books generally say that Colonel Johnson was the one who likely took him out in hand-to-hand combat. This became so generally accepted that a depiction of Johnson versus Tecumseh is part of the historic timeline encircling the Rotunda of the US Capitol building. Johnson's political allies even came up with a clever campaign slogan used in his bid for the vice-presidency in 1836. It rhymed: "Rumpsey-dumpsey, rumpsey-dumpsey; Colonel Johnson killed Tecumseh!"

However, a plausible case can be made for several other men to have taken down the famed Tecumseh, and a strong one exists for Whitley.

In spite of his age, Whitley had volunteered to participate in this conflict along the Thames River. It was well beyond what anyone would have expected of him. He went so far as to choose to be one of the twenty men on the very front line of the Americans' attack. This group was dubbed the "forlorn hope" because the chance of their survival was so slim. They were to draw the first fire of the Indians as they ran onto the battlefield. In so doing, a second line of men could rush forward from behind them, and shoot at the Indians while they were re-loading. Only four of the twenty forlorn men lived to see another day. Whitley was not one of them.

One who did survive was a man named Richard Spurr. His testimony is the only one given as an eye-witness to Whitley's part in the action of that day. Per an affidavit provided by Spurr's great-nephew, the men of the forlorn hope had come forward and

> among them [were] Col. Whitley, my old uncle Richard Spurr, and John McGunnigle. They were ordered to advance to attract the Indians, to keep well in line with spaces of twenty to thirty feet between them. When formed in line, McGunnigle was on the right of Richard Spurr and Col. Whitley on his left... Almost simultaneously they were fired upon by the Indians from the opposite side of the slough [swamp]. Mr. McGunnigle fell dead shot thru the heart. Col. Whitley instantly threw himself behind the body of a large tree that had fallen diagonally to the slough, its branches reaching it. Spurr threw himself behind the stump of a fallen tree, and near, as he thought, to the dead body of Col. Whitley. Just as the Indian got near the log Whitley raised his gun and shot him dead. Then turning on his back he reloaded his gun. After doing this he crawled along behind the log to its end near where the dead Indian lay, as supposed to scalp him.
>
> While doing this another Indian broke out of the brush at the farther side of the slough. When he got about half way across Col. Whitley jumped up, threw up his gun to his face and the Indian seeing him raised his gun and both fired sounding like the report of one gun, and both fell dead. At this time Johnson's Battalion came up in force, a charge was ordered and a sharp skirmish ensued. The Indians retreating scattered in the bushes and this part of the Battle of 1813 was over... Richard Spurr, an officer, was ordered to take a squad of men and bring in the dead to the camp, which he promptly did. He found the body of McGunnigle in a thicket of briars, and the body of Col. Whitley lying where he saw him fall, with the two fresh Indian scalps at his belt. Just

over the log he found the Indian Whitley had slain, lying on his back and having a piece of skin two inches wide and more than a foot long taken from the middle of his back. These four they carried into camp and laid side by side. General Harrison was present and looked at the four bodies and stated "That body with the strip of skin taken from its back was that of Chief Tecumseh" as he had seen him often and knew him well. [19]

Whitley and the others were buried with honors near the battlefield. He had earlier asked his friends that if he should fall that they would protect his body from being scalped, which they did. He also always said that when it was his time to go, he hoped it would be while fighting for his country. He did that. A friend of the family returned Whitley's rifle, powder horn, and his aged horse, Old Emperor, to a grieving Esther and their ten-year-old daughter, Ann. General Harrison himself gave Esther a small brass cannon as a tribute to her husband. She was known to fire it as a salute to William on the anniversary of his death every October until she passed away herself some twenty years later.

Commendations could, and should, go to most of the men and women who strove for a new life in the wilds of Kentucky when the country was just in the midst of its birth. The Boones and McGary's, the Logans and Harrods, and so many more, proved as patriotic and protective of their fellow man as any other; and the Whitley's were just another one of these historic couples. However, this pair seemed to have repeatedly gone above and beyond what most would expect of them. Still, their names are seldom recollected when a discussion of frontier America is had. They deserve our, and our future generation's, appreciation. As this sampling of their deeds proves, they lived what they believed. It's said that actions speak louder than words, well the Whitleys were people of action. Jesus said, "Greater love hath no man than this, that a man lay down his life for his friends." William and Esther Whitley did just that whenever it was necessary, and without complaint. Little wonder that their friends and neighbors viewed them as their guardian angels. ♦

HMMM...

Although Indian attacks are the subject of many frontier stories, it is infrequent that a woman ends up as the heroine. This tale was included in a volume of Theodore Roosevelt's history books of the frontier and was compiled by someone that he had trusted to be a truthful source because the teller had interviewed the settlers himself.
At a settlement in Kentucky during the mid-1780s...

...the cabin of a man named John Merril was attacked at night. He was shot in several places, and one arm and one thigh broken, as he stood by the open door, and fell calling out to his wife to close it. This she did; but the Indians chopped a hole in the stout planks with their tomahawks, and tried to crawl through. The woman, however, stood to one side, and struck at the head of each as it appeared, maiming or killing the first two or three. Enraged at being thus baffled by a woman, two of the Indians clambered on the roof of the cabin, and prepared to drop down the wide chimney; for at night the fire in such a cabin was allowed to smolder, the coals being kept alive in the ashes. But Mrs. Merrill seized a feather-bed and tearing it open, threw it on the embers; the flame and stifling smoke leaped up the chimney, and in a moment both Indians came down, blinded and half smothered, and were killed by the big resolute woman before they could recover themselves. No further attempt was made to molest the cabin or its inmates.

In Theodore Roosevelt's, The Winning of the West, Part IV, 1905 [20]

IV.
THE WINDS OF CHANGE.

> The stormy wind comes from its chamber,
> and the driving winds bring the cold.
> God's breath sends the ice,
> freezing wide expanses of water.
> He loads the clouds with moisture,
> and they flash with his lightning.
> The clouds churn about at his direction.
> They do whatever he commands throughout the earth.
> He makes these things happen either to punish
> people or to show his unfailing love.
>
> Job 37:9-13

If you subscribe to the fact that the Bible is the inspired word of God, this quote from the book of Job, circa 2,000 BC, may persuade you that God does indeed have the ability to show His hand through Nature. If your view of the Bible's authenticity is less than absolute, you may chalk most of our climate's twists and turns up to another diety, chance, or nature's mother herself. Wherever your understanding lies, it is a fact that several confrontational events in the early history of the United States turned in favor of the burgeoning nation by some quite unusual meteorological means.

In the mid-1750s, still almost a quarter of a century before the Revolution had erupted, the border lands of the frontier were becoming the site of ever more frequent armed conflicts. We're speaking of the wilderness territories just west of the Appalachians; what would eventually become portions of the states of Ohio, Michigan, Indiana, Pennsylvania, West Virginia, and Kentucky. In the mid-eighteenth century, this acreage had overlapping claims made to it by two perpetually adversarial countries – France and England.

The rights to the land meant the that the owner had rights to trade with the Indians of the land. Animosity between the two countries was percolating over this issue. Up until this time period, most of the Indians of the region had sided, and traded, with the French. Now the British were getting a piece of the action. Military contests, to decide who owned what, were inevitable.

In the midst of one of the more significant early confrontations over this matter, something rather surprising happened. It wasn't a weather-related mystery, but none-the-less, many people of that day considered it to be a supernatural phenomenon. That sentiment holds true for scores of people today who, in hindsight, see how one man was spared by his Creator early in life for a very special purpose. Years later, during the Revolution, the man we're speaking of would lead the Americans to victory after victory, and escape after escape, often with the aid of unexpected and unexplainable weather anomalies. Because of this, his first miraculous battlefield experience deserves to be taken note of.

It happened in the summer of 1755, just a few miles southeast of present-day Pittsburgh and it became known as the Battle of the Monongahela, or Braddock's Defeat. Historians would later say that it was the precursor to the French and Indian War.

Two years previous to the battle, several French forts were erected across the disputed region of the West as a means of defending their claims to the land. One of these garrisons was named Fort Duquesne and it was situated at the juncture of three major rivers; the Ohio, the Allegheny, and the Monongahela – today's downtown Pittsburgh. Major-General Edward Braddock, the commander-in-chief of the British forces of North America, didn't much care for this new French presence on what he deemed to be land owned by his king. He made his way to evict the foreign tenants.

As his force of nearly fifteen hundred British and Colonial troops made their way to Fort Duquesne, they were ambushed by several hundred warriors of various tribes, as well as by a smaller contingent of French regulars. Braddock's men were sitting ducks; the British regulars in their red coats and the colonials in their blue ones, were all trapped in a ravine and surrounded by hidden Indian marksmen and snipers. The fighting would last for several hours. Some of the British troops broke off from the group and, deciding to counter their enemy in the same Indian fashion by which they were being attacked, hid behind trees and rocks. Others remained in the formal ranks, leaving themselves more vulnerable to a direct hit. There was a good deal of disorder throughout the foray.

Braddock had been rallying the troops fearlessly as bullets flew all about him. So had all the other officers. Unfortunately for the British, it seems that the men on horseback, the officers, were the primary aim of the enemy who took full advantage of them being the more conspicuous targets.

On the whole, the battle was not good for the British, and especially not for Braddock. After already having a couple horses shot out from under him, to his credit, he kept mounting another one and proceeded to parade through the scene shouting out his orders. Finally, a ball found its way through his right arm and came to rest in one of his lungs. His aide-de-camp was the one that came to his rescue; carrying him out of the immediate line of fire. That man was a twenty-three year old Lieutenant-Colonel named George Washington.

Braddock, for the moment was down, but not out. Though he couldn't walk or ride, he was cognizant of the situation and so orally gave directives to his right-hand man. These commands were dutifully followed by Washington and in-turn passed on to the troops. Braddock had called for a regrouping of the soldiers in order to make a counter-attack; however, in spite of Washington's heroic efforts to reassemble the scattered men, there were too few of them to make a sufficient stand. As a result, a full retreat had to be ordered by the general; and that too cost even more lives.

Washington took on his new leadership role as if he had been doing it for a lifetime and he became a national hero for his efforts. As bad as the British losses were, the survivors recognized that they could have been among the dead if not for Washington stepping up as proficiently as he had. Nearly a third of the English forces were killed. Another third were wounded. It was an undeniable disaster. General

Braddock himself passed away a few days later as the army was still retreating. Washington buried him along the road that they had just cut on their way into the fight.

For nearly twelve straight hours during this event, Washington was astride his horses. That's plural, "horses," because, like Braddock, he had several steeds shot out from under him. Additionally, Washington was still suffering with a fever throughout the battle, as many of the men had been, primarily due to a poor supply of substantive food and water on the journey to the fight. Of the more than sixty mounted officers in the battle that day, only one had escaped being killed or even wounded by the enemy's fire. That one was Braddock's adjunct, George Washington.

In a letter to his younger brother, John, and another to his mother, Washington spoke of his miraculous fate. Seemingly, rumors of his death had preceded his arrival at Fort Cumberland where his troops took some respite.

> To John Augustine Washington
> Fort Cumberland, July 18, 1755
>
> Dear Jack: As I have heard since my arriv'l at this place, a circumstantial acct. of my death and dying speech, I take this early oppertunity of contradicting both, and of assuring you that I now exist and appear in the land of the living by the miraculous care of Providence, that protected me beyond all human expectation; I had 4 Bullets through my Coat, and two Horses shot under me, and yet escaped unhurt.
>
> We have been most scandalously beaten by a trifling body of men; but fatigue and want of time prevents me from giving any of the details till I have the happiness of seeing you at home; which I now most ardently wish for, since we are drove in thus far. A Weak and Feeble state of Health, obliges me to halt here for 2 or 3 days, to recover a little strength... [1]

Four bullets had pierced his coat. Others took out two of the horses he was riding. George was barely spared to fight another day.

Washington had a lifelong friend with him in this battle. His name was James Craik and he had afterwards become Washington's personal physician. Some fifteen years later, Craik had joined Washington on a trip back to the site of the battle. The two of them were exploring lands there in which to invest. According to a trusted historian of the early 1800s, Craik had once told the story that while on this excursion to the vicinity of the battleground

> a company of Indians came to them with an interpreter, at the head of whom was an aged and venerable chief. This personage made known to them by the interpreter, that hearing Colonel Washington was in that region, he had come a long way to visit him, adding, that, during the battle of the Monongahela, he had singled him out as a conspicuous object, fired his rifle at him many times, and directed his young warriors to do the same, but to his utter astonishment none of their balls took effect. He was then persuaded, that the youthful hero was under the special guardianship of the Great Spirit, and ceased to fire at him any longer. He was now come to pay homage to the man, who was the particular favorite of Heaven, and who could never die in battle. [2]

Though this Indian story was never documented in writing by Washington, it was told repeatedly by Craik. It may have simply been a politically spun tale that helped to bolster patriotism and Washington's importance as the Revolution loomed in the early 1770s. Then again, it could have been all of that, and still true. Washington's adopted grandson, George Washington Parke Custis gave the story national attention in 1827 when he produced a play titled, "The Indian Prophecy," which depicted the encounter and gave the credit for George's survival to God Himself.

Just a month after the battle, Washington was already rounding up companies of men to fight yet again against the now proven to be formidable French and Indian alliance. In a sermon at one such company's camp, a Reverend Samuel Davies preached a word of encouragement to the troops. After praising their zeal and faith he ended his patriotic sermon with a reference to the man who survived the Battle of the Monongahela.

> I may point out to the public that heroic youth, Colonel Washington, whom I cannot but hope Providence has hitherto preserved in so signal a manner for some important service to his country. [3]

And as we all know, the rest is history.

Shortly after the French and Indian War, rumblings of dissent were beginning to be heard across the colonies. This time, however, it was different. The opposition was not toward another country or the Indians, but against their own British government. In large part, the animosity began when a series of taxes known as "acts" were imposed on them by the King in 1765. Tensions rose as fast as their resentment to these levies. By 1775, it had erupted into an all-out rebellion.

All things considered, the most, and most-consequential, battles were fought in the colonies. However, the Revolution was fought on the frontier with just as much courage and determination as it was elsewhere. It simply took a bit of a different form in the wilderness.

There were only a few outright battles between British regulars and the disaffected Americans, who on the frontier were primarily composed of militia. The English had occupied a few key fortresses across the West. Detroit was perhaps the strongest, along with a handful of others like Vincennes and Kaskaskia. The few large-scale engagements that did occur were against the latter of these posts. They were successfully led by the primary American military commander on the frontier, George Rogers Clark. The British had allied with several Indian tribes who most often comprised the front line of attackers in their offensives.

Flurries of raids were carried out by both sides during the Revolution; often times to recover stolen horses, other times to recover stolen people. Stories of settlers being kidnapped and forced to live on a long-term basis with the Indians abound. Often, it was children who were taken and adopted into a tribe. Many of these youth, as well as some of the adult captives, grew to love their new way of life. Even when offered the chance to return to their natural families, some were reluctant to do so. At the very onset of their being taken, however, most could do nothing but contemplate a means to escape. Such was the case of one of the most heroic men of these frontier times, Simon Kenton.

Kenton was a contemporary of the iconic Daniel Boone. He was also his friend. Thanks in large part to authors of historical books from the mid-twentieth century onward, Kenton has finally come to be appreciated for his intrepidity, patriotism, and fidelity. That goes for Daniel Boone as well, who has enjoyed a few more than the usual fifteen minutes of fame. The life of Kenton, just as Boone's, was instrumental in the founding of our nation and the achievements of each are much too lengthy to fully recount here. Many times over, these heroic men had brushes with death. There were two particular life-saving episodes, one in each of these rugged men's experiences, which they and many since have deemed to be acts of Divine intervention. Ironically, both began on September 7, 1778.

On that day, Chief Blackfish and a band of his Shawnee warriors were approaching Boonesborough making ready for a major assault on the settlement. Meanwhile, Kenton was leaving Logan's Station, some forty miles southwest of Boonesborough, on a mission to a village north of the Ohio River. There he planned to recapture horses that had been stolen by the Shawnee living in Chillicothe. He left with two other men, Alexander Montgomery and George Rogers Clark. After several days, the Indian village and their horses came into view. They patiently waited until the deepest hours of the night to make their move. It proved an easier task than anticipated. They successfully rounded up the stolen horses, as well as a few of the ones owned by the Indians. However, as they led the horses away, something roused one of the Indians and he noticed them missing. Though they had a head start in making their escape, the Kentuckians knew by the ensuing commotion that they would soon be pursued. After two days of slow travel, guiding the horses through dense woods to avoid capture, they reached the Ohio River. It was here that the will of God, as evidenced by the winds and rains, seemed to go against Kenton. An author and descendent of Simon, Edna Kenton, has noted that while they were at the river

> the weather by now was stormy, the wind was high, the river was smothered with white caps, driftwood was floating thick, and although they tried repeatedly they could not make their horses take the water. Knowing the wind often stilled at sunset, they went back upon their trail and waylaid it at so advantageous a place that from their ambush they could have easily repulsed a party much larger than theirs. There they hoppled their horses and turned them loose among the river hills to graze, while they lay concealed, waiting for their pursuers and for the evening.
>
> But the wind did not abate and they stayed there all night. The next morning Kenton tried to swim two or three of the horses across but the animals, frightened by the water the day before, utterly refused to cross.

Portrait of Simon Kenton. Artist unknown.

Knowing they could delay no longer, they decided to gather up the rest of the horses, move down the river to the falls... [4]

Well, for safety's sake and diversion from pursuit, the men decided to split up on their way downriver. Before moving on, Kenton first went back up on a ridge to see if the Indians had caught up to them. They had. Kenton fired at one of the five approaching on horseback, but he suffered only a flash in the pan. Before he knew it, his hands and feet were being bound and he was tied to a nearby tree. Montgomery had heard the commotion from a ways off and ran back toward Kenton. He fired into the scene, but he didn't find a target so he fled. A couple of the captors gave chase to Montgomery. When they returned, Kenton learned of his friend's fate as he was repeatedly slapped in the face with Montgomery's bloody scalp. Clark was the only one to have successfully made his escape.

From this point on, Kenton was under the constant threat of death, but it would be slow and delayed because the Indians knew they had a great catch. Kenton's reputation was well-known to them and likened to that of Boone, whose recent escape from their clutches, made Kenton's captivity even more prized.

The tortures inflicted on Kenton were unending and unbearable. The first night the group camped along the Ohio River on their way back to Chillicothe. After being lectured about the vileness of horse stealing, his punishment was imposed.

> They laid him flat on his back, with his arms extended their full length and his wrists tied securely to a pole laid transversely across his breast. A rope passed under his body and around the pole was used to lash his elbows to it likewise. A halter placed about his neck was fastened to a tree near by and stakes were driven in the earth at his feet to which his ankles were tied. He was almost literally unable to move during the long night, and the pain of his bonds made sleep impossible — the pain of his injuries as well, for the Indians had spared no pain of cuffing, beating, and kicking. [5]

Things only got worse. In the morning they all mounted their horses for the rest of the ride to their village. They took extra measures to amuse themselves by putting Kenton on a feisty, unbroken, young horse.

> They fastened his hands behind him and his feet under the colt's belly. A halter was passed about his neck and its ends fastened to the colt's neck and rump. Then, all made ready, with Kenton powerless to ward off branches and underbrush from his face and body, they gave the colt a smart blow as they released it, and as it dashed off they roared with mirth at the spectacle… The colt pitched, reared, and rolled to rid itself of its burden; the ragged bushes tore its rider's legs and feet; the tree limbs raked and scourged his face and body. If he dropped forward on the colt's neck to avoid being blinded by branches, his back was lashed by them. Every leap of this ride was a hairbreadth escape, for if he once lost his balance he was finished — the halter would hang him. [6]

Kenton was a gentle friend to horses and therefore in spite of the tortuous ride, the young steed eventually settled down and was ridden the next day with little incident.

The travels continued into a third night until the entourage found themselves close enough to the village to send a runner ahead of them announcing that they would be coming in with a captive in the morning. The celebration deserved to occur in the daylight. However, a number of the villagers came out into the woods that night to see Kenton. For their preliminary amusement, they tied his hands over his head to a pole they had set into the ground and for hours they jeered at him as they circled his naked body.

When the sun rose, Kenton was led into the village only to see the residents lined up before him in two seemingly unending rows with a six foot gap between them. He was to run this gauntlet as many times as it took to successfully get through to its end; all the while withstanding the blows of clubs, branches, stones, and fists. He faltered in two attempts, always near the end of each run. Too weak to continue with a third, he would be nourished and mended so he could run again tomorrow.

But on the following day, the Indian leaders, after a council, decided to celebrate the death of Kenton on a broader scale. They would make the forty-mile trek to Wappatomika, near today's Bellefontaine, Ohio where a larger audience would witness his death sentence of being burned at the stake. On the way to Wappatomika, two more stops were made and two more gauntlets were run by Kenton. On the second run, he leapt over an Indian at the finish and was suddenly on his way to freedom. Then fate, or chance, or Divine Providence, intervened to Kenton's disadvantage. He ran directly into an approaching Indian party, led by Blue jacket, that was coming in to witness the celebrity captive. They promptly caught him and the game plan was resumed.

Insults to Kenton were non-stop, often the most degrading coming from children and women. One account given by Reverend Asal Owen, a grand-nephew of Kenton, details a very graphic and disturbing event perpetrated by an Indian squaw. While pinned to the ground, spread eagle, with no use of his hands or feet, a female of the tribe

> deliberately seated herself upon the face of our hero who with the vigor and fierceness of a tiger, he gave his teeth a death-like set somewhere in the reagion of her inexpressibles and held a deathlike grit with his teeth and his mouth was well filled with her sporting flesh. Alass, she began to screach and yell like a loon. Now the Indians were convulsed with frantic and savage laughture, loud and sportive yells and howlings; all their mirth was at the expense of the unfortunate squaw – the Indians love fun even at the misfortune of their own friends. Our hero held his holt until he disengaged his mouth and face from her flesh. [7]

Finally, their destination was reached; Wappatomika. Here more and more Indians were arriving to view the anticipated spectacle of Kenton burning at the stake. After Kenton's face was painted black, giving evidence of his fate, an old friend appeared in the crowd; Simon Girty. Though a vehement adversary to the Americans, Girty came to recognize the man he long admired. Through a series of speeches to the Indian leadership, Girty made a case for Kenton's freedom. Their eventual vote was to spare his life. For the moment, he was free to recuperate from his numerous assaults and was technically adopted into the tribe by an older squaw, who along with Girty, nursed him back to health.

Kenton's reprieve was short-lived. A few weeks into his recovery, a dour Indian war party returned to Wappatomika having lost many of their friends in a battle against Americans in Virginia. Learning of Kenton being among them, they made the case, and won, to have the death penalty re-imposed as compensation for their recent lost fellows. This time Girty could not come to his rescue, except for buying him some time. He convinced the chiefs that by executing him in (Upper) Sandusky, some fifty miles away, an even broader audience could take part and they would gain the others' accolades as well.

Again the captors made their way northward. Along the route, two more random individuals made their personal feelings known to Kenton. One man wielded the pipe-end of his tomahawk into Kenton's head, which left an impression for the rest of his life. Later on the same day, another Indian grabbed an axe and cracked it into his collarbone. The march continued in spite of his agony. When they stopped for the night it was at Chief Logan's hunting camp. This unexpected destination boded well for Kenton who had previous encounters with Logan and knew him to be a fair man.

Logan conversed with Kenton and then discreetly sent two runners ahead of the group in order to put in a good word for him at Sandusky. Kenton had one more day to recoup from his injuries before heading out on the last twenty-mile trek to the village where he would surely meet his maker. Halfway there, a band of Indians had formed and forced him to run the ninth gauntlet of his ongoing nightmare. As they resumed their travel, he expected yet another beating when they finally reached the village. That didn't occur, only because the Indians at Sandusky considered that another attack might actually kill the already weakened Kenton; hence ruining the anticipated fiery spectacle.

The following day again, fate intervened. Everything was ready for the burning: the stake was planted; there even hung on it a horn containing water for him to drink during the process of his torture. When the morning came and the fire was about to be lighted — indeed, according to one account, when the fire was lighted and "just as he felt the flame and began to circle around the stake amid the shouts of the savages" – Kenton raised his eyes in hopelessness to the heavens which were blue and almost cloudless. But suddenly, from a sky so clear as to make the sequel miraculous, there fell "the heaviest rainstorm he had ever experienced, as though a rain cloud had burst over his head. An awe-stricken silence fell upon the noisy throng," at the marvel of "water poured from a cloudless sky."[8]

In silent bewilderment, the Indians untied Kenton. So extraordinary was this event that it caused many to wonder if they had offended the Great Spirit by trying this second time to take what seemed to be a divinely protected life.

None-the-less, the council would stand by their decision for his death. It was agreed that when the wood had sufficiently dried, the execution would again be attempted. However, before that time arrived, a seemingly distinguished British officer made an appearance at the village. Unbeknownst to Kenton, his arrival came as a result of the runners that Chief Logan had sent ahead days earlier.

Peter Drouillard was actually a French-Canadian trader hired by the British for his knowledge of Indian languages. His flashy uniform, however, and the promise of multiple gifts impressed the Indians. Mr. Drouillard explained that the British wanted to question Kenton for his knowledge of any of the Americans' plans for attack on the frontier. It was agreed Kenton would be temporarily loaned to the British for interrogation in exchange for numerous gifts.

At Detroit, Kenton was interrogated and then remained a loosely guarded prisoner. After several attempts to have Kenton returned to them, the Indians realized that they had forever lost their captive to the British authorities and made no further attempts to have him returned. Months later, in the summer of 1779, Kenton and two other prisoners managed to escape from Detroit. To avoid any Indian or British pursuit, they took a highly divergent route westward, well into Indiana lands, before heading south to Kentucky. Finally, after nearly a year, Kenton's ordeal had ended.

As one reviews all the events of Kenton's captivity, there is an obvious dichotomy. Just the fact that he was captured, let alone having to suffer so many tortures that would have killed lesser men, seems horrific for God to have allowed. On the other hand, there was the rain, from a cloudless sky, arriving at precisely the most opportune moment for Kenton. Likewise, the arrivals of Girty and Drouillard came exactly at the right moments to secure a reprieve from certain death. Perhaps God is misunderstood in tragedies like this. The misery Kenton had to bear ended up giving witness to the Great Spirit's presence in his affairs. At least that is how Kenton viewed it. Rather than curse God for all his misfortunes…

… He himself, who for seven weeks had seen life and death flash before his eyes in dazing succession, held always a belief in a special providence exerted in his behalf – a belief "so deep," said one of his friends, "as to appear almost superstitious." [9]

A year and a half before Kenton's capture, he had saved the life of Daniel Boone. Since its establishment in April of 1775, Boonesboro bore the brunt of numerous assaults and raids on its inhabitants, cattle, and horses. The Shawnee Chief Blackfish, from the Chillicothe settlements north of the Ohio River, was often behind the attacks. On one such occasion, April 24, 1777 to be exact, a couple of men went out from the walls of Boonesborough to see what was spooking the cows from going out to pasture. The men had wandered a bit too far from the gate when they were discovered and fired upon by a handful of Blackfish's warriors. The two men raced back toward the fort, but one of them was felled and scalped. As the Indian attacker raised his trophy with a yell, Simon Kenton, who was running onto the scene from the fortress, stopped, aimed, and shot the Indian dead.

The remainder of the Indians dispersed, or so Kenton, Boone and the other men on the scene had thought. As they turned to make their way back, while still at some distance from the fort, the men discovered that they had been led into a trap by several dozen other Indians who now appeared between them and their protective garrison. There was no choice for the Kentuckians but to charge their way against these warriors if they were going to have any chance of getting to the fortress.

Shots rang out in all directions. In due course, Boone was one of the men to fall with a ball landing in, and shattering, part of his ankle. Just as an Indian crouched over Boone and lifted his tomahawk to strike a fatal blow, Kenton yet again took immediate aim and abolished the assailant. Before he could even reload, a warrior came charging toward Kenton brandishing a knife. Kenton dismissed him as well, by abruptly swinging the butt of his musket to his head. With no hesitation, he then raised Boone's disabled body onto his shoulders, and carried him swiftly and safely into the fort; all the while dodging the enemy's flurry of deadly flying balls. Later, as Boone began to recover, he is reported to have called the mere twenty-one year old Kenton to his bedside, thanking him with the words, "Simon, you have behaved like a man today. Indeed, you are a fine fellow." [10]

In September of the following year, 1778, on the very day that Kenton had left for Chillicothe to retrieve his stolen horses from the Shawnee, Chief Blackfish and a large force of warriors reappeared within sight of Boonesborough. This was not going to be just another random skirmish, it was a planned attack with over four hundred warriors ready to destroy Daniel Boone and his community should he not agree to give it up peacefully. The settlement would resist for nearly two weeks, and would survive to see many more days due in large part to yet another critically timed meteorological event.

Like Kenton, Boone had only recently escaped from Indian captivity. In January of 1778, he and a few dozen other men had been working at a salt lick when they were surrounded and captured by the Shawnee. During his time as a prisoner in the Indian camp, Boone was adopted by Blackfish who took a fatherly liking toward him. Boone is believed to have manipulated those feelings into a faux friendship before he made his escape in June. He is said to have even promised the peaceful surrender of Boonesboro to Blackfish when the time was right. This he used as a bargaining chip to secure the lives and safe transport to Detroit of his friends who had been captured along with him. Now, just a couple months after Boone's return to Boonesboro, the two men were meeting under very different circumstances. Blackfish had expected Boone to keep his word and to give up the settlement without

Old Fort at Boonesborough, 1775. In book, *The Loyal West in the Times of the Rebellion*, by John Barber and Henry Howe.

a fight; but Boone was not about to surrender anything or anyone. All he could do was stall for time in the hope that reinforcements might arrive from nearby stations. Thanks to a false report from an American captive, the Indian aggressors were under the impression that Boonesboro had a significant number of defenders within its walls. It did not.

After Boone made clear that the residents of Boonesboro would fight to the death, it was decided that talks would be held to diffuse the situation. Along with Boone and Blackfish, several other dignitaries on both sides joined in the discussions. Contrary to Blackfish's request to meet within the confines of the fortress, the talks were held outside the walls. A table was set up and the parties cordially discussed their options for two days; always well within range of the sharp shooters perched along the walls of Boonesboro.

On September 9,

> ...Both parties, unarmed, sought the shade of the great sycamores near the Lick Spring, where the pioneers were invited to seat themselves on deerskins and pantherskins spread on the ground by their hospitable enemies, who passed around the pipe and the whisky. The day was spent in pow-wows, which the settlers protracted, and in feasting — the besiegers seeking, with suspicious generosity, to beguile the half-starved "rebels" with eatables and drinkables from the British commissary department at Detroit, such as most of them had not seen, much less tasted, in many a long month. By sunset a compact, inscrutable to this day, was agreed to, which was to be signed the next morning. The settlers seemed completely hoodwinked, hilarity reigned, and DeQuindre [the French lieutenant representing and advising the British authorities at Fort Detroit] was confident that the royal standard of England would quickly float over the wooden walls of Boonesborough. Neither party was sincere. [11]

The compact referred to in this account was believed to state that the Indian force would depart with no aggressive action being taken, if the settlers would agree allegiance to the British until higher authorities officially ratified the said treaty. The frontier signing was to take place the following morning. As a precaution, it was agreed by Boone's men beforehand that a wave of their hats would be the signal that the meeting had failed and the sharpshooters should take out the enemy. On September 10,

> the sham treaty was signed, and Blackfish then declared that it must be confirmed by what he said was the Indian custom a handshake all around, two braves to each white brother. It was the signal for treachery. The young Indians, in apparently high good humor, seized the hands of the pioneers, but in the very act they betrayed their purpose by too tight a grasp and by a sudden movement toward the underbrush. Suspicious, alert, and quick, with the quickness of desperation the hunters freed themselves almost as soon as touched, and in the same thrilling moment, as they sprang aside and waved their hats, came the deadly crack of the ready rifles from the blockhouse, and the unarmed savages vanished in the surrounding thickets. Then up the steep hill dashed the fleeing pioneers, bounding from tree to tree and from stump to stump to protect themselves from the hail of bullets sent after them by the enraged ambuscaders... [12]

The fight was on. The truth was that Boonesborough only had about forty men and a few boys that could handle a gun. The two-day pause for these talks inadvertently gave the community in the fortress time to gather some extra water and to make ammunition which were both in short supply. In spite of this extra time to prepare, their supplies were still limited. The odds were nearly ten-to-one against their survival.

The Indian attack was made with arrows and gunshots aimed at men along the walls and at every other opening they could perceive. The assaults took a physical toll on the small band within as they continued their effort to appear to be more than they were. Women were instructed to wear hats and men's shirts to embellish the illusion. Some Indians ran toward the fort with lit torches which they aimed to hurl over the walls, but that tactic was soon stopped as they made themselves easy targets for the Boonesborough marksmen before they could fling their firebrands. Any flaming sticks that did make it into the fort were quickly swept off the combustible rooftops by women wielding long poles.

Squire Boone, Daniel's brother, turned out to be a budding engineer. He managed to lash two black gum tree logs together with the metal strapping from a wagon wheel, and thus created a couple of wooden cannons. One fired as planned. Its resounding blast alone intimidated the Indians; but it cracked upon firing and couldn't be reused. The second cannon exploded when lit. Luckily only the men's pride was injured as they drew the taunts of a few Indians who witnessed the combustion from just outside the walls. In spite of the constant onslaught, for the moment at least, Boonesboro was surprisingly holding its own.

Several days into the fight, men noticed the river water near the fort turning muddy. Hidden from the fort's view by its angle and high brim, it was soon discerned that the Indians were beginning to dig a tunnel into the river's bank. By constantly firing upon the fortress, the Indians hoped to muffle the sound of the digging. Daniel Trabue, a frontiersman at the site reported:

> This fort was close on the bank of the Kentucky River, and it was Descovered from the fort that their was an old cedar stick or pole that come up out of the bank perpendecular and it was observed to shake: our men knew then the endeans was Digging a passway (this was a project

of a Canadian french man, [DeQuindre] as was thought) under the fort from the River under the bank but they could not be seen from the fort. Col. Calleway imediately had our men at Diging a ditch oppersite the Indians' Ditch. [13]

So from about seventy yards out, the Indians proceeded for several days to tunnel toward the fortress. The plan was to lay gunpowder at the wall when it was reached and blow open a devastating entry hole. Unbeknownst to the Indians, the men of Boonesboro began burrowing their own tunnel in their direction in the hopes of intercepting them underground. This digging would go on for days.

The combatants not involved in the tunneling, on both sides, spent the following days randomly trying to pick off whoever they could from a distance. On the Lord's day, the thirteenth of September, the Indians returned to their plan of burning the residents out of Boonesborough. This time, they didn't get their torches into the fort, but managed to get a few strewn against the outside of the wooden walls. They also added lit arrows to their arsenal. The heads were sheathed in oily hickory bark and flax allowing them to burn aggressively. As they landed on the combustible roofs, the residents tried again to sweep them away; but they just couldn't keep up. Besides, they were dodging a barrage of bullets at the same time. As the fires took hold in spots, the end seemed near.

For a brief period the disheartened frontiersmen gave in to their worst fears. But then they witnessed a surprising turn in their situation. The fires were actually extinguishing themselves. When the fiery arrows landed, the dampness in the roofs soon prohibited them from progressing beyond a brief ignition. Light rains that had been drizzling on and off over the previous two days had created the moistness.

Rain grew heavier over the next two days, as the tunnels grew closer and closer to each other. On Tuesday, September 15, the men were beginning to hear the quarrying of the Indians from inside their own burrow. Their meeting up seemed imminent. All waited in anticipation of a breakthrough, but none came. The tensions weighed on the men and women of Boonesborough as heavily as the downpours that persisted through the dark, foreboding night. If the enemy was still chipping away at the earth below ground, the sound of it was deadened by the torrents of rain.

When morning broke, the silence was unsettling. The noisy precipitation had stopped and so had the sounds of the enemy beyond the walls. In utter bewilderment, the occupants took stock of their surroundings and concluded that the Indians were gone. How could that be possible? Historian, George W. Ranck, writing in 1901 sums it up like this:

> The wet weather had done more to balk the Indians than rifles or wooden walls. The rain had not only strengthened the thirsty garrison and saved the fort from destruction by fire, but, as the settlers soon discovered, it had caused such quantities of the saturated earth to cave in and obstruct the mine as to effectually ruin it, and the fickle savages, who never willingly engaged at all at any manual labor, had abandoned the siege in inexpressible disgust.[14]

Reinforcing this view was Peter Drouillard, the same French-Canadian working for the British who would save Simon Kenton's life. He had come onto the scene at Boonesborough with Blackfish as an interpreter and participated in the negotiations with Boone before the siege commenced. Some time later, he stated to Kenton that the collapse of the Indian tunnel was the final disheartening blow to the Indians, causing them to finally withdraw from Boonesborough.

Daniel Boone had survived what became known to the people of that day as "the great siege of Boonesborough." He would go on to have many more notorious adventures over the next forty-some years of his life. The settlement he had established, as well, would continue on, enduring as a small village for a few more decades before dwindling back to only sixty-eight residents in 1810. Both the community and its founder were forever grateful for the very timely heavenly rains in September of 1778.

As the years passed, more communities would be established by families in the wilderness; and the Native Americans, backed by the British through the Revolution, would continue to resist them. Some of the conflicts between the two sides were random and only involved a few individuals. But others were major, preplanned, offensive measures aimed at destroying the larger settlements. Although most did not have any surprising or dramatic changes in the weather that would

Print by Nagel Weingartner, circa 1851, depicting the women of Bryan Station bravely getting water while acting as if they hadn't noticed Native Americans looking on from the woods.

suddenly reverse their anticipated outcomes, there is one such attack that is worth mentioning before we turn to the incredulous events that affected several of the more consequential battles that took place in the colonies.

It happened at Bryan's Station; a community similar to Boonesboro and located only twenty miles northwest of it. There were forty houses within its walls and a few other buildings just outside of them. In the fall of 1782, a major attack was made upon it, much like the one at Boone's community four years earlier. This one boasted a force of over five hundred Indians under the leadership of the notorious Simon Girty.

It began on August 15, 1782, when the Indian army, hiding in the distance, was detected by the inhabitants of the fort. Rather than react rashly, the people of Bryan's Station tempered their anxiety and strategized their best next move. Meanwhile, still assuming that they were undiscovered, the Indians confidently planned their attack. The fortress residents went so far with their supposed unawareness of these Indians that by evening several very brave women dared to casually walk for water from the well that was located a short distance from the fort. The water they collected would prove essential in case of an extended siege against them. Likewise, it might become a vital necessity to douse any fires that the Indians might attempt to ignite. The residents continued their forced casualness through the night. In the meantime, two men from the fort were sent under the cover of darkness through a cornfield and onward to other fortresses in the region to seek reinforcements.

The next morning, the attack began. The Indians sent a small party of warriors to one side of the fort who began firing on the structure. This was a ruse designed to draw out most of the men so that the bulk of the Indian force could afterwards attack the opposite side of the fortress en masse with supposedly little if any resistance. The residents, knowing of their presence, played along by sending several men out to confront the small band. The men ran and fired ferociously managing to scatter and wound a few of the attackers. Rather than remain in close contact and continue to pursue the Indians, these men abruptly stopped a short distance from the fort, turned, and ran as fast as they could back to the fort's gate.

It was the sound of the gunfire from this ruse that was the signal for Simon Girty and his greater force to come out from hiding and attack the other side. One can imagine their surprise when they were met with a hail of gunfire from the bulk of the men who had remained along those back walls in anticipation of this very strategy being employed. As one shot was made, each frontiersmen swapped out his rifle for another, already loaded by his wife or kids and ready to be fired. They had a system.

The Indians suffered a heavy loss, but they were successful in one regard; their torches and lit arrows had ignited several buildings. These were the structures just outside of the fortress. With flames rising high and mighty, for a few tense moments the inhabitants feared th worst. The timbers of Bryan's Station were eager to ignite. According to an eyewitness, Joseph Ficklin, who was a boy in the station at the time:

> There were a few houses about 60 feet outside of the Pickets which were abandoned at the first alarm and occupied by the Indians for a short time and set on fire. A favorable and sudden change of the wind to N. E. blew the flames the opposite direction and saved the whole population from the flames and death or capture. [15]

This time it was the wind that suddenly changed direction and swept the fires away from the dry walls of the fortress. Had that shift not occurred, the fort would surely have been lost. As it happened, the Indians were gone the following morning. With that brisk wind at their backs, they moved on to the Blue Licks region some forty miles away. It would be there, before the Revolution officially ended the following year, that they would finally garner some success against these men of the frontier.

The fighting in the colonies was primarily between the British loyalists and the American rebels. Native Americans had become involved in the colonial engagements as well, though in lesser numbers than on the frontier. In fact, the Revolution caused a divide in loyalties within many of the tribes. Some were faithful to the British who had already been trying to keep the colonists from settling over the mountains. Others allied with the Americans. Still others remained neutral. The battles occurring between the Atlantic and the Appalachians were often on a much grander scale than those on the frontier; involving thousands of men rather than a handful or a few hundred. None-the-less, unusual weather-related events again came to play a significant role in several of these conflicts, just as they had on the frontier.

In March of 1776, the British fleet was still positioned in the Boston Harbor. They had been there since the previous June when their forces had defeated the Americans at Bunker Hill. Additional British troops were stationed on some of the hills that surrounded the city. One of the three most strategic of these mounds happened to overlook the south side of the city. It was known as Dorchester Heights. It had remained unoccupied by either side in spite of the fact that both knew it was probably the most critical point to hold should another conflict ensue.

To gain it, the British feared that they would have to suffer a potentially large loss of lives, as they just recently had at Bunker Hill. They projected that they would attempt it only if and when the Americans tried to occupy it first. The Americans were successfully holding another hill, Cambridge, which was located east of Boston proper.

This was a time of stalemate. As time passed, Washington, in command of the Americans who were still positioned outside of Boston, had as his goal a further fortification of the harbor area in order to force the departure of the British fleet. Henry Knox, the future Secretary of War, had a plan to help him do so.

Knox wanted to have the arsenal of cannons and other supplies, recently captured at Fort Ticonderoga, transported to Boston. This was a daunting proposal because Ticonderoga was three hundred miles away from Boston; but Washington trusted Knox to do it. Over several brutally cold and snowy months, the mission was completed. Numerous hefty cannons were pulled on sleds over rugged, frozen trails and on boats through icy waters. The fact that this feat was successfully accomplished is itself miraculous.

Upon Knox's arrival in Boston at the end of January, Washington concluded the time to attack was imminent. In a special council on February 16, he proposed an all out assault. He was overruled, however, by his fellow officers. Instead, a bold move of intimidation and provocation was agreed to. It was decided that they would secretly, and very quickly, take possession of Dorchester Heights. Such a sudden occupation of this hill would draw the British out against them while they held the advantage of being on the high ground.

In order to avoid notice or attack, possession would have to be taken overnight. As an emotional incentive, Washington purposely chose the anniversary of the Boston Massacre, March 5, as the day that would shine its first light on his men surprisingly being stationed at the top of this strategic hill.

From the time this decision was made the men had only a little over two weeks to get things in order to accomplish it. All preparations had to be done in secret. One consideration was that there would be no time to build a wall of protection in front of the cannons once they were hauled into position atop Dorchester. Therefore, a very keen strategy was employed. Portable fortifications, built in sections, would be moved up the hill and quickly pieced together to create an abatis. Barrels, too, were built. Once at the top, they would be filled with earth and then rolled down the hill, as needed, to dislodge any enemy troops climbing toward them. Clever. One might wonder if the creators of the twentieth century arcade game, "Donkey-Kong" were students of this historical event!

As a decoy to the noise and commotion created during the construction of all these materials, several lengthy firings of the American cannons from Cambridge were made. These were an audible and directional diversion because Cambridge was ninety degrees off the mark of Dorchester Heights. The tactic did produce the desired distraction; allowing the noise of sawing and hammering near Dorchester to go unnoticed. Even the process of moving the multiple cannons from Cambridge to Dorchester was a complicated task. Hay bales had to be stacked along an extended causeway in order to block the view of the artillery being transported from the distant enemy's spyglasses.

Finally the night of March 4 arrived and all was in readiness to proceed. The men began a most incredible effort, all with great swiftness, and right under the nose of the British. Teams of men and oxen hauled the arsenal of cannons upwards. Likewise, the redoubts, or portable barricades, were pulled up the one hundred foot tall mound. The Reverend William Gordon wrote a letter to a friend a short time after the event explaining how the hill was secured:

> The covering party consisting of 800 men led the way; then the carts with the entrenching tools; after that the main working body under Gen' Thomas consisting of about 1200; a train of more than 300 carts loaded with fascines, presst hay, in bundles of seven or eight hundred, etc. closed the procession...
>
> ...The night was remarkably mild, a finer for working could not have been taken out of the whole 365. It was hazy below so that our people could not be seen, tho' it was a bright moon light night above on the hills. [16]

Isn't that interesting? On the very night that had been decided upon weeks in advance for this feat to be attempted, the men ended up with plenty of illumination in the middle of the night once at the top of the hill. And, at the same time, any view of them from the ships was obscured by low hanging clouds at the bottom. The Reverend went on to explain that

> when the ministerialists [supporters of the Crown] discovered in the morning early what we had been after, they were astonished upon seeing what we had done. Gen'l How was seen to scratch his head and heard to say by those that were about him, that he did not know what he should do, that the provincials (he likely called them by some other name) had done more work in one night than his whole army would have done in six months. In this strong manner did he express his surprise. [17]

Indeed, the British were shocked at the overnight change of circumstances precipitated by the previously supposed incompetent, rag-

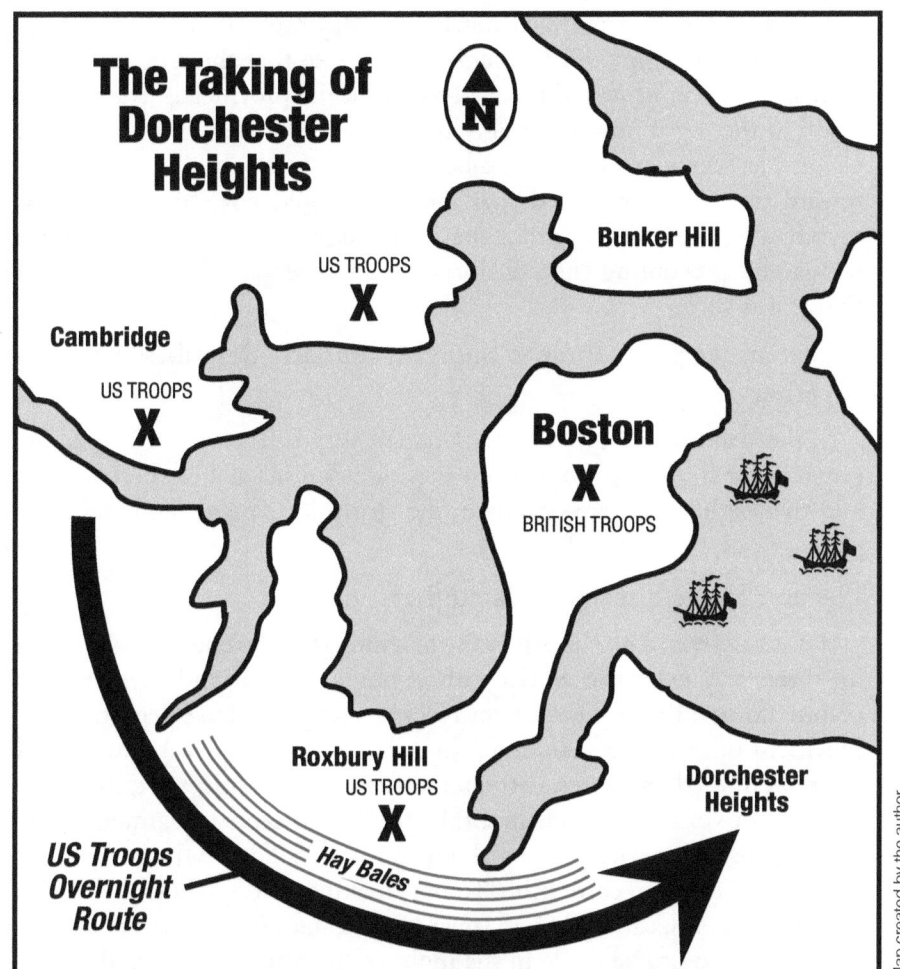

tag rebels. Three stations were now in play atop the Heights with the potential to reach the fleet with their cannons. General Howe had to decide his next move.

He ordered, several thousand troops to be boarded onto boats and head to the base of Dorchester Heights. But as the force progressed toward the hill something happened. Rev. William Gordon who was on site, testified that

> the wind was very unfavourable to the design carrying on by the ministerialists, blowing pritty fresh and almost full against them…
> … I expected that the men of war would get as near to Dorchester

hills as possible, that the next morning at day break a most heavy cannonade would begin; and I thought it probable that the regulars would land under cover of it, and proceed to attack the provincials. But when I heard in the night how amazingly strong the wind blew (for it was such a storm as scarce any one remember'd to have heard) and how it rained toward morning, concluded that the ships could not stir, and pleased myself with the reflection that the Lord might be working deliverance for us and preventing the effusion of human blood. The event proved that it was so. [18]

A British sergeant, Thomas Sullivan, similarly describes the change of weather:

... the wind blowing hard and it rained very heavy so that it was impossible for the troops to land on the intended place. For the two days and two nights we were on board, the storm lasted and the wind blew right a head. [19]

General Howe himself declared that

It was discovered on the 5th in the morning that the enemy had thrown up three very extensive works with strong abbatis round them on the commanding hills on Dorchester Neck, which must have been the employment of at least 12,000 men. In a situation so critical I determined upon an immediate attack with all the force I could transport; the ardor of the troops encouraged me in this hazardous enterprise; regiments were expeditiously embarked on board transports to fall down the harbor, and flat-boats were to receive other troops, making in the whole 2400 men to rendevous at Castle William [near Dorchester Heights] from whence the descent was to be made in the night of the 5th. But the wind unfortunately coming contrary and blowing very hard the ships were not able to get to their destination, and this circumstance also making it impossible to employ the boats, the attempt became impracticable.

The weather continuing boisterous the next day and night gave the enemy time to improve their works, to bring up their cannon and to put themselves in such a state of defence that I could promise myself little success by attacking them under all the disadvantages I had to encounter; wherefore I judged it most advisable to prepare for the evacuation of the town upon the assurance of one month's provision ... [20]

From the moment of Howe's announcement, there was a frenzy about Boston as preparations were made for the British to leave. It was no small operation. Not only did it require the collection of military goods, men, and foodstuffs; but also the gathering and collating of over a thousand Loyalist families who immediately wanted out of Boston. It took nearly two weeks to get all in order aboard the one-hundred and twenty ships of the fleet. The British needed that time, but they might have left sooner if not for the winds that had continued to blow against their ability to make a safe departure. It wasn't until St. Patrick's Day, the seventeenth of March, that the winds had finally changed and the retreat commenced. It was marked with a tremendous volley of cannon firings from each of the British ships as a salute to themselves in spite of their forced departure. Ardent cheers echoed from the hills of Boston, especially from the incredibly determined men atop Dorchester as they realized their success. As of this writing, that date is still observed as Evacuation Day in Boston's Suffolk County.

Though they had abandoned Boston, the armada soon joined up with even more British ships in the harbor of New York. By late July of 1776, over a hundred and seventy-five ships had come under General Howe's command, making their base in the waters surrounding Staten Island, Brooklyn, and Long Island. Another battle, the most significant to date in the Revolution, was in the offing. It would come to be known as the battle of Brooklyn Heights at the time, and later as the Battle of Long Island. And, yet again, the wind and weather played a timely role in the Americans' favor.

Over several weeks through late July and early August, the ships continued to sail into the New York Harbor. Crowds gathered all across the higher grounds of the seaport to see the spectacular show of force. Over 30,000 British troops were aboard their majestic vessels. One can only imagine the magnificence of so many tall ships in one place with their sails glistening in the summer sunlight.

The American land forces were gathered on Manhattan Island, New York. From there they moved southward across the East River and into Brooklyn. Two entrenchments were established; one in the interior of Brooklyn around today's Flatbush region and the other to the north in Brooklyn Heights which was closer to the East River.

The British began their offensive with the landing of troops along the southwest shores of Brooklyn on Thursday morning, August 22.

By afternoon, some 15,000 soldiers were in motion toward Washington's front lines. For several days the forces on both sides strategized their next moves and finally positioned themselves for the inevitable fight. On Monday night, August 26, with twice the number of troops than the Americans had presented, the British inched forward under the cover of darkness ever closer to the rebels. Before dawn on Tuesday, shots were being fired on three fronts.

General Washington's men were prepared for a frontal attack, but General Howe opted for a plan that not only called for a head-on confrontation, but also one that would flank the Americans on both sides. The British strategy proved successful. After much fighting throughout the day, the Americans were almost completely surrounded; almost, because once again the winds favored the Americans. Through the days leading up to the engagement, Washington's biggest concern was whether British ships could and would make their way into the East River north of the battleground. It was this waterway, between Manhattan and Brooklyn, which if occupied by British ships would mean that the Americans' fate was sealed because they would be totally surrounded on all four sides. In the beginning, the winds had remained still; keeping the enemy vessels stagnant and preventing any maneuvers.

On Wednesday, the twenty-eighth, the sun rose over a battlefield where only random gunshots rang out from scattered skirmishes. The Americans had suffered their heaviest casualties in the major land assault of the previous day in which hundreds were taken captive as well. It was generally believed that another all out British attack was imminent, and that it might be the crushing blow that the Americans feared. That is why, overnight, Washington had brought more troops over the East River to reinforce those already in Brooklyn. It was in mid-afternoon when the weather came into play. Heavy, rolling clouds, claps of thunder, lightning, and the howling winds of a nor'easter soon superseded the din of the gunfire. A young chaplain of a New Jersey regiment kept a journal of his experiences and on August 28 entered:

> Our Enemies enlarge their Appearance; show us more Tents & begin a Breastwork — The Riffle-Men went out in Parties & are perpetually firing; the Balls come buzzing over our Lines. Yet no Execution as we hear of done. Afternoon, at three, a Alarm in the midst of a violent Rain.

Drums heavily calling to Arms. Men running promiscuously, & in Columns to the Lines. All the Time the Rain falling with an uncommon Torrent. The Guns of the whole Army are wetted. And after the Alarm was over, which was occasioned by the Regulars coming in a greater Body than usual to drive our Riffle-Men, our Troops fired off their Guns quite till Evening so that it seemed indeed dangerous to walk within our own Lines — for we could from every Part hear perpetually Firing, & continually hear the Balls pass over us. [21]

Another American minister kept a diary as well and testifies to the unusual rains and the retreat that they helped to disguise.

From one of the Forts of the Continental army on Long Island, two alarm guns were fired in the midst of the heavy rain; supposing that the regulars would attack their line somewhere between Flatbush and Brockland; all the men were ordered out though it rained prodigiously; it was found, after some time, that it was a false alarm. The sound of these alarm guns had just ceased, when, immediately after, a flash of lightning came, followed by a clap of thunder. It was awful. The very heavy rain, with intermixed thunder, continued for some hours till towards evening. In the night the battling on Long Island continued, and likewise, [on] Thursday 29th; and in the afternoon such heavy rain fell again as can hardly be remembered; nevertheless the operations on Long Island went on more or less; and behold, in the night, the Americans thought it advisable to retreat, and leave Long Island to the King's troops. They found that they could not stand their ground, and feared to be surrounded, and their retreat cut off. The great loss they had sustained, the want of provision and shelter, in the extraordinary Wet; the unfitness of many of their troops for war, &c.; undoubtedly contributed to this resolution. [22]

Though the weather dampened weapons and spirits on both sides, it came as a blessing for the Americans. The winds of this storm were continuously pushing southward against the attempts of the British ships to move up through New York Bay and into the East River. The downpours of rain continued through Thursday and still into Friday, preventing any significant British aggression by land. Troubling Washington was that the winds could change, and when they did, the enemy ships would sail into the East River and cut them off from Manhattan. Some gunboats eventually did get close enough to fire, but little actual damage was done. All of this prompted Washington

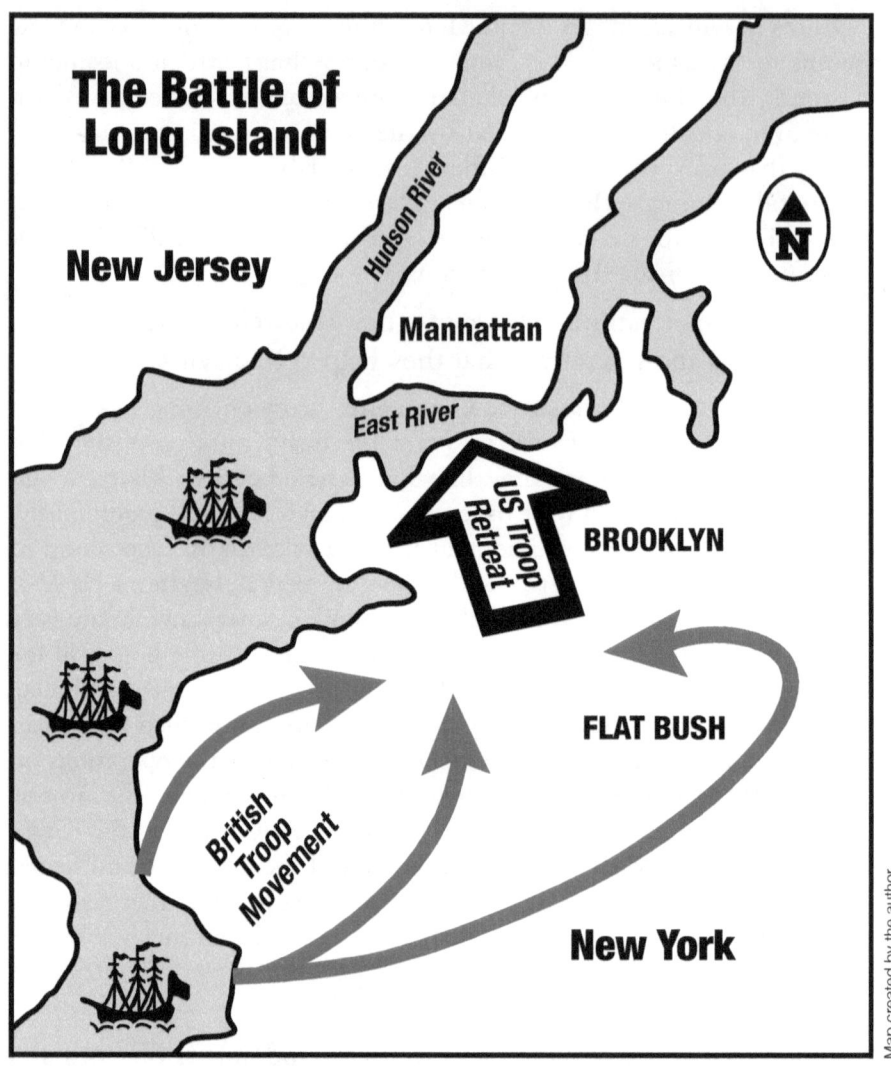

to make a tough decision. He was going to have the men retreat back to Manhattan; and do so as discreetly as possible. An army lieutenant wrote to his father that

> our Retreat [from Long Island] before an Enemy much superior in Numbers, over a wide River, and not very well furnished with Boats certainly does Credit to our Generals. The thing was conducted with so much Secrecy that neither subalterns or privates knew that the whole Army was to cross back again to N. York, they thought only a few Regiments were to go back.[23]

Washington wanted the withdrawal to be so stealth that he presented it to many of his officers as a mere swapping out of some men with fresher reinforcements, rather than the full retreat that it was. All the while, under the cover of Thursday evening's darkness, company after company moved north across the East River. Major Benjamin Tallmadge, one of Washington's most-trusted officers later documented:

> Gen. Washington was so fully aware of the perilous situation of this division of his army, that he immediately convened a council of war, at which the propriety of retiring to New York was decided on. After sustaining incessant fatigue and constant watchfulness for two days and nights, attended by heavy rain, exposed every moment to an attack from a vastly superior force in front, and to be cut off from the possibility of retreat to New York, by the fleet, which might enter the East River, on the night of the 29th of August, Gen. Washington commenced recrossing his troops from Brooklyn to New York. To move so large a body of troops, with all their necessary appendages, across a river full a mile wide, with a rapid current, in the face of a victorious, well disciplined army, nearly three times as numerous as his own, and a fleet capable of stopping the navigation, so that not one boat could have passed over, seemed to present most formidable obstacles. But, in the face of these difficulties, the Commander-in-Chief so arranged his business, that on the evening of the 29th, by 10 o'clock, the troops began to retire from the lines in such a manner that no chasm was made in the lines, but as one regiment left their station on guard, the remaining troops moved to the right and left and filled up the vacancies, while Gen. Washington took his station at the ferry, and superintended the embarkation of the troops. It was one of the most anxious, busy nights that I ever recollect, and being the third in which hardly any of us had closed our eyes to sleep, we were all greatly fatigued. [24]

Tallmadge then went on to explain what happened at sunrise on Friday.

> As the dawn of the next day approached, those of us who remained in the trenches became very anxious for our own safety, and when the dawn appeared there were several regiments still on duty. At this time a very dense fog began to rise, and it seemed to settle in a peculiar manner over both encampments. I recollect this peculiar providential occurrence perfectly well; and so very dense was the atmosphere that I could scarcely discern a man at six yards' distance.

> When the sun rose we had just received orders to leave the lines, but before we reached the ferry, the Commander-in-Chief sent one of his

Aids to order the regiment to repair again to their former station on the lines... where we tarried until the sun had risen, but the fog remained as dense as ever. Finally, the second order arrived for the regiment to retire, and we very joyfully bid those trenches a long adieu. When we reached Brooklyn ferry, the boats had not returned from their last trip, but they very soon appeared and took the whole regiment over to New York... [25]

As if the winds and rains slowing down the advancement of the British forces wasn't fortuitous enough, a dense fog rolled into the region just as the sun began its rise. It obscured from the enemy's view the last of the US troops who were abandoning Brooklyn. Tallmadge concludes:

> As soon as they [the British] reached the ferry, we were saluted merrily from their musketry, and finally by their field pieces; but we returned in safety. In the history of warfare, I do not recollect a more fortunate retreat. After all, the providential appearance of the fog saved a part of our army from being captured, and certainly myself among others who formed the rear guard. Gen. Washington has never received the credit which was due to him for this wise and most fortunate measure... [26]

An anonymous letter from an American soldier reiterates Tallmadge's observations.

> ... Our battalion, with the other Pennsylvania troops and the Maryland Regiment, were ordered to cover the retreat of our Army, which must have consisted of ten thousand men. Our Army began to embark in boats about ten o'clock, and continued till daylight. We received orders to quit our station about two o'clock this morning, and had made our retreat almost to the ferry, when General Washington ordered us back to that part of the lines we were first at, which was reckoned to be the most dangerous post. We got back undiscovered by the enemy, and continued there until daylight. Providentially for us, a great fog arose, which prevented the enemy from seeing our retreat from their works, which was not more than musket shot from us. Had we been discovered, we must have been unavoidably cut off, as we were on a neck of land which could have been taken possession of by them before we could have got out. [27]

Still another commentary comes from an officer under Washington's command who testifies to the particulars of the retreat and nicely sums up how the Battle of Long Island had concluded.

> ... we moved with celerity, we guarded against confusion, and under the friendly cover of a thick fog, reached the place of embarkation

without annoyance from the enemy, who, had the morning been clear, would have seen what was going on, and been enabled to cut off the greater part of the rear... On attaining the water, I found a boat prepared for my company, which immediately embarked, and taking the helm myself, I so luckily directed the prow, no object being discernible in the fog, that we touched near the centre of the city. It was between six and seven o'clock, perhaps later, when we landed at New York; and in less than an hour after, the fog having dispersed, the enemy was visible on the shore we had left.

Next to the merit of avoiding a scrape in war, is that of a dexterous extrication from it; and in this view, the removal of so great a number of men, stated I think at nine thousand, with cannon and stores, in one night, was, no doubt, a masterly movement... [28]

Over the next three months, Washington would lose, or be forced to retreat from, four more engagements with the British forces who remained in endless pursuit. By mid-December of 1776, the Americans found themselves camped on the western side of the Delaware River. Having retreated through New York, and then New Jersey, they decided to camp in Pennsylvania with the river as a barrier between them and the enemy who was giving chase. On the eastern side of the river was Trenton, New Jersey. Here the British troops with their leaders Howe and Cornwallis, as well as their Hessian allies, had established their presence.

Washington had an uncomfortably small army. It may have approached five thousand as they moved into this region, but as recently as the first of December their number was reduced by two thousand men who had left the war effort because their terms of service had expired. Few would blame them. They had suffered through a brutal year of severe physical hardships and few successful fights which left them weak and demoralized. With only a handful of troops remaining to confront an enemy force assumed to be much larger, Washington made constant solicitations for reinforcements. Even further complications were in the offing because many of the remaining enlistments were about to expire come January 1 of the new year. It was a hard-sell to keep these men on board any longer than the date agreed to. The fact that many wore mere rags, most of them bloodied, instead of shoes on their feet, was evidence enough of the horrific condition of the troops.

As the days of December passed, the weather would again come into play. Until the middle of the month the temperatures had been bearable. But, it was December after all, and Washington fully expected that if the river were to freeze those British troops just might march right across it and destroy them. On the thirteenth of December it indeed grew much colder and Washington's concern about the firmness of the river water intensified.

The sudden cold wave did change the plans of the British Generals, but it wasn't a decision to cross the frozen river and make an assault on the Americans. Howe determined that the war could be paused for the winter. After all, it was generally accepted that winter offensives were downright offensive to the sensibilities of the English soldier. Besides, Howe believed that he had done quite well over the past year, putting the enemy seemingly on the cusp of defeat. Therefore, on December 14, both Cornwallis and Howe dismissed their men until spring and retired themselves to cozier confines in New York.

As the next few days passed, General Washington was still making calls for reinforcements, unaware that the bulk of the enemy forces had left Trenton. Only fifteen hundred Hessians remained in the town. His repeated plea for more troops was finally answered on December 20. The number was less than hoped for, but still very welcomed. The additional men swelled the army roles to nearly seven thousand, though over a thousand were too ill or disabled to fight, suffering from the effects of the cold, snows, and long marches to get to the Delaware River.

At this time, word had finally come from spies that the British had left Trenton, but Washington and others questioned the truth of it, sensing that it could be a ruse. Should they dare to cross the river and attack the British, it was not unreasonable to believe that the enemy would come out of hiding and overpower them. None-the-less, with the increase of men in the ranks, and opportunity at hand, a plan was conceived by Washington to attack on Christmas night.

The assault would be carried out from three different crossing points along the Delaware River. One contingent would cross at Bristol, Pennsylvania, about ten miles south of Trenton. Another would go directly into Trenton from their present camp on the west side of the river. The third set, led by Washington, would take boats across at McKonkey's Ferry, ten miles north of Trenton. As it happened, at midnight of December 25, over a twenty mile stretch, the assault began. So too, began a change in the weather; yet again in a precise and timely manner. It was another nor'easter that blew in just as the crossings were beginning. This time, as before, it proved to be a blessing for the Americans, but somewhat in disguise.

The men at Bristol were crossing at a point in the river where the ice had broken up into dangerous floating chunks which were difficult to see and avoid in the darkness. After several attempts, only a few men made it safely across. It was decided that this southern flank would have to cancel its attack. An officer crossing at Bristol stated that

> on arriving at the ferry, some of the light infantry pushed over in the first boats, and landed on the opposite shore. The weather was very cold. An effort had been made to keep the troops from kindling fires before they embarked, but it was found impossible… the ice had drifted in such quantities on the Jersey shore that it was impossible to land the artillery. It was with difficulty they were enabled to get on shore with their horses. Advice being sent over to the Pennsylvania side, the troops, which by this time were mostly in the boats, were ordered to disembark, and the ice beginning to drive with such force as to threaten the boats with absolute destruction, and a heavy storm of hail and snow setting in, the expedition was reluctantly abandoned, and the troops, with the exception of a few of the light infantry, were marched back to Bristol. [29]

Similarly, the troops venturing across the Delaware at the Trenton campsite, faced the same extreme weather conditions. After a few efforts were made to cross the treacherous waters, this detachment also had to forego the plan. Two of the three prongs of attack were now abandoned.

At McKonkey's Ferry, today known as Washington Crossing, the situation was extreme as well. The ice was not flowing in huge chunks, but the waters were freezing. and the boats acted as cutters; breaking the ice as they moved forward. The vessels used to cross here were believed to be of two types. Most were Durham boats, used in that region to transport iron ingots. These were usually flat bottom boats with straight, high, side walls that would begin to bow as they neared the stem and stern. They could carry over forty standing men and their accoutrements. These boats were in common use up and down the river and so Washington was able to secure several of them for his purposes this night. Per a letter from Major General Nathanael Greene to General James Ewing, Washington had ordered his generals to gather more boats just days before the crossing:

> I am directed by his excellency George Washington to desire you to send down to Meconkea ferry, sixteen Durham boats & four flats. Youl send them down as soon as possible. [30]

The "flats" referred to by Greene were presumed to be large ferry boats that were also in use at the time to transport people and goods across the river. These were more like a large raft, but with low sides that created a shallow interior depth. It's presumed today that Washington likely would have made the crossing on a flat.

A testimony of the weather conditions at the McKonkey's Ferry location comes from a fifer, John Greenwood, who was in the company that later guarded the Hessian POWs after the successful assault. But first, referring to Christmas Day, Greenwood begins…

> If I recollect aright the sun was about half an hour high and shining brightly, but it had no sooner set than it began to drizzle or grow wet, and when we came to the river it rained… Over the river we then went in a flat-bottomed scow, and as I was with the first that crossed, we had to wait for the rest and so began to pull down the fences and make fires to warm ourselves, for the storm was increasing rapidly. After a while it rained, hailed, snowed, and froze, and at the same time blew a perfect hurricane; so much so that I perfectly recollect, after putting the rails on to burn, the wind and the fire would cut them in two in a moment, and when I turned my face toward the fire my back would be freezing. However, as my usual acuteness had not forsaken me, by turning round and round I kept myself from perishing before the large bonfire. The noise of the soldiers coming over and clearing away the ice, the rattling of the cannon wheels on the frozen ground, and the cheerfulness of my fellow-comrades encouraged me beyond expression… During the whole night it alternately hailed, rained, snowed, and blew tremendously. I recollect very well that at one time, when we halted on the road, I sat down on the stump of a tree and was so benumbed with cold that I wanted to go to sleep; had I been passed unnoticed I should have frozen to death without knowing it; but as good luck always attended me, Sergeant Madden came and, rousing me up, made me walk about.

Washington's Crossing the Delaware. Print by Paul Giradet after painting by Emanuel Leutze. 1853.

We then began to march again… [31]

Washington's two thousand-plus troops all made it safely over the Delaware. However, no one knew that the other two groups had failed. The plan was also hours behind schedule which had called for them to attack at dawn. Surprise was of the essence. The troops moved very slowly toward their foe in order to lessen the sounds of their march. The storm raged on through the night. The troops split into two fronts about halfway along their eight mile trek. Near the eighth hour of the morning the Hessians were met.

It was now that the mixed blessings of the weather conditions became evident. The scathing winds, sleet, snows, etc., that had been pelting the Americans' backs as they made their way southward to Trenton, were now lashing into the faces of the enemy. It was a couple hours after sunrise that the Americans came rushing into the town in the midst of this storm. The Hessians had a difficult time distinguishing them and their number in the white-out conditions. With the winds and hail gusting directly against them, they were deterred from making a significant defense.

Many of the Americans' guns and powder had become wet and unusable due to the long hours of marching through these horrific conditions. Obviously, that was a downside of the storm from their point of view, but with orders from General Washington to fix their bayonets they proceeded to attack. Most of the regular Trenton residents had long fled the area, leaving their homes open to be occupied by the Hessians. The bayonetted American soldiers readily ran through the streets attacking or capturing the surprised British allies.

Another seemingly negative effect of the storm on the Americans was the failure of the two other groups to cross the river. However, if they had crossed, especially the group directly across from the town, they would have alerted the Hessians before Washington's men had arrived. As it happened, the element of surprise was maintained and thus the enemy's resistance was kept to a minimum.

It's likely that the Hessian commander, Colonel Rall, had some clue that Washington's attack was in the works; but he did little to prepare for it. An assumption was apparently made that the blinding snows would prevent any substantial assault. That said, when a band of Americans appeared and took their first shots into the enemy camp, it was further assumed that this was merely a small band of troops that would create only a minor skirmish, but little else. Obviously, they misjudged the situation.

It also bears noting that this was a holiday. There were indications that the bulk of the Hessians had partied quite heavily in celebration of Christmas that night; leaving them less than battle-ready when the Americans arrived in the early morning.

When all was said and done, a handful of Hessians were killed, several more wounded; but nearly a thousand taken prisoner. The remainder escaped. The Americans lost only two men who sadly had frozen to death.

The battle at Trenton was technically over, but the whole episode didn't really conclude for another two weeks. A series of skirmishes between recalled British troops and the American forces continued into the new year. The changes in weather during these following days was not necessarily as dramatic as what happened the night of the Delaware River crossing, but none-the-less, they had a significant effect.

The British came back into the Trenton area by January 2. Washington's forces were still in place, anticipating another confrontation. Over the last days of 1776 and the first of 1777, there was a bit of a winter thaw. This had turned the roads into muck, which impeded the progress of the British troops under Cornwallis back into Trenton. Horses, artillery, and men repeatedly became bogged down in the muddy, rutted roads. On the flip side, their delay gave the Americans a little extra time to establish defensive works.

When the forces met, it was across from each other at a creek known as Assunpink. It wasn't long before Washington found himself in a dire situation. The British outnumbered him, and a final blow from this superior force could have undone all the success of just a few days earlier. The only option left was another retreat, but those muddy roads that had delayed the entrance of the British troops, were now an impediment to the Americans' exit as well. Having gained the upper hand through the day, Cornwallis opted to cease fire as darkness fell. He did not want to risk unforeseeable problems by fighting at night. Besides, he was confident that victory would quickly be his in the morning. Washington appeared trapped.

Then, the weather changed again. Washington having lived in this region his whole life, took note of the atmospheric signs. As temperatures started to drop, he predicted a hard freeze overnight, and he was correct. Though seemingly insignificant, the cold had hardened the ground, which meant the troops could move the equipment and themselves quickly out of harm's way. Once again under cover of darkness the troops retreated. Fires were kept burning through the night to foster the illusion that the camp was still occupied. It wasn't until the morning as the British prepared to finish their attack that they discovered the Americans were gone. Washington led them toward Princeton, about ten miles northeast of Trenton, where a smaller contingent of the British forces had remained. Against this lesser enemy detachment the Americans had the edge, and would prove to win the day. Once again, due in no small part to some subtler, yet timely, changes in the weather, the rebels were the victors.

In July of 1779, a smaller action took place along the Hudson River in New York. This assault was launched by the Americans in order to protect West Point, their most strategic post in the region The actual site of the conflict was known as Stony Point, appropriately named for its appearance as it jutted into the river about fifteen miles downstream

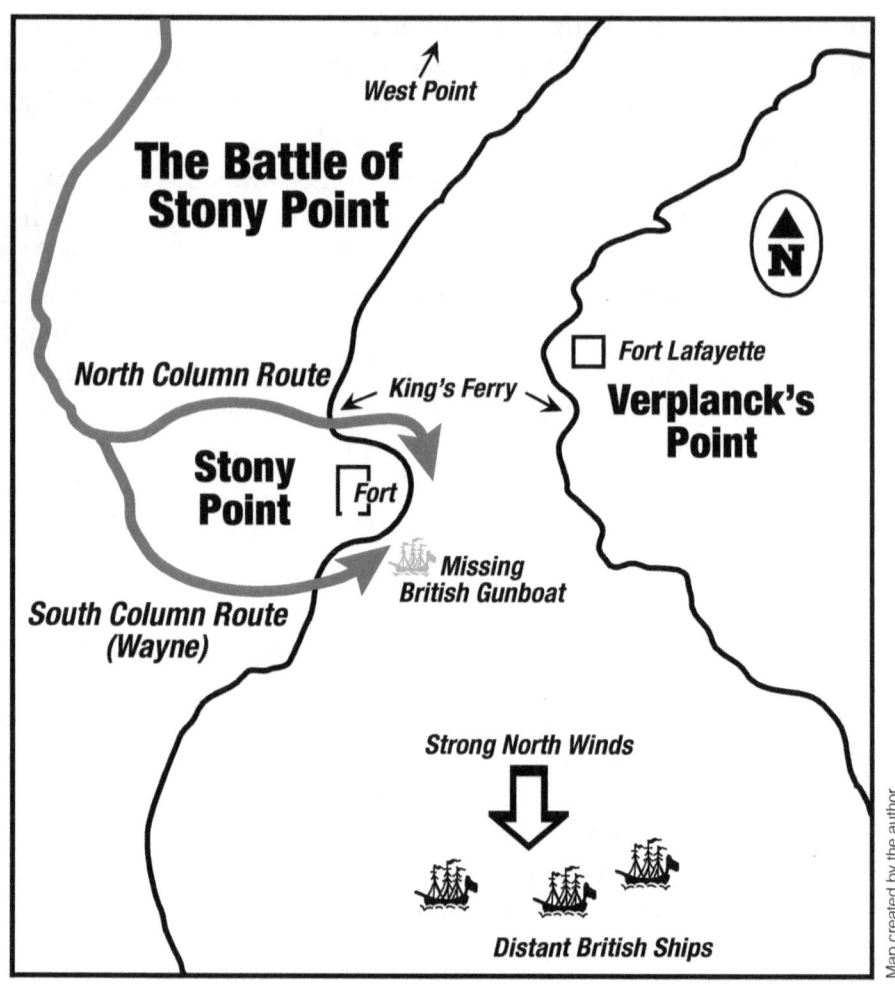

from West Point. The Hudson River was the highway of the Northeast; a literal lifeline for the transport of supplies and men. Whoever held control of it had a huge advantage in the war. Stony Point was one of several strategic locations along this river and the Americans needed to maintain it.

King's Ferry was a crossing point which ran between Stony Point, on the west side of the river, and Verplank's Point on the east. Through May of 1779, the Americans had held control of it. However, on the first day of June, a British fleet carrying six thousand men had arrived in the river. When sighted, the mere forty American soldiers who happened to be building a blockhouse atop

Stony Point, immediately set fire to it and headed out. Across the river, the seventy troops who were in Fort Lafayette atop Verplanck's Point had to surrender. In a metaphorical heartbeat the British had full control of this location which had been regularly used to cross the river.

The British were itching for more of a fight; but they wanted it to come to them. The bulk of Washington's men were ten miles north of West Point, twenty-five miles from Stoney Point, at this time and the British preferred not to venture so far northward just yet. After six weeks of deliberation, Washington executed a plan to regain the two high points downriver where the British waited. The Americans were seemingly giving the British what they had hoped for.

As was his style, Washington devised an operation that would be as aggressive as it was stealthy. He sought out Brigadier General Anthony Wayne to lead his troops. A corps of elite soldiers would be hand-picked for this mission; seasoned and skilled in the use of the bayonet. The troops would be divided into three columns; one to attack from the north, one from the south and one from the middle of the Stony Point. Only the middle column would be allowed to carry ammunition for their muskets. When in position, it would be their firing that was to draw the attention of the British to themselves, allowing the other two columns to advance undetected. Washington would not allow anyone in the north or south columns to carry ammunition for fear that an anxious or accidental shot would be fired and eliminate the critical factor of surprise. It would be hand-to-hand combat for these men.

The clandestine operation began to unfold a little before midnight on the fifteenth day of July. The columns moved ever so slowly through the darkness. The weighty clouds above them added to the murkiness of the night and made their movements ever more precarious. However, those same clouds that blocked the moon and starlight had also helped to obscure them from the enemies sight.

When they reached the base of Stony Point they found themselves in marshlands with waters at times sloshing against their chests. Luckily, as they progressed, the tide was receding. At the same time, the winds which had been blowing all day and night, continued to gust. In fact, the winds were so strong that they had kept the ships of the British fleet from coming any further upriver.

The columns were close to being in their appointed positions around the precipice when suddenly a few shots from the top were fired in their direction. It was a brief flurry of gunfire that quickly ceased because the British patrol had attributed the noise they had shot at to be nothing more than the winds rustling through the brush below.

Wayne, who was leading the southern column, had the most difficult task before him. He had anticipated having to silently ambush a British guard boat that they knew to be anchored at the point where they planned to begin their climb. It was typically moored along the first of two sets of dense abatises erected by the British. To their surprise, and relief, there was no boat present as they approached the area. The heavy winds had kept the ship from holding anchor and so the site was left unguarded on this particular night. An ensign later testified that, "had the Gun Boat been at her station, and the People in her Vigilant, I do not think it possible for a Column of Men to have waded thro' the water without being heard." [32]

And so it happened that Wayne and the other two columns, with the help of the winds, overcame the natural and the British-built obstacles. It was no easy feat, but they scaled the steep one hundred and fifty foot bluff of Stony Point, while shots were fired at them. When they reached the top, most of the combat was hand-to-hand using the bayonet, knife, and sword. On the way up, Wayne himself was grazed by a bullet that had streaked across his forehead. Though stunned and severely bloodied by the wound, he quickly gathered himself and rallied his men to continue their climb. The grit he displayed that day was one of many reasons that the "mad" moniker was attached to his name.

Within a half hour, the fortress on Stony Point was surrendered to the secretive team of climbers. Fifteen Americans and twenty British lost their lives. The rest of the wounded and able-bodied enemy were led away as prisoners. Over the next two days Washington's men hauled off their booty of supplies and artillery as well. Before they were rolled away, some of the cannons were put to good use. They were turned toward the British across the river on Verplank's Point and fired. It was the last amount of convincing the soldiers on the opposite bluff needed to abandon their post as well.

Washington knew he could not hold control of this crossing point for long. The winds were bound to change and those British ships being held downriver by them would be released to attack. In fact, the winds did shift after a few more days and the fleet moved to the American's position. The British Lieutenant General Sir Henry Clinton reported on the whole of the event ten days after it had begun. In a letter he penned to Lord George Germain, the Secretary of State for the Colonies, Clinton explained that Brigadier General Stirling, commanding the British fleet, had been trying to come to the relief of their men at Stony Point but

> the northerly winds, rather uncommon at this season, opposed Brigadier General Sterling's progress till the 19th, when upon his arriving within sight of Stony Point, the Enemy abandoned it with Precipitation, and some Circumstances of Disgrace. [33]

Clinton went on:

> Having been apprehensive that the delay occasioned by the contrary Wind might have given the Enemy time to collect a Force at the Points too powerful for Brigadier General Stirling, and being anxious that no step should be omitted for the security of Verplancks and Recovery of Stony Point, I had embarked with light infantry and joined General Stirling in Haverstraw Bay. My whole Army being within my reach, I had some hopes of being able to betray Mr. Washington into an Engagement for the Possession of Stony Point. Possibly he suspected my view, and declined adventuring any Measure which might bring on an action in a country unfavorable to him.
>
> Brigadier General Stirling is now at Stony Point with five Battalions repairing the Works, which are a good deal damaged. [34]

The British held the Hudson River posts until October when the war operations had made a definitive move to the south. The crossing suddenly took on less importance. The Battle of Stony Point would prove to be the last conflict of significance in the northern colonies. Although the Points were held for only a few days by the Americans, the boost that their capture gave to their morale lasted far longer – and the British soon caught wind of it.

1781 marked the seventh year of the American Revolution. It began with a significant fight on January 17 that became known as the Battle of Cowpens. An odd name to many, but in that day it was a common term for open prairie lands that were usually defined as an area of a couple thousand square yards where cows were penned-in to graze. It was in such a location about fifty miles southwest of Charlotte, North Carolina, that the Americans made yet another stand against the British. This one was considered a logistical masterpiece designed and executed by General Daniel Morgan; and it proved to be a significant turning point in the war.

Lieutenant Colonel Banastre Tarleton, leading a seasoned force of British soldiers and dragoons into the area, had anticipated a quick and decisive victory over Morgan's men. He presumed the Americans to be quite foolish for making their stance here with the Broad River at their back; thus leaving no possible avenue for a potential retreat. With no undergrowth in the cowpen to trip up the horses, the British cavalry confidently began the fight by charging the line of American militia before them. Morgan's front line of men were ordered to fire two rounds at the dragoons before making a faux retreat. With their exit, battlefield left, the main body of the American line, who had been hidden behind them, was exposed.

The retreat of that front line was also a signal for a surprise attack to be made to one of the British flanks. As it happened, an American cavalry force that had been hidden from the British view came about just as the supposed retreating front line ran in their direction. The clever militia, who were the stars of this opening scene, had simply circled behind the main body and came back out on the other side, battlefield right. They returned with reloaded muskets and fixed bayonets ready to attack the opposite British flank. It wasn't long before Tarleton's men were surrounded and surrendered. Over seven hundred of their troops, two hundred of them wounded, were suddenly POWs. Over a hundred British troops were killed, while only twenty-five Americans lost their lives. Tarleton managed to escape; but with only a handful of his dragoons.

Morgan retreated from Cowpens almost immediately after his victory. His large contingent of British prisoners were under guard. He knew that when Cornwallis learned the news, he would come seeking to take back his captives. Word of the embarrassing defeat did come to Cornwallis the next morning while camped along Turkey Creek some

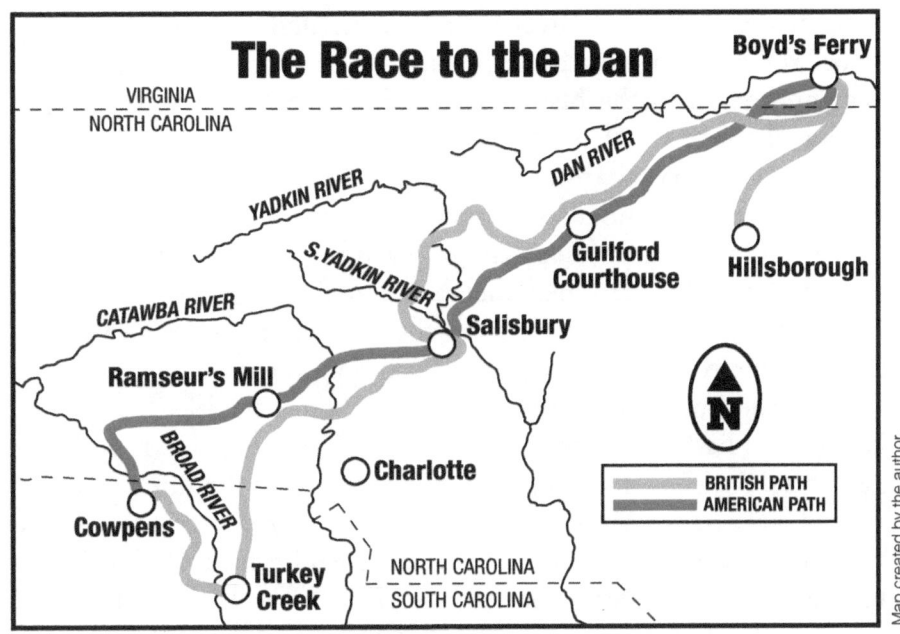

thirty miles southeast of Cowpens. As the story goes, the general's temper was so strained while listening to Tarleton report on the debacle, that as he leaned so heavily on his sword that was pinioned to the ground, it snapped in two.

Cornwallis was determined to pursue Morgan, and it was from this Battle of Cowpens forward that numerous surprising and timely weather coincidences again favored the Americans. It seemed that Mother Nature had the patriots' back throughout 1781, ultimately helping to bring the war to its conclusion at Yorktown, Virginia later that year.

Since December of 1780, the Carolinas had been experiencing heavy winter rains, resulting in swollen rivers across the entire region. Even before the battle at the cowpens had begun, Morgan had a difficult time crossing the flooded Broad River. After positioning his troops in front of it and winning the day, it was no small feat that he successfully retreated across it yet again. This time he had the addition of hundreds of British prisoners to maneuver as well.

The same was true for Tarleton. His remnant band of soldiers had to be threatened by his sword to make the dangerous crossing of the raging Broad River on their way to Cornwallis at Turkey Creek. These crossings of the Broad River were just the first of many to be made across the rivers of North Carolina. The "Race to the Dan," as it has become known in the history books, had begun. From the moment Cornwallis learned of the Cowpens defeat, an inter-colony chase of the retreating Americans had begun toward the Dan River; the doorway to the rebel-sympathetic colony of Virginia.

Begrudgingly, Cornwallis delayed any immediate pursuit of Morgan because he had determined that he needed a larger force to engage him. Those reinforcements arrived the following day, January 19, and that is when the race to the northeast began in earnest.

From the outset, the British ran into some trouble. Surprisingly, Cornwallis had made some wrong turns. Eventually, he found Morgan's track, but his mistakes had left them further behind their prey.

The Catawba River was about seventy-five miles northeast of Cowpens, and it was the first of three major rivers both parties would have to cross in the coming weeks as they drove toward Virginia. Six days out from the battle, Morgan had already safely crossed it. Cornwallis was lagging well behind and wouldn't reach it for several more days. In a letter to Lord George Germain, he referenced the natural hazards that had hindered his ability to catch up to the US troops.

> … great exertions were made by part of the army, without baggage, to retake our prisoners and to intercept General Morgan's corps on its retreat to the Catawba [River], but the celerity of their movements and the swelling of numberless creeks in our way rendered all our efforts fruitless. [35]

The previous and ongoing rains presented everything from an inconvenience to an outright impediment to Cornwallis. Creeks grew deeper and roads turned into muddy quagmires. He went on to explain how he had decided to make a daring and unusual maneuver to hasten the pursuit of his foe. That action was to severely lighten the load that his army had to transport.

> I therefore assembled the army on the 25th at Ramsoure's Mill on the South Fork of the Catawba, and as the loss of my light troops [at Cowpens] could only be remedied by the activity of the whole corps, I employed a halt of two days in collecting some flour and in destroying superfluous baggage and all my wagons except those loaded with hospital stores, salt, and ammunition and four reserved empty in readiness for

sick and wounded. In this measure, tho' at the expense of a great deal of officers' baggage and of all prospect in future of rum and even a regular supply of provisions to the soldiers, I must in justice to this army say that there was the most general and chearfull acquiescence. [36]

Maybe. One can only imagine the true lamentations of the soldiers as they not only saw their belongings go up in flames, but also watched as numerous barrels of their ardent spirits saturated the grounds about them.

Cornwallis assessed the Catawba for a safe crossing point, but he was continually foiled by the weather. On the day he had finally determined to attempt it, the rains came. Heavy rains. He was delayed another two days because of how they had aggravated the Catawba River waters. Finally, after a brief lull in the precipitation, he was determined to make the crossing. He continued in spite of showers that were beginning to intensify once more.

… the rains had rendered the North Catawba impassable… The morning [February 1] being very dark and rainy… however, as I knew that the rain then falling would soon render the river again impassable and I had received information the evening before that General Greene had arrived in General Morgan's camp and that his [Greene's] army was marching after him with the greatest expedition, I determined not to desist from the attempt… [37]

An American General, Nathanael Greene, had been sent for by Morgan to support his efforts against his British pursuers. The reinforcements he supplied, though not as numerous as Cornwallis may have believed, would none-the-less strengthen the American's presence and make an attack by them on the British a more distinct possibility.

In conference with Morgan, Greene weighed several options. He could have the whole of his troops join Morgan's and attack Cornwallis at the Catawba River. Or, Morgan could move thirty miles to the east, to make a stand at Salisbury, where Greene had already sent the bulk of his reinforcing troops. However, because his force was smaller than he really preferred, Greene decided on a third option. He ordered his men, stationed at Salisbury, as well as Morgan's men, presently at the Catawba, to both begin a retreat even further to the northeast. They were all to head for the Guilford Courthouse near today's Greensboro, North Carolina. It would be here that a battle would soon ensue.

At this point, General Morgan was ailing severely from back and hip problems. He had sciatica. Because it had become such an intense disability, General Greene relieved him of his duty and sent him north to Winchester, Virginia along with the British prisoners that were taken at Cowpens. Greene was now in full command.

When both American and British forces were east of the Catawba, another natural obstacle presented itself. It was the Yadkin River, situated approximately midway between the Catawba and Guilford. It too was high and raging, but Greene had planned ahead. He had ordered boats to be made available at the crossing point by the time the troops arrived. The people of the region, being sympathetic to the rebel cause, readily obliged. It was still a treacherous crossing; even Greene's vessel was severely tossed about. In the end, he and the rest of the Americans successfully made it to the other side.

When Cornwallis arrived at this same ford, he saw the Americans' boats abandoned and moored on the opposite bank.

> … the ford had become impassable. The river continuing to rise and the weather appearing unsettled, I determined to march to the upper fords after procuring a small supply of provisions at Salisbury. This and the height of the creeks in our way detained me two days…[38]

And so the British suffered another delay of several days due to another flooded river and the incessant rains. Finally, the Yadkin receded enough for them to cross without boats and the chase resumed for another forty miles toward Guilford.

It was at the courthouse in Guilford that Greene held a war council with his officers. Since the Americans were still outnumbered, it was decided that the troops would continue heading for Virginia rather than stop to challenge Cornwallis here. The Dan River marked the state border.

In a shrewd move, Greene decided to split the American force. One group, under Colonel Otho Williams, headed toward the upper fords of the Dan, while Greene and his troops marched toward the lower fords, specifically, to Boyd's Ferry. Williams' troops were sent in a different direction as bait for Cornwallis, and it worked. He pursued William's troops because the British scouts had reported that there were no boats at the ford Williams was headed toward.

However, to Cornwallis's surprise, as preplanned by the American officers, Williams made a sharp turn before he reached the river and marched directly to Boyd's Ferry. It was there that Greene's troops were already crossing in boats; vessels that Greene had again prearranged to have at the ready. A day after Greene had crossed, William's men did likewise, just hours ahead of the pursuing Cornwallis. Greene wrote to George Washington:

> Lord Cornwallis has been at our heels from day to day ever since we left Guilford; and our movements from thence to this place have been of the most critical kind, having a river in our front, and the enemy in our rear. But, happily, we have crossed without the loss of either men or stores.[39]

By the time Cornwallis arrived at Boyd's, they witnessed the last of the Americans climbing the opposite banks. The race to the Dan was over. Cornwallis and his men could not possibly ford the raging waters without boats. The British force would head about fifty miles south to a town named Hillsborough, North Carolina where they hoped to find food and reinforcements from the Tories living in the region. That didn't happen, at least not on the scale Cornwallis was desperate to find. His men were so extremely fatigued and starving that the residents' oxen and some army horses had to be slaughtered for food. Even more troublesome for Cornwallis was that the people came out of their homes to gawk at the British soldiers, but few signed on to join the fight.

Greene, after only about a week of relative security north of the Dan, decided to recross that river back into North Carolina and become the aggressor. This was due in no small part to his having gained significant reinforcements from Virginia militias. He set his sights on Guilford once again as the best place to engage Cornwallis. It was there, on March 15, that an outright battle took place between the two adversaries.

A military strategy similar to what worked at Cowpens was once more employed by Greene. The US troops formed into three lines on the cleared ground in front of the Guilford Courthouse, which gave its name to the engagement. The fighting was heavy. After more than two hours, Greene and his men ended up retreating, and so the victory was attributed to Cornwallis and the British. But, the history books call it a "pyrrhic victory"; one in which the winner suffered extreme losses. British survivors were so severely exhausted that they were unable to continue any pursuit of Greene. Instead they retired to the Atlantic port city of Wilmington, North Carolina to regroup and resupply themselves.

Greene reevaluated the American's situation after this battle and soon made plans for his forces to attack the smaller, scattered British posts throughout the southern colonies. Cornwallis had become dismayed over the toll his efforts in the South had taken on his troops, but realized that more actions would need to be taken there rather than in the northern colonies. Just a few weeks after his so-called victory at Guilford, he confided to a fellow British general:

> I assure you that I am quite tired of marching about the country in quest of adventures. If we mean an offensive war in America, we must abandon New York, bring our whole force into Virginia. We then have a stake to fight for and a successfull battle may give us America. [40]

And so it happened that a new base was soon established by Cornwallis in Virginia at a place known as Yorktown. It would be here, in the fall of a year which had already seen a good deal of fighting and a good deal of marching, that the most significant battle of the Revolution would take place. And, once again, the weather would play a very consequential role.

Up and down the Atlantic coast throughout the war, the British fleet had been in control. It was one of their major advantages to keeping their enemies confined and their supplies coming in. Though some challenges had been made to this behemoth of the seas, it wasn't until September of 1781 that one of them was finally successful.

It was the French, who had already been allied with the Americans for over three years, that now sailed a fleet of their own toward Virginia. Admiral François Joseph Paul de Grasse was in command and upon arrival his twenty-eight ships slipped into place in the Chesapeake Bay and established a blockade of the rivers that were the essential water routes into and out of Yorktown.

The French and British were among several countries that had colonized various islands of the West Indies, or Caribbean, by the time of the Revolution. The naval fleets of these two countries were based at their respective island ports, from which they could sail north to the fight on the continent.

As still occurs today, in the 1700s this region was annually riddled with hurricanes; especially through the peak season of September and October. As it happened, in October of 1780 a series of intense hurricanes rolled across the Caribbean every few days. They were recorded to have been devastating in the extreme. Tens of thousands of people were killed and much of anything upright was leveled. After-the-fact, one of these tempests received a name, "The Great Hurricane of 1780." Like the others which hit that autumn, this hurricane had inflicted severe casualties of both lives and ships.

The French fleet took a beating, but the British were particularly hard hit. The difference was that the Royal Navy lost more of its war ships, including an extraordinary sixty-four gun vessel and another with seventy-two cannons. The French had only lost some of its non-military vessels.

When Washington asked the French Admiral de Grasse for help in the fall of 1781, it was out of their loyalty to each other that he agreed to assist. However, it can't be ignored that there was another practical reason for de Grasse to get his ships out of the Caribbean. Hurricane season was approaching and memories of the previous year's havoc were still fresh in his memory. Harboring his fleet in the Chesapeake Bay sounded like a much safer option, in spite of the probability of them having an engagement with the Royal Navy.

The British had caught wind of the French fleet's movement toward Virginia to aid the Americans. They responded by sending Admiral Hood from their island harbors with fourteen "ships-of-the-line" (those ships designed for in-line battles at sea) in the hope of intercepting the French vessels before they reached the mainland.

As it turned out, rather than catching up to de Grasse, the British had sailed so fast that they arrived at the Chesapeake Bay four days before him. With no one to fight when the harbor came into view, and knowing that the American land forces were based in New York, they chose to sail further north and assist their land troops from that port.

Admiral de Grasse had been given two options by Washington. He could come to the New York harbor and assist Comte (Count)

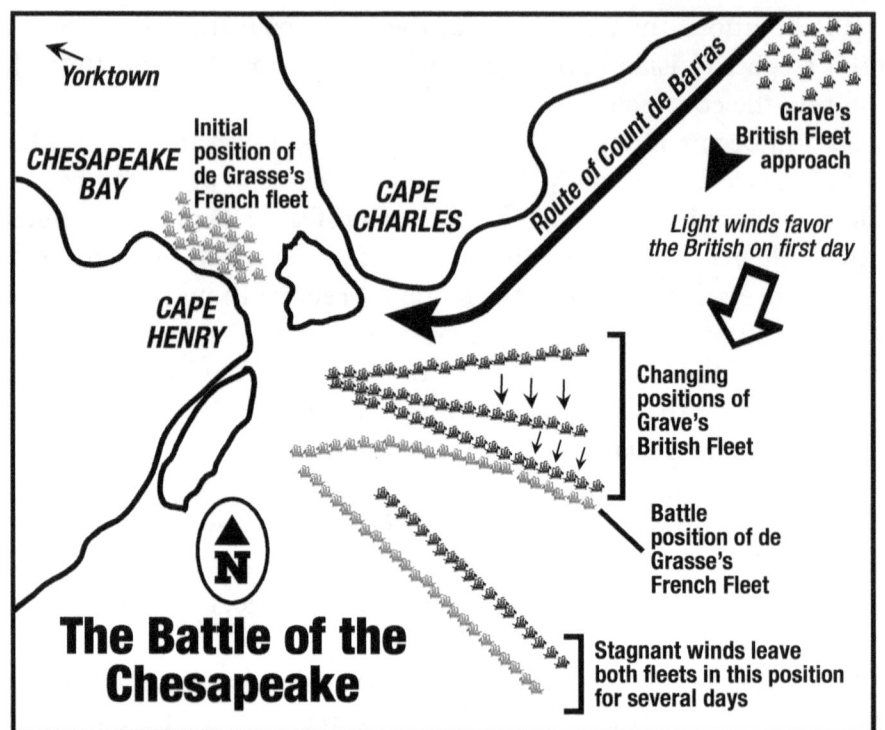

Rochambeau and himself in their planned attacks on British forces in and around New York City or he could anchor in the Chesapeake Bay to block supplies from getting to Cornwallis at Yorktown. His presence in Virginia waters would also hinder the British from escaping their base camp via ships should the need arise. De Grasse chose the Chesapeake harbor which his fellow countryman, Rochambeau, had also favored.

In mid-August, Washington and Rochambeau, now knowing that de Grasse was headed for Virginia, began marching their troops from New York southward toward Cornwallis's camp. Their ultimate plan was to encircle Cornwallis by land, which they soon accomplished. On August 31, when de Grasse dropped anchors, unopposed, across the entrance of the bay, the British camp at Yorktown became isolated.

One can only imagine the annoyance that Admiral Hood, who recently arrived at the New York harbor from the Chesapeake region, and Admiral Graves, who had command of the British fleet already in New York, must have felt when they learned that the fight was moving to the Chesapeake waters.

While the American land troops and the French fleet were already enroute to Virginia, Admiral Graves took command of his ships as well as those of Admiral Hood and began the sail to Cornwallis's aid. The British now presented a combined force of nineteen ships of war, but they were playing catch-up. It wasn't until five days later, on the morning of September 5, that they were within a few miles of the Chesapeake Bay. Their scout ship had reported back the news of the large French presence that was already ahead of them in the harbor.

A few days before the British fleet had arrived, the American regulars, militia, and the French soldiers who had come along on de Grasse's ships, had already begun to flank the numerous rivers flowing around Yorktown in order to deter any enemy movements upon them.

> On the evening of the same day [September 2], M. du Portail, a French officer, dispatched by Generals Washington and Rochambeau, announced the departure of the squadron of Count de Barras, escorting the artillery and munitions necessary for the projected siege… [41]

This deployment of men under the French Count de Barras, was the second French fleet sent on its way to assist the Americans. They and their cargo would prove crucial to this effort. De Barras was headed south from Newport, Rhode Island with six warships, a few armed frigates, and several more transport vessels carrying artillery and supplies that would be essential to the anticipated siege of Yorktown. This backup French task force had discreetly followed the British fleet at an unnoticeable distance and lingered behind when Graves first stopped outside of the Chesapeake Bay.

The French presence, blockading entrance to the harbor, forced Graves to make a strategic decision. He became determined to draw the French into a fight in the open ocean waters. He ordered his ships into battle formation some ways out from the bay. De Grasse, was eager to engage the enemy, and opted to file out into the Atlantic for an imminent confrontation. All participants had positioned themselves for a traditional one-on-one ship battle.

The winds were light, but in favor of the British, giving them the so-called "wind gauge," or advantage. It took hours for the ships to align themselves into the desired formation with still a few miles separating them. A northeast wind continued letting the British decide when to move in closer to their foe. Hours later, as the sun was well below its maximum height, the first cannon was fired against the French ships of de Grasse.

For nearly two hours the shots were exchanged. The sun had set and the shooting ceased. The winds had only slightly shifted. At sunrise, although both sides would have preferred to reignite the cannonading, extensive repairs were needed to many of the ships of both fleets. Additionally, the winds continued quite calm. This made any strategic maneuvering of the ships very difficult. Meteorologically speaking, the engagement was being undertaken while a high pressure system was in place producing only very light winds. When you are on ships requiring wind-filled sails to move, this is a problem.

From the night of the fifth of September through the eighth, the enemies were essentially in a stalemate, unable to maneuver into advantageous positions because of the dead air. What wind there was only kept the parties out at sea; gradually moving them further and further away from the Chesapeake Bay. Unbeknownst to the British, this was actually part of de Grasse's hope and plan. If they engaged each other far enough out to sea, then the arrival of de Barras's French fleet, which was laden with those stocks of desperately needed artillery and supplies, might not be noticed entering the bay.

On September 9, the weather became foggy. The winds were still light, but were now giving the French the ability to sail back into the bay. And they did. The British could have attacked again, but having suffered more damage to their ships than the French had, they opted to retire back to New York. There they planned to make repairs and return with reinforcements.

As de Grasse reached the bay, he was gratified to discover that de Barras and his ships had successfully eluded any notice by the enemy and were safely at the ready. The lack of wind in the deeper Atlantic had kept the fleets away from the harbor long enough to make the French presence in the Chesapeake Bay quite formidable. Cornwallis was in a serious predicament.

The American and French land troops used a strategy of digging successive trenches to move themselves and their artillery forward in short jaunts until they were in range of the Yorktown camp. Thanks to the dark, moonless, night of October 14, they had finally gotten themselves into a commanding position, in range of their enemy. They commenced firing A few days later, completely circumvented on land and by sea, Cornwallis himself explained his desperate situation as he had decided to attempt an escape through a less guarded section of the York River.

> I therefore had only to chuse between preparing to surrender next day or endeavouring to get off with the greatest part of our troops, and I determined to attempt the latter, reflecting that, tho' it should prove unsuccessfull in its immediate object, it might at least delay the enemy in the prosecution of further enterprizes. Sixteen large boats were prepared and upon other pretexts were ordered to be in readiness to receive troops precisely at ten o'clock. With these I hoped to pass the infantry during the night, abandoning our baggage and leaving a detachment to capitulate for the town's people and the sick and wounded, on which subject a letter was ready to be delivered to General Washington. After making my arrangements with the utmost secrecy, the light infantry, greatest part of the Guards, and part of the 23rd Regiment embarked at the hour appointed and most of them landed at Glouchester, but at this critical moment the weather, from being moderate and calm, changed to a most violent storm of wind and rain and drove all the boats, some of which had troops on board, down the river. It was soon evident that the intended passage was impracticable, and the abscence of the boats rendered it equally impossible to bring back the troops that had passed, which I had ordered about two o'clock in the morning. In this situation, with my little force divided, the enemy's batteries opened at daybreak. [42]

That same day, October 19, having been delayed at New York making repairs and facing more opposing winds, Admiral Graves finally departed the New York harbor on his return trip to Virginia in support of Cornwallis. However, while Graves was enroute, General Cornwallis noted in a letter to Lieutenant General Sir Henry Clinton dated October 20:

> I have the mortification to inform your Excellency that I have been forced to give up the posts of York and Gloucester and to surrender the troops under my command by capitulation on the 19th instant as prisoners of war to the combined forces of America and France. [43]

Although independence was declared on July 4, 1776, and that date is recognized as the birthday of the United States, the new country really began its life, uncontested, on September 3, 1783, when the Treaty of Paris, ending the Revolution, took effect. However, less than thirty years later the fight was on once again. The War of 1812 began in June of that year and would be executed until February of 1815. This fight has been considered by most historians to have resulted in a draw; but the fact that the United States continued to exist at its conclusion seems to suggest that the Americans were once again the victors. Like many of the Revolution, several of the battles over this three year conflict have become legendary. And, in this second war for independence, once again, many of the engagements seem to have evidence of God's hand at work for the Americans.

Things did not go well for the United States at the outset. General Hull was already on the move toward Canada with troops in anticipation of war when it was declared on June 18. Within the first two months of the conflict, he would fail on two counts. First, he aborted the sure capture of a British fortress known as Fort Malden, near today's Windsor, Ontario. Then, and even worse, he surrendered the strategic American garrison at Detroit. This meant that the British were in an excellent position to simply cross Lake Erie with their fleet of ships at will. The Americans had no vessels to speak of on the Great Lakes when the war broke out. That soon changed as Oliver Perry and Daniel Dobbins would get busy building warships in the harbor of Erie, Pennsylvania, toward the southeastern end of the lake. Another shipbuilding site would be established at the burgeoning village of Cleaveland.

Founded by Moses Cleaveland while he surveyed the lands along the Erie shores in 1796, the community numbered less than a hundred inhabitants in 1812. However, many more small settlements were growing across the region with new souls arriving almost daily. The attraction to the area was the Cuyahoga River which flowed through parts of northern Ohio before it emptied into the lake at Cleaveland. It was expected that the village would soon grow into a major Great Lakes port, and history has made that prediction a fact.

By 1813, with the war raging more furiously than the waves of Lake Erie, waterfront property was being evacuated for the safer confines found inland. Those who stayed near the lake were mostly young men who had united into a militia in case the enemy should make an appearance. Supplies for these and other armed forces of Ohioans were regularly being transported into the area, turning Cleaveland into a major storage depot.

In May, the Governor of Ohio, Return J. Meigs, came to town to inspect the military preparations. While he was there, a company of regular soldiers arrived and were heartily welcomed by the authorities and citizenry alike. Their presence meant that there were now several hundred troops and several hundred more militia on guard. But many of these men were either ill or injured. The healthy ones were ordered to construct a hospital. The twenty by thirty foot structure they built provided shelter and comfort to the disabled. Then

> all the men of the company were set at work building a small stockade, about fifty yards from the bank of the lake, near the present Seneca street [today's West 3rd Street]. Cutting down a large number of trees twelve to fifteen inches in diameter, they cut off logs some twelve feet long each. These were sunk in the ground three or four feet, leaving the remaining distance above the surface. The sides of the logs adjoining each other were hewed down for a few inches, so as to fit solidly together. This made a wall impervious to small arms, and the dirt was heaped up against the outside so as somewhat to deaden the effect of cannon balls. Next a large number of trees and brush were cut down, and the logs and brush piled together near the brink of the lake; forming a long abatis, very difficult to climb over, and which would have exposed any assailing party who attempted to surmount it to a very destructive fire from the fort while doing so. The post was named Fort Huntington, in honor of the ex-governor [Samuel Huntington]. [44]

As the war evolved, the small community of Cleaveland was not only being transformed into a small military post for defense of the area; but also a place for troops to rendezvous, and to build ships. Yes, just a couple miles up the Cuyahoga, schooners and smaller flatboats were being built for transportation of men and goods. One of the larger ships built here was christened the *Ohio*. It was later captained by the lead engineer of the warships built at Erie, Pennsylvania, Daniel Dobbins. The *Ohio* was not in the Battle of Lake Erie itself, but it was a vital transport vessel in use immediately after the fight.

The activity on the lakeshore of Cleaveland drew the attention of the enemy. In May of 1813, British forces, under General Henry Proctor and the Indian alliance led by Tecumseh, had attacked Fort Meigs at the eastern end of Lake Erie. They were rebuffed, but a few weeks later, on June 19, 1813,

> the British fleet, consisting of the "Queen Charlotte" and "Lady Provost," with some smaller vessels, appeared off the coast and approached the mouth of the [Cuyahoga] river with the apparent intention of landing. Major Jessup [commander of Fort Huntington] had left, but expresses were sent out to rally the militia, and as soon as possible every man in the vicinity was hastening with musket on his shoulder toward the endangered locality. When the fleet had arrived within a mile and a half of the harbor the wind sank to a perfect calm, and the vessels were compelled to lie there until afternoon. Meanwhile the little band of regulars made every preparation they could to defend their post... [45]

The two British warships were certainly on a mission to at least do some detective work for their superiors regarding the ship building efforts about the Cuyahoga. It's likely they were prepared to attack if it was called for. The people on land were a bit panicked, but none-the-less ready to defend themselves. A local judge, in service to the army at the time, knew of a lone, small cannon in the town. It was unmounted, however, and so couldn't be transported to a defensive location. That didn't stop the judge, who dismantled a wagon and used its wheels and axle to roll the piece of artillery to the waterfront and aim it at the ships offshore. To wait and to watch was all the Americans could do as the ships rested in place on the windless lake.

> At length the calm ceased, but the succeeding weather was no more propitious to the would-be invaders. A Terrific thunder-storm sprang up in the west and swept furiously down the lake, and the little fleet was soon driven before it far to the east-ward; relieving the Clevelanders of all fear of an attack, at least for that day. [46]

The ships were blown some fifteen miles to the east, near today's Euclid, Ohio. From there, they vanished, not to be seen again until September 10, 1813. It was on that day that Master Commandant Oliver Perry, later titled "Commodore," with his newly constructed fleet of ships, would challenge them and the rest of the British naval force to a fight near the islands of the lake.

It became known as the Battle of Lake Erie. Through the summer before the fall engagement, ships from the British base at Fort

Malden in Amherstburg, Ontario, cruised the lake to assess what their enemy was up to. Amherstburg was on the Detroit River and had immediate access to the lake. It was a British shipbuilding yard. Many of the settlers of the town were employed in the construction of vessels that would see action in the famous upcoming contest. Specifically these were the *Queen Charlotte*, *Prevost*, and *Detroit*. At the other end of the lake, at Erie, Pennsylvania, was the American counter-construction site of ships. From this harbor, known as Presque Isle, sailed the *Lawrence, Niagara*, and *Ariel*. Both sides added additional ships to their fleets at the time of the battle.

The Americans had the advantage of numbers with nine ships to the British with six. But some of the ships of Admiral Robert Barclay, the commander of the British fleet, had longer range cannon capabilities. This was a serious disadvantage for the American fleet since their ship walls were typically only two inches thick; highly susceptible to destruction by artillery. The British hulls ranged upwards of a foot thick. The Americans frequently overloaded their cannons to try to compensate.

The face-off began just before noon. The winds were light and from the southwest. Perry was on the *Lawrence*, standing below a bold, blue flag that was waving stoically above him. He had raised that banner just minutes earlier to the cheers of his men. It flaunted the dying words of the recently killed American naval hero, James Lawrence, for whom this vessel was named. It read, "Don't Give Up the Ship!"

There was strategy to how ships engaged each other at sea. Typically they would sail into parallel lines across from each other. Most times it would be a ship-on-ship formation, sometimes more of a zone approach, to use a sports analogy. Maneuvers were not as easy as one might assume since the winds were the only means available to get into a desired position; and the winds were wholly unpredictable.

This day, the British ship *Detroit* fired the first shot. The primary target was Perry on the *Lawrence*, who had come up to the enemy fleet with three other ships and was soon in range of their guns. The remaining five American ships, including the *Niagara*, lined up as well, but at a distance behind Perry's line. They remained out of the range of fire. The *Niagara* was captained by Perry's second in overall command, Master Commandant Jesse Elliott. His action of lining up behind

Perry's line was contrary to the directive Perry had established beforehand. As the fight ensued, the *Lawrence* took an unceasingly severe beating. First the *Detroit*, but soon the *Queen Charlotte*, which should have been targeted by Elliot from the *Niagara*, was left free to move-in on the *Lawrence* and fire at will. For two hours Perry and his crew shot back; but with much less effect than the enemy had on them.

> The Niagara had taken a station… which prevented her from firing, except her long gun, on the sternmost of the enemy's vessels. The small [American] vessels at the rear of our own line were too remote to do more than keep up a cannonade with the nearest vessel of the enemy. [47]

Finally, at two o'clock, Elliott had begun moving toward the *Lawrence*. He suspected that the casualties were high and feared that Perry may be among them. As he drew closer, to his surprise, Perry was on his way to him.

> … the last gun of the Lawrence became useless, and the ship, now an unmanageable wreck, was beginning to drop astern, Captain Perry was looking round, as the smoke cleared away, to estimate the real condition of his resources, when Lieutenant Forrest [the officer of the deck] again called his attention to the strange manoeuvres of the Niagara, at this time on the larboard [port] beam of the Lawrence, directly opposite to the enemy. "That brig," said Forrest, "will not help us; see how he keeps off; he will not come to close action." "I'll fetch him up," was the commodore's reply; and he immediately ordered his boat. He remarked that the Niagara did not appear to be much injured, and that the American flag should not be hauled down from over his head on that day. Giving Mr. Yarnall [a lieutenant] command of the Lawrence, Perry stepped down the larboard gangway into his boat, telling his officers, as he shoved off, with prophetic confidence of a hero conscious of his powers, "If a victory is to be gained, I'll gain it!" [48]

Perry had ordered the stars and stripes to remain flying at the discretion of the officers who remained aboard the tattered *Lawrence*. However, he did order his blue flag to be lowered. It was bundled under his arm as he made his way to the *Niagara*. Three officers and the last of the sailors of the *Lawrence* stood on its deck; now a horrific scene of death and destruction. They watched until they saw their leader board the *Niagara*. Only then, holding their honor, would they surrender their ship.

THE WINDS OF CHANGE

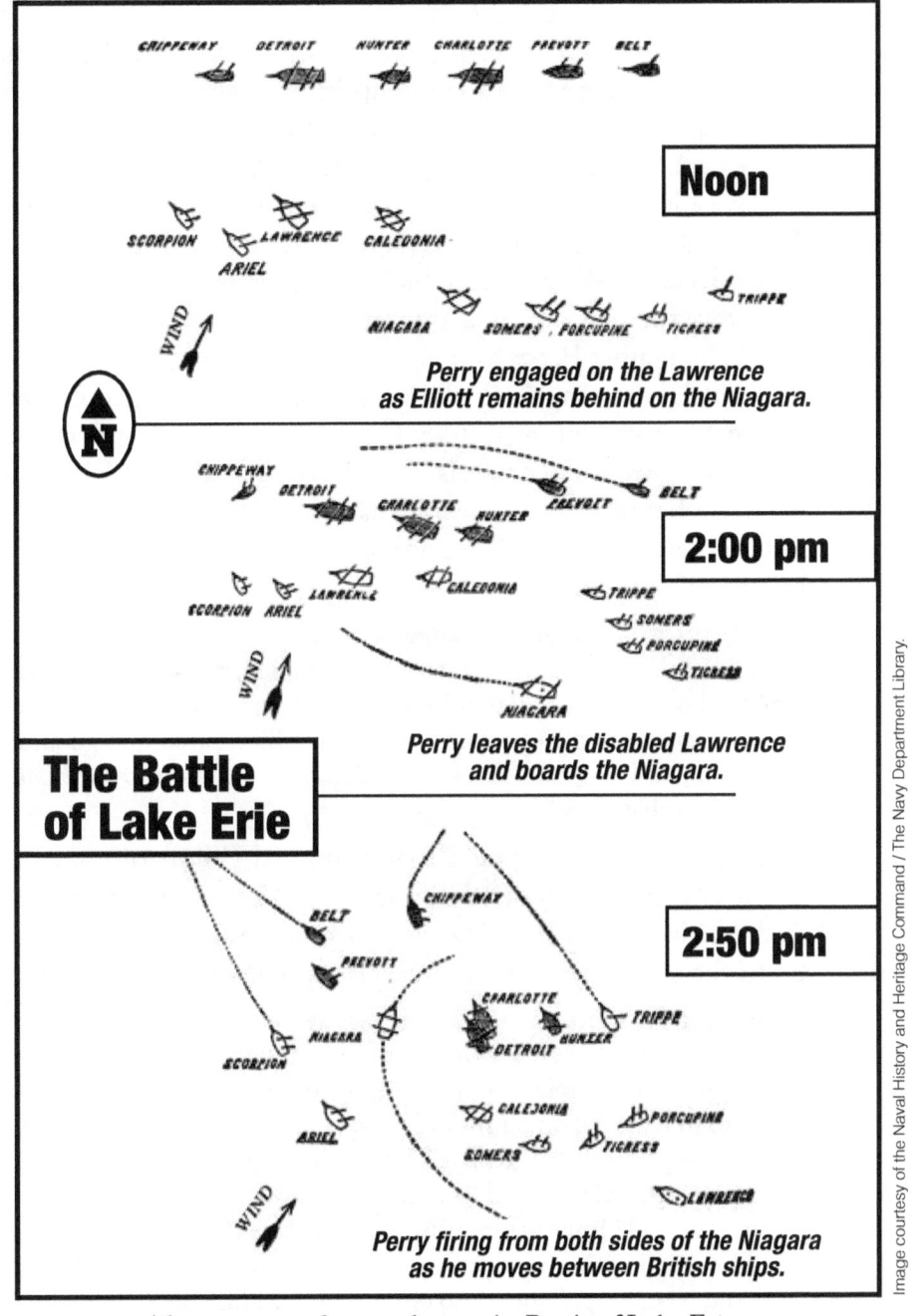

The sequence of action during the Battle of Lake Erie.
Original drawings in *The Naval War of 1812*, by Theodore Roosevelt, 1897.

The British thought the fight was over. However, in a small boat, rowed by a handful of his surviving crewmen, the commander of the *Lawrence* is said to have actually stood upright for at least a portion of the trip as a signal to his fellows that the fight was not over.

The fact that Elliott kept the *Niagara* out of a position from which he could have adequately assisted the *Lawrence* was a controversy that had a life of its own; continually debated publicly and privately for three more decades. Why Elliott took the actions, or better stated lack of actions that he did, is a mystery. Whether it was a jealous grudge he held against Perry for being passed over for Perry to command this battle, or something else of a professional or deeply personal nature, has to be left as a study for another time. Simply stated, Elliott and Perry were not friends. In fact, the greeting of Elliott to Perry when he boarded the *Niagara* was almost callous according to Samuel Hambleton who had been onboard the *Lawrence* as its purser and who was a friend of Perry.

> ... he [Perry] was met at the gangway by Captain Elliott, who "inquired how the day was going. Captain Perry replied, badly: that he had lost almost all of his men, and that his ship was a wreck; and asked what the gunboats were doing so far astern. Captain Elliott offered to go and bring them up; and, Captain Perry consenting, he sprung into the boat and went off on that duty." [49]

So it was in this manner that Perry dismissed Elliott of his command of the *Niagara* and allotted him the job of getting the four ships that had remained out of harm's way to now come forward. However, officially, to the secretary of the Navy, Perry made a report that was

> admirable for the modesty which everywhere pervaded it, so far as he was himself concerned; merely confining himself, with regard to his own movements, to a simple relation of the most important facts; and evincing his desire to make all under his orders appear advantageously. To this desire was owing the notice which he took of Captain Elliott, which, without being very eulogistic, was suited, on whole, to prevent conveying any unfavourable impression of his conduct. He stated that, "at half past two, the wind springing up, Captain Elliott was enabled to bring his vessel, the Niagara, gallantly into close action. I immediately went on board of her, when he anticipated my wish by volunteering to bring the schooners, which had been kept astern by the lightness of the wind, into

close action." He leaves to Captain Elliott the benefit of the inference that, more than two hours after the Lawrence had been in close action, he actually did what he was enabled to do; which, by the concurrent testimony of the officers of the squadron, except a few of those of the Niagara, he never did. [50]

Possibly overlooked in this generous description of Elliott's behavior was a truth that was very significant to the outcome of the battle — the wind had intensified. It was this fact that few historians even mention.

It should be acknowledged that there are many factors involved in the way this battle unfolded and concluded. As just referred to, there were personality conflicts, various types and numbers of ships, the competency or incompetency of the crews, and more; but it was the wind that allowed Perry to make his next and most decisive move against his foe.

Beyond any possible ulterior motives Elliott may have had, if the winds had not been almost still for the first two hours, the *Niagara* would likely not have been held behind the *Lawrence* which, as it happened, left it in excellent condition for Perry's use. And had the winds not begun "springing up" when they had, Perry could not have attempted what he did next.

> Perry's first order on board the Niagara was to back the main topsail, and stop her from running out of the action; his next, to brail up the main trysail, put the helm up, and bear down before the wind, with squared yards, for the enemy, altering the course from that which Captain Elliott had been steering [by] a whole right angle; at the same time, he set top-gallant-sails, and hove out a signal for close action. As the answering pendents were displayed along the line [of ships], the order was greeted by hearty cheers, evincive of the admiration awakened throughout the squadron by the hardy manoeurve of the Niagara, and of renewed confidence of victory. By great efforts... the Trippe soon closed up to the assistance of the Caledonia, and the remaining vessels approached rapidly, to take a more active part in the battle, under the influence of the increasing breeze. [51]

One can see from this early account that Perry immediately took charge of the *Niagara* and redirected her. His aim now was to cruise straight into the midst of the British fleet. And, we see from this account, that was only able to be done because of the increasing winds. It was forty-five minutes after two in the afternoon when Perry boarded the *Niagara* and by three o'clock the enemy had surrendered.

One historian of 1816 wrote:

> During the first two and a half hours, the American squadron fought to a great disadvantage, the action being chiefly sustained all that time by the Lawrence. The fresh breeze which sprung up, about the time that vessel was entirely disabled, turned the fortune of the day in our favor, by enabling all our vessels to press on the enemy, break through his line, and rake him effectually in every direction. [52]

Another chronicler of the day noted:

> With increased breeze, seven or eight minutes sufficed to traverse the distance of more than half a mile which still separated the Niagara from the enemy. As the enemy beheld her coming boldly down, reserving her fire until it could be delivered with terrible effect, they poured theirs upon her in a raking position… [53]

The *Niagara* came charging into the enemy fleet with, as they say, guns-ablazin'. From both sides of the ship their cannons fired their arsenal. On one side the *Prevost* and the *Belt* took the assault and on the other the *Queen Charlotte* and the *Detroit*; the two ships who had destroyed the *Lawrence* earlier. Confounding the British situation was the fact that the *Queen Charlotte* had trouble maneuvering into a proper position as the *Niagara* approached and had gotten its booms intertwined with some of the rigging of the *Detroit*. It certainly diminished the ship's ability to fire back.

> in this unfortunate predicament, when the Niagara, having shortened sail to check her velocity, passed slowly under the bows of the Detroit, within half pistol-shot, and poured into both vessels, as they lay entangled, a deadly and awfully destructive fire of grape[shot] and canister; the larbord guns, which were likewise manned, were directed with equally murderous effect into the sterns of *Lady Prevost*, which had passed to the head of the line, and the Little Belt; the marines at the same time, cleared their decks of everyone to be seen above the rails. The piercing shrieks of the mortally wounded on every side showed how terrific had been the carnage. [54]

The firings continued for a few more minutes from the *Niagara* and some of the smaller American vessels until

> all resistance now ceased: an officer appeared on the taffrail of the

Queen, to signify that she had struck [lowered her flag]; and her example was immediately followed by the Detroit. Both vessels struck in about seven minutes after the Niagara opened this most destructive fire, and about fifteen minutes after Perry took command of her... at three [o'clock] the Queen Charlotte and Detroit surrendered, and all resistance was at an end. [55]

Just an hour after the smoke of the cannons had cleared the lake air, Perry wrote a note to William Jones, the Secretary of the Navy. It read very similar to the more famous version that was scribbled on the back of an old envelope and delivered to General William H. Harrison as he awaited the result of the battle at the mouth of the Portage River in today's downtown Port Clinton, Ohio. This one stated:

Sir:
It has pleased the Almighty to give to the arms of the United States a signal victory over their enemies on this Lake – the British squadron consisting of two ships, two brigs, one schooner and one sloop have this moment surrendered to the force under my command, after a sharp conflict. [56]

Over the next few weeks the wounded survivors would be cared for and the ships refitted. Perry, as commander of the Navy's Great Lakes fleet would move on to assist William Harrison as he led his Northwest Army toward Canada in pursuit of the British ground troops and his Indian allies.

General Henry Proctor and the celebrated Tecumseh were based at Fort Malden where they could hear the guns of the lake battle. When they learned of Perry's victory, they opted to retreat along the Thames River toward Lake Ontario for reinforcements. Harrison led his troops in hot pursuit for several days. Perry sailed a ship alongside them carrying supplies for the troops. Finally, the American forces caught up to their enemy and a heated engagement took place. The Americans would win the day. This event, in which Tecumseh was killed, became known as the Battle of the Thames.

A noted historian, Robert McAfee, who was a participant in this battle, makes an interesting statement. Apparently, in the early stretch of this famous chase, Harrison may have had a Providential sign of good fortune to come his way; one that Perry, as well, had received before his conflict.

The campaign was not without auspicious omens, which in the superstitious times of ancient history, would have had a more powerful effect on the minds of both officers and men, than the circumstance of capturing a small detachment of the enemy. When the army arrived at the mouth of the Thames, an eagle was seen hovering over it, which General Harrison observed was a presage of success, as it was our military bird. Commodore Perry, who had condescended to act as a volunteer aide to the general, remarked that a similar circumstance had occurred to the fleet, on the morning of the 10th of September. [57]

Life is replete with the unanticipated. As we have just seen in this sampling of events which molded the early United States, their were plenty of unexpected occurrences. As things go, they all could be explained away as merely chance. Curiosity is piqued, however, when a compilation of such a number of victorious American episodes seems to have had the same common denominator — sudden and unexpected changes in the weather.

No one of the 1700s or early 1800s had a forecast to consider as they planned their next moves. Weather just happened. Sure, there were signs in nature, as there are today, which people may have been attuned to; but their observations only gave general clues to what may be in the meteorological offing. In the events just recalled, the actions taken by men were not made in anticipation of predicted weather conditions. Plans were put in motion based on any number of other important factors. The Indians and inhabitants of Boonesboro battled and dug their tunnels with little concern over how much rain might fall. The date to take Dorchester Heights had been set with no expectation of a foggy night. Washington began his attack on the Hessians in Trenton with no knowledge that a storm would blow into the enemy's faces as they approached. And you've read the rest.

Perhaps this is all coincidence, but it is intriguing to consider that Providence just may have intervened dramatically and repeatedly in the events that shaped America. ♦

HMMM...

Along the Thames River of Upper Canada was a stretch of unbroken wilderness forest that was as spectacular and romantic a setting as ever existed. It was known as the Long Woods. In the early 1800s the land was pristine with no signs of man's presence. Not even a bridge had been built yet to traverse the Thames River. Over forty river miles, only a small Moravian village of missionaries and a quaint little inn had been built in the otherwise undisturbed natural surroundings. A visitor at the inn on Christmas Night of 1819 had a very remarkable experience. The gentleman said:

When it was midnight, I walked out and strolled in the woods contiguous to the house. A glorious moon had now ascended to the summit of the arch of heaven and poured a perpendicular flood of light upon the world below. The starry hosts sparkled brightly when they emerged above the horizon, but gradually faded into twinkling points as they rose in the sky. The motionless trees stretched their majestic boughs towards a cloudless firmament; and the rustling of a withered leaf, or the distant howl of the wolf, alone broke upon my ear. I was suddenly roused from a delicious reverie by observing a dark object moving slowly and cautiously among the trees. At first I fancied it was a bear, but a nearer inspection discovered an Indian on all fours. For a moment I felt unwilling to throw myself in his way, lest he should be meditating some sinister design against me: however, on his waving his hand and putting his finger on his lips, I approached him, and notwithstanding his injunction to silence, inquired what he did there. "Me watch to see the deer kneel," replied he: "This is Christmas-Night, and all the deer fall on their knees to the Great Spirit, and look up." The solemnity of the scene, and the grandeur of the idea, alike contributed to fill me with awe. It was affecting to find traces of the Christian faith existing in such a place, even in the form of such a tradition.

In George Monro Grant's, Picturesque Canada, 1882 [58]

V.
NO MORE SQUABBLING.

"Yuakoowas! Yuakoowas!"

From the early 1600s on, that cry echoed through the woodlands of western New York alerting the tribes that lived there that the guests they had expected were on their way. Almost every year, there would be at least one visit from this mass of birds. The first Indian to see the flock approaching would run through the village announcing their arrival. However, as the twentieth century dawned, the exclamation would not be heard again. It was the Seneca, members of the Iroquois nation, that used this name "yuakoowas" for what we know as the "passenger pigeon." Other tribes had their own names for this magnificent bird as well. In the South, the Choctaws called them the lost doves, the Ojibwe to the north named them "omiimii." The whitemen derived their name from the French word "passager" meaning "a bird of passage." These were wild pigeons that migrated incessantly across, or "passed over," the eastern two-thirds of North America in numbers that still sound exaggerated; but they aren't.

Jesuit missionaries, working with the Seneca who lived around Onondaga Lake (near today's Syracuse, New York), made note of the passenger pigeons in their journals as early as 1656. They stated that the birds were particularly attracted to the salt springs of the region where the Indians would erect net traps for their capture. It was noted that, "sometimes as many as seven hundred are caught in the course of one morning."[1] Several additional accounts of this period speak similarly to the large numbers of these birds being captured by the Indians using either nets or birdshot.

From these early days, when the English colonies were just getting established on the Atlantic coast and New France's traders and missionaries occupied the middle of the continent; these birds not only provided a visual and audible spectacle, but they became an easily accessible and vital food source for numerous generations to come.

The passenger pigeon typically spent its winters in the warmer, southern climates. But, when things heated up beyond their comfort level, they would head north to procreate; choosing sites abundant in the foods they preferred. When they arrived on the scene, wherever it might be, there was nothing subtle about it. The flocks were beyond massive. Credible scientists and writers of history over the years have expounded on the awe that the event stirred in their hearts and minds; whether they witnessed them passing overhead on their journeys, or if they watched them coming down to roost, or even nest, in their vicinity.

In the autumn of 1813, John James Audubon, the famous artist and naturalist, recorded his observations of flocks of wild pigeons as they flew along the Ohio River. He encountered them while on a trip from Henderson to Louisville, Kentucky. Knowing how fanciful their performance might sound to those who never saw it, he prefaced his remarks with an oath to their sincerity.

> The multitudes of Wild Pigeons in our woods are astonishing. Indeed, I even now feel inclined to pause, and assure myself that what I am going to relate is fact. Yet I have seen it all, and that too in the company of persons who, like myself, were struck with amazement.

He went on to explain that it was

> a few miles beyond Hardensburgh [Hardinsburg, Kentucky] I observed the pigeons flying from north-east to south-west in greater numbers than I thought I had ever seen them before... I travelled on, and still met more the farther I proceeded. The air was literally filled with Pigeons; the light of noon-day was obscured as by an eclipse; the dung fell in spots, not unlike melting flakes of snow; and the continued buzz of wings had a tendency to lull my senses to repose.

A few hours later, while stopped for his dinner about forty miles further into his journey, Audubon said:

> I saw, at my leisure, immense legions still going by, with a front reaching far beyond the Ohio on the west... I cannot describe to you the extreme beauty of their aerial evolutions, when a Hawk chanced to press upon the

Passenger Pigeon, Hand-painted engraving by John James Audubon.

rear of a flock. At once, like a torrent, and with a noise like thunder, they rushed into a compact mass, pressing upon each other towards the centre. In these almost solid masses, they darted forward in undulating and angular lines, descended and swept close over the earth with inconceivable velocity, mounted perpendicularly so as to resemble a vast column, and, when high, were seen wheeling and twisting within their continued lines, which then resembled the coils of a gigantic serpent…

After another fifteen miles of travel, Audubon reached his destination of Louisville. It was just before sunset and he noted that "the pigeons were still passing in undiminished numbers, and continued to do so for three days in succession."[2]

Simon Pokagon, the last chief of the Potawatomi tribe living in the region of Michigan, was a prolific author as well as a renowned leader. Amongst his writings is an article about the wild pigeon of North

America. In it he explains that

> when a young man I have stood for hours admiring the movements of these birds. I have seen them fly in unbroken lines from the horizon, one line succeeding another from morning until night, moving their unbroken columns like an army of trained soldiers pushing to the front, while detached bodies of these birds appeared in different parts of the heavens, pressing forward in haste like raw recruits preparing for battle. At other times I have seen them move in one column for hours across the sky, like some great river, ever varying in hue; and as the mighty stream, sweeping on at sixty miles an hour, reached some deep valley, it would pour its living mass headlong down hundreds of feet, sounding as though a whirlwind was abroad the land. I have stood by the grandest waterfall of America [Niagara] and regarded the descending torrents in wonder and astonishment, yet never have my astonishment, wonder, and admiration been so stirred as when I have witnessed these birds drop from their course like meteors from heaven.[3]

Even the renowned novelist of the nineteenth century, James Fenimore Cooper, vividly described passenger pigeon scenes through the dialogue of characters in several of his novels. One such description is given in *The Chainbearer* when Mr. Mordaunt Littlepage explains:

> I scarce know how to describe that remarkable scene. As we drew near to the summit of the hill, pigeons began to be seen fluttering among the branches over our heads, as individuals are met along the roads that lead into the suburbs of a large town. We had probably seen a thousand birds glancing around among the trees, before we came in view of the roost itself. The numbers increased as we drew nearer, and presently the forest was alive with them. The fluttering was incessant, and often startling as we passed ahead, our march producing a movement in the living crowd that really became confounding. Every tree was literally covered with nests, many having at least a thousand of these frail tenements on their branches, and shaded by the leaves. They often touched each other, a wonderful degree of order prevailing among the hundreds of thousands of families that were here assembled. The place had the odor of a fowl-house, and squabs just fledged sufficiently to trust themselves in short flights, were fluttering around us in all directions in tens of thousands. To these were to be added the parents of the young race endeavoring to protect them, and guide them in a way to escape harm…
>
> …Not one of our party spoke for several minutes. Astonishment

seemed to hold us all tongue-tied, and we moved slowly forward into the fluttering throng, silent, absorbed, and full of admiration of the works of the Creator. It was not easy to hear each others' voices when we did speak, the incessant fluttering of wings filling the air. Nor were the birds silent in other respects. The pigeon is not a noisy creature, but a million crowded together on the summit of one hill, occupying a space of less than a mile square, did not leave the forest in its ordinary impressive stillness. [4]

Citations like these are as endless as the flights of the pigeons themselves. Not only were these birds seen migrating seasonally from north to south and back again, they also moved about as necessary to find food and adequate nesting locations. The reports of their travels have come from all sectors of the continent: the New England states, Canada, the Midwest, and the South.

By all accounts, the passenger pigeon was a beautiful bird. In fact, it was quite a distinguished species due to its colorings, grace, and intelligence. It was one of the now more than three hundred species of wild pigeons, who are not to be confused with the current, nor the ancient, domesticated varieties. Homing, or carrier pigeons, have garnered most of the historic attention because they have been trained since the earliest days for racing and the delivery of messages. These special breeds are genetically tuned-in to their geographic homes. Even Queen Elizabeth II was an avid pigeon racing enthusiast; carrying on an English tradition ever since King Leopold II of Belgium gifted racing pigeons to the Royal Family in 1886. As recently as World War II, domesticated homing pigeons were used to discreetly send vital messages. Other breeds have been, and still are, raised for food or for show. However, these domesticated pigeons could not survive in the wilds that the passenger had dwelt in.

The male passenger pigeon had a body somewhat longer than most species, averaging over sixteen inches; his mate was an inch or so shorter. Both had slender bodies; a small head and neck balanced with a long, straight, feathered tail. However, it was their breasts that enveloped muscles of great strength for flight. This physique gave them the power to race at fantastic speeds through the air. Perhaps Audubon said it best. "When an individual [passenger] is seen gliding through the woods and close to the observer, it passes like a thought, and on

Winter Sports in Northern Louisiana, Shooting Wild Pigeons.
Illustration by Smith Bennett, 1875.

trying to see it again, the eye searches in vain; the bird is gone."[5]

It may be that the passenger's most striking feature was its coloring. Working down from the male's blue-grey head and neck, this pigeon had purple, green, and copper iridescence that soon blended into its famed breast of red. Often referred to as a rose blush, it would gradually change to white as it extended toward the tail. The female was similarly colored, but the hues were muted. Both sexes had bright red eyes and short dark beaks. Many consider today's mourning doves to be closest to them in appearance.

Because of their staggering abundance, the passengers quickly became the easy prey of, well, almost anyone. And, for a long time that was a good thing. Food was not sitting on store shelves or in butcher shops ready to be purchased on the American frontier of the early 1800s. Hunting was still a lifelong, almost daily activity, until late in the century.

The techniques used to capture the pigeons were as numerous as they were uncomplicated. One approach couldn't possibly be any easier since it was the mere act of bending over to pick them up. A geologist, George Featherstonhaugh, traveling through the southern states in 1844 testified to this as well as some additional aspects of a passenger pigeon's life cycle.

A new and very interesting spectacle now presented itself, in the incredible quantities of wild pigeons that were abroad; flocks of them many miles long came across the country, one flight succeeding to another, obscuring the daylight, and producing a rushing and startling sound, that cataracts [waterfalls] of the first class might be proud of. These flights of wild pigeons constitute one of the most remarkable phenomena of the western country. I remember once, when amongst the Indians, seeing the woods loaded from top to bottom with their nests for a great number of miles, the heaviest branches of the trees broken and fallen to the ground, which was strewed with young birds dead and alive, that the Indians in great numbers were picking up to carry away with their horses: many of their dogs were said to be gone mad with feeding upon their putrefied remains. A forest thus loaded and half destroyed with these birds, presents an extraordinary spectacle which cannot be rivalled; but when such myriads of timid birds as the wild pigeon are on the wing, often wheeling and performing evolutions almost as complicated as pyrotechnic movements, and creating whirlwinds as they move, they present an image of the most fearful power. Our horse, Missouri, at such times, has been so cowed by them, that he would stand still and tremble in his harness, whilst we ourselves were glad when their flight was directed from us. 6

The enormous flocks moved across the continent in search of several vital needs: food, a place to rest, or roost, and a place to procreate. Though they seemingly had little trouble finding these locations, their presence at them usually caused the land to be left devastated by the time they re-took flight.

Their favorite foods were beechnuts and acorns. Other seeds, grains and berries sufficed in a pinch. If a woodland of beech trees was found, the flocks would dive in for a feast. Like acorns, beechnuts fell to the ground and were usually in as much abundance as their consumers. Flock after flock would scour the grounds loading their crops, the internal pouches at the base of their necks for storing food, with the tasty seeds. If they decided to roost, they crowded every possible limb of these trees. More than a few such branches would snap under the excessive weight, injuring the tree and the pigeons dining below.

It was during nesting that all these factors worked together for the greatest benefit of the hunter. About a week and a half after the parents had mated, a single egg would be laid. It would take a little over two weeks for it to hatch. In earlier days, the Indians had left the families alone to feed the newborn. It was the babies, or squabs, who grew plump with fat over their first few weeks of life that were the prize catch. Though the adult pigeons were leaner than the squabs, they too were taken for food as the years went by; primarily because they were so easy to trap.

An account from a renowned ornithologist of early America, Alexander Wilson, details a nesting that took place along the Kentucky River in 1810.

> As soon as the young were fully grown, and before they left the nests, numerous parties of the inhabitants, from all parts of the adjacent country, came with wagons, oxen, beds, cooking utensils, many of them accompanied by the greater part of their families, and encamped for several days at the immense nursery. The noise was so great as to terrify their horses, and it was difficult for one person to hear another speak without bawling in his ear.
>
> The ground was strewn with broken limbs of trees, eggs and young squab pigeons which had been precipitated from above, and on which herds of hogs were fattening. Hawks, buzzards and eagles were sailing about in great numbers, and seizing the squabs from their nests at pleasure; while from twenty feet upwards to the tops of the trees, the view through the woods presented a perpetual tumult of crowding and fluttering multitudes of old pigeons, their wings roaring like thunder, mingled with the frequent crash of falling lumber. For now the axemen were at work cutting down those trees which seemed to be most crowded with nests of the young birds, and contriving to fell trees in such manner that in their descent they might bring down several other trees. The felling of one large tree sometimes produced two hundred squabs, little inferior in size to old birds, and almost one mass of fat.
>
> On some single trees upwards of a hundred nests were found, each containing one young only, a circumstance in the history of this bird not generally known to naturalists. It was dangerous to walk under these flying and fluttering millions of birds, from the frequent fall of large branches, broken down by the weight of the multitudes above, and which, in their descent, often destroyed numbers of the birds themselves. [7]

When flocks came to roost, or even while simply flying low to the ground, the simple wielding of long sticks could randomly take down large numbers of the passengers. Such use of poles could also dethrone those who chose to perch on lower branches. However, beyond this swatting maneuver, the primary method of catching the birds was with nets.

The art of trapping prey in a net had its own series of techniques, depending on the local hunter's preferred method and their history of success or failure. In the early days of the seventeenth century, the Indians were using techniques that they had perfected over time. Sometimes on each side of a cleared lane they would string a net between two trees, a vertical sandwich of sorts. With strings that stretched to a secluded blind, the Indians would drop the nets when the area was sufficiently populated. Other tribes set their nets on high between trees and likewise dropped them over the unsuspecting birds as they ate. These methods were generally adopted later by the settlers.

Unless a spot was chosen where nature had already provided a forest floor of tasty seeds or salt, the traps usually needed to be baited to attract the passengers. These lures changed as the years went by. Early on, the scattering of beechnuts or acorns, or even salted mud, was sufficient. Later the idea of a decoy to attract the rest of the flock was employed. Though a bit gruesome, the eyelids of a randomly caught pigeon would be sewn shut. He would then be fastened by short ropes and stakes to the ground, or to a box or stool that could be pulled about by attached strings. Set in the midst of the strewn nuts and seeds, this "stool pigeon" would draw the attention of his fellows, for when he heard them flying above he would take flight for the few yards allowed by his hunter's strings. The flock above suspected that there was food on the grounds of the stool pigeon and so descended. Sooner or later the visitors to the feeding ground would increase in number, until, with a quick tug of the lead lines, the net would envelope them.

A popular author of the nineteenth century, Samuel Goodrich recalled how in his youth he partook in a pigeon hunt. His group waited silently as the sun rose when

> finally the rushing sound of the pigeons, [came] pouring like a tide over the tops of the trees.
>
> By this time of course our nets were ready, and our flyers and stoolbirds on the alert. What moments of ecstacy were these, and especially when the head of the flock – some red-breasted old father or grandfather – caught sight of our pigeons, and turning at the call, drew the whole train down into our net-bed. I have often seen a hundred, or two

hundred of these splendid birds, come upon us, with a noise absolutely deafening, and sweeping the air with a sudden gust, like the breath of a thundercloud. Sometimes our bush-hut, where we lay concealed, was covered all over with pigeons, and we dared not move a finger, as their red, piercing eyes were upon us. When at last, with a sudden pull of the rope, the net was sprung, and we went out to secure our booty – often fifty, sometimes even a hundred birds – I felt a fullness of triumph, which words are wholly inadequate to express! [8]

As this account relates, the catches were usually in the hundreds. Once the nets were dropped however, the birds had to be silenced. Sometimes the catch was so large and powerful that they would manage to raise up, netting and all, and try to fly away. This was intolerable. The squabs, especially, in short order would spoil if their engorged crops were not removed. As cruel as it may seem, as their heads popped up through the mesh, their crops and skulls would be pinched between the captors forefinger and thumb. Others used the blacksmith's pinchers to this end. Sometimes the hunters would even crush the heads between their teeth; why, is uncertain.

By the mid 1800s, pigeons remained so abundant and easy to capture that they had almost became a staple food, especially for the poor. Then the railroads came, crossing the entire country by the 1860s, and making the passenger pigeon available almost anywhere they were wanted. The trains allowed the birds to be delivered to remote locations quickly, so they didn't spoil. Demand skyrocketed. It was now big business. The birds could be crated live or iced and packed to be sent by rail to cities large and small. Dining establishments and chefs for high-class clientele began creating premier dishes with the lowly passenger. The growing demand meant that even more pigeons needed to be caught and shipped as swiftly as possible. This in-turn led to new techniques of capture; often unsavory ones.

An example comes by way of the Indian chief, Pokagon, who was taken aback by one of these methods.

In May 1880, I visited the last known nesting place east of the Great Lakes. It was on Platt River in Benzie County, Michigan. There were on these grounds many large white birch trees filled with nests. These trees have manifold bark, which when old hangs in shreds like rags or flowing moss, along their trunks and limbs. This bark will burn like paper soaked

Illustration titled, *Netting Wild Pigeons in New England*, in Frank Leslie's *Illustrated Newspaper*, 1867. Netting on ground is covered with grains as bait. Stool pigeons tied to strings that are pulled by hunters in the blind at left are made to flutter close to the ground as if feeding. When the flock descends to eat, strings attached to the net are pulled and the catch is made.

in oil. Here for the first time I saw with shame and pity a new mode for robbing these birds' nests, which I took upon as being devilish. These outlaws to all moral sense would touch a lighted match to the bark of the tree at the base, when with a flash more like an explosion the blast would reach every limb of the tree and while the affrighted young birds would leap simultaneously to the ground, the parent birds, with plumage scorched, would rise high in the air amid flame and smoke. I noticed that many of these squabs were so fat and clumsy they would burst open on striking the ground. Several thousand were obtained during the day by that cruel process.

Ironically, Pokagon had told this story to an old man whom he stayed with that same night. The man was appalled upon hearing it. After a short period of contemplation, the ol' hunter said that he would show Pokagon

a way to catch pigeons that will please any red man and the birds too.

Early the next morning I [Pokagon] followed him a few rods from his hut, where he showed me an open pole pen, about two feet high, which he called his bait bed. Into this he scattered a bucket of wheat. We then sat in ambush so as to see through between the poles into the pen. Soon they began to pour into the pen and gorge themselves. While I was watching and admiring them, all at once to my surprise they began fluttering and falling on their sides and backs and kicking and quivering like a lot of cats with paper tied over their feet. He jumped into the pen saying, "Come on, you redskin."

I was right on hand by his side. A few birds flew out of the pen apparently crippled, but we caught and caged about one hundred fine birds. After my excitement was over I sat down on one of the cages, and thought in my heart, "Certainly Pokagon is dreaming, or this long-haired white man is a witch." I finally said, "Look here, old fellow, tell me how you did that." He gazed at me, holding his long white beard in one hand, and said with one eye half shut and a sly wink with the other, "That wheat was soaked in whisky." [9]

Of course, besides these unorthodox methods and the simple knocking of birds out of their nests with a long pole, the firing of tiny lead balls out of a shotgun was a standard technique that would soon evolve into a sport. An Englishman named William Faux came to the United States in 1819 to see what was drawing his fellow countrymen to move here. Amongst his many travels he stopped at various locations in Ohio. One day near Zanesville, his diary recorded that he

> wandered in the fields shooting pigeons, which is here fine sport, they fly and alight around you on every tree, in immense flocks, and loving to be shot. They are rather smaller than English pigeons, and have a lilac breast, but in other respects are blue, or blue grey. They breed in the woods, and seem to court death by the gun, the sound of which appears to call them together, instead of scaring them away, a fowling-piece well charged with dust shot might bring down a bushel of these willing game dead at your feet. [10]

By the late 1800s, while the demand had already increased for passenger pigeons as food, another market was also growing for these birds — trap-shooting contests. A live pigeon was kept in a box trap which would suddenly open with the pull of a rope, releasing the bird into the air. Competitors would have only seconds to take aim with their shotguns and dispatch their target. The sport grew rapidly, becoming a favorite activity across the land. Thousands of birds would be purchased for competitions. The pigeons needed to be healthy so that they would take flight quickly when their trap was sprung open. As well, they were kept well-nourished so they would be plump, and hence marketable, after they were shot. This gun play evolved into the trap and skeet shooting we know today; only now it is with clay pigeons in lieu of the live passengers.

As it happened, whether for food or for fun, demand eventually eclipsed supply. By the late 1870s the passenger pigeon's future was in serious peril. The professional hunter had taken control and routinely moved from one nesting site to another wiping out flocks by the millions. In 1878, in Petoskey, Michigan, a famously thorough elimination of the passenger population took place. It was reported that on each day, over the course of one month, multiple railroad boxcars were loaded with the birds. Though a few laws were passed to try to curb such mass slaughter of the birds, as well as their use in sporting events, it was too little too late.

The last migrations of the passenger pigeons were seen in scattered regions of Michigan in the early 1890s. As the twentieth century dawned, only handfuls of them were still viewable in their confines at a few zoos across the country. The zoos were making a desperate effort to maintain their propagation, but the passengers didn't do well in captivity. Finally the population, that once was in the billions, had dwindled to one lone female at the Cincinnati Zoo. Rewards as high as one thousand dollars were offered for anyone bringing in a passenger that could be preserved with her, but none were found. Martha, so named in honor of Martha Washington, eventually passed away in 1914 and with her death came the official end of the species. Today the preserved body of Martha is in the collection of the Smithsonian Institution.

It's been quite well-documented that these birds were over-hunted for decades with little thought ever given to the fact that they could face extinction. They were so incredibly abundant that such a fate was inconceivable. However, of course, they have disappeared and man does have to take much of the blame; but maybe not all of it.

Other factors cannot be ignored as contributing to this tragedy. One weather-related theory is that a significant number of the last flocks may have been wiped out by catastrophic winter storms over the Great Lakes during their migrations. Another point to consider is that after so many decades of roosting, nesting, and foraging in such massive numbers at particular locations, they destroyed the very woodlands they needed to occupy. It took years for the forests to sufficiently regrow after their all-encompassing visits. As well, the number of settlers arriving through the 1800s increased logarithmically and they were clearing their share of woodlands to build their homes and villages. Mother Nature, too, provided the pigeon with plenty of natural predators. Hawks and owls would prey on them through the sky, while skunks, wolves, foxes, badgers, and even snakes took aim on the ground. Perhaps these animal attackers may not have had much effect when the population of the passengers was in the billions; but in later years, when their numbers were already severely diminished, they had an impact.

Though forever gone, this pigeon lives on today through numerous cultural venues. The lore runs deep. Novels have been written about them or at least have addressed the hunting of them; as can be seen in the stories of James Fenimore Cooper. Poets and lyricists have created compositions that range from light-hearted prose to sentimental ballads. Paintings and sculptures from greats like Audubon and many others have been created to preserve their memory and for scientific documentation. Memorials have been erected including one at Martha's former residence in the Cincinnati Zoo.

For generations the passenger pigeon was primarily viewed as a food source. From the 1600s until settlers arrived in the late 1700s, the appearance of the flocks was reason for the Indians to put on a grand feast. Horatio Jones, an Indian agent to the tribes of western New York, described their arrival along the Genesee River, near Buffalo, in 1782. Jones

> beheld a sight that he never forgot. The pigeons, in numbers too great to estimate, had made their temporary homes in a thick forest. Each tree and branch bore nests on every available spot. The birds had exhausted every species of nesting material in the vicinity, including the small twigs of the trees, and the ground was as bare as though swept with a broom...
>
> As the annual nesting of the pigeons was a matter of great importance to the Indians, who depended largely upon the supply of food thus obtained, runners carried the news to every part of the Seneca territory, and the inhabitants, singly and in bands, came from as far west as Seneca

Lake and as far north as Lake Ontario. Within a few days several hundred, men, women and children gathered in the locality of the pigeon woods...

The Indians cut down the roosting trees to secure the birds, and each day thousands of squabs were killed. Fires were made in front of the cabins and bunches of the dressed birds were suspended on poles sustained by crotched sticks, to dry in the heat and smoke. When properly cured they were packed in bags or baskets for transportation to the home towns. It was a festival season for the red men and even the nearest dog in camp had his fill of pigeon meat. [11]

The Chippewa Indians had a few different methods of cooking fresh pigeons. They often boiled the cleaned birds in a stew of potatoes and other meats, or alone in a pot with rice. At other times they would skewer them onto a stick which was then positioned over the edge of a fire and turned frequently to cook all sides. In a rush, they sometimes covered the still feathered pigeon in the ashes of their fire until they were cooked.

It was the squabs, the newborns if you will, that were considered the tastiest catch. They were so stuffed with food by their parents during their first few weeks, that they grew very round and engorged with fat. These youngsters got the best price in the marketplace.

As noted, the birds were preserved for use in the winter by a drying and smoking process. The fat of the squabs was used to make the most luscious butter. And little else was wasted. The feathers were saved and stuffed between cloths to make pillows and true feather beds. It was said that few were the young girls of Canada who married without bringing a dowry that included pigeon feather bedding. Some accounts claim medicinal cures from pigeon's blood, gizzards, and even their dung.

A testament to the curative powers of the lowly passenger pigeon comes in a story from the first person to settle in the vicinity of Cleveland, Ohio; Judge James Kingsbury. He came to the region with his wife Eunice, three children, and a teenage nephew in the spring of 1796 just after the surveyors had finished their work of delineating the area's former wilderness into lots. Kingsbury tells how after establishing his family's residence in the region during the spring, he had to return to New Hampshire in November; leaving his pregnant bride and family alone. While separated, both spouses suffered an attack of fever. Both recovered, albeit weakened from the ordeal. Struggling physically to travel through neck-deep snows as a result of the death of his horse to the elements, Kingsbury finally arrived at the home of his family on Christmas Eve. He found that he had a new son, Albert, who was born while he was gone, but his wife had since relapsed into a feverish state. She had become unable to feed the infant. Kingsbury made a treacherous trip to Erie, Pennsylvania to find food. He returned with some grain for his family, but it was too late. Soon thereafter, the baby had succumbed to starvation. His wife, Eunice, was said to have briefly sat up in her sickbed, only to witness through a cabin window the burial of her infant. She then fell into unconsciousness. The fever and lack of nutrition had taken its toll. In a very feeble state himself, from the arduous treks across the country for food, Kingsbury was hardly able to walk; yet

> he loaded an old "Queen's Arm," which his uncle had carried in the war of the revolution; and which is still in the keeping of the family. He succeeded in reaching the woods, and sat down upon a log. A solitary pigeon came, and perched upon the highest branches of a tree. It was not only high, but distant. The chances of hitting the bird were few indeed, but a human life seemed to depend upon those chances. A single shot found its way to the mark, and the bird fell. It was well cooked and the broth given to his wife, who was immediately revived. For the first time in two weeks she spoke in a natural and rational way, saying, "James, where did you get this?" [12]

Through the latter years of their existence, the passengers were turned into a delicacy at premier restaurants along the east coast. Even as early as 1838, the menu at the famous Delmonico's of New York featured several pigeon entrees. There was Pigeon aux petis pois, braised pigeon with peas; Pigeon en Macedoine, braised pigeon with mixed vegetables; Compote de pigeon, stewed pigeon; and Pigeon en crapaudine, so named because the pigeon is presented in such a way as to resemble a frog – crapaud in French meaning toad. Over their early years, Delmonico's had some extravagant banquets for the likes of Charles Dickens in 1842 and President Andrew Johnson in 1866; and passenger pigeon was on their menu in even more variations. Some of these original French dishes are still served today in more exclusive restaurants, albeit using other varieties of pigeon.

Though a culinary delight in some circles, the pigeons inhabiting today's cities are generally frowned upon. They are no longer coveted as a source of food. Many municipalities are overrun with various breeds that have adapted to eating discarded human food scraps. As a result of their need to stay close to their supply of nourishment, they have taken up residence in the nooks and crannies of tall buildings. Frequent flights about the city create the further, and very bothersome, problem of defecation. Because these unhealthy living conditions can invite disease, the city-dwelling pigeons are generally not safe for consumption. There are, however, many sources that still raise various breeds under strict conditions to be sold to restaurants or individual consumers.

A sentimentality for the lowly passenger pigeon was evident in some segments of the population during its many years of flight over the continent, and some still lingers today. There were people with a religious background who felt that the pigeons should be left alone because they were a breed of bird that had been around since the days of the Old Testament. Cultures of those ancient times did raise them for food, but they were more importantly esteemed and used as a sacrificial offering to God. Other cultures felt that the passengers were so majestic in their aerial dances that they should simply be admired rather than destroyed.

One sentimental yet eccentric story comes from a young clergyman, James Clarke, who had been newly located to the frontier station of Louisville, Kentucky in 1834 at the outset of his ministry. On one particular evening he was feeling a bit melancholy as he peered into the embers of his fireplace. He had been less than well-received by his new congregation and was contemplating his future when a knock came at his door. A young boy was there and he handed Clarke a note that read:

> Sir, – I hope you will excuse the liberty of a stranger addressing you on a subject he feels great interest in. It is to require a place of interment for his friend(s) in the church-yard and also the expense attendant on the purchase of such place of temporary repose.
>
> Your communication on this matter will greatly oblige, sir, your respectful and obedient servant,
>
> J. B. Booth

Photograph of Junius Brutus Booth Jr. circa 1855.

The young preacher felt that ministering to the needs of the grieving Mr. Booth was just the type of work he was here to perform. That night he went to the mayor and then another gentleman of the area to find out the availability and cost of a burial. Neither man had an answer. Therefore, Clarke decided to go to the hotel where Mr. Booth was staying to at least show him that he was trying to help. Upon his arrival he was directed to a parlor where Mr. Booth and another man were sitting. Clarke then recognized the famed actor who he had briefly met some time previous. He explained that he was unable as yet, to secure the burial information that had been requested, but would have it in the morning. Booth acknowledged the effort and invited Clarke to join them. Attempts at consolation were lightly rebuffed by the actor, but Clarke pursued by asking if the death of his friend was a sudden occurrence.

"Very," he replied.

"Was he a relative?"

"Distant," said he, and changed the subject.

Booth then invited Clarke to sit as he and the other gentleman returned to reading aloud the story of the *Ancient Mariner*. Later Booth queried of Clarke whether he was familiar with a certain author's opinion on a particular topic.

"Did you ever read," said he, "Shelley's argument against the use of animal food, at the end of 'Queen Mab'?"

"Yes, I have read it."

"And what did you think of the argument?"

"Ingenious, but not satisfactory."

"To me it is satisfactory. I have long been convinced that it is wrong to take the life of an animal for our pleasure. I eat no animal food. There is my supper," – pointing to the plate of bread.

Booth went on at length citing example after example from the bible, in particular, to make his case for vegetarianism, and he did so convincingly. Then

Booth rose, and, taking one of the candles, said to me, "Would you like to look at the remains?"

I assented... he led me into an adjoining chamber... spread out upon a large sheet, I beheld to my surprise, about a bushel of wild pigeons!

Booth knelt down by the side of the birds, and with evidence of sincere affliction began to mourn over them. He took them up in his hands tenderly, and pressed them to his heart. For a few moments he seemed to forget my presence. For this I was glad, for it gave me a little time to recover from my astonishment, and to consider rapidly what it might mean.

Clarke dismissed the idea that this was some odd joke being played on him and believed Booth's sincerity. Over the previous week there had been a visit from a massive number of passengers as they roosted in the area. They were taken in large quantities by many of the residents who never flinched at what they were doing. The thought that their actions were somehow wrong never crossed their minds. Booth felt otherwise.

"You see," said he [Booth], "these innocent victims of man's barbarity. I wish to testify, in some public way, against this wanton destruction of life. And I wish you to help me. Will you?"

"Hardly," I [Clarke] replied. "I expected something very different from this, when I received your note. I did not come to see you, expecting to be called to assist at the funeral solemnities of birds."

"Nor did I send for you," he answered. "I merely wrote to ask about the lot in the graveyard. But now you are here, why not help me? Do you fear the laugh of man?"

"No," I returned. "If I agreed with you in regard to this subject, I might, perhaps, have the courage to act out my convictions. But I do not look at it as you do. There is no reason, then, why I should have anything to do with it. I respect your convictions, but I do not share them."

"That is fair," he said.

This discussion continued at some length until it concluded with a mutual respect for each other's stance. A few days later Booth had purchased a plot in the cemetery. With the deceased secured in a special coffin he had purposefully made, they paraded in a horse-drawn hearse to the final resting place. Soon after the burial scene, Booth began showing further signs of mental unrest. Over the next few days he was often found sitting at length staring into space, getting lost on long walks in the woods, and randomly feeding horses around the town while lecturing the carriage drivers to be humane in their treatment of their steeds. The stray from sanity proved to be only temporary and soon Booth was back to himself performing on stage as usual. Yes, this man, Junius Brutus Booth, was the father of the infamous John Wilkes Booth who likewise was a stage actor with a passionate streak laced with a bit of instability.

Perhaps the poetic lines, which Clarke mentions to have been Booth's favorite, are the perfect way to eulogize the legacy of the passenger pigeon in North America. They are from the poem of Samuel Taylor Coleridge, titled, He Prayeth Best Who Loveth Best.

> He prayeth well, who loveth well
> Both man, and bird, and beast.
> He prayeth best, who loveth best
> All things, both great and small;
> For dear God, who loveth us,
> He made and loveth all. [13] ♦

NO MORE SQUABBLING

Frontispiece of book, *Our Vanishing Wild Life*, by William Hornaday, 1913. Illustration depicts *Martha*, the last known Passenger Pigeon who survived until 1914 in the Cincinnati Zoo.

The 1857 Senate's lack of foresight on the fate of the pigeons is countered by its correct prediction about the Snipe. This bird has survived, and because it is so elusive to hunt, only a person who is a great shot with a gun can take one down — hence our term "Sniper" for a skilled marksman.

HMMM...

Along the Ohio River on July 7, 1792, what should have been a simple canoe trip of the few miles from Fort Washington to the nearby community of Columbia became a story for the ages. The short excursion resulted in tragic deaths, captivity, injury, and a hilariously bouyant account of survival.

Oliver M. Spencer [of nearby Columbia], a lad of eleven years of age, on the 3rd of July, 1792, went down to Fort Washington with some other members of the family to witness the celebration of the Fourth. He remained at Cincinnati until about 3 o'clock in the afternoon of the 7th, when he went on board of a canoe lying in front of the fort, in which Jacob Light, Mrs. Mary Coleman, a Mr. Clayton, and a soldier of the garrison were about going to Columbia. The canoe was small and unsteady, hardly fit to carry such a load. When they had proceeded a few rods above the mouth of Deer creek, the soldier, who was much intoxicated, nearly upset the canoe, and finally fell overboard. He reached the shore, however, and sat down on the bank. Young Spencer, who could not swim, became uneasy at the unsteadiness of the canoe, and at his own request was set to shore. He walked up the beach keeping opposite the canoe and conversing with the party. Mr. Light propelled the boat with a pole, keeping her close in shore. Mr. Clayton sat in the stern with a paddle, which he used sometimes as an oar and sometimes as a rudder.

Mrs. Coleman, a woman about fifty years of age [and obese], sat in the middle. When they had proceeded about a mile up the river, Mr. Clayton, looking back, discovered the drunken soldier staggering along the shore, and remarked that he would be good bait for Indians. Just then two rifle shots were fired from the willows. Mr. Clayton was struck and fell out of the boat on the shore side. Mr. Light was wounded by a ball, which glanced from his pole, and sprang into the river on the other side. The Indians now rushed to the edge of the water, one of them seized Clayton, who was struggling in the water, dragged him ashore, then tomahawked and scalped him, and held up the scalp in fiendish exultation. The other Indian made a prisoner of Spencer.

Mr. Light, although wounded in the left arm, struck out boldly with his right for the Kentucky shore, and Mrs. Coleman, who preferred being drowned to falling into the hands of the Indians, jumped overboard, and, buoyed up by her clothes, floated down the river. The Indians would have reloaded and fired at them, but the report of their rifles had brought some persons to the Kentucky shore, and fearing to create further alarm, they decamped in haste with their prisoner. Mr. Light, seeing them retreat and finding that in his wounded condition he could not cross the river, turned and reached the Ohio shore. He fell from exhaustion as soon as he landed, but soon revived and proceeded to Fort Washington. The most remarkable circumstance connected with the transaction was the manner of Mrs. Coleman's escape. Her underclothing spread out on the surface of the water

The 1700s style of dress that saved the life of Mrs. Coleman.

and prevented her from sinking, while she floated down with the current. At length finding herself nearing the shore, she made use of her hands as paddles and landed just above the mouth of Deer creek, having floated more than a mile.

Mrs. Coleman survived; reaching the fort and telling her tale as well as getting a dry change of clothing. She was soon reunited with her family in Columbia. Young Oliver Spencer, whose father was a Revolutionary war hero, was taken to Detroit and held in captivity until his release late that same year. The negotiations were heavily influenced of George Washington, a close friend and admirer of the senior Spencer. Oliver went on to become a renowned Methodist preacher, a successful businessman, and an author of a book recounting his captivity.

In Theodore Roosevelt's, The Winning of the West, Part IV, 1905 [14]

VI.
I SPY...

On April 30, 1789, George Washington rested his left hand on the Bible, raised his right hand toward heaven, and recited a simple oath to faithfully execute the Office of President of the United States. It was a grand moment and a foreboding one, as it would be no small task to manage the multitude of circumstances facing the burgeoning nation. After nearly six years of a floundering existance without a designated leader at its head, the country was more than ready for some sound direction. From day one, numerous, sometimes overwhelming, problems were laid at the president's feet. One of the most-pressing issues that Washington would have to wrestle with was the on-going conflict between the Native Americans and the new Americans who were settling in the West.

Since the end of the Revolution in 1783, many citizens had already moved from the established states along the Atlantic coast and established themselves in the lands of today's Midwest. Most were squatters. They laid claim to acres of land which were bounded by nothing more than a specific tree, boulder, bend in a creek, or other such landmark. Then they proceeded to build and self-righteously defend their homesteads. Eventually counter-claims to lands and legal issues caught up with the practice of free settlement and things got ugly. The government had to step in.

The new country was having a very difficult time getting on its financial feet. The Revolution had been expensive, and the countries who helped finance the revolt against the King were now calling for repayment. The government didn't have the money. In the states, there was chaos. The former colonists were a divided group. Loyalists to

Britain and the new United States citizens had to sort out ownership of properties and goods. Businesses needed to be established or re-established under new laws. The commodities exchanged in business often had to be acquired from new sources. Many families, neighbors, and business partners were now at odds with each other because of their chosen loyalties and people were moving in and out of communities. It was a mess.

All these factors, and more, worked together to create an environment that was ripe for federal intervention. The authorities soon used the frontier to do just that; and in a very novel way. Ordinances were drawn up and approved in 1784, 1785, and finally again in 1787. These laws had several purposes, but one of the most important was to sever any and all former claims by east coast states to these lands which sat north of the Ohio and east of the Mississippi Rivers. The territory that this encompassed was then segmented into a handful of districts that governed themselves rather than having any obligations to the existing states. As soon as the ink had dried on these legal documents which declared the lands to now be the federally controlled Northwest Territory, officials got to work on the bigger issue which had prompted this legal move in the first place – the generation of income. Surveyors were ordered to the frontier and the land was quickly divided into lots which would be put up for sale. The government had become a real estate broker.

Though sales accelerated as the months went by, the settlers were soon coming to a realization that beyond the natural challenges of wilderness survival, they had to defend themselves against the resistant Indians. As the country's first president took control, the Indian opposition to any settlement north of the Ohio River was escalating, as well as the death counts in both cultures.

Of course opposition to the whitemen of any nation making permanent homesteads in lands west of the Appalachians was nothing new. Before the Revolution, in 1768, the first Treaty of Fort Stanwix was agreed to between the Iroquois and the British; granting settlement rights south of the Ohio River. After the Revolution, in 1784, the second Treaty of Fort Stanwix was signed between the Iroquois and the Americans. This one said that much of the land north of the Ohio River was free to be settled. The catch to this agreement was that the

Iroquois were not living in the lands they had given away. The many tribes who did dwell and hunt upon them were not consulted about their sale and so never acknowledged the validity of the treaty.

As the Americans moved in, and attacks increased, more talks between the adversaries were held. One of the most noteworthy took place at Fort McIntosh. It was more of an announcement, rather than a discussion. The US representatives explained that their ownership of Ohio lands was a result of the British signing them over to them as part of the terms that ended the Revolution. As with the previous treaties, the other tribes of the region, who did not attend the talks, did not accept this premise.

In the summer of 1789, just a couple months after his inauguration, President Washington ordered the construction of a fortress to be built along the northern banks of the Ohio River. This was in the area that would soon grow to become Cincinnati. Construction was led by the then general, Josiah Harmar; who was likely the one to name it Fort Washington in honor of the president. Its initial purpose was to establish a permanent American presence along this important river. It also provided a site for incoming settlers to pause after their long journeys from the east, and become acclimated to their new wilderness surroundings. Their safety against any immediate Indian aggression was another of its critical functions.

It didn't take long, however, before the structure took on a much more significant military role; one that Washington surely had expected. Even after the fort's completion, the settlers of the Ohio Valley and regions northward were screaming louder and louder for a more significant number of troops to be on the scene. The Indian attacks were still prolific and Washington knew he had to adjust his plans.

Some diplomacy was attempted by the then governor of the Northwest Territory, Arthur St. Clair. In early 1790, he sent offers to various Indian leaders to meet and discuss ways to resolve the situation; but he was generally rebuffed or ignored. With little success, St. Clair came to the conclusion that the attackers had to be attacked. As chief advisor to Washington on frontier activities, St. Clair wrote to the president reiterating that his motive for advising a military strike against the Indians was

> to chastise the Indian Nations who have of late been so troublesome

to the Frontier, of Virginia, and upon the Ohio River; and to impress proper Notions upon the others with respect to the United States. 1

During the last week of September 1790, per Washington's orders, some fifteen hundred men under the command of General Josiah Harmar began their move northward from Fort Washington. They were headed toward the Indian villages of the lower Great Lakes basin. This was the beginning of what many historians call "Washington's Indian War" – a series of three serious confrontations with the Native American tribes who had resisted American settlement of lands north of the Ohio River. Before the third battle had ended, the Indian forces had grown into a collective of more than a dozen tribes. The battles occurred between the years of 1790 and 1794, along and about the Wabash and Maumee Rivers, in today's Indiana and Ohio.

Over the course of world history, to gain an advantage over one's enemy, a warring party often employed a simple, time-tested technique — spying. This stratagem has expanded today to the point that almost every country on earth, even through times of peace, has such an organization of secret operations. Their designations more often use the term "intelligence" in their titles instead of the more crude expression of "spy." Movies have glorified some of the most prominent agencies like the CIA of the United States, the Mossad of Israel, and the MI6 of England. During Washington's Indian War of the Northwest, spying may not have had the technology of today's broad networks of espionage, but it was employed no less fervently at the scenes of battle.

The American spys were more often referred to as scouts, and though their purpose was to discern the position and future plans of the enemy, they were charged with additional strategic duties. Perhaps the best word to explain their overall objective is "reconnoiter." They were to inspect the land as well as those about it; especially those who were of a less than friendly disposition. Much of the land traversed by Harmar's men during their first episode of conflict was a wilderness with which they were unfamiliar. Geographical features and potential obstacles to their travel needed to be brought to the commander's attention before those areas were reached. With the knowledge of what was ahead, they could then determine if they should plot a new course

Portrait of Arthur St. Clair. Engraving by Edward Wellmore.

or confidently continue on an established route. A few of the natural hinderances that often had to be reckoned with were creeks or streams that were too wide or too deep to forge. Sometimes broad patches of marshlands and swamps would not allow equipment or men to move through. Even established enemy villages or camps were frequently discovered where they were not expected.

Before Harmar's troops moved out of Fort Washington, the scouts had already been days on their way to secure the course ahead of them. Ultimately, the American force was headed to Kekionga, at today's Fort Wayne, Indiana. It was this expansive Indian village which was known to be the primary base for the Indian resistance. Unfortunately, the names of most of the men employed as scouts or spies in this first effort, as well as those in the rest of Washington's Indian War, are lost to history. A few, however, have survived; and what we know of their actions has luckily been, at least sketchily, recorded.

In one documented instance, about ten days into the journey of Harmar's troops toward Kekionga, the spies reported back that they had discovered an ominous sign. In a clearing a short distance ahead, they had found chunks of bear meat purposefully displayed on numerous, scattered tree stumps. This was recognized by the scouts to be a deliberate warning left by the enemy with the intention of scaring the Americans off once they realized that they were being watched. And they were being watched. Further evidence of the enemy's presence came from repeated random thefts of some of the American's pack horses. These animals were mostly laden with supplies and had brought up the rear of troops' march. While feeding in the evenings, they were frequently snatched away either singly or in groups by Indians who were obviously following alongside through the surrounding woods.

In another instance, as the troops had progressed northward, a few of the scouts had come upon several Indians uncharacteristically wandering through the woods. They managed to kill all but one of them. Then, through interrogation of that lone, detained captive it was learned that though the residents of Kekionga had initially planned to defend their village from the impending attack of Harmar, they had recently changed their strategy and opted to burn the village down themselves and retreat elsewhere.

As a result of this disclosure by the captive Indian, Harmar decided to forego any delays and immediately head for their destination so he could dispense of anyone who may be lingering there about. When they arrived, the grounds were still smoldering and no residents were in sight. The men plundered what goods they could find, and further destroyed any structures and crops the Indians had left standing.

A few days later Harmar sent out a detachment of three hundred men to canvass the broader, outlying region of Kekionga for the Indians who had deserted the village. The force acted as a large patrol of scouts. Unfortunately, the only intelligence they gleaned for all their effort had come from an old Frenchman who they happened to cross paths with during their search. This man shared that the Indians were still lingering en masse in the area, but he did not know exactly where. When Harmar received this report, he immediately sent out yet another larger than normal scouting party of forty men under Colonel James Trotter to find that Indian force; but they too returned with no precise information of where the Indians had secluded themselves.

Harmar was beside himself with frustration over not being able to find the tribal coalition. He decided to give the search a third try. A few hundred militia men under Colonel John Hardin were sent out. Finally, they had some success. Major John Fontaine, with a handful of scouts who ran ahead of Hardin's troops, reported back to him that the Indians were sighted and seemed to still be in a full retreat. Hardin moved out quickly in pursuit. It wasn't long, however, before the troops discovered that the Indian retreat had been a ruse. The Americans had been led into a trap and were suddenly being ambushed from several directions. Heavy casualties were suffered before the troops could make a successful retreat. While the entire campaign of 1790 became known as Harmar's Defeat, this episode was similarly labeled as Hardin's Defeat.

From the outset, Harmar had been tasked with disabling the Indian's capability of executing any further attacks on American settlers. That order did not mean that he was required to take the lives of the warriors themselves through battle. In truth, he essentially was ordered to send a message of the Americans' capability to inflict serious pain on the Indians should they continue their harassment on the frontier.

After the trouncing of Hardin's men, Harmar refocused on this main objective. He proceeded to burn down and destroy the crops of several more of the nearby Indian villages. The devastation would seriously jeopardize the Indians' attempts to survive in the area. While these smaller villages were being ravaged, two Indians were spotted watching from the woods. Though they were not approached, it warned Harmar that the Indians were still spying on them as well.

Feeling that he had done a reasonably good job of fulfilling his duty, Harmar ordered the men to begin gathering up the supplies and to prepare for the march back to Fort Washington. He surmised that the destruction of several villages, especially Kekionga, in spite of the men he had lost, had given him the right to consider the mission as accomplished. But it wasn't over just yet. Another group of scouts led by a man named Daniel Williams came back into the camp the evening that they were packing up. His report stirred Harmar and the men. Williams had discovered that over a hundred Indians had returned to Kekionga. The temptation to take vengence for the deaths of Hardin's men was too hard to resist. Harmar decided to send yet another set of troops back to the Indian village. This time, unfortunately, the scouting

Portrait of Josiah Harmar.
A photographic reproduction of an engraving by John Sartain
based on a painting by Raphael Peale circa 1790-1799.

report was not as thorough as had been assumed.

Companies of regulars and militia headed to Kekionga in separate detachments, each targeting a different side of the village. It was hoped that they could surround and surprise the returned inhabitants in much the same way that Hardin's men had been. When they arrived, fighting broke out in various locations around the site. Many of the engagements were hand-to-hand, but the fighting didn't last long. The Indians surprisingly began to retreat. Believing that they could easily be chased down, the Americans pursued. Before they knew it, the troops discovered themselves in the middle of a sprawling, open patch of flattened, drying cornstalks. They had just been purposefully led into another Indian trap. Ironically, the Americans were in the very cornfield that they had earlier leveled; leaving nothing to shield themselves from the bullets that were now flying toward them from the Indian guns encircling them. The Native Americans had masterfully executed their strategic plan. The few who escaped scrambled back to Harmar's base camp, thoroughly shaken by the experience.

Soon, the troops made their way back to Fort Washington. In spite of the dreadful ambushes that took so many lives, General Harmar claimed that his campaign had been a great success. He had hung his hat on the fact that Kekionga and several other Indian villages were now out of commission. However, the series of confrontations that were had under his general command also resulted in nearly two hundred men killed or wounded. Horrific stories told by the survivors to government leaders and to the general public presented the true toll of what had transpired. Their gruesome accounts of the fighting far overshadowed the successful destruction of property cited by Harmar.

Though intimidation was the goal of this campaign, which in-turn was supposed to stop the Indians from pursuing future raids on settlers' homes, that was not the result. In fact, the effect was just the opposite. The sloppy performance of the Americans during the fights near Kekionga only emboldened the Indians.

There were several factors contributing to the poor results of Harmar's campaign. One that received some attention was the drinking habits of Harmar himself. Government authorities were apparently aware of some of his previous indulgences and had warned him to not let it affect the mission. Afterwards, some men alluded, but never proved, that his intoxication was a contributing factor to the defeat.

Another issue of the day was the lingering tension between the Americans and the British. It was only seven years since the Revolution had ended, and contrary to the terms of the treaty ending that conflict, the British were maintaining a fortress at Detroit and were trading with the Indians of Kekionga and other tribes along the entire Maumee River Valley. It was for the profits from trade with the Indians that the British had maintained their presence at Detroit and elsewhere. In this frontier location they were distant from the states, and so they were confident that they could abide there safely; unchallenged by the Americans. They were correct. It was only now, as the recent American settlements in the wilderness began to increase in the Ohio Valley, that their illegal presence and business dealings with the Indians were potentially threatened.

There was an underlying fear before this action by Harmar was undertaken that it might anger and nudge the British toward another major war. Afterall, the Americans were heading toward an attack on the key Indian trading partners of the British at their primary exchange post. At least that's how Governor St. Clair saw it. In fact he was so concerned that he sent a messenger to the British alerting them that this strike by Harmar was in the offing. Along with the apprisal was a request that the British keep this information under their tall, cylindrical hats. The move was incredibly naive. The Indians were, of course, promptly tipped off by the British. That is why Kekionga and other nearby villages had been abandoned and partially destroyed before Harmar had arrived.

Perhaps the most significant factor affecting the disastrous performance of the American forces in Harmar's effort was that they were not a trained military. As the country got off the ground, the Confederation Congress viewed the defense of the country as something to be handled by the militia of each state, who would be called into action only if and when they were needed. The regular army was purposely small; less than a thousand trained soldiers. There was little money to support a standing army. This is why a call for additional volunteers and militia was made to serve in the Harmar campaign.

Unfortunately, the respondents were less than qualified to fight. Most had very little training in military affairs, if any. Several showed up with rifles, muskets, and pistols that were in such disrepair that they were unable to be fired. Some had no weapons at all. A good number of these men had been living in extreme poverty and simply came on board for the free food and clothing. A few deserted once they had acquired some garments and a few good meals. Though payment for their service may have been an inducement to sign on as well, even that had failed. None of the troops were paid through the entire year of 1790. The term rag-tag was often applied to this volunteer portion of the force, and rightly so.

Though few in number, the trained soldiers despised this militia. They viewed them as disorganized, undisciplined, and unskilled marksmen. The only exceptions were the Kentuckians who signed on later in the war. Those men living south of the Ohio River were generally acclaimed for their skills with a gun, even on horseback. Officers, as well as the regulars, held the militia in contempt for their unruliness and disregard for authority. Although the militia may have had some appreciation for the discipline that the officers and regular troops adhered to; they still viewed most of them as pompous and arrogant. When these underlying adversarial attitudes were added to the mix of an already life-and-death situation, even desertion became an enticing option to many.

With so much disorder, inexperience, and lack of foresight, it is no wonder Harmar's campaign had such disastrous results.

It was just a few weeks after Harmar and his survivors had returned to Fort Washington that President Washington addressed Congress and in due course noted that

It has been heretofore known to Congress, that frequent incursions have been made on our frontier settlements by certain banditti of Indians from the northwest side of the Ohio. These, with some of the tribes dwelling on and near the Wabash, have of late been particularly active in their depredations; and, being emboldened by the impunity of their crimes, and aided by such parts of the neighboring tribes as could be seduced to join in their hostilities or afford them a retreat for their prisoners and plunder, they have, instead of listening to the humane invitations and overtures made on the part of the United States, renewed their violences with fresh alacrity and greater effect. The lives of a number of valuable citizens have thus been sacrificed and some of them under circumstances peculiarly shocking, whilst others have been carried into a deplorable captivity.

> These aggravated provocations rendered it essential to the safety of the western settlements, that the aggressors should be made sensible, that the government of the Union is not less capable of punishing their crimes, than it is disposed to respect their rights and reward their attachments. [2]

The language was strong enough to lay the groundwork for planning another campaign into the Wabash and Maumee River Valleys. Unfortunately, the problems from within that had debilitated the efforts of Harmar were still not addressed. Undisciplined militia, regulars insufficiently trained in Indian warfare techniques, internal dissension and disorder, as well as many others issues remained. Regardless, the need to provide a safe environment for the settlers on the frontier was the primary objective. It was as much a political and financial requirement as it was a practical one of saving lives. The United States desperately needed the money from sales of frontier property and the Indian threat was seriously impeding that revenue stream. And to be fair, the lands being sold were, on paper, owned by the United States, per the tribes who signed the treaties. The objecting tribes made another battle inevitable.

Before such an engagement would take place, talks were held on several fronts to negotiate a peace; but none produced any tangible results. It bears repeating that the stated strategy of the government was to put on such a display of strength that the resistant Indian tribes would almost beg for peace. Washington did not want to militarily wipe them out. In fact, at this point in time he had introduced what became known as his "civilizing" program, which enticed the Indians to assimilate into the American culture by accepting the concept of private property ownership as well as animal and crop farming. The idea took root with some of the older generation, but not in large numbers until a few more years had passed. The younger generation adamantly resisted any such proposal.

With little progress made in the peace talks, the frequency of raids escalated all along the Ohio River. The death count rose on both sides of the fight. The assaults were not all initiated by the Indians. Settlers were known to attack Indians as well. One can imagine how tensions and frustrations remained high as vengence was sought for previous confrontations.

One incident, though not deadly, ruined what was a nugget of progress that had been made with some members of the Iroquois nation. The leader of the Seneca tribe, Cornplanter, had just completed months of friendly talks with American officials in Philadelphia, when on his way back to his village he was stopped by a rogue band of Pennsylvania militia men. Under the threat of being shot, the frontiersmen confiscated a literal boat-load of goods that Cornplanter was transporting back to his village — canoes laden with gifts given to him by the US government for his willingness to act as a mediator with the confrontational tribes northwest of the Ohio River. Cornplanter's allegiance to the US was shaken by the incident. It was one of many blows to the ongoing peace efforts.

The successor to General Harmar, as commander of the US Army, was the already heavily involved governor of the Northwest Territory, Arthur St. Clair. By the autumn of 1791, he would be leading the second major offensive into the Maumee River Valley. But before launching the main thrust of the assault, which was set for October, a preliminary confrontation with the Indians was planned for springtime. Many of the settlers throughout the Ohio River Valley could not wait to avenge the recent and ongoing attacks across the region. They were living in such constant fear that many had made, or were at least contemplating, a move back east. Others huddled together for a little safety in numbers, albeit an uncomfortable stratagem for most. Rants against the government for its continuing lack of substantial military protection of the frontier people were increasing each day.

St. Clair secured the services of Brigadier-General Charles Scott from the Kentucky lands for his first raid on the Indians. In late May of 1791, Scott led roughly a thousand-man militia northward to the cheers of the frontier families. Word of the troops movement came to the Indian leaders from their scouts who had been hiding in the woods north of Fort Washington. After successfully capturing and interrogating an American, these Indian spies reported to their leaders that Scott's large force was on its way. However, their assumption that the Americans were on their way to Kekionga, as Harmar had done the year previous, was incorrect.

A massive Indian force, drawing warriors from far away villages, formed at Kekionga. There they waited for Scott's approach and a major conflict. After the fact, they were told that halfway into his march, Scott had made an abrupt turn from the route Harmar had taken. He was headed to the Wabash and Eel River region near today's Lafayette, Indiana; not Kekionga. This was the area where Tecumseh and his brother would establish Prophetstown some twenty years later. However, this day, Scott found mostly deserted villages because the resident warriors had all headed nearly a hundred miles away to do their part in the predicted fight at Kekionga. Scott, as was planned, proceeded to destroy any structures and crops in the Wea village of Ouiatanonas and a few other small Indian sites in the area. His actions were intended to show the capability of US forces to reach even the tribes living in these more remote locations.

With this initial success, St. Clair decided to send out a second company to the Wabash region just two months later. This time the troops were under the command of another brigadier-general, James Wilkinson. He proceeded about fifty miles further up the Wabash River from where Scott had done his damage. And, he too accomplished his mission; successfully destroying the Miami village of L'Anguille. Though more tribes were becoming involved in the resistance effort, they were still mistakenly on guard at Kekionga. When the actions of Wilkinson were learned, the Indian leaders were in some disagreement about what to do next. The attacks by the Americans had caused both concern and dissension among them. Some wanted to seek peace, some sought vengence.

Faced with the challenging logistics of feeding and caring for their swollen force which was now standing ready at Kekionga, the Native Americans found themselves in need of more extensive aid from the British. They were especially in want of food and arms due to the devastation of their crops and the inevitable battle with the Americans on the horizon. Even Joseph Brant of the Mohawks in the Iroquois nation asked the British to play a larger part in the frontier conflicts by recommending that a fortress be built at the rapids of the Maumee River, in today's Maumee, Ohio, just south of Toledo. It was reasoned that a post there would be an impediment to Americans who might try to get to Detroit. Perhaps even more important to the Indians was that such a permanent presence would make a much more accessible food and weapon depot for the tribes living in the vicinity. The fortress was built, but not for another two years. At this point in time, circa 1791, the British aid was still being handled with discretion. In fact the British themselves walked a fine line between the Indians and the Americans. They tried to persuade the Indians toward peace with the Americans. The king did not want another war so soon after the last one had ended. All the British desired was for the profits from their trade with these Indians to not be impeded.

It wouldn't be too much longer before the two large opposing forces would finally meet. Each side had grown to over a thousand men by the time of the climactic event on November 4, 1791. Over the autumn months leading up to it, as the US troops slowly progressed northward, the old, internal dissension had again become a distraction. Everything, from the bad weather, to sparse food, to disease, to poor equipment, to whatever, had all come together to sour the disposition of nearly everyone in camp. Militia were close to calling for a mutiny and the regulars despised them for it. Officers had lost almost all

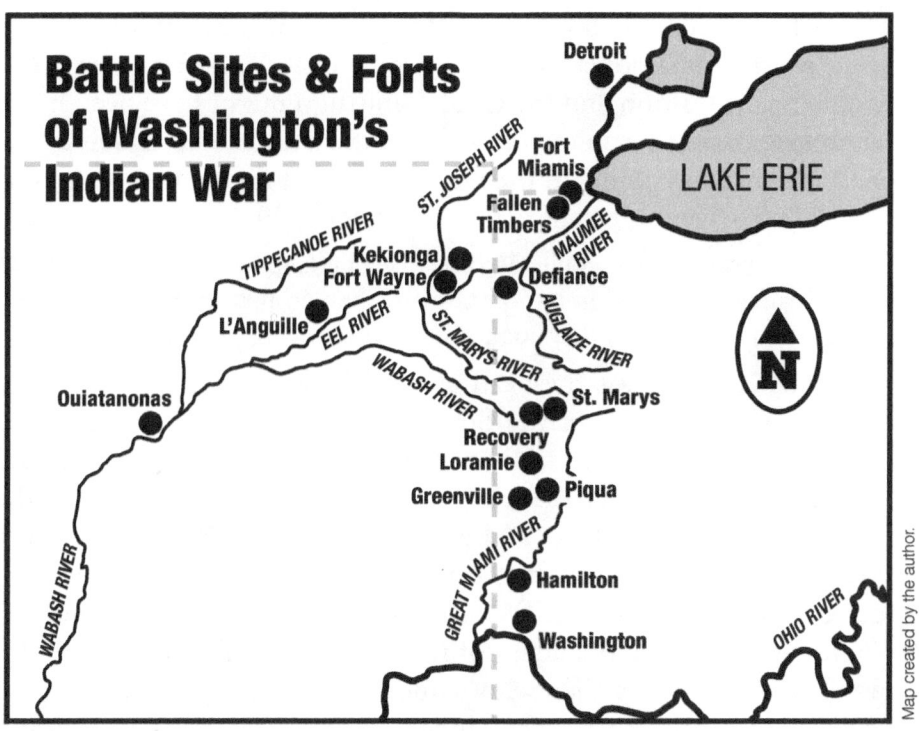

control. Even the horses were not being cared for properly. Nearly a hundred were lost because they were repeatedly set in the woods without being properly hobbled or otherwise secured. Some of the horses injured each other while fighting for food that was improperly strewn about the ground.

The situation was coming to a head, and even some sobering disciplinary actions taken by St. Clair did not seem to eleviate the problems. From a letter of the general to the Secretary of War, Henry Knox, we learn that on October 23

> ...two men taken in the act of deserting to the enemy, and one for shooting another soldier and threatening to kill an officer, were hanged upon the grand parade, the whole army being drawn out. Since the army has halted, the country around this, and ahead for fifteen miles, has been well examined. It is a country which, had we arrived a month sooner in it, and with three times the number of animals, they would have been all fat now. [3]

The latter comment sarcastically referred to the many delays that the troops had endured before getting adequate food and provisions from the government suppliers. Had they come in the timeframe expected, the men's disposition and the whole campaign might have been much improved. St. Clair also mentioned that the land had been well examined which again points to the fact that at least the scouts were doing their job. He went on to note that on October 29

> Piamingo and his people, accompanied by Captain Sparks and four good riflemen, [were] going on a scout; they do not propose to return under ten days, unless they sooner succeed in taking prisoners.[4]

Chief Piamingo was the head of the Chickasaw tribe that lived in the Mississippi region of the South. He was a trusted friend of the Americans and his appearance at this time bore that out. His arrival also highlights the fact that certain tribes were in the corner of the United States at this time and even worked as spies for their white neighbors. Piamingo and his sect of Chickasaws were at odds with the Creeks and Cherokee. Tribes living in his region of the southern wilderness were in a quandary of who to seek out for aid. The choice was between the Spanish, who while based in the Louisiana region still had eyes on securing the lands of Kentucky; or the Americans, who were just starting to spread their wings westward. Piamingo chose the US.

On his scouting foray, Piamingo was joined by several other Indians and Americans. One of those among the Americans was Colonel Richard Sparks, a white man who had been kidnapped by the Shawnee when he was but a toddler. Perhaps the most intriguing part of his story is that the person who adopted him into the Shawnee way of life was a leader known as Pukeshinwa, the father of Tecumseh and the Prophet. Sparks grew up with the soon to be famous brothers.

In his late teens or early twenties, Sparks was returned to his white roots as a result of the terms that had established for the exchange of captives after the Battle of Point Pleasant in 1774. In that confrontation, his adopted father, Pukeshinwa, was killed. Against all odds, after the swapping of captives, Sparks had found and returned to life with his biological mother. He went on to serve in the US military for several decades until the end of the War of 1812. He even fought alongside Colonel Crawford during his attacks on the Wyandot and Delaware, for which Crawford famously suffered a horrific death.

Sparks' upbringing in the Indian ways of fighting, hunting, tracking, etc., made him a perfect scout. These same traits became highly sought after on the resumes of the men being recruited as scouts in the future. Ironically, through the battles of Washington's Indian War, Sparks would end up fighting against the very Shawnee tribesmen he had been raised by. This included his step-brother, Tecumseh, who had taught him most of his skills. In 1815, in his mid-sixties, Sparks was honorably discharged. He had made a lifetime career of military service and resented being released. He was certain that he still had a lot to offer. So distraught was his soul, that he passed away a mere two weeks afterwards.

An entry in the diary of Colonel Winthrop Sargent, the Adjunct General of the Army, notes the arrival and the attitude of the "Mountain Leader," as Piamingo was known, two days before his group left the US camp.

> The twenty Chickasaw Indians mentioned to have been at Fort Washington arrived in camp this day [October 27], Piamingo, who is now their king, with Colbert and some other character of distinction, are among the number. These people have the most inveterate animosity to all the Indian tribes northwest of the Ohio, but most particularly to the Kickapoos, and have been at war with the whole of them from time immemorial.⁵

Piamingo was well known and much admired by the Chickasaw and several tribes in the South. The main land route through Tennessee and Mississippi, and extending from the Ohio River Valley to the Louisiana Territory, was known as the Natchez Trace. However, before it bore that name, it was known as Mountain Leader Trace, testifying to Piamingo's celebrity. He had frequently traveled the road between tribal communities. During October of 1791, he was actually on his way to address Congress about some Chickasaw matters, but took a temporary detour. To show his good faith to President Washington, he opted to give a hands-on effort to the Americans in the field. He was persuaded to do so in part by his fellow Chickasaw leaders, George Colbert and his brother William, who wanted their own personal vengence on the tribes of the North. One of their brothers had been killed, and another wounded, by the bands now attacking the settlers. When Piamingo and his team had set out, it was on a mission to not

Statue of Piominko, leader of the Chickasaw from 1783-1799. Memorial is in front of the Chickasaw National Capitol Building; Tishomingo, OK.

Image of Colonel Richard Sparks who had been raised by the Shawnee through his youth, then had a lifetime of US military service.

only scout the area ahead, but to capture at least one enemy Indian and bring him back to St. Clair for questioning.

We learn from St. Clair's chief assistant, Major Ebenezer Denny, that while Piamingo's party was still making plans to go forth, the insubordination and unprofessionalism of the troops was again bubbling to the surface.

One of the sentries, which form the chain round the encampment, alarmed the troops last night [October 28] about nine o'clock, and put them all under arms. He imagined that he saw an Indian, and fired three times at some object. The First and Second regiment of regulars compose about one-third of the army, and although chiefly recruits, are tolerably well disciplined, but the remainder (excepting the few militia), being levies and raised but for six months, and their times expiring daily, they take great liberties. This morning there was a constant firing kept up round the camp, not withstanding it is known there is a general order against it; in fact, at present they are more troublesome and far inferior to the militia. [6]

The militia were the rowdy bunch; but Major Denny notes that the levies were becoming even more difficult to keep in line. The levies were an idea that was new to St. Clair's campaign. Because the militia were generally undisciplined, and Washington wanted a more massive force than Harmar had presented, the levies were men who were recruited to serve with the regulars, but only for a six-month stretch, and for a set pay. They were barely trained because after only a few weeks into their service, the fighting had begun; and no matter the situation, when their time was up they were heading home.

As it happened many of the levies were scheduled to leave over the first few days of November; coincidentally the time when a confrontation with the Indians seemed imminent. St. Clair was aware of the contract expirations and so he tried to put as much physical distance as possible between them and any secure fortress that the levies could retreat to. Longer forced marches took the troops several days deeper into the woodlands as their terms were expiring. St. Clair reasoned that the levies might think twice about heading back alone or in small groups while Indians lurked in the miles of wilderness between them and their home. As it happened, most of the levies were on hand when the assault began on November 4.

The words of Major Ebenezer Denny, St. Clair's aide-de-camp, are lengthy, but they are a raw, unscripted record of what he and the others experienced that historic Friday morning.

> 4th – ...The troops paraded this morning at the usual time, and had been dismissed from the lines but a few minutes, and the sun not yet up, when the woods in front rung with the yells and fire of the savages. The poor militia, who were but three hundreds yards in front, had scarcely time to return a shot — they fled into our camp. The troops were under arms in an instant, and a smart fire from the front line met the enemy. It was but a few minutes, however, until the men were engaged in every quarter. The enemy from the front filed off to the right and left, and completely surrounded the camp, killed and cut off nearly all the guards, and approached close to the lines. They advanced from one tree, log, or stump to another, under cover of the smoke of our fire. The artillery and musketry made a tremendous noise, but did little execution. The Indians seemed to brave every thing, and, when fairly fixed around us, they made no noise other than their fire, which they kept up very constant, and which seldom failed to tell, although scarcely heard.

Our left-flank, probably from the nature of the ground, gave way first; the enemy got possession of that part of the encampment, but, it being pretty clear ground, they were too much exposed, and were soon repulsed. Was at this time with the General engaged toward the right; he was on foot, and led the party himself that drove the enemy and regained our ground on the left. The battalions in the rear charged several times and forced the savages from their shelter, but they always turned with the battalions and fired upon them back; indeed, they seemed not to fear any thing we could do. They could skip out of reach of the bayonet, and return as they pleased. They were visible only when raised by a charge. The ground was literally covered with the dead. The wounded were taken to the center, where it was thought most safe, and where a great many who had quit their posts unhurt had crowded together. The General, with other officers, endeavored to rally these men, and twice they were taken out to the lines.

It appeared as if the officers had been singled out; a very great proportion fell, or were wounded, and obliged to retire from the lines early in the action. General Butler was among the latter, as well as several other of the most experienced officers. The men, being thus left with few officers, became fearful, despaired of success, gave up the fight, and, to save them selves for the moment, abandoned entirely their duty and ground, and crowded in toward the center of the field, and no exertions could put them in any order even for defense; perfectly ungovernable. The enemy at length got possession of the artillery, though not until the officers were all killed but one, and he badly wounded, and the men almost all cut off, and not until the pieces were spiked. As our lines were deserted the Indians contracted theirs until their shot centered from all points, and now, meeting with little opposition, took more deliberate aim and did great execution. Exposed to a cross fire, men and officers were seen falling in every direction; the distress, too, of the wounded made the scene such as can scarcely be conceived; a few minutes longer, and a retreat would have been impracticable.

The only hope left was, that perhaps the savages would be so taken up with the camp as not to follow, Delay was death; no preparation could be made; numbers of brave men must be left a sacrifice — there was no alternative. It was past nine o'clock, when repeated orders were given to charge toward the road. The action had continued between two and three hours. Both officers and men seemed confounded, incapable of doing any thing; they could not move until it was told that a retreat was intended. A few officers put themselves in front, the men followed, the enemy gave way, and perhaps not being aware of the design, we were for a few minutes left undisturbed. The stoutest and most active now took the lead, and those who were foremost in breaking the enemy's line were soon left behind. At the moment of the retreat, one of the few horses saved had been procured for the General; he was on foot until then; I kept by him, and he delayed to see the rear. The enemy soon discovered the movement and pursued, though not more than four or five miles, and but few so far; they turned to share the spoil...

...By this time the remains of the army had got somewhat compact, but in the most miserable and defenseless state. The wounded who came off left their arms in the field, and one-half of the others threw theirs away on the retreat. The road for miles was covered with firelocks, cartridge-boxes and regimentals. How fortunate that the pursuit was discontinued; a single Indian might have followed with safety upon either flank. Such a panic had seized the men, that I believe it would not have been possible to have brought any of them to engage again...

...The remnant of the army, with the first regiment, were now at Fort Jefferson, twenty-nine miles from the field of action, without provisions, and the former without having eaten any thing for twenty four hours. [7]

The survivors, one-third of the force that had started out, found little more than a physical wall of protection against the Indian force when they finally reached Fort Jefferson. Luckily, they were not pursued that far. As Denny cites, there were few supplies, and scarce food on hand. The wounded had to suffer without any medical help. Stragglers continued to show up well into the night. Eventually, those who managed to survive the days afterwards would get to Fort Washington and then home; but never to be the same. Nearly nine hundred people, including almost one hundred women who were camp followers, were killed in what is the largest defeat of Americans by the Native Americans in our history. That was more than three times the number who would be killed at Custer's Last Stand decades later.

The scouting team of Piamingo and company were almost a week into their venture when unbeknownst to them, the fury of warriors under the command of Little Turtle, the Miami chief, and Blue Jacket of the Shawnee, had been unleashed on St. Clair's men. Another entry in the diary of Colonel Sargent reports the outcome of Piamingo's expedition; given when they returned to camp a week after the battle on November 11.

> Piamingo, Colbert and the other Chickasaws, with the white people mentioned to have gone out from our Camp of the 29th ultimo, have returned with five scalps, having been twenty miles beyond the Miami Towns on the road to Detroit. Here they fell in with an Indian, who, mistaking them for friends, gave so vaunting an account of the late unfortunate Action and Defeat, that before he had completed his narrative they shot him through the body. He told them that they had but seven hundred warriors engaged, and that his "own arm was quite weary with tomahawking." [8]

For their service, all three of these Chickasaw leaders were later awarded silver medals by Washington. Piamingo and George Colbert continued on for many years as primary spokesmen for their tribe. William was honored with a commission in the American military as a major-general.

A few days after the battle, Denny noted in his diary:

> The prediction of General Harmar, before the army set out on the campaign, was founded upon his experience and particular knowledge of things. He saw with what material the bulk of the army was composed; men collected from the streets and prisons of the cities, hurried out into the enemy's country, and with the officers commanding them totally unacquainted with the business in which they were engaged; it was utterly impossible they could be otherwise. Besides, not any one department was sufficiently prepared; both quartermaster and contractors extremely deficient. It was a matter of astonishment to him that the commanding general, who was acknowledged to be perfectly competent, should think of hazarding, with such people, and under such circumstances, his reputation and life, and the lives of so many others, knowing, too, as both did, the enemy with whom he was going to contend; an enemy brought up from infancy to war, and perhaps superior to an equal number of the best men that could be taken against them. [9]

Like salt in a wound, the defeat stung the Americans, dearly. The final stroke of this tragic scene is related by an early historian:

> Very few escaped the carnage of the 4th of November, and after the flight of the remnant of the army, the Indians began to avenge their own real and imaginary wrongs by perpetrating the most horrible acts of cruelty and brutality upon the bodies of the living and the dead Americans who fell into their hands. Believing that the whites, for many years, made war merely to acquire land, the Indians crammed clay and sand into the

eyes and down the throats of the dying and the dead.[10]

The war was not over.

Before another confrontation occurred, both sides stepped back to take stock of their situations. It was a new and somewhat complex footing on which the Indians found themselves. They had just been victorious. Not that they hadn't had success in the past, but this time it was different. They had beat down a huge American force and only lost a relatively small number of their own men in the process. The question that now presented itself before the coalition of area tribes was whether to strike again, and if so, when? Or, should they use their current display of power to negotiate from their perceived advantage for terms of peace. Ironically, this would be the exact leverage the Americans had been striving to attain.

One of the earliest councils to be held over the matter took place just a few weeks after the defeat of St. Clair. Numerous tribal leaders met at a spot overlooking the Ottawa River, near present-day Lima, Ohio. The guests were of varied opinions on how to proceed. At length, one of the elder war chiefs of the Ottawa rose and offered his perspective for continuing the fight.

> Chiefs, warriors, and friends, listen –
>
> This is the proper time, whilst your tomahawks are lying on the ground, and whilst you are smoking your pipes with composure, to talk over the business before you; whether to offer peace to your elder brethren of the United States; or, whether to wait until they propose it to you? This is the question now before you; and it merits your serious attention…
>
> …I am of the opinion, (as I believe every warrior present is, for what I say is at their request), you ought not to give peace to your enemy until they ask it, or until they first retire out of your country: nor ought you to give them peace, nor listen to any proposition from them, whilst that cloud in the east shall be held over your country, should it advance into it! But let us adhere to the maxims of our wise ancestors, never to meet around the council fire with my nation, tomahawk in hand. So sure as you consent to alot the armies of your enemy, in your own country, to talk of peace, so surely will you repent of it! Our wise ancestors have cautioned us against such foolish conduct! Our wise men have always told us, never to treat of peace with an enemy advancing and holding

his tomahawk over our heads! It is not a time then to talk, or to think of peace! That is only a time to act like men and as warriors! [11]

Countering this opinion, another chief rose and argued:

I hope you will excuse me, when I tell you, that all the injuries and injustice imposed upon you by the United States, were they, if possible, tenfold more iniquitous, will not add to your strength, nor lessen the numbers or the power of your oppressors: compared to them, your numbers are so few, that were you to lose one warrior for each hundred you may destroy of theirs, they would in time extirpate you from your country; and fill it by the influx which has already astonished you...

...Were your numbers ten times greater than they are, you would not be equal to the contest you have entered into: it is true that whenever you attack double, or treble, the number of your enemy, you can beat them; but what avails it to destroy an hundred of them, when you see ten hundred immediately arise like locusts from the earth! And, let me tell you, that you possibly beat your enemy until you teach him your own manner of warfare – What then will be the consequence? Think of it, I beseech you! [12]

This council discussion ended without any of the participants coming to an agreement and thus led to further councils being held over the next year. Physical deprivations from disease and poor crops added to the uncertainty of the Indian condition. The Miamis and a few other tribes, decided to abandon Kekionga and moved to the Maumee River Valley, near today's Defiance, Ohio. There they were nearer to the other tribes with whom they were allied and in closer proximity to the British stores of goods which they were so direly in need of. The area became the new headquarters for the gathering tribal force. It was known as "The Grand Glaize," so named by earlier French traders who noticed the high clay banks of the river flowing into the Maumee River at this point. "Glaize" being the French word for clay, the tributary was christened the AuGlaize, or "at the clay."

Like the Indians, the Americans were in a flux as well. Washington was beside himself in anger at the defeat handed to St. Clair. He knew that the frontier families could not continue to live on the defensive. Along with other government leaders, he came to the realization that they were in an all out war whether they liked it or not. That meant that a much more calculated effort and a real army was going to be essential to bring an end to it. By late December, just six weeks after the battle, such a proposal was presented to Congress. It first outlined how the country got to this point in their relations with the Indians, and then went into what was required to resolve the situation. The conclusion was:

...Hence, it will appear that an Indian war, of considerable extent, has been excited, not only contrary to the interests and intention of the General Government, but by means altogether without its control.

That it is in the public interest to terminate this disagreeable war, as speedily as possible, cannot be doubted; and it will be important to devise and execute the best means to effect that end. That, upon due deliberation, it will appear that it is by an ample conviction of our superior force only, that the Indians can be brought to listen to the dictates of peace, which have been sincerely and repeatedly offered to them. The pride of victory is too strong at the present for them to receive the offers of peace on reasonable terms. They would probably insist upon a relinquishment of territory, to which they have no just claim, and which has been confirmed by the several before recited treaties...

...Hence, it would appear, that the principles of justice as well as policy, and, it may be added, the principles of economy, all combine to dictate, that an adequate military force should be raised as soon as possible, placed upon the frontiers, and disciplined according to the nature of the service, in order to meet, with a prospect of success, the greatest probable combination of the Indian enemy...

...That the military establishment of the United States shall, during the pleasure of Congress, consist of five thousand one hundred and sixty-eight non-commissioned officers, privates, and musicians.

That the said non-commissioned officers and privates shall be enlisted to serve three years, unless sooner discharged...

...That in addition to the foregoing arrangement, it would be proper that the President of the United States should be authorized, besides the employment of militia, to take measures, for the defensive protection of the exposed parts of the frontiers, by calling into service expert woodsmen, as patrols or scouts, upon such terms as he may judge proper...[13]

Leaders in Congress argued over the entire situation for months; but by March the proposal was signed into law and the military numbers and discipline issues were finally going to be addressed.

With a substantial army on the brink of formation, Washington continued to attempt diplomacy, as is evidenced in a speech given a month later to all the tribes of the northwest region through Henry

Knox, the Secretary of War. In part, it read:

> Brothers,
>
> The President of the United States entertains the opinion, that the War which exists is founded in error, and mistake on your part. That you believe the United States want to deprive you of your Lands, and drive you out of the Country. Be assured, this is not so – On the contrary that we should be greatly gratified with the opportunity of imparting to you all the blessings of civilized life, of teaching you to cultivate the earth and raise Corn, to raise Oxen sheep and other domestic animals, to build comfortable houses and to educate your children, so as ever to dwell upon the Land.
>
> Brothers,
>
> The President of the United States requests you to take this subject into your serious consideration, and to reflect how abundantly more it will be for your Interest, to be at peace with the United States, and to receive all the benefits thereof, than to continue a war, which however flattering it may be to you for a moment, must in the end prove ruinous. [14]

This speech presents evidence that Washington had reached out with his so-called "civilizing" program as a means of creating coexistence without warfare. In reality it only created more internal strife among the Indians who were already indecisive about what to do next. They also sought aid and advice from the British.

While talks continued for months, the Americans began to rebuild their forces. Anthony Wayne, a hero of the Revolution, was chosen by Washington to recruit and train the new military. He took the job very serious and in the end became the perfect choice because of his strict disciplinarian attitude. Composure, obedience, and training were qualities that were in dreadfully short supply in the previous troops.

Over the next two years, from St. Clair's defeat in late 1791 through late 1793, the Indian attacks on the frontier hadn't stopped, but were far less frequent. During this period, the practice of using spys to garner information about the enemy's plans was being taken to a new level – by both sides.

The Indians sent runners regularly to see what Wayne and his men were up to. They would report back to the chiefs at the Glaize on whatever they had discovered, be it troop movements, the building of new fortresses, or overheard plans of a future attack. They found their fair share of stragglers who had deserted the American cause or who happened to be hunting or tending horses too far from the main camps. Obviously, the idea of bringing in an enemy as a captive for questioning was loved by both sides in this fight. And, it's worth noting that the British worked on some of these scouting missions with the Indians so their officers were always kept abreast of the Americans' position.

Within weeks of Knox having suggested the need for "expert woodsmen, as patrols or scouts," the American authorities were finding and employing them. As early as January 1792, a fur trader and explorer named Peter Pond was hired to do some secret surveillance of the Indians who were still living near British posts at both the far western, and the distant eastern, shores of Lake Erie – Detroit and Niagara. Another scout by the name of William Steedman was to accompany Pond. All that is known of Steedman's background comes from Pond himself who noted that he was "a land jobber, a politician, and a historian." [15] Pond on the contrary is known to have had a somewhat storied history. He was just the kind of man the army needed as a spy.

The men chosen as scouts had to possess more extreme character traits in the sense of being rougher, tougher, and more seasoned than the ordinary enlisted man. The American authorities now demanded it. Frequently, men who had previous trade experience with the Indians were solicited. Even more often, men who had been kidnapped and raised with Indians until they had made their escapes were sought out. These former captives had an understanding of the enemy that ran deep. All the scouts needed to have a strong grasp of the Indian ways and be able to communicate with them. Further, they had to have a good knowledge of the landscape, be self-sufficient, adventurous, and brave.

Pond in particular was aggressive and energetic in all his affairs. He had travelled, explored, and hunted the sparsely populated regions of western Canada and even had the skill to map uncharted river systems. He also had some nefarious events occur during his time up north. Some people held him in suspicion of murdering two men on two separate occasions; but no convictions occurred. Due in part to his alleged crimes, as well as business dealings that had soured, he had returned to his homeland of the United States just a couple years before he was hand-picked for this scouting expedition.

The mission of the two spys was to infiltrate the Indian and British camps under the guise of wanting to trade with the Indians. This was no stretch for Pond because he had been doing just that for a good portion of his life. The only difference for him was that most of his earlier dealings were with tribes in northwest Canada. It's assumed Steedman had to stretch his acting talents a bit, but if he was all that Pond said he was, than he had to of been knowledgeable of the territory and an astute observer of people. Once taken into the Indian communities, the two spies were to glean information from the inhabitants as to the nature and timing of future assaults against the Americans, the general attitude of the tribes toward the alliance that they had formed, and the extent of the British influence.

The scouting mission was ordered by Knox himself. An excerpt of his instructions to the two hired spies reads:

> This war is irksome to the President and General Government, as well as to the people, generally, of the United States. It has, however, been brought on by events which the government could not control.
>
> We wish to be at peace with those Indians – to be their friends and protectors – to perpetuate them on the land.
>
> The desire, therefore, that we have peace, must not be inconsistent with the national reputation. We cannot ask the Indians to make peace with us, considering them as the aggressors: but they must ask a peace of us. To persuade them to this effect is the object of your mission…
>
> …While among the Indians, or at Niagara, or Detroit, endeavor to find out the numbers and tribes of the Indians who were in the attack of General St. Clair, and their loss killed and wounded; what number of prisoners they took, and what they did with them; what disposition they made of the cannon taken, arms, tents, and other plunder; what are their intentions for the next year; the numbers of the association; how they are supplied with arms, ammunition, and provisions. [16]

Beyond the intelligence gathering, the pair of men was supposed to try and nonchalantly drop innuendos, based on overtures that they had supposedly heard from varied sources, that the Americans were open to working toward a friendly relationship with the Indians. The men did all they could toward their goal, but after a short time in the camp at Niagara, they were viewed suspiciously by the British authorities. It was there that Pond and Steedman were turned away and their progress halted.

Efforts like this continued through 1792. Individuals or groups of men were sent to various tribes on the Wabash, Maumee, Sandusky and other rivers where the northwestern tribes were settled. Some of the men approached the Indians as the messengers or diplomats which they truly were, while others were much more covert in their affairs.

Brigadier-General Wilkinson, while at Fort Washington, was ordered by Knox to informally send out another set of scouts to the Indians to follow up on Pond and Steedman's attempt. The Americans wanted the Indians to come to the fort for peace talks. Restless for results, Knox decided to take a more direct approach. This time he sent an official representative of the government with a document endorsed by the president, as a request for a meeting. Captain Alexander Trueman was the officer given this mission and he went in full military attire with two other men to request the meeting. Even another pair of officers, one of whom was Colonel Hardin who had fought with Harmar two years previous, were sent out separately with peace overtures. All these attempts failed. All these men were killed.

A private in the US troops by the name of William May, was the next man to be called upon to perform some daring service. Again, it would be a spy mission. May was a bit of a rogue soldier. With two friends, he had tried to desert during the disastrous defeat of St. Clair the year previous, but was caught. His buddies received the penalty of death, but May was spared, at least for the moment. Wilkinson offered the young man only a potential death sentence. Ironically, May was now going to be ordered by his superior officer to desert! May must have had some expertise as a woodsman and knowledge of the Indian culture which caused Wilkinson to offer him such an option. As part of a scheme to once again extract information from the Indians about their plans and to learn the fate of the previously sent envoys, May was to assume this role of a deserter. In so doing, he was supposed to win the confidence of the Indians. He was at Fort Hamilton when this plan was hatched. A letter from Wilkinson to the commander of that fort in April of 1792 explains the plan, and also highlights the real dangers involved in the art of scouting at this time.

> ...You must order William May to desert in a day or two, or must cover his departure by putting him in a way to be taken prisoner – as you deem best. I consider the first preferable in one point of view; that is, it

would guard him effectually against any real desertion which may hereafter take place. It will be exceedingly difficult, if not impracticable, for him ever to make a second trip with success. However, that will depend, in a great measure, upon the fertility of his own genius.

He should cross the Miami at or near your post, and keep a due north course – remarking critically, the distance, ground, and watercourses over which he may pass, until he strikes the St. Mary's, the site of the old Miami village, and the first town. His first business will be to find out what has become of my messengers. If they have been received and well treated, he may authenticate the sincerity and good faith which has prescribed their journey. For this purpose, he must be made acquainted with the departure of the messengers, and the order restraining offensive hostilities. But if they have been killed, or made prisoners, and the enemy positively refuse to treat, then, so soon as he clearly ascertains these facts, he must return to us, by the nearest and safest route. If this occasion should not present, he is to continue with the enemy – and is, at all events, to acquire their confidence. To this end, he must shave his head – assume their dress – adopt their habits and manners – and always be ready for the hunt, or for war. His greatest object, during his residence with the enemy, will be to find out the names of the nations which compose the confederacy now at war, – their numbers, and the situation of their respective towns, as to course and distance from the old Miami village, and the loyalty of each. He will discover the names, residence, interests, and influence of all the white men now connected with those savages; and whether the British stimulate, aid, or abet them, and in what manner – whether openly, by the servants of the government, or indirectly, by traders. He will labor to develop what are the general determinations of the savages, in case the war is continued, and we gain possession of their country. Having made himself master of these points, or as far as may be practicable, he will embrace the first important occasion to come in to us. Such will be the moment when the enemy collectively take the field and advance against our army, or a detachment of it, and have approached it within a day's march.

Should he execute this mission with integrity and effect, I pledge myself to restore him to his country, and will use my endeavors to get him some little establishment, to make his old age comfortable. [17]

William May set out as ordered. It was only a matter of days before he discovered the murdered bodies of several of the men who were sent out before him. He was soon captured by Indians as well, but was spared his life in return for a promise of helping the Indians' effort against the Americans. After five months of service to the British traders and Indians along the Maumee Valley, he managed to escape to Pittsburgh. There he fell in with Wayne's camp and found favor with the commander by providing good intelligence on the Indian and British condition. May would go on to serve as a scout for Wayne on the upcoming campaign.

The US overtures toward peace continued inspite of so many failed attempts. It should be noted that, as we just witnessed, the literal message of the Americans' desire to hold talks was often never received by the Indians for whom it was intended because the messengers were killed enroute. One offer that did get through led to a treaty being signed by some of the tribes living in the region of Vincennes in the Indiana territory. However, it never got through official approval in Congress. This treaty effort was assisted by a man named William Wells who acted as an interpreter at the discussions.

Wells was a white man who, like many others, had been kidnapped from his home in the vicinity of Louisville when he was just a child of ten or twelve. He was adopted into the Miami tribe of which Little Turtle was the chief. He grew up in age and prestige within the tribe. Little Turtle took a keen interest in Wells and later permitted him to marry his daughter, Sweet Breeze. Wells was sharp. He understood both cultures and quickly became proficient in several Indian dialects. The name "Black Snake" was attributed to him among the Miami because of his ability to act quickly and astutely. This is why he was trusted to act as an interpreter at the Vincennes treaty negotiations. It was during these talks that the Americans took special note of his talents. Coincidentally, at the same time, Wells's thoughts had drifted to his previous life. He wondered if in the battles against Harmar and St. Clair he had unknowingly killed some of his own relatives. After much deliberation, he felt compelled to return to his biological family. Tradition has it that

> Taking with him the War Chief, Little Turtle, to a favorite spot on the banks of the Maumee, Wells said, "I now leave your nation for my own people; we have long been friends, we are friends yet; until the sun reaches a certain height (which he indicated), from that time we are enemies. Then if you wish to kill me, you may. If I want to kill you, I may." [18]

The separation had to of been extremely difficult, but Wells did leave and went to find General Wayne to offer him his services. He would be intensely scrutinized by Wayne before being accepted into the American troops. He was made the leader of a small, but elite, group of scouts who acted as a special force to be used at Wayne's discretion.

In September of 1793, already a year into his American service, Wells was sent as a representative of the American cause to a major Indian Council along the Maumee River. As was becoming the norm, his true mission was to covertly collect information on the plans of the Indians and British. He returned with an alarming report. The peace talks had not achieved their desired conclusion, and further, the Indians were aggressively continuing to prepare for war. As a result, Wayne shifted his preparations into a higher gear as well.

The American general was still encumbered with too few men to function as he had felt the situation demanded, but now even more trouble was at hand. The supply chain of desperately needed food was in jeopardy of arriving anytime soon. Government vendors had been very lax in their jobs of getting supplies in motion; and when they were finally enroute, Indian raiders were often successfully stealing them and the pack horses on whose backs they were being carried. These two issues combined to convince Wayne that he needed more help. He accepted the assistance of many more of those rugged woodsman types who happened to live right around Fort Washington.

Ephraim Kibbe and over forty other men, who had just a few years previous established the village of Columbia near Fort Washington, persuaded Wayne to hire them as hunters and scouts. They were well acquainted with surviving in this wilderness and had honed their skills of hunting, tracking, and trail-blazing. Additionally, they had a keen knowledge of Indian habits. Kibbe and his hearty neighbors provided much needed fresh meat and fish to the soldiers, and when the troops went into motion toward the Maumee Valley, they were running a few miles ahead and to the sides of the main body as official spies.

While Kibbe's large contingent of scouts performed their service on foot, Wells's handful of men moved on horseback and were used for special endeavors. It is likely that no matter which team these scouts were on, they came away from these days of service with plenty of their own breath-taking tales to tell their families. Unfortunately, only a few

Image of William Wells from a family medallion portrait.

such stories, from a couple of the key players, have been recorded for posterity. And, they come from members of William Wells' elite corps. Their names were Robert McClellan, Henry Miller, Chris Miller, and the already cited, William May.

It was likely the winter season of 1793-94 that came very close to being the last one Robert McClellan would ever live through. Had he died that winter, it would have been a national shame. He went on to have quite a full life as an explorer, trader, and a key member of John Jacob Astor's Pacific Fur Company in the wild west of the early 1800s. His story became forever etched in readers' minds in Washington Irving's famed novel "Astoria."

McClellan did survive a dire situation during the winter before the battle amongst the fallen timbers. According to Captain Jacob White, the builder of White's Station which served as a supply depot to nearby Fort Washington,

> McClellan and one [William] May were out on duty during some excessive cold weather – May discovered McClellan was nearly frozen. An effort was made to strike fire – which for some time was unsuccessful. McClellan had become stupid – at this crisis May dismounted, killed his horse, tore out its bowels and put McClellan in – this expedience gave May time to strike and build a fire and McClellan recovered. [19]

One has to wonder if this very curious true story from two hundred years ago might have become the inspiration for some of the fictional Hollywood stories of the present time. Afterall, Hans Solo saved Luke Skywalker's life by stuffing him into the cavity of a dead tauntaun after spilling its guts in the 1980 classic, *The Empire Strikes Back*. And, the character Hugh Glass, played by Leonardo DiCaprio in the 2015 movie, *The Revenant*, uses his dead horse in an extraordinarily similar manner.

McClellan continued in service to Wayne as one of his elite scouts. In fact he was a key player in an attempt to capture an Indian who would be taken back to camp for interrogation. Beyond his capacity for extreme endurance, McClellan had an uncanny ability to jump very high and to run quite fast. It's likely he would have been a hall-of-fame running back if he had been born in the modern era. One account of his feats say that

> …While at Fort Hamilton he would frequently leap over the tallest horse without apparent exertion. In the town of Lexington, Kentucky, when passing along a narrow sidewalk with the late Matthew Heuston, a yoke of large oxen happened to be drawn up on the sidewalk, instead of walking round them as Colonel Hueston did, he, without hesitation leaped over both at a bound. When with the army at Greenville, at a trial of feats of strength among the soldiers and teamsters, he leaped over a wagon with a cover top, a height of eight feet and a half… the above reported to me [James McBride of Hamilton County, Ohio] by eye-witnesses are enough to show his extraordinary strength and agility. [20]

In June of 1794, while the bulk of Wayne's troops were at Greene Ville, present-day Greenville, Ohio, William Wells was ordered to find still another Indian captive for interrogation. He took with him Robert McClellan and Henry Miller, who had himself been a prisoner of the Indians through most of his youth. What happened on their search would be hard to make up. As they proceeded through the woods and up the Auglaize River,

> …they discovered a smoke, dismounted[,] tied their horses and cautiously reconnoitered. They found three Indians encamped on a high, open piece of ground, clear of brush or any undergrowth, rendering it difficult to approach them without being discovered. While reconnoiter-

ing, they saw not very distant from the camp, a fallen tree. They returned and went round, so as to get it between them and the Indians. The tree top being full of leaves would serve to screen them from observation. They crept forward on their hands and knees with the caution of the cat, until they reached it, when they were within 70 or 80 yards of the camp. The Indians were sitting or standing about the fire, roasting their venison, laughing and making merry antics, little dreaming that death was about stealing a march upon them. Arrived at the fallen tree, their plans were settled. M'Clellan, who was almost as swift of foot as a deer, was to catch the center Indian, while Wells and Miller were to kill the other two, one shooting to the right and the other to the left. Resting the muzzles of their rifles on a log of the fallen tree, they aimed for the Indian's hearts. Whiz went the balls, and both Indians fell. Before the smoke had risen two feet, M'Clellan was running with lifted tomahawk for the remaining Indian, who bounded down the river, but finding himself likely to be headed if he continued in that direction, he turned and made for the river, which at that place had a bluff bank about 20 feet high. On reaching it, he sprang off into the stream and sunk to his middle in the soft mud at its bottom. M'Clellan came after and instantly sprang upon him, as he was wallowing and endeavoring to extricate himself from the mire. The Indian drew his knife: the other raised his tomahawk and bade him throw down his knife, or he would kill him instantly. He did so, and surrendered without farther opposition. By this time, Wells and his companion came to the bank, and discovered the two quietly sticking in the mud. Their prisoner being secure, they selected a place where the bank was less precipitous, went down, dragged the captive out and tied him. He was sulky and refused to speak either Indian or English. Some of the party went back for their horses, while others washed the mud and paint from the prisoner. When cleaned, he turned out to be a white man, but still refused to speak, or give any account of himself. The party scalped the two Indians whom they had shot, and then set off for headquarters. [21]

The more the captive looked at the men transporting him back to the fort, the more he detected something familiar in one of them. Henry Miller was getting the same feeling. At last, Henry called out the Indian name of his brother who had been captured with him so many years ago. The prisoner responded and the siblings were joyously reunited once again. This was Christopher Miller who had chosen to stay behind when Henry had escaped from the Shawnee. He was quite young when they were first taken, and so the Indian life was all he really knew. When the scouts arrived at Greene Villle, Christopher was separated and guarded as a prisoner. After some time, and repeated questioning by Wayne and his brother, he offered to stay with his natural white brothers and work as a spy. Perhaps he was counting his blessings, for by the grace of God, if he hadn't been the one standing between his two Indian friends at the moment that Wells and Henry Miller had fired, he would have been one of the dead Indians, possibly unknowingly killed by his own brother.

Wells' team members were the restless type, and so after a few weeks, they were off again to find another Indian. Christopher Miller and McClellan quickly and successfully did so; catching an unsuspecting Indian chief who was roaming the area. Christopher handled the situation as he was expected to, and thus was proving his allegiance to the Americans.

Soon, the crack team of scouts was sent out again. On this July expedition, Wells would have a special, chance encounter. When the spies reached the St. Mary's River, Wells

> discovered a family of Indians coming up the river in a canoe. He dismounted from his horse and concealed his men, while he went to the bank of the river, in open view, and called to the Indians to come over. As he was dressed in Indian costume and spoke in that language, they crossed to him, unsuspicious of danger. The moment the canoe struck the shore, Wells heard the nicking of the cocks of his comrades' rifles, as they prepared to shoot the Indians; but who should be in the canoe but his Indian father and mother, with their children! The others were now coming forward with their rifles cocked and ready to pour in a deadly fire upon this family. Wells shouted to them to desist, informing them who the Indians were, solemnly declaring that the first man who attempted to injure one of them should receive a ball in his head. "That family," said he to his men, "had fed him when hungry, clothed him when naked, and nursed him when sick, and had treated him as affectionately as their own children." This short speech moved the sympathetic hearts of his leather-hunting-shirt comrades, who entered at once into his feelings and approved of his lenity. Dropping their tomahawks and rifles, they went to the canoe and shook hands with the trembling Indians in the most friendly manner. [22]

The scouts would continually go out in search of Indians to question and were usually successful. The prisoners provided some keen insights into the Indian affairs, giving Wayne a huge strategic advantage. Just nine days before what would become known as the Battle of Fallen Timbers, Wells and several of his regulars went out for another look at what was happening in the Indian village at the rapids of the Maumee River. They mingled in the town garnering as much information as they could. Brazen as this was, they were not suspected of being anything but new Indians who had come to the camp for the fight. Just outside of the village, they found and took hostage an Indian couple and proceeded back to Fort Defiance. However, along the way they just couldn't reign in their impetuous desire to tempt fate.

Somewhere between the Maumee rapids and Fort Defiance,

> they came near a large encampment of Indians, merrily amusing themselves around their camp fires. Ordering their prisoners to be silent, under pain of instant death, they went around the camp until they got about half a mile above it. They then held a consultation, tied and gagged their prisoners, and rode into the Indian camp with their rifles lying across the pummels of their saddles. They inquired when they heard last of Gen. Wayne and the movements of his army, and how soon and where the expected battle would be fought? The Indians standing about Wells and his party were very communicative, and answered the questions without any suspicions of deceit in their visitors. At length an Indian, who was sitting at some distance, said in an undertone, in another tongue, to some who were near him, that he suspected these strangers had some mischief in their heads. Wells overheard it, gave the preconcerted signal, and each fired his rifle into the body of an Indian, at no more than six feet distance. The moment the Indian had made the remark, he and his companions rose up with their rifles in hand, but not before each of the others had shot their man. The moment after Wells and party had fired, they put spurs to their horses, lying with their breasts on their animals' necks, so as to lessen the ark to fire at, and before they had got out of the light of the campfires, the Indians had fired upon them. As M'Clellan lay in this position, a ball entered beneath his shoulder blade and came out at the top of his shoulder; Wells's arm was broken by a ball, and his rifle dropped to the ground; May was chased to the smooth rock in the Maumee, where, his horse failing, he was taken prisoner. The rest of the party escaped without injury and rode full speed to where their prisoners were confined, and mounting them upon horses continued their route. Wells and M'Clellan being severely wounded, and their march slow and

painful to Defiance, a distance of about 30 miles, ere they could receive surgical aid, a messenger was dispatched to hasten to that post for a surgeon and a guard. As soon as he arrived with the tidings of the wounds, and perilous situation of these heroic and faithful spies, very great sympathy was manifested. Wayne's feeling for the suffering soldier was at all times quick and sensitive. [23]

As a result of their injuries, neither Wells nor McClellan were able to participate in the battle on the twentieth day of August. Likewise, William May was unavailable. He was dead. From the testimony of a white boy who was in the group of Indians that Wells and his party had approached, we learn that

> ...They [the Indians] then took May to camp. They knew him; he had formerly been a prisoner among them and ran away from them. They told him, "We know you – you speak Indian language – you not content to live with us: tomorrow we take you to that tree, (pointing to a very large burr oak at the edge of the clearing which was near the British Fort [Miamis]), we will tie you up and make a mark on your breast, and we will try what Indian can shoot nearest it." It so turned out. The next day, the very day before the battle, they tied him up, made a mark on his breast, and riddled his body with bullets, shooting at least fifty into him. Thus ended poor May. [24]

In due course, the American troops moved up from Fort Defiance to an old, abandoned Indian site known as Roche de Boeuf, or Rock of the Buffalo in present-day Waterville, Ohio. The name referred to a large rock formation in the Maumee River that resembled the hump of the common beast. The Indians had retreated from the Grand Glaize region where Fort Defiance now stood, to just a few miles north of Roche de Bouef. They were along Swan Creek in present-day Toledo, Ohio.

In a last ditch effort to avoid a fight, just days before the battle, Wayne entrusted Christopher Miller to act as his emissary to the Indians with a final offer to meet and discuss peace. It was a futile attempt. The message delivered by Christopher Miller only caused further discord among the Indian forces, especially because it included a note of caution from Wayne that the British would not follow through on their promises of support. Already the Indian coalition was wary and indecisive. Little Turtle, of the Miami, who had led the previous victories over Harmar and St. Clair, now saw the futility of taking on a much more formidable force under Wayne. As well, he noted the inevitable influx of more and more Americans. Generally, Little Turtle represented the opinion of the older generation, while the younger warriors, primarily led by Blue Jacket of the Shawnee, were ready to engage. Christopher Miller returned to Wayne just a couple days before the fight with an Indian request that they be given more time to consider the situation. Wayne viewed this response as a simple stalling ploy for them to gain more time to coalesce their plans.

On the morning of August 20, 1794, the American troops marched nearly four miles to the northwest from their camp on the banks of the Maumee River. When they reached an area that had been ravaged some time previous by a tornado, they met their enemy. Behind and among the broken limbs and uprooted trees which had been strewn all about, the Indians had taken their positions. A handful of British Canadians, disguised in Indian attire, were also in the mix. The work of the scouts had been masterful. The scene was just what Wayne had anticipated.

Over one thousand men were present on each side. The battle lasted a little over an hour with some back and forth maneuvers. Once Wayne determined that only a bayonet charge on foot could dislodge the Indians from their positions behind the fallen timbers, the Indian fate was sealed. They fled on foot to the British fortress, expecting protection. It was a long five mile run to their rear. This was Fort Miamis, built just a few months earlier. It had given the Indians a feeling of more sincere British support; something they were in dire need of. However, when the exhausted retreating Indians reached the British post, they were denied both entrance and military support against the Americans. The commander was not authorized to overtly get involved.

At first, some of the more belligerent officers who survived the battle had considered this whole event along the Maumee River as nothing more than a skirmish. However, over thirty Americans, including a few officers, lost their lives that day. Somewhere between twenty and forty Indians were killed as well. It would seem that the death toll alone, would warrant this being considered a significant event.

The tangible evidence of how historic this engagement had been came a year later. One of the most course-altering treaties of the day, the Greenville Treaty, was signed almost a year to the day of the battle by General "Mad" Anthony Wayne and all the participating tribes in the conflict. This document stated that the previously resistant tribes, who had been rampaging against the settlers of the region for the passed many years, were finally agreeing to allow the Americans to, once and for all, peacefully settle on what would become nearly three-quarters of the state of Ohio.

The journey to this consequential breakthrough required a huge transformation in the structure of the US Army. It had begun its existance on such an unbelievably flimsy footing that something inevitably had to change in order for the country to survive. A literal handful of soldiers were considered the standing national defense force. They were theoretically supported with a mere promise of an on-call, untrained, militia from each state, should a major conflict erupt. Because of the way Washington's Indian War had unfolded, the serious shortcomings of the military were exposed. The government authorities could no longer linger in denial. Over four short years, the army of the United States was truly born, as a bunch of mostly undisciplined volunteers were transformed into what General Anthony Wayne named his legion; a salute to their caliber having been raised to the level of the famed Roman forces.

In the histories of war there are always unsung heroes. Through the series of conflicts of the early 1790s on the northwestern frontier, those overlooked combatants were the very special men known as scouts. They were a distinguished breed, ever willing to put their life on the line by spying on the enemy. And once a mission was completed, they would do it again and again and again. One has to wonder how things may have played out differently had these fearless men not gathered the intelligence that they had. They proved to be the secret weapon on which much of the war's success would hinge. A salute to the many overlooked, daring scouts of our earliest United States military is certainly in order; and very long overdo. ♦

HMMM...

Roche de Bouef is a tall, hump-shaped rock outcropping in the Maumee River whose name translates to the, "Rock of the Buffalo," due to it's unusual formation. Paul Manor was a Frenchman trading with the Ottawa and numerous other Indian tribes of the Maumee River Vallley in the 1812 era.

Legend of Roche de Bouef.

The following legend of the Roche de Bouef, was told by Peter Manor, the celebrated Indian scout and guide. Evidences of its truth are found in the many relics and skeletons found in the vicinity:

"At the time when the plum, thorn-apple, and wild grape were the only products, and long prior to the advent of the pale-faces, the Ottawas were camped here, engaged in their games and pastimes, as was usual when not clad in war-paint and on the lookout for an enemy. One of the young tribe, engaged in playing on Roche de Bouef (Rock in the River), fell over the precipice and was instantly killed. The dusky husband, on his return from the council fires, on being informed of the fate of his prospective successor, at once sent the mother in search of her papoose, by pushing her over the rocky sides into the shallow waters of the Maumee. Her next-of-kin, according to Indian law, executed the murdering husband and was in turn executed in the same manner, until the frantic passions were checked by the arrival of the principal chiefs of the tribe. This sudden outburst cost the tribe nearly two-thirds of its members, whose bodies were taken from the river and buried with full Indian honors the next day."

In Henry Howe's, Historical Collections of Ohio, 1907 [25]

VII.
THE LORE OF LORAMIE CREEK.

Along today's highways, unobtrusive little signs are often posted at certain overpasses in order to identify the rivers that are being crossed. Few of us think much about these waterways as we speed along to our destinations. However; in the not too-distant past, these rivers were themselves the highways. Of course there were land paths as well, but until they evolved into smoother, wider roads it was the rivers that provided the most expedient travel. In the Ohio country of the 1700s, the particularly intricate network of rivers provided a magnificent system of transportation. Besides sustaining the region's abundant vegetation and wildlife, this river system seemed to have been preordained to encourage settlement by providing easy access across its wilderness.

In the midsection of what became the state of Ohio, several rivers have their origins. Most are within a reasonable distance of one another and some happen to bend or have tributaries that stretch into close proximity of another. Thus, nature often provided the would-be boater with only a short distance to carry, or portage, his vessel and goods between two waterways before continuing on across the region.

Of course they twist and turn in all directions, but for the most part, rivers in the lower half of the Ohio country flow southward and empty into some part of the Ohio River, while many of the rivers in the northern half eventually pour into Lake Erie. Therefore, the only concern with making a long trip across the area was the switch between coasting with the current of a river in one direction or paddling against it in another. Villages were always established at a fresh water source

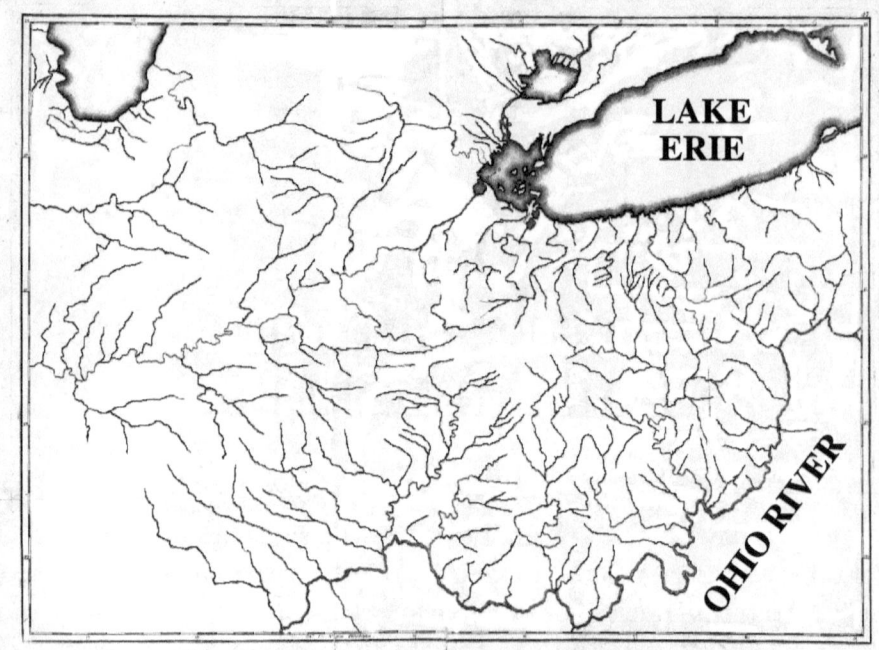

The extensive river system across the current states of Ohio, Indiana, Illinois and southern Michigan.

and very often that was along a river bank where not only essential water was provided, but also quick and easy access to travel.

Just north of Piqua, Ohio, is one end of a creek that originally emptied into the opening stretch of the Great Miami River. Today this waterway still bears the name given to it by Anthony Wayne shortly after his victory at Fallen Timbers in 1794. The General christened it, Loramie's Creek, for reasons soon to be discovered. During the second half of the 1700s, at both the origin and the terminus of this once large stream of twenty miles, several significant historic episodes of frontier life played themselves out.

By the middle of the eighteenth century, a large portion of the Miami Indians lived in a village known as Kekionga. This was in present-day Fort Wayne, Indiana. For hundreds of miles around, it was the largest community of Indians to be found, and it was continuously growing. For many generations previous, it had been the residence of the Miamis, but other tribes settled there as well. This was due in large part to its strategic position at the confluence of the St. Mary's, St. Joseph, and Maumee Rivers. This location provided easy access to travel in almost any direction, be it to the Great Lakes, the Mississippi River, or the Ohio Valley. For this reason it was also the most active site of trade between the Native Americans and the men from European nations. Over the years, Kekionga saw its share of physical trading posts erected and run by the Spanish, French, and English.

As of 1747, it was the French who were holding the monopoly on business dealings with most of the western Indians, but their grip was weakening. They occupied Fort Miamis, a structure erected twenty-five years earlier adjacent to Kekionga. It was built for their own protection against any outside Indian attacks, but more importantly it established a tangible French presence and a sense of permanence to the trade center. That held true for decades, but in recent years the French were falling out of favor with the Miamis.

By applying the old idiom of "follow the money" one can discover the true reason for the growing enmity at this time between the Native Americans and their long-time "fathers" the French. For that matter, the money trail also explains the escalating tensions between England and France on the whole.

The big money for European businessmen was to be found in trade with these Indians. Animal pelts, especially those of the beaver, which were supplied by the expert Indian hunters, yielded tremendous profits in Europe for the clothing and felt into which they were transformed. In turn, the Indians had grown more and more dependent on metal goods which they had little skill to produce for themselves. Firearms, ammunition, cooking utensils, and other items had gone beyond being novelties and were now becoming essentials to the eighteenth-century Indian way of life. Demand and supply was high on both sides of the bartering table.

There had been generations of conflict between the French and English up to this point in time, and more was on its way. In 1740, an armed conflict had broken out in Europe. It was called the War of Austrian Succession and as usual, though each was allied with other world powers, England and France were on opposite sides of the fight. Over the last four years of this conflict it had extended into America, and here it became known as King George's War. Most of the action escaped the Ohio Valley; taking place primarily in regions of New York and Nova Scotia. The outcome was essentially a draw as far as the French and English were concerned; but through its eight year duration, 1740 through 1748, the British Royal Navy had established a blockade of French ships. This proved disastrous for the trading efforts of King Louis XV in North America. The result was that the French had fewer goods to offer the Indians; and even when they did, the prices had risen and the quality had diminished. England was gaining an upper hand. Other circumstances were festering among the western Indians which were disturbing the established order of trade with the French as well.

One factor was the disarray many tribes found themselves in after struggling through several decades of conflict amongst themselves. After long-term domination by the eastern nations known as the Iroquois, the western tribes allegiances to them were beginning to waiver. Some tribes were completely disassociating themselves from the powerful coalition, while others were newly signing on. These changes in tribal alliances caused tensions to rise. Some Indian villages uprooted themselves and resettled in new locations to distance themselves from tribes that they had disagreements with or whom they feared. It was a time of uncertainty with division on the rise; even between clans of the same tribe.

Another issue of the day was that colonial traders from the East had often acted independently in their negotiations with each of the western tribes; not necessarily acting in the sole interests of the colonial government as they were supposed to be doing. These traders came primarily from Virginia and Pennsylvania and viewed the western lands of the Ohio Valley as mere extensions of their own colonies, and therefore fair game in their pursuit of lucrative business ventures. However, the westward movement of these British traders' was actually seen as an encroachment by France, who also laid claim to the land. Official policies of England regarding any such movement into the territories were somewhat vague. In at least one instance, King George II went so far as to grant a substantial amount of acreage to wealthy investors who would in-turn form the Ohio Company. This land speculation enterprise was aimed at drawing English settlers into the West. Several similar companies like the Loyal Company and the

New River Company soon sprang up as well and created competition and confusion over land ownership claims — arguments that were not only between the land companies, but between the countries of England and France.

Many decades previous to the 1740s, France had laid claim to the vast inner third of the North American continent. New France stretched east to west between the Appalachians and the Mississippi River; and from the middle of Canada in the north down to the Gulf of Mexico in the south. However, in the Ohio Valley, the borders between British and French possessions were somewhat vague. Even though the boundaries of ownership could have been better defined in the course of peace talks ending the War of Austrian Succession in 1748, they weren't. This negligence only furthered the confusion and the tension.

The British colonial population was expanding rapidly and many had their sights on the West for settlement and financial gain. The lands they viewed, while inhabited in clusters by Indian tribes, had very few French residents. Only in its Canadian region was the French population on the rise. So while France was claiming possession, and had long-running trade agreements with various Indian nations, with little permanent, local presence they were hard-pressed to defend their claims of ownership.

In the end, it was the combination of internal tribal friction, discontent and disagreement over established trade alliances, ill-defined western borders of the English colonies, insufficient French settlement in the Ohio Valley, and a colonial population boom; which all coalesced to position the British for huge profits in New France.

While many of the Miami Indians at Kekionga were frustrated with the French trade situation, they were not alone. Other tribes across the region were beginning to prefer doing business with the British. One of these Indian communities was newly established on the south shores of Lake Erie near today's Sandusky, Ohio. The Wyandot chief of this village was Orontony and in 1747 he had formed a coalition of tribes who would implement a multi-pronged attack on the French. Ironically, by engaging in these actions, Orontony was turning his back on longtime French friends, whose Jesuit missionaries had baptized him twenty years previous and had even given him the name of Nicholas, by which he was often known.

Nicholas's plan was to send an Indian force to each of the three most strategic French trading posts in the region. One group went north to Fort Michilimackinac (in present-day Mackinaw City, Michigan), another to Fort Detroit, and another to Fort Miamis, (in present-day Fort Wayne, Indiana). Two of the three assaults had failed. Only the attack on Fort Miamis was partially successful. It was there that a few Frenchmen were captured and part of the fortress burned down.

This Fort Miamis attack was lead by a Miami Indian who was chief of his Piankashaw band. He went by many names. The Indian version is Memeskia, or Meemeehsihkia, which translates into English as "dragonfly." That seems usual and customary, as many Native Americans names were of animals. However, because of his ever-growing allegiance to Great Britain in later years, the English gave him the nickname, "Old Briton." The French, however, were a bit sly in their epithet for the chief. They called him "La Demoiselle." That word does mean "dragonfly" in some circles, but it is more often defined as meaning "young girl." The chief must not have picked up on the innuendo because the French used it to address him directly and repeatedly; which further suggests that perhaps their use of it was a little inside joke that reinforced their disgust of his English leanings.

Details are sketchy, but Memeskia may have originally come to the Kekionga region from Canada, and more recently from the Vincennes area at the southern end of the Wabash River. In 1747, he had a small settlement in or very near Kekionga and his following had been convinced for some time that continuing to trade with the French was a mistake. He, and other chiefs including Nicholas, had been courted by the likes of George Croghan, an influential trader and agent of the British who worked with the Iroquois. It didn't take much for Croghan to persuade them to the British point of view.

After his attack on Fort Miamis, Memeskia learned that he was the only one in Nicholas's plan to have had any amount of success. Memeskia's fear of retribution from the French for his actions was not unwarranted and so he and his followers left Kekionga for a new home. They travelled southeast down the St. Mary's River some eighty miles until they reached a spot that they found to be flat, fertile, and well watered. It was between the west bank of the Great Miami River and, at that time, the mouth of an unnamed creek. It was both a prime cross-roads and cross-rivers location, providing easy access to all the trade routes in any direction; whether along the Great Miami, St. Mary's, Auglaize, or Scioto Rivers.

The place came to be known as Pickawillany. The origin of the name and whether it is related to the nearby town of Piqua is still debated in scholarly circles. Many conclude that Pickawillany was a derivation from the Shawnee pronunciation of Memeskia's Miami tribe name. Regardless, Pickawillany was a very influential location in its own right over its short five years in existence.

Within a matter of months, Memeskia had formed friendships with tribes across the region, garnering support for shifting trade preferences away from the French and toward the English. More and more Miami traders from Kekionga came around to his point of view and Pickawillany grew to several hundred people in its first year. In July of 1748 a conference to affirm good will and good trade between various tribes and the British was called for by Memeskia, Croghan, and others. It was held at Lancaster, Pennsylvania and hosted by commissioners and council members of that colony. In attendance were chiefs of the Iroquois nation, as well as representatives of the Delaware, Shawonese, Nanticoke, and Twightwee (the British name for Miami) tribes. In a matter of days their purpose was fulfilled as an official Alliance of Friendship was agreed upon; thus opening the door to prolific trade between the British and western Indians.

It's interesting to find that in the treaty's concluding statement, the appointed spokesman for the Indians, an Iroquois leader named Suchraquery, cunningly asks their new business associates to tip the scales in the Indians' favor as a good faith gesture.

> It seems that the Commissioners then enquired if the Indians had any particular News to communicate, and, after some Time spent in Conference, Suchraquery spoke as follows:

> The Indians of the several Nations, living at Ohio, return you Thanks for your Acceptance of their good Offices in conducting the Twightwees, and admitting them into your Alliance; likewise for your Goodness in accepting their Mediation on Behalf of the Shawonese, and thereupon forgiving their late Breach of Faith. Our new Brethren the Twightwees tell us, that they have brought a few Skins to begin a Trade, and they desire you will be pleased to order the Traders to put less Stones into their

Scales, that their Skins may weigh more, and that they may allow a good Price for them, which will encourage them and their Nation to trade more largely with you. This the Commissioners promised to do.[1]

Of course news of this agreement did not sit well with French authorities. The benefit to the British was two-fold: more trade, and a strong defense of that trade by this Indian coalition which essentially acted as a physical buffer to potential French hostilities against the British.

The threat that the growing anti-French sentiment could spread across the Ohio Valley was very real, so the French decided to reiterate their ownership of the land and of the commerce that transpired upon it. In June of 1749, the governor of Canada sent Captain Pierre Joseph Celeron de Bienville, generally referred to as Celeron, to the region. In a caravan of twenty-three canoes he led soldiers, Canadians, Indians, and at least one missionary on a journey of French affirmation. From the town of La Chine, near Montreal, they paddled against the current of the St. Lawrence River and then through the Great Lakes of Ontario and Erie. Just east of today's Erie, Pennsylvania, they landed and began heading south; repeatedly alternating between land and water travel. Eventually they were floating down the Conewango River to the point where it emptied into the Allegheny River. Here Celeron buried the first of his six leaden plates which were meant to physically declare French ownership of all the lands fed by these rivers.

Five more plates were buried at the mouths of rivers that emptied into the Ohio or Allegheny River (which eventually met the Ohio at Pittsburgh, Pennsylvania). They included French Creek, near today's Franklin, Pennsylvania; Wheeling Creek at Wheeling, West Virginia; the Muskingum River in Marietta, Ohio; the Kanawa River near Point Pleasant, West Virginia, and the final one at the terminus of the Great Miami River's run near Cincinnati, Ohio. An additional plate was to be buried at the mouth of the Scioto River, in present-day Portsmouth, Ohio, but it was stolen by an unknown Indian while enroute.

The only plate to survive completely intact is the one Celeron planted at the mouth of the Kanawa River and it is currently in the Virginia Museum of History and Culture. It's smaller than one may have expected, roughly the size of today's standard letter. However,

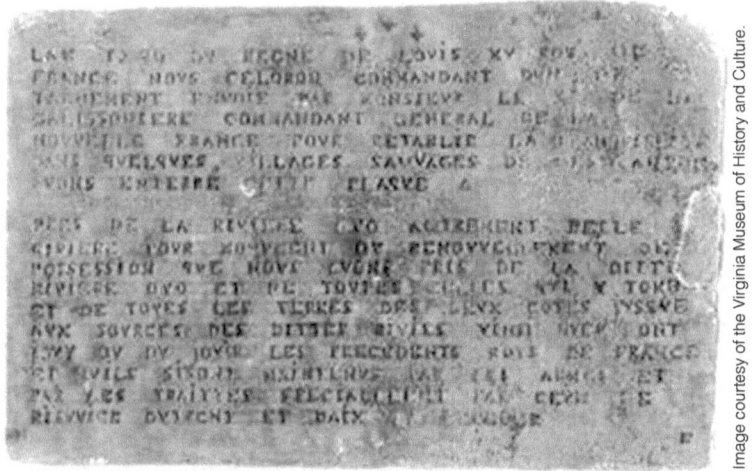

The lead plate discovered at the junction of the Kanawha and Ohio Rivers. Planted by Captain Pierre Joseph Celeron de Blainville in 1749, it was found by a young boy playing along the riverbank in 1846 and is now on display in the Virginia Museum of History and Culture in Richmond, Virginia.

at an eighth of an inch thick and roughly eleven by seven-and-a-half inches across, it's a hefty piece of metal. All the plates were engraved beforehand with space left in the appropriate location for the date and river name to be added by the scribe who had come along on the journey. The full inscription on the recovered plate reads:

"In the year of 1749, of the reign of Louis the 15th, King of France, we Celoron, commander of a detachment sent by Monsieur the Marquis de la Gallissoniere, Governor General of New France, to reestablish tranquility in some Indian villages in these provinces, have buried this plate at the mouth of the River Chinodahichiltha [Kanawa] on the 18th of August near the River Ohio, otherwise Beautiful River, as a monument of the renewal of the possession we have taken of the said River Ohio, and of all those which empty into it, and of all the lands on both sides as far as the sources of said rivers, as enjoyed or ought to have been enjoyed by the kings of France preceding, and as they have there maintained themselves by arms and by treaties, especially those of Ryswick, Utrecht, and Aix la Chapelle." [2]

In addition to burying the plates near the banks of certain river mouths, a sheet of tin, emblazoned with the Coat of Arms of France, was sometimes nailed to a nearby tree. During some of these procedures, Celeron had ordered his men into formation and with just a bit of pomp and ceremony King Louis XV was loudly proclaimed lord of these lands.

Joseph Pierre de Bonnecamps was a Jesuit missionary who made the six-month excursion with Celeron through the Ohio Valley in order to chronicle its geographic features. He also kept a thorough diary of the events he experienced, as can be seen in one of his entries:

> We encamped at the mouth of riviere Blanche ("White River"), where we found a small band of Miamis with their chief named le Baril ("the Barrel"). They had established themselves there a short time before, and formed a village of 7 or 8 cabins, a league distant from the river. Monsieur de Celeron requested them to accompany him to the village of la Demoiselle ("the young Lady"), and they promised to do so. We passed two days waiting for them. Finally, on the morning of the 31st, they appeared, followed by their women, their children, and their dogs. All embarked, and about 4 o'clock in the afternoon we entered riviere a la Roche [Great Miami River], after having buried the 6th and last leaden plate on the western bank of that river, and to the north of the Ohio. [3]

The itinerary of this extended trip was now nearly completed. The plates had all been planted. Only one final piece of business needing tending. Celeron wanted to show himself to Memeskia. Since this chief was the key instigator of Indian rebellion in the Ohio Valley against the French, Celeron wanted to try to appease him with in-person promises of friendship, gifts, and better trade practices in the future. However, the unspoken, primary objective was to coax, cajole, and ultimately convince Memeskia, and the Barrel as well, to return with Celeron, immediately, to Kekionga; the home which they abandoned two years previous.

From Celeron's own diary we learn about the difficulties of traveling the Rock River, as they had called what we refer to as the Great Miami River. Besides having to paddle upstream, the river had many shallow areas where its flat-rock bottom often scraped the undersides of the canoes. He also gives us a keen glimpse into the protocol they were expected to follow before meeting Memeskia. Twelve days after leaving the Ohio River, Celeron wrote:

> The Miamis of the village of the Demoiselle, having learned that I was on the point of arriving among them, sent four chiefs to meet me with pipes of peace to have me smoke; as the half of my people were

on land, there not being water enough in the river to float the freighted canoes. I was informed by M. de Courtemanche, the officer of the detachment, of the arrival of his [la Demoiselle's] messengers. I landed at the place where they were, and when we were all seated they began the ceremony of presenting the pipe. I accepted it. They then brought it to M. de Contrecoeur, second captain of the detachment, and to all the officers and the Canadians, who, worn out for a smoke, would have wished that the ceremony had continued longer. The hour having come for camping, we passed the night in this place. The messengers remaining with us, I was obliged, despite the scarcity of provisions then in my possession, to give them supper. [4]

The next day, September 13, Celeron set up camp with expectations of speaking directly to Memeskia. However, the interpreter which he had requested to be sent to him from Fort Miamis had not arrived. In fact, four days later, he had still not shown up, much to the chagrin of Celeron.

Wearied at the fact of the interpreter not arriving, and because my provisions were being consumed while thus waiting, I [Celeron] determined to speak to the Demoiselle by means of an Iroquois who knew Miami well. I showed them magnificent presents on the part of M. the General [the Governor of New France] to induce them to return to their villages, and I explained to them his invitations… [5]

Speaking to both Demoiselle and the Baril, as the chiefs were referred to, Celeron read a pre-written letter of the governor to both tribes. Eight wampum belts were also included as gifts. In part, the letter read:

My children: The manner in which I behave toward you, despite all you have done to the French whom I sent you to maintain your wives and your children, ought to be a sufficient proof of the attachment which I have for you and the sincerity of my feelings. I forget what you have done to me, and I bury it in the depth of the earth in order to never more remember it, convinced that you have acted only at the instigation of a people whose policy is to trouble the land and destroy the good disposition of those with whom they have relations, and who avail themselves of the unhappy ascendency which you have let them get over you. They make you commit faults and they incite you to an evil course without their seeming to have any part in it, in order to ruin you in my estimation.

> It is then to enlighten you that I send you my message; listen carefully to it, and pay attention to it, my children; it is the word of a father that loves you, and in whose eyes your interests are dear. I extinguish by these two belts of wampum the two fires which you lighted during the last two years, both at the Rock River and at the White River. I extinguish them in such a way that not a single spark can escape... [6]

The governor's speech continued on, explaining that whatever transgressions he felt these tribes had made against the French were now completely forgiven. He was interrupted at times only by the distribution of belts of wampum to both of the chiefs. The governor invoked the Miami's memories of previous French friends like Monsieur de Vincennes, whom they sincerely admired. As well, he pointed out the fact that many of their ancestors were still buried at Kekionga. The message oozed with words of how good the French had been to the Miamis and how much more they would provide in the future. All that they asked was for Memeskia and the Barrel to abandon their villages and to return with them to Kekionga — now. If they acquiesced, the French hoped the growing and threatening ties with the English in the valley would be severed.

The Indians were given time to respond and did so early on the following morning when they approached Celeron's camp with peace pipes in hand.

> It is an ancient custom among us when one speaks of agreeable affairs to present, first of all, pipes. We earnestly entreat you to listen to us. We are going to answer what you have asked of us. This pipe is a token of the pleasure which we have in smoking with you, and we hope to smoke the very same pipe with our father next year. [7]

A belt was passed from the Indians to Celeron followed by the pipe. When the calumet had completed its journey through the dignitaries present, the Indian response was given.

> My father: Yesterday, we listened with pleasure to your speech. We have seen clearly that you are come only on a good mission. We have none other but good answers to give you. You have made us recall to memory the bones of our forefathers, who mourn to see us in this place, and who remind us continually of it. You have made us a good road to return to our ancient home, and we thank you for it, my father, and we promise you to return thither immediately after the coming spring.

> We thank you for the kind words which you have addressed us. We see clearly that you have not forgotten us. Be convinced that we will labor to deal fairly with the Chauanones [Shawnees]. We still remember the good advice which M. de Vincennes gave us. My father, you have to treat with people without spirit, and who are, perhaps, unable to answer you as well as you hoped; but they will tell you the truth, for it is not from the lips that they speak to you, but from the bottom of their heart. You bid us reflect seriously upon what you told us. We have done so, and we shall continue to do so during the whole winter. We hope to have the pleasure of making you a good speech this spring if the hunting is abundant. We will correct our faults, and we assure you, my father, that we will not listen to evil counsel, and that we will pay no attention to the rumors we hear at present. [8]

In other words, Memeskia and the Barrel said, "Thanks, but no thanks" to the proposal of moving back to Kekionga, at least for the moment. They did promise to uproot themselves in the spring. The response annoyed Celeron, so he tried to re-explain the seriousness of the situation and the power of the French with a "Look here..." reproach.

> I have listened to you my children, and I have weighed your words. Whether you may not have understood me, or that you feign not to have done so, you do not answer to what I asked of you. I proposed to you on the part of your father Onontio [Indian term for Governor], to come with me to Kiskakon [Kekionga] to light there your fire and to build up your wigwam, but you put off doing so till next spring. I would have been delighted to be able to say to your father Onontio that I had brought you back. That would have caused him great pleasure on account of the interest he takes in all that concerns you. You give me your word that you will return there at the end of the winter. Be faithful then to your promise. You have assured him of this, because he is much stronger than you, and if you be wanting to it, fear the resentment of a father, who has only too much reason to be angry with you, and who has offered you the means of regaining his favor. [9]

Memeskia cordially assured Celeron that they spoke in truth of returning to Kekionga in the spring; at which point the council meeting ended. The following day, the interpreter from Fort Miamis had finally arrived. Even though the talks had concluded and the interpreter was six days late, through him Celeron made a final pitch for Memeskia

French Exploration of the Ohio Valley, a 12 x 20 foot mural by Mark Missman at the Wheeling Civic Center in West Virginia. It depicts the ceremony held by Celeron and his men during the burial of each plate.

and the Barrel to leave this place in their company. The badgering only angered Memeskia who repeated his previous answer. Through thinly veiled sarcasm he told Celeron that he would heed his suggestion at a more opportune time.

The next day, September 20, the Celeron entourage left Pickawillany behind and headed for Fort Miamis. So damaged were the canoes by the trip up the Rock River that they were deemed useless and so were burned. Most traveled on foot; some officers went on horses that were likely secured from Indians of the area. Six days later the group settled in for a rest having reached their destination. Celeron met with the commander of Fort Miamis, Captain Charles DeRaymond, and the local chief of the Miamis named Cold Foot. He told them the details of his council with la Demoiselle and the Barrel, repeating the gist of his speeches and the responses of the Indian chiefs. When finished, the reaction of Cold Foot, recorded in Celeron's journal, confirmed the true status of French interests in the region.

> I hope I am deceived, but I am sufficiently attached to the interests of the French to say that the Demoiselle is a liar. It is the source of all grief to be the only one who loves you, and to see all the nations of the south let loose against the French. [10]

Neither Memeskia, nor the Barrel, nor any other of the Ohio Valley tribes returned to Kekionga. Instead trade was shifted into the next gear between them and the British. A few months after Celeron's departure, George Croghan negotiated with Memeskia to have the British build walls around the cabins used for trade at the village and thus what became known as Fort Pickawillany was completed by early 1751.

> Having obtained permission from the Indians, the English, in the fall of 1750, began the erection of a stockade, as a place of protection, in case of sudden attack, both for their persons and property. When the main building was completed, it was surrounded by a high wall of split logs, having three gateways. Within the inclosure the traders dug a well, which furnished an abundant supply of fresh water during the fall, winter, and spring, but failed in summer. [11]

It was then in February of 1751 that Christopher Gist, one of the earliest white explorers of lands west of the Appalachians, visited Pickawillany as a member of the Ohio Company. While noting the area's geography for later settlement, he took part in a council with Memeskia. Croghan and other English traders participated as well. The discussions were very friendly with thanks and goodwill exchanged by all. That was until four Ottawa Indians walked into the camp. They explained that they were there at the behest of the French commander at Detroit who wanted to extend an invitation for Memeskia and others to visit him there. They bore gifts, but that did not tamp down Memeskia who addressed them with obvious outrage:

> Brothers the Ottawas, we let you know, by these four strings of wampum, that we will not hear anything the French have to say, nor do anything they bid us. [12]

With his English friends all around, Memeskia looked into the distance, and went on with an address whose words were seemingly carried on the winds to the French authorities.

> Fathers, we have made a road to the sunrising, and have been taken by the hand by our brothers the English, the Six Nations, the Delawares, Shawanoes, and Wyandots. We assure you, in that road we will go; and as you threaten us with war in the spring, we tell you that we are ready to receive you. [13]

Through the remainder of 1751, after Memeskia's defiant speech to these Ottawa representatives, trade continued to escalate between these Indians and the British. So too, the tension between them and the French and Ottawa tribe grew proportionately. As bold as his "bring it on" attitude was, Memeskia, the English, the Miamis, and other tribes had all feared the Ottawa; who they knew had gone to the extreme of cannibalizing several of the British traders they had captured in the past. Memeskia was also concerned that should the French indeed attack, the English were not in a military pose to help defend them. He suggested the British erect a fort nearby along the Ohio River. Though British authorities liked the idea, disputes over who would pay for it, and who would benefit from it, was in constant dispute between the colonies of Pennsylvania and Virginia. They all knew, as well, that the French would not take kindly to such a structure being erected in what they saw as New France.

By the end of the year, the French had enough. The governor general of New France, La Jonquiere, ordered Celeron to gather a new force together with which to attack the English trading post at Pickawillany. The reasons are not definitive, but Celeron soon decided to not follow through on his orders to recruit. There are indications that it was the refusal of the Indians at Detroit to sign on, who he felt were critical to making an attack such as this successful, that changed his mind. Additionally, Celeron had expected to bolster his numbers with a large force of Frenchmen who were supposed to be sent from Canada. When less than fifty of these Canadians arrived under the leadership of Sieur de Bellestre, far less than the number he required, Celeron deemed the endeavor to not be feasible.

However, by the fall of 1751, Bellestre became confident that he could accomplish the goal on his own. His chances of victory were slim. He ignored the local Indians who warned him that such a small force would have difficulty against a village that was much larger and more fortified than he was anticipating. Making matters even worse, only eighteen of his fifty Canadians were willing to accompany him. None-the-less, they moved out.

Memeskia had caught wind of the fumbling situation the French troops were experiencing, and so assumed that an attack was unlikely, at least for the present time. Therefore, he joined most of his villagers on a hunt outside of the Pickawillany village proper. When Bellestre's French Canadians arrived, they successfully captured two British traders and randomly killed an older Miami couple who were working in a field. However, even with many of the Indians gone on the hunt, there were enough left in the British fortress to make Bellestre forego any further confrontation. The so-called attack was a farce, but it drew the ire of Memeskia when he had learned of it upon his return.

Memeskia redoubled his efforts to gain the allegiance of more tribes in the region to oppose the French. A gathering was held in Pickawillany early in 1752 and several new tribes did sign on to the cause. To intimidate the governor of New France, and to raise his stature as head of the coalition, Memeskia decided to get a little dramatic. He ordered that one of the four French prisoners, that they had previously captured in an ambush, have his ears cut off. The said prisoner was to be sent to the governor as a harbinger of Indian retaliation to the French aggression led by Bellestre. The other three captives were ritually killed. Over the next few months, other French traders and soldiers were also steadily and secretly attacked.

Governor La Jonquiere's frustration with Celeron's seeming disobedience, and Bellestre's failure at Pickawillany, had taken a grave toll on his health. He passed away in March of 1752. With that, Baron de Longueuil was put in the governor's seat. From the moment of his appointment, notices of trouble brewing across the Ohio Valley were being sent to him on a regular basis. Commander DeRaymond at Fort Miamis reported to Longueuil how dire things had become for him at Kekionga.

> My people are leaving me for Detroit. Nobody wants to stay here and have their throat cut. All the tribes who go to the English at Pickawillany come back loaded with [English] gifts. I am too weak to meet the danger. Instead of twenty men, I need five hundred... We have made peace with the English, yet they try continually to make war on us by means of the Indians; they intend to be masters of all this upper country. The tribes here are leaguing together to kill all the French, that they may have nobody on their lands but their English brothers. This I am told by Coldfoot, a great Miami chief, whom I think is an honest man, if there is any such thing among Indians... If English stay in this country we are lost. We must attack, and drive them out. [14]

Still, no firm plan of attack on Pickawillany was able to be devised. Compounding Celeron's dismal effort to assemble a sufficient number of troops was an outbreak of smallpox at Detroit; and it was spreading across parts of Canada.

Finally, help for the French dilemma came from Fort Michilimackinac. A young man named Charles Langlade, whose father was French and mother was Ottawa, had united an Indian force of Ottawa and Ojibwa. Langlade was a French trader and had a significant amount of influence with tribes around Michilimackinac. Nearly two hundred and fifty warriors were assembled. They had no qualms about attacking the English traders at Pickawillany as well as the Miamis who lived there.

En masse, they moved out. As much as possible they used waterways to get to their destination. First they paddled along the shores of Lake Huron, through the St. Clair River and the lake of the same name, to Detroit. After a short respite, they entered the mouth of the Maumee River and went upstream to Fort Miamis. From there it was a lesser jaunt along the St. Mary's River to its source. After a short portage, they were in sight of Pickawillany.

Ironically, while Langlade expeditiously led his force onward to certain battle, the governor of New France had cancelled his mission. The government authorities reconsidered the situation on the whole and strategized that if they began blocking the influx of the British into their lands in the first place, Indian trade opportunities in the valley would dissipate. With no Englishmen present to trade with, the Miamis would have no reason to remain there. Thoughts were turning toward building a string of defensive forts along the eastern river boundaries of New France throughout the Ohio Valley. This was to be a strategic alternative to attacking Pickawillany or any other rebellious Indian camps, which could cause them to suffer further embarrassing defeats. However, as they say, Langlade never got the memo.

It was mid-morning of June 21, 1752.

> The first to observe the enemy were the squaws who were working in the cornfields outside the town. They rushed into the village giving the alarm. At this time the fort was occupied by the English traders as a warehouse. There were at the time but eight traders in the place. Most of the Indians were gone on their summer hunt, so that, in reality, Pickawillany was almost deserted; only Old Briton, the Piankeshaw king, and a small band of his faithful tribesmen remained. So sudden was the

attack that but five of the traders (they were all in their huts outside the fort) could reach the stockade, and only after the utmost difficulty. The other three shut themselves up in one of their houses. At this time there were but twenty men and boys in the fort, including the white men. The three traders in their houses were soon captured. Although strongly urged by those in the fort to fire upon their assailants, they refused. The enemy learned from them the number of white men there were in the fort, and having taken possession of the nearest houses, they kept up a smart fire on the stockade until the afternoon.

The assailants now let the Miamis know that if they would deliver up the traders that were in the fort they would break up the siege and go home. Upon consultation it was agreed by the besieged that, as there were so few men and no water inside the stockade, it would be better to surrender the white men with a pledge that they were not to be hurt, then for the fort to be taken and all to be at the mercy of the besiegers. The traders, except Thomas Burney and Andrew McBryer, whom the Indians hid, were accordingly given into the hands of the enemy. One who had been wounded was stabbed to death and then scalped. Before getting into the fort fourteen Indians were shot, including Old Briton, one Mingo, and one of the Shawanese nation.

The savages boiled and ate the Demoiselle (Old Briton) as he, of all the others, because of his warm attachment to the English, was most obnoxious to them. They also ate the heart of the dead white man. They released all the women they had captured, and set off with their plunder, which was in the value about 3,000 pounds.

The captured traders, plundered to the skin, were carried by Langdale to Duquesne, the new governor of Canada, who highly praised the bold leader of the enterprise, and recommended him for such reward as befitted one of his station. [15]

Shortly after this tragic event, a letter from the Miamis was delivered to the Governor of Pennsylvania by Thomas Burney, a blacksmith of Pickawillany and one of those two British traders who was hidden by the Miami during the siege. It too details how the attack concluded.

We your brothers, the Twightwees, have sent you, by our brother, Thomas Burney, a scalp and five strings of wampum, in token of our late unhappy affair at the Twightwees' town, and whereas our brother always been kind to us, hope he will now put us in a method how to act against the French, being more discouraged for the loss of our brother, the Englishman who was killed, and the five who were taken prisoners, than for the loss of ourselves; and, notwithstanding the two belts of wampum which were sent from the governor of Canada as a commission to destroy us, we still shall hold our integrity with our brothers, and are willing to die for them, and will never give up this treatment, although we saw our great Piankashaw King (which commonly was called Old Britain by us) taken, killed, and eaten within a hundred yards of the fort before our faces. We now look upon ourselves as lost people, fearing that our brothers will leave us; but before we will be subject to the French, or call them our fathers, we will perish here. [16]

Soon the French began building the chain of forts that they had decided upon to aid in their defense of the Ohio Valley. Four fortresses were completed over a stretch of nearly one-hundred and fifty miles; from the shores of Lake Erie near today's Erie, Pennsylvania to present-day Pittsburgh where Fort Duquesne was erected. The British responded to the appearance of these new French fortresses in the summer of 1754. King George called upon another George, a young lieutenant-colonel named George Washington, to take his first command of troops into battle and drive the French away. Washington failed. As a result, more and more organized battles occurred between the two countries and soon it all evolved into the French and Indian War. The fight continued for nine more years, ultimately ending in England's favor.

Pickawillany never recovered as a trade center. The warriors who were out hunting the day of the attack briefly attempted to rekindle the village, but without financial and military support from the eastern tribes and the British, their efforts soon died out. Eventually they moved back to Kekionga or other villages. British trade with the Miamis and others was reduced to a trickle. The French had temporarily regained much of their control. On occasion they would use the former Pickawillany post to handle a simple transaction of goods or gifts. Sometimes the Miami would rendezvous at the site before or after hunting forays. However, over the next forty years, no activity approached the hustle and bustle of the trade hub Memeskia had created. It can also be argued that what happened on June 21, 1752, at Pickawillany, on the south end of Loramie Creek, was in actuality the unofficial beginning of the French and Indian War.

It wasn't until 1769, six years after the war had ended and seventeen years after the site was destroyed, that any substantial trading center was resurrected anywhere near Pickawillany. It began again with the arrival of a French father and son team from the small town of Lachine near Montreal, Canada. They set-up a post near the northern end of Loramie's Creek, approximately fifteen miles upstream from Memeskia's former village. It was in their honor that this waterway was so named.

Claude-Nicolas de Lorimier de La Rivière, we'll refer to him as Claude, had a long, distinguished military career in Canada. However, with the loss of the French and Indian War to the English, French officers like himself were often made scapegoats for the defeat. Further, the change in governments created an economic malaise in the land. This combination of a slightly tarnished military record and a poor economy caused Claude and his family to suffer financially. He had dabbled in a few business ventures through his life, enough to give him some confidence that at sixty-five years of age he could make a fresh go of trading among the Ohio Valley tribes.

Forging good, lasting relationships with the indigenous people of Canada, primarily the Iroquois but with other tribes as well, was part of Claude's previous military assignment. It was in his nature as well. His knack for easy communication with Native Americans was rewarded by his appointment as captain of a garrison known as the Lake of Two Mountains near Montreal. The fortress was attached to a trading station and a Jesuit mission that served the local Indians. The whole community was known as Kanehsatake. Such a complex, consisting of an Indian mission, a fortress, and a trading post, was somewhat common across New France. The Jesuits were supported by the government and Catholic Church to promote the faith; but as well to foster friendship, protection, and trade between the two cultures. Later in his military career, Claude was transferred to a very similar environment as commandant of Fort La Presentation, in present-day Ogdensburg, New York.

When the trek to Ohio began, Claude brought his son, Pierre-Louis de Lorimier, with him. Only twenty-one years old at the time, Peter Loramie, as he generally became known with the English version of his name, arrived as an apprentice to his father. However, within a year of establishing the new business, Claude went back to Lachine for unknown reasons. It's likely that poor health caused him to return home, as shortly thereafter he passed away. Loramie's Station was now under the sole management of Claude's young, but enterprising son, Peter.

Like his father, because he was raised in the environment of places like Kanehsatake, Peter developed the same understanding of the indigenous people's way of life. It was second nature for him to befriend and mingle with the Native Americans. Some believe he came to the valley with his father as a Jesuit missionary. While his upbringing at the Jesuit posts may have induced a desire to convert other indigenous peoples, it is disputed whether that was his official vocation. In fact, once Britain took control of New France in 1763, Jesuit properties like Kanehsatake were absorbed by the new government. Furthermore, due to suspicious political dealings by Jesuit communities across the globe at this point in time, Pope Clement XIV had officially abolished the Jesuit Order in 1773; though it was revived in 1814. If Loramie had come to the Ohio country as a Jesuit missionary as well as a trader, his spiritual role would have been eliminated with the pope's decree just four years after his arrival.

Peter Loramie may have had Indian ways down pat and he may have already learned several of their languages, but he was illiterate. For this reason, another fellow named Louis Largeau had made the trip to this region as well, acting as a scribe and accountant in lieu of Peter's limitations. Beyond his inability to read, he also had no military experience; something his three older brothers and father did have. Loramie's resume was light, and it's likely that this was the reason Claude chose Peter over his other children for his new business venture. He was a high-spirited soul, but at this time, the social and business atmosphere of the French-Canadians in which the Lorimer family had circulated offered little opportunity for an uneducated, civilian, young man like Peter.

The particular creek chosen as the site of their new trading post was purposefully selected for its accessibility. Like Pickawillany, it was in the region of the Ohio Valley where rivers and paths from all directions crossed. Anyone wanting to, could easily get to Loramie's Station. Additionally, the location had numerous springs and was on a high ground; providing safe, fresh water and a protective view of the

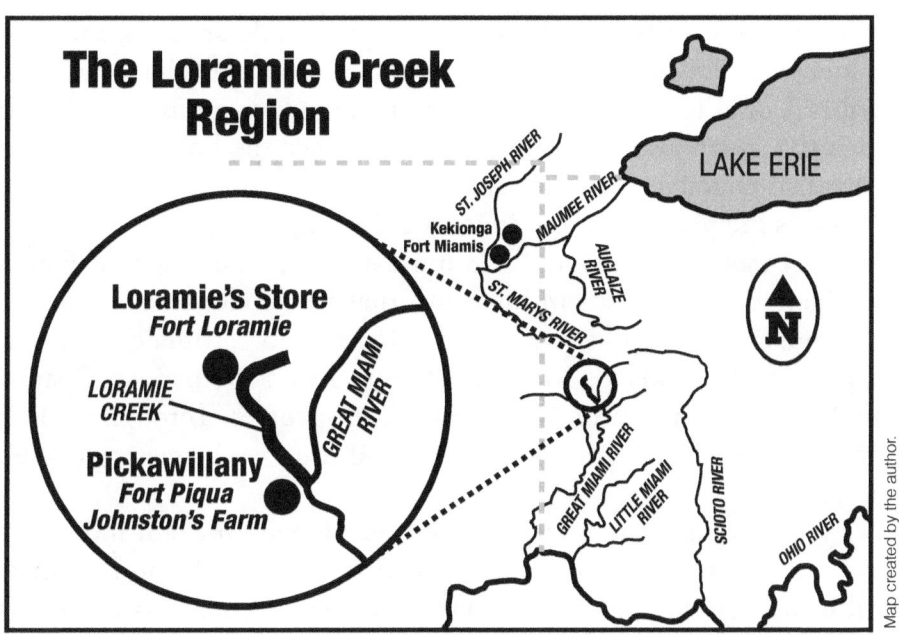

surrounding's activity. The Shawnee were the first and primary people to trade with Loramie. Their villages were scattered across the region. There were still some Miami, Wyandot, and others in the area as well. With his high level of comfort among the indigenous people, it didn't take long for Loramie to make lasting friendships and a good profit in business.

Loramie also quickly picked up on the angst that was festering all around him. While in Memeskia's day, the Indian struggles were over which country to trade with; when Loramie arrived they were upset with the growing number of white people settling on what was supposed to be their land. A Royal Proclamation by King George, issued just months after the war had ended in 1763, was supposed to keep colonists in the colonies. That wasn't happening. Loramie's arrival in 1769 came at a time when unrest over this situation was on a dangerous uptick amongst the Indians in the West and sparks of a revolution were catching fire in the colonies to the east.

As the 1770s began to unfold, it became more and more apparent that the British were getting ever closer to an armed conflict with the colonists. No one could predict the result. The Indians had to gamble when picking sides. Based on their previous trade dealings, and being a known entity, the British were the choice of most of the Ohio Valley tribes. Loramie, though French by birth, opted to continue serving the British Crown just as he always had ever since the French and Indian War had ended in their favor.

As his life played out, Loramie would pledge allegiance to many nations. It was a testament to the cultural influences amongst the French, Indigenous, and Jesuits of his youth that he developed extraordinary diplomatic skills and savvy. Always sincere and spiritually grounded, he eventually managed to assimilate into British, American, Spanish, and untold numbers of Native American peoples. Through it all, he would take on more and more responsibilities; ever increasing his stature and prominence.

By 1774, just before the Revolution officially began, indigenous people of the Ohio Valley were growing angry with the British for allowing settlements in their land; but even more frustrating was that fellow tribes were selling land out from under them. The eastern Iroquois were signing over hunting grounds of the valley to the British. In the minds of the Ohio tribes, these Iroquois had no such authority to sell their lands, especially because they did not live anywhere near them. As time went on, animosity grew between the western tribes and those to the east. Tensions likewise rose to new heights between the local Indians and the new homesteaders. Things got so bad that finally, in late fall of 1774, the Virginia militia was called out to the valley to quell the disturbances. The Battle of Point Pleasant ensued.

On paper the colonists won this conflict along the Ohio River, as another treaty was soon signed to reaffirm where settlement would be allowed. Just a few months afterwards, in the east, Minutemen of the Massachusetts Bay colony stood their ground against British soldiers at Lexington, and the Revolution had begun. The anger of the Shawnee and other tribes against the British over the treaties didn't last long. When large scale war broke out, the army of the king was seen as the stronger force; most able to aid in the defense of their lands against the now rebellious colonists.

As the war progressed, Loramie became an advocate for the British cause as well and his post evolved into a strategic supply depot for them. His store was strategically located. For generations of French, Indian, and British travelers, the region where Loramie's store now stood provided easy access to the Ohio country in any direction.

Loramie acted primarily as a logistics person and quartermaster for Indian affairs during the Revolution. However, early in the war, in spite of his having no previous military experience, Loramie volunteered to engage in at least a few of the frontier fights. Most famously, he was in the contingent of Indians led by Blackfish that captured Daniel Boone and others along Kentucky's Licking River in 1778. After joining the Shawnee on two previous unsuccessful raids into Kentucky, Loramie dictated to his scribe, Largeau, an entry for his journal:

> Seeing that these two campaigns had not been at all advantageous for me and desiring ardently to see the enemy, I set out about Christmas from the village of the Miamis in order to go to those of the Shawnee in company with Sieur Beaubien [Charles Beaubien, British Indian Agent] where we raised a party and attacked in February 1777 [1778] a salt lick, where there were twenty-seven men, whom we took prisoner. This little affair began to swell my courage and gave me better hope for the next campaigns that I had planned to make…[17]

This "little affair" has since become one of the many legendary stories about Boone. In this event, he was one of those captured and held by Blackfish's Shawnee tribe for over seven months. Boone finally managed to escape and returned to Boonesborough. The Shawnee soon staged a major attack against his fortressed community. Again, in the simplest of terms, Loramie mentions his participation in the now famous siege of Boonesborough.

> Monsieur Fontenoy de Quindre, Lieutenant of the Indian Department, passed by my place on his way to the Shawnee villages. I joined with him and we went to attack a fort in Kentucky. After eleven days of siege, we withdrew. The enemy having found out our weakness of our party, was not willing to surrender at our summons…[18]

Loramie also acknowledged how the British Lieutenant Governor Hamilton of Detroit had done him a great service. For Loramie's aid in capturing the Kentuckians at the salt licks, he was awarded a hatchet. This trophy signified Loramie's courage under fire, similar to our presenting medals to our soldiers. Having been presented this honor in front of the Shawnee, who alongside he had fought, his stature with them was raised.

> ... he honored me with a hatchet, which he gave me at a council in the presence of many (Indian) nations, and said to the Shawnees: "I gave him [Lorimer] this hatchet on account of the good testimony that you render about him. It is for going to service with you, whenever he judges it apropos." [19]

One thing was certain, Loramie's allegiance to the British and Indian alliance was strong and his station became the center of their supply operations on the frontier during the Revolution. Through each attack, British guns and ammunition flowed to the tribes through Loramie's. One of the brothers of the infamous Simon Girty, James, aided Loramie at the post in the funneling of goods and supplies to the Indian allies. Later, James would establish his own trading post. Known as Girty's Town, at today's St. Marys, Ohio, it was only about ten miles north of Loramie's. Other notorious anti-Americans, like Simon Girty and Alexander McKee, were also strategic players in this supply chain.

In August of 1782, the Americans suffered a severe thrashing at the hands of the Shawnee and other tribes at what became known as the Battle of Blue Licks. One of the fallouts of that defeat, was a tremendous amount of criticism heaped on General George Rogers Clark, who wasn't even there. In retaliation, and to save a fall from grace, Clark quickly organized and executed a raid on Shawnee villages up and down the Great Miami River. The attack's denouement was Clark's order for the thorough destruction of Loramie's Station. Ben Logan led the charge of a combined force of soldiers and vengeful Kentucky militia. It would be the last major campaign Clark was to make in his celebrated career. In a letter from him to Benjamin Harrison, then governor of Virginia, the general explained

> Sir
>
> ... I left the Ohio the fourth [November] with one Thousand and fifty men and supprised the principal Shawonee Town on the Eavening of the Tenth Inst amediately Detacking off Strong parties to difierent Quarters in a few Hours two thirds of their Towns was laid in ashes and everything they ware possess'd of destroy'd except such articles most usefull to the Troops the Enemy not having time to Secret any part of

their Riches that was in ye Villages the British Trading post [Loramie's] at the Portage on the Head of the Miami shared the same fate by Col' Benj. Logan and a party one Hundred and fifty Horse whare property to a great amount was burnt the Quantity of provisions destroyed far surpassed any Idea we had of their Stores of that kind the loss of the Enemy was Ten scalps Seven prisoners and two whites Retaken ours one kiled one wounded... [20]

As stated, the buildings and commodities were all torched. As of this writing, hard evidence is beginning to be uncovered at the site in the form of ashes that are still holding their shape as the posts that were once the walls of Loramie's store. Any trade goods of potential use to the troops were confiscated as spoils of the raid. Historian Henry Howe found one story of how the booty was dispersed; providing a moment of amusement in an otherwise brutal situation.

The store contained a large quantity of goods and peltry, which were sold at auction afterwards among the men by the general's orders. Among the soldiers was an Irishman named Burke, considered a half-witted fellow, and the general butt of the whole army. While searching the store he found, done up in a rag, twenty-five half-joes [coins], worth about $200, which he secreted in a hole he cut in an old saddle. At the auction no one bid for the saddle, it being judged worthless, except Burke, to whom it was struck off for a trifling sum, amid roars of laughter for his folly. But a moment elapsed before Burke commenced a search, and found and drew forth the money, as if by accident; then shaking it in the eyes of the men, exclaimed, "An' it's not bad a bargain after all!" [21]

Loramie had lost everything, except his life. He had managed to physically survive Clark's wrath, but now faced the tough question of what to do next. The war was evidently winding down. The Americans, whom he had been supplying the Indians with arms to defeat, were about to own the frontier lands he was living upon. Rebuilding along the creek was a precarious option. Historians speculate that he could have returned to Canada where he had old, but good, relations with family, Indians, and British friends from his younger days. However, he didn't take that road. Instead, the still relatively young man went west with his Shawnee family.

At least part of the reason for his decision was that Loramie had eyes on a lady named Charlotte Pemanpieh Bougainville. She was half Shawnee, her father French and her mother Metis (a nation of people in Canada whose ancestors were of both European and Indigenous descent). Their marriage in 1783 sealed Peter's connection to the Shawnee. Charlotte eventually bore him eight children.

The Loramie family first settled with the Shawnee in a village along the White River near Vincennes. Soon they would move to Ste. Genevieve on the Spanish side of the Mississippi River. Here Loramie established himself as a diplomat with the Spanish officials and acted as an Indian agent. Over the years he acquired more and more lands along the Mississippi River. Trade was always his forte and with his contacts and persuasive skills amongst all peoples, he prospered. Along the way, Peter Loramie became known by his original French name, without the first appellation. Louis Lorimier was even bestowed the title of "Dom" by the Spanish government. The town of Cape Girardeau, Missouri, grew from a trading post he started. He passed away in 1812 and along with his wife is buried in a prominent memorial in the city he founded.

After Clark's destruction of Loramie's Trading Post in 1782, like Pickawillany three decades earlier, the site became a ghost town of sorts. A year later, the Revolution had officially ended and it was then that the Americans picked up where the colonists had left off of expanding into the Ohio Valley, only to face more Indian resistance. By 1790, the fighting grew to the scale of war.

General Josiah Harmar was the leader of the first of three major waves of attack on the hostile Indians. From Fort Washington (Cincinnati, Ohio) his course would take him over the deserted sites. They crossed the Great Miami River just south of the former Pickawillany and camped one night seven miles up Loramie Creek. The following morning they were marching over the grounds of Loramie's old post on their way to a battle that they would lose.

In the following year, General St. Clair suffered an even more horrific defeat just a hundred miles outside of Fort Washington. As a result, the third assault would be led by General "Mad" Anthony Wayne who was sent north with a more highly trained force.

On his way up to, and back from, his victory in today's northwest

Ohio, Wayne built a string of fortresses and supply depots. At the outset of his march, he erected the largest of his forts at present-day Greenville, Ohio. About the same time, he decided to also construct a supply depot that could easily and safely store goods headed westward for Greenville and other nearby sites, some yet to be built. He chose the high ground of old Pickawillany, just twenty miles to the east, because of its strategic location along the same network of rivers that Memeskia had appreciated nearly fifty years earlier. It became known as Fort Piqua and was staffed at least through 1795.

On the trip back from his successful battle, Wayne passed through the grounds of Loramie's old store. He ordered the construction of yet another fortified supply station at this spot so that it could support garrisons to the west like Forts Recovery, Defiance, Adams, and Wayne. This depot became known as Fort Loramie by Wayne's order, testifying that the French trader's memory was still in the hearts and minds of the settlers and Indians a dozen years after he had been forced out. The creek too, was christened as "Loramie's" at this time.

In 1795, the Greenville Treaty gave the United States free access to much of what would become the state of Ohio. The document itself also bears witness to how important Loramie's former trading post had been; as it is referred to as a demarcation point of the lands involved. Article 3 of the treaty reads:

> The general boundary line between the lands of the United States and the lands of the said Indian tribes, shall begin at the mouth of Cayahoga river, and run thence up the same to the portage, between that and the Tuscarawas branch of the Muskingum, thence down that branch to the crossing place above fort Lawrence, thence westerly to a fork of that branch of the Great Miami river, running into the Ohio, at or near which fork stood Loromie's store, and where commences the portage between the Miami of the Ohio... [22]

Unlike Fort Piqua to the south, Fort Loramie would remain manned, at least periodically, through the War of 1812, though without much incident. It was used for storing military supplies, but also functioned as a stopping point for both government and private convoys, as did the other forts between the Ohio River and Lake Erie. In 1815, it was sold to a private citizen, James Furrow, who turned its timbers into a tavern and a post office. The village of

Fort Loramie has flourished ever since, boasting of its rich history through its name and its populace.

By the end of Wayne's foray through the territory, the site of old Fort Pickawillany and then Fort Piqua had become known as Upper Piqua. Just a bit farther down the Great Miami River from there was the new Shawnee village of Piqua. When Fort Piqua was abandoned by the military in 1795, a former sutler named Job Gard, who had been selling his wares to the soldiers of Fort Greenville, moved into the fortress. He didn't stay long. By the summer of 1797, he was floating many of the timbers that had formed the fort walls down river to a spot in Piqua where he used them to build himself a new home.

During these Indian wars of the early 1790s, a teenager by the name of John Johnston was enlisted by Anthony Wayne as a wagoner. He was held responsible for transporting army supplies between military posts while maintaining the wagon and tending the horses. As Johnston had criss-crossed the Ohio countryside, he kept a keen eye out for both job opportunities and for a future homestead. One day, in the course of his duties, he approached Fort Piqua. The view of the landscape struck at his heart and mind. He immediately knew he would one day live there.

The job he held with the army exposed him to numerous savvy buyers and sellers. He quickly picked up on the art of negotiation. Eventually his skills of persuasion were taken note of. A few years after Washington's Indian Wars, in 1801, Johnston was appointed as a clerk for the war department. Just a few months later he landed a position as a factor, a government authorized merchant and deputy, at Fort Wayne. This was the fort built and named for Wayne near the site of the former Fort Miamis at Kekionga.

Before reporting for his new job at Fort Wayne in September of 1802, Johnston had some important business to attend to. He was in love. However, having been raised as an Episcopalian, the twenty-six year old Johnston was forced to elope with his sixteen-year-old Quaker girlfriend, as her parents were not approving of their marriage. Soon after the July wedding, they made the long trek from Pennsylvania to Fort Wayne. Johnston's duties there were broad-based. He managed incoming and outgoing supplies, as well as the comings and goings of the people living in the fort and surroundings. Business dealings revolved around the Indians living at Kekionga and the neighboring villages. It was through his work with the Indians, on matters of importance to them, that he earned their respect; and that achievement was again taken note of by the military officials. When William Wells left his position as the Indian Agent at the fort, Johnston was given the job. That occurred in April of 1809. He held the new post for the next two years. Worth noting is the fact that during his tenure at Fort Wayne, Johnston did make one significant personal business transaction. Back in 1804, he bought that land along the Great Miami River that he had spotted years previous. Pickawillany was eventually going to have a new inhabitant.

Late in 1811, Johnston decided to retire to his long vacant home in what was then referred to as Upper Piqua. He planned to raise crops and kids. But it wasn't meant to be so simple. Apparently, his talents of diplomacy and efficiency were not to be squandered. Just a few months into a quiet life on his farm, yet another war broke out. In June of 1812, Johnston was called out of retirement to act as a Federal Indian Agent once again; first to the Shawnee and soon after to the Wyandot, Lenape, Seneca and Delaware. His homestead became an official Indian Agency – a hub where residents of the nearby Indian villages could gather. Here he attended to their needs as a representative of the United States government.

Ohio, already established as a state for nearly a decade, was at the heart of the conflicts in the whole of the Northwest Territory throughout the War of 1812. President Madison's keen awareness of this powder keg area, relied heavily on Johnston's abilities to quell as much Indian resistance as possible. However, the war, by its very nature, heightened the potential for more chaos. Madison viewed Upper Piqua as the most natural site to be elevated to the status of a station of central intelligence for Indian affairs. He appointed Ohio's then governor, Return J. Meigs, along with two of its future governors, Thomas Worthington, and Jeremiah Morrow as commissioners to the Native Americans. It should be noted that just a mile or two downriver from Johnston's farm and agency was Lower Piqua which eventually evolved into the present-day Piqua, Ohio. The two

Portrait of John Johnston, Indian Agent. Artist unknown. Shown here as it appeared in book: *History of Ohio: The Rise and Progress of an American State*, 1912.

locations were often referred to jointly and interchangeably as Piqua, though they were separated by a few miles.

Madison wanted as many of the Indians to be on his side of the conflict as he could possibly persuade to do so. In the least, he wanted them neutral; not on the British side. He ordered a meeting to be scheduled as soon as possible between the US officials and the Indian leaders living in the Ohio Valley. In an extract from a letter of the then Secretary of War, William Eustis, to the commissioners, we learn some of the council's objectives.

> ... The President having been pleased to appoint you commissioners to meet the chiefs and head men of the several Indian tribes from the western frontier in council at Piqua town, in the State of Ohio, on the 1st of August next, I have the honor to communicate his pleasure that you, or any two of you, explain to them the views of the President in ordering the council. He has heard of their determination to preserve peace with the United States, and he is desirous of saving them from

the destruction which would inevitably ensue in case of their hostility. The conduct of some of them would justify him in lifting his hand against them and destroying them, but he is informed that the tribes disapprove of what has been done, and he will not punish the innocent with the guilty. You will hear all their complaints, and learn from them the course they desire to pursue in the war with Great Britain. You will inform them that the President stands in no need of their assistance. For their own sakes he desires them to remain quiet and to pursue their usual occupations. In case they shall give satisfactory assurance that they will pursue peace with good faith they may be assured that the President will take them by the hand – that he will protect them – that they shall have their annuities according to treaty – that their lands shall be held sacred, and that, being at peace with the United States, they will be reconciled to and will preserve the chain of friendship with all their Governors and Agents. It must be distinctly explained to them that the chiefs will be held responsible for the good conduct of their tribes, and if a single murder be committed on the frontier the murdered [murderer?] shall be forthwith delivered up or the tribe to which he belongs shall be driven beyond the Mississippi, their lands shall be forfeited, and their annuities shall cease forever. Upon a perfect understanding of the agreement to these several points the goods sent to Piqua as presents may be delivered, in whole or in part, according to the discretion of the commissioners. Twelve or fifteen chiefs may be invited to visit the President, and receive from his own mouth a confirmation of your engagements, and have them formed into a regular treaty. If, on the contrary, they are not disposed to friendship, or there is good reason to doubt the sincerity of their professions, the council will be immediately broken up, with a warning of the consequence... [23]

Reinforcing the need for a council is evidenced by a letter written in mid-July of 1812 by Johnston himself. He warned the commander of nearby Fort Greenville that danger was in the air.

Dear Sir: I send you for perusal a letter which I last night received from the Shawanoes Indians. It appears that a war party was seen near [Fort] Recovery, you will of course take proper measures to prevent mischief happening to any of our citizens or their property within your command. I think an officer and 10 or 12 men from your company or VanCleve's should occupy Capt. Perry's Block House, a few of the men could sleep in my barn at night to guard the United States goods. The property is too valuable to remain as it is, now that we are at war with the British... [24]

On August 15, 1812, delayed a couple weeks from its originally scheduled date, the commissioners, along with Johnston and others, held a general council with representatives of the Indian nations at the new military headquarters established on Johnston's property. Even Little Turtle of the Miamis attended. The discussions continued over several days, concluding with an agreement by the tribes attending to not take sides in the fight. It was a major coup for the Americans.

Just weeks after the council, news of the loss of Fort Michilimackinac and Hull's defeat at Detroit threw previously laid military plans into chaos. Rumors of attacks planned against the only two major American strongholds left on the northern frontier, Fort Dearborn (Chicago) and Fort Wayne, were running rampant. These threats soon became a reality that William Henry Harrison would have to deal with.

In the fall of 1811, Harrison made a one-day camp with his troops in Upper Piqua on their way to Tippecanoe. He became very comfortable with the commissioners and agent Johnston. A year later, in early September of 1812, he returned. At this time, tensions were growing throughout the region. Harrison began putting matters in motion for a fight; ordering both supplies and men to move in several directions. Before he had even arrived at Johnston's agency, he had sent a proclamation to be read to the men of Piqua:

VOLUNTEERS WANTED

Any number of volunteers, mounted and prepared for active service to continue for twenty-five or thirty days, will be accepted to rendezvous at the towns of Dayton, on the Big Miami on the 15th inst. It is expected that the Volunteers will provide themselves with salt provisions and a proportion of biscuits.

Those brave men who may give their services on this occasion may be assured that an opportunity of distinguishing themselves will be afforded. I shall command the expedition in person; and the number of troops employed will be entirely adequate to the object proposed.

I wish also to hire a number of substantial horses. Fifty cents per day will be allowed for each horse which is provided with saddle and bridle. Those patriotic citizens who are unable to afford their personal subsistence, will render essential service to their country by furnishing the horses, which must be delivered in Dayton on the 14th inst. to a person who will be authorized to receive and receipt for them.

William Henry Harrison [25]

While this call for militia was urgent, a second request came just three days later while Harrison was still at Upper Piqua.

> Headquarters, Piqua
> September 5, 1812, 4 o'clock, A.M.
>
> MOUNTED VOLUNTEERS!
>
> I requested you, in my late address [Sept. 2 above] to rendezvous at Dayton on the 15th instant. I have now a more pressing call for your services! The British and Indians have invaded our country and are now besieging (perhaps have taken) Fort Wayne. Every friend to his country, who is able to do so, will join me as soon as possible, well mounted, with a good rifle and twenty or thirty days provision. Ammunition will be furnished at Cincinnati and at Dayton - and the Volunteers will draw provisions (to save their salted meat) at all the public deposites: the Quartermasters and Commissaries will see that this order is executed.
>
> William Henry Harrison [26]

Soon the general had left Upper Piqua for an anticipated fight at Fort Wayne. As it turned out he and his troops had indeed arrived there in time to save the fortress from capture.

John Johnston remained at his home until the end of the war, continuing to serve as an agent of the government to those Indians who promised their neutrality. In fact, he would remain in this diplomatic role well after the war had ended in 1815. It was politics, as they often do, that caused him to lose his position. Andrew Jackson and the Democratic party won the election of 1828 and they soon appointed one of their own to the position. Johnston had been an appointee of the Whig party. Thereafter, his homestead may not have been an official Indian Agency, but unofficially Johnston maintained regular contact and friendships with his long-established Indian friends.

A man of diverse interests, Johnston remained active through his later years, having a special interest in promoting both civil and military education. Most notably he co-founded Kenyon College in central Ohio. He also served on boards at Miami University and West Point. In addition, Johnston served on the Ohio Canal Commission. He was influential on determining the route that the Miami-Erie Canal would take through Ohio, especially through his neighborhood at Upper Piqua.

In a sad twist of fate, on October 6, 1846, the last known members of the Miami nation were unwillingly boarded onto canal boats at the former Kekionga village in Indiana for a one-way trip west of the Mississippi River. They first sailed northeasterly up the Wabash-Erie Canal until they connected with the Miami-Erie Canal in the vicinity of today's Defiance, Ohio. From there they moved southward, on their way to the Ohio River, which would then take them westward to their final destination. The canal route that this last remnant of the Miami nation had followed traced sections of Loramie's Creek until it reached the point where it met the Great Miami River at old Pickawillany. One can only imagine their despair as they drifted by their forefathers' former villages for the last time. Johnston himself, likely couldn't bear the scene that played out that day; just a hundred yards in front of his always sympathetic homestead.

The network of streams and rivers, and even former canals, across the Ohio Valley hold many stories that are now long forgotten. Some are tales of ordinary people simply surviving day to day. Others are of great men and great conflicts. All are seemingly washed away by the waters still flowing over the Ohio country and by time itself. Loramie Creek is one of those waterways with an eventful and life-changing past that should be remembered and appreciated. Should your travels take you across the Ohio countryside, take note of those little identification signs of the rivers being traversed. Give a thought to who may have canoed down or up them over the past three hundred years. Wonder what their lives were like. Then find a book or website or historical society which has documentation of the real stories of those real people and discover how their lives may have unknowingly had an impact on the life you lead today. ♦

HMMM...

This recollection of John Johnston, Indian Agent at Piqua, Ohio and longtime friend of William H. Harrison, was published in the mid-1800s.

God Knew.

Pending the Presidential election in 1840, Gen. Harrison was occasionally an inmate at Upper Piqua. He was there a few months previous to the death of my beloved wife. She had enjoyed his acquaintance for almost forty years, and took a deep interest in all that concerned his happiness and fame. She was an humble, pious and devout Christian, and cherished a sincere desire to see all others in possession of those hopes which sustained her through a life spent in the wilds of the West, under circumstances of more than ordinary trial and difficulty.

She sought an opportunity of conversing with the General on the subject of religion, urging upon him that as he was getting old it was time he should turn his attention to the close of his earthly career and seek his peace with God in the gospel of his Son.

He replied that he was long convinced it was his duty to make a public confession of Christianity, that the people of the United States had made him a candidate for the Presidency, that if he was then to unite with the church it would be ascribed to a desire of popularity, and would do the cause of religion a serious injury and make himself the subject of uncharitable remarks in the political journals, but, he said, as soon as this contest for the Presidency is over, let it be adverse or prosperous to myself, it is my purpose if my life is spared to make a religion after the inauguration.

It is well known that the President had the proper understanding with the Rev. Doctor Hawley of St. John's Church in Washington to become a member of that church on Easter Sunday, April [11], 1841. The Doctor stated this fact over his remains [April 4, 1841].

Late in March, 1841, I [Johnston] went to the President's house on a Sunday evening. The whole house was filled with visitors of all sorts. I was pained to see this, on account of the character of its incumbent; at last an opportunity occurred of my speaking to the President. I told him I was sorry to see the house the resort of such a multitude of idle persons on the Sabbath Day, that I feared those matters would get into the newspapers and injure his character. He said he regretted much himself that persons would visit him on that day, that the city was full of people and all wanted to see him, but as soon as the crowd dispersed and went home, that house in future would be closed against all visits on the Sabbath Day.

Harrison passed away just one week before the date he had set to make his Christian faith public knowledge.

In Leonard U. Hill's, John Johnston and the Indians, 1957 [27]

VIII.
ONE FOR THE ROAD.

In the northern region of today's Iraq, archaeologists have discovered an artifact known as a cylinder seal – a stamp of sorts which when rolled onto a slab of soft clay leaves a decorative impression. This cylinder depicts two ancients of that region sipping beer from a large clay vessel through very long straws. These were Sumerians living in the formerly festive lands of Mesopotamia, circa 1500 BC. How do we know it was beer they were enjoying? That's because a poet of that same era, and area, etched a series of verses about beer in stone, and we're not speaking metaphorically. A tablet exists with a hymn of praise to an ancient diety named Ninkasi and it contains what is considered to be the oldest recipe for beer, as well as some applause for its effect when consumed. Afterall, Ninkasi was the goddess of beer in Sumeria; and in a land with a god for everything vital in life, including water, air, and earth; shouldn't she be given a little adulation of her own?

The hymn's poetry style is a bit repetitive, perhaps meant to be sung, but parts of it read:

> You are the one who handles dough [and]... with a big shovel,
> Mixing, in a pit, the bappir [barley bread] with sweet aromatics.
> Ninkasi, you are the one who handles dough [and]...with a big shovel,
> Mixing, in a pit, the bappir with [date]-honey.
>
> You are the one who bakes the bappir in the big oven,
> Puts in order the piles of hulled grain.
> Ninkasi, you are the one who bakes the bappir in the big oven,
> Puts in order the piles of hulled grain...

> ...You are the one who soaks the malt in a jar,
>   The waves rise, the waves fall.
> Ninkasi, you are the one who soaks the malt in a jar,
>   The waves rise, the waves fall.
>
> You are the one who spreads the cooked mash on large reed mats,
>   Coolness overcomes...
> Ninkasi, you are the one who spreads the cooked mash on large reed mats,
>   Coolness overcomes...
>
> ...When you pour out the filtered beer of the collector vat,
>   It is [like] the onrush of the Tigris and the Euphrates.
> Ninkasi, you are the one who pours out the filtered beer of the collector vat,
>   It is [like] the onrush of the Tigris and the Euphrates...
>
> ...In the...reed buckets there is sweet beer,
> I will make cupbearers, boys, [and] brewers stand by,
> While I circle around the abundance of beer,
> While I feel wonderful, I feel wonderful,
> Drinking beer, in a blissful mood,
> Drinking liquor, feeling exhilarated,
> With joy in the heart [and] a happy liver... [1]

With a careful clink of our ancient ceramic mugs, let's toast ol' Sumeria's ingenuity, give cheers to our human heritage, and jump in time and place to the early American frontier. From the days of the Revolution through the early 1800s, the country grew up and out from its confines east of the Appalachians; and alcohol went with them. Those former colonials had well-established protocol for the consumption of intoxicating beverages. Behavior was based on the heritage they had brought with them from Europe centuries earlier. As evidenced from the Sumerian records those practices in-turn had a long history of their own. This is all a long way of saying that alcohol has been a part of human culture forever. The inhabitants of early America were simply carrying on as those who had come before them. The differences were only in what type of alcohol was drunk as well as some of the reasons for its consumption.

With the end of the French and Indian War in 1763, the migration from the Atlantic coast into the wilderness had begun in earnest. Vague paths into the lands of Kentucky, and soon thereafter Ohio, were eventually worn into defined roads as more and more people arrived. The wayfarers along these thoroughfares had many needs as;

An ancient cylinder seal found in Khafajeh, Iraq dating from the early Dynastic period, circa 2600-2350 BCE. Its rolling depicts two figures drinking beer through long reed straws.

both as they travelled and after they had arrived at their destinations.

Food, water, shelter, and clothing were of course vital to survival, but so too was alcohol. Beyond the obvious relaxation it could provide, as well as the havoc it could wreak when used excessively, fermented spirits were also employed as a preventative and cure of disease.

Alcohol played two broad roles on the frontier. One was based in biology, the other in psychology. The first was to ensure physical health. The second was to enhance social health. In both capacities there was the ever-present danger of its abuse; but that was a risk worth taking.

The human body was begging for trouble when it ventured into the wilderness. Due to the adverse conditions, injuries were more frequent, either by accident or through conflicts. Disease was spread by insects, water, and general lack of hygiene. Problems like these were not uncommon in the towns that the frontiersmen had come from, however in the wilderness, survival from them was much more difficult to achieve.

The physician on the frontier was, more often than not, the woman of the house. Trained doctors were scarce, especially over the first decade or two of settlement. If there was a physician in the region, he regularly made rounds from village to village. If you broke your arm while he was a hundred miles away, your friends or family were going to assume the doctoring role with limited hope of success. Likewise, the few medicines known in the states were hard to come by in the wilderness. One of the few treatments readily available for any health issue was alcohol.

It was generally believed throughout the medical community, and society on the whole, that alcohol promoted good health. It was prescribed, frequently in large doses, to relieve fever and pain. In the treatment of wounds, one can imagine the violent sting of hard liquor being poured on an open wound. Well, one can only imagine it, because the reality is that it was rarely used in that way. There was no understanding of microorganisms causing the complications of infection. In fact, whoever was tending a wound had no idea that using their bare hands and unwashed instruments could cause further problems for the afflicted person. Therefore, along with a stick to bite down on, the alcohol was given to the patient internally as a sedative.

In the absence of doctors, it was fortunate that many of the Indians who had befriended the Americans shared their knowledge of herbal remedies. For internal problems, one might make a tea from specific plants indigenous to the region. In the treatment of wounds, poultices were made by combining various local herbs, grasses, and barks. Known remedial drugs used in the states were not often available on the frontier. For the most part, even if those established medicines could be acquired, they generally treated symptoms rather than providing a cure. And, the number of such drug treatments available during this era was minuscule when compared to today's pharmaceutical industry.

That availability started to change a bit once the number of settlements had increased. As the population grew, they became a burgeoning market for the sale of medicines. This prompted entrepreneurs to get in on the action. They began by running advertisements in the frontier newspapers that offered medicines that were made in the eastern states as well as some imported from other countries. Some were patented. Others were the creations of the so-called "snake oil" salesmen. Bottles full of herbs, flower petals, berries, and who knows what else, were promised to remedy almost every ailment known to man at the time; with no legitimate medical oversight of their claims. Since it was a given of this time period that alcohol alone had medicinal benefits, it is no surprise that it was added as the base ingredient to almost all the real and so-called medicines. Most blends had at least five percent alcohol content, some as much as twenty-five. That translates to being ten to fifty proof. There's little doubt that more often than not it was this secret main ingredient in the charlatan's potions that was providing the real relief, at least mentally.

Disease was plentiful. By far, it was the primary cause of death on the frontier. Afflictions came through the stings of mosquitoes and bites of critters, for certain. However, it was water that posed the biggest problem. The lakes and rivers that appeared to be so pristine actually harbored invisible enemies of man. Today we know that it was bacteria and viruses, swimming freely in those waters since time began, that caused their problems. The only thing that the pioneers knew was that drinking water right from the source often caused illness; sometimes just momentary discomfort, sometimes death.

With this in mind, when choosing a permanent site to call home, a family would often pick one near a fresh spring. Otherwise, they would soon dig a well. Waters from these underground sources were the only ones naturally purified. Settlements typically bloomed along rivers and streams, but the residents quickly learned that these above-ground waters needed some attention before they could be safely drunk.

Of course there were plenty of occasions when thirst had to be quenched by dipping directly into a stream, but that was usually when away from home on a long hunt, or on an expedition to a new location. When thirst hit hard in those situations, it was easy to risk having some discomfort later, in lieu of the pains of dehydration.

The pioneers had long ago learned from their life in the colonies that boiling and sifting water would sometimes strain out any unknown demons lingering therein. However, though they didn't understand the science of it, they learned that fermenting water with grains or fruits produced beverages that satisfied thirst, tasted good, did not make them ill, and made them feel pretty darn good. Fermentation became the best solution yet. And so, beer and cider, the quickest and easiest libations to brew, became the drinks of choice.

The recipes varied depending on what grains, vegetables, or fruits were available. One had to make do with what one had. It was apples that were rather plentiful across the wilderness; especially bitter crab apples which were not the best tasting of fruits when eaten fresh off the tree. They were, however, excellent for fermenting into cider. The famous travels of Walter Chapman, aka Johnny Appleseed, add to the lore of the frontier and apples used for cider. The fact that Chapman

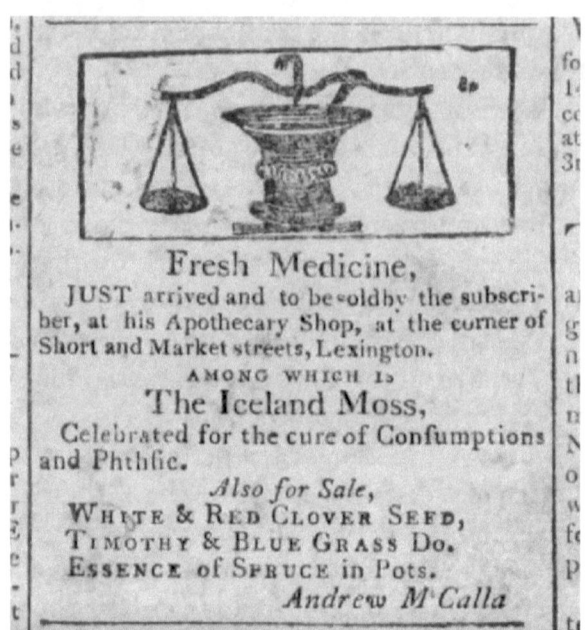

An advertisement in the *Kentucky Gazette* dated January 16, 1799 for medicines. A lichen known as Iceland Moss was imported for common discomforts of cough, sore throat, bronchitis, and indigestion. It is still available today, usually as a tea.

was primarily on a mission of spreading the gospel along the frontier is often glossed over, but that was his foremost purpose. In the course of his missionary trips across the frontier he also created a business of selling apple seedlings. The apples he planted were not the varieties we enjoy crunching into today. His were those bitter types best suited for making cider. Though arguments can be made that his real goal was to promote the consumption of alcoholic ciders for profit, it can likewise be cited that cider was already being produced as a necessity to survival due to the poor quality of the water on the frontier. It's more likely that Chapman was fulfilling two vital life-saving needs at the same time: spreading the knowledge of Christ through his preaching and spreading the fruit required to make safe beverages.

Over time, the frontier folks learned a clever trick that enabled them to make a more potent cider. It only worked during the cold days of winter when the cider was left outside of the cabin in order for it to freeze. When that happened, only the water in the batch of cider had succumbed to the temperature. The brewer would discard the ice thus formed, leaving behind a much more concentrated alcoholic drink. The finished product had been "jacked," or increased in potency and hence became known as "Applejack." Whereas stills were generally used to separate water from alcohol by employing heat, the homesteader let mother nature's coldness do her thing through the winter season.

Others opted to brew their beer. It was crafted in homes and surely varied in flavor from batch to batch because, again, whatever was available was used. In most cases it was wheat, corn, or oats that would be mixed with yeast. However, sometimes vegetation that would be considered unusual to today's taste was used. This included persimmons, squash, and spruce. The full-potency, finished product was generally saved for the adults; especially for times of celebration or relaxation. A very low alcohol beverage was brewed for the children and for general adult thirst quenching. These batches of beer would be brewed a second or even third time, which reduced the alcohol content of the finished product. In one of his early journals, our future first president, George Washington, recorded his own recipe for "small beer," which he likely had made and served to the troops that he was leading during the French and Indian War of the 1750s.

> To make Small Beer Take a large Siffer full of Bran Hops to your taste - Boil these 3 hours. Then strain out 30 Gall[ons] into a Cooler[.] put in 3 Gall[ons] molasses while the Beer is scalding hot or rather draw the molasses into the Cooler & strain the Beer on it while boiling Hot[.] let this stand till it is little more than Blood warm then put in a quart of Ye[a]st[.] if the Weather is very Cold cover it over with a Blank[et] & let it Work in the Cooler 24 hours then put it into the Cask - leave the Bung open till it is almost done working - Bottle it that day week it was Brewed[.] [2]

The rugged character of some children and their tolerance for alcohol in the early 1800s becomes evident in a report that an aged frontiersman sent to a newspaper on the Western Reserve.

> He (old Dr. J. B. Harmon) more than fifty years ago pulled a tooth for me, in the summer of 1834. I found him at the old court house. Then he took an old dull jack-knife and cut around the tooth. That hurt some, but I was a boy then and had not learned to chew tobacco, but I could take a pretty stiff horn of whisky, a common article in every family." [3]

Beer, small beer, and cider were staples of frontier life and were consumed between and with most meals. The barley and hops of the wilderness were not of the same quality as those found across the Atlantic which were hard to secure and pricey. Therefore, local varieties of vegetation were used or even skipped in the home-made batches. Wine was made from the fruits of the land as well, but quality grapes were less abundant in the early days. For this reason, some wines were imported, but their consumption was less because of their cost and availability.

Of course there were also the more ardent spirits of rum and whiskey which were consumed by the frontiersmen. From early colonial days, rum was imported from the British-ruled West Indies, today's Caribbean Islands. Later the molasses used to create that rum was imported as well, so that the colonists could make their own batches at a lesser cost. That practice held until the American Revolution began. At that point the British stopped the export of both finished rum and its key ingredient, molasses, from the islands. An alternative to rum was needed and it came through the Scots-Irish who made up a large percentage of the frontiersmen heading west.

Whiskey became the next strong drink of choice. As farming expanded, it was difficult to transport large quantities of grains to the east coast. There was plenty of excess corn, rye, wheat , etc.; and transforming the surplus into whiskey was a strategic business move. The liquid distillations were much easier to transport, didn't spoil, and drew a larger profit. It wasn't long before farmers across the wilderness were distilling what became the rye and corn whiskies, as well as the bourbons, still enjoyed to this day.

A historian of the mid-1800s explains how alcohol was viewed and used by the early settlers of the Ohio country:

> Alcoholic liquids were considered a necessity of life; a sort of panacea for all ills; a crowning sheaf to all blessings; good in sickness and in health; good in summer to dispel the heat, and good in winter to dispel the cold; good to keep on work, and more than good to help on a frolic.
>
> So good were they considered, that their attributed merits were fixed by pleasant names. The first dram of the morning was an "eye-opener;" duly followed by the "eleven-o'clocker" and the "four-o'clocker;" whilst the very last was a "night-cap;" after which one was supposed to take no more drinks that day, unless he was unexpectedly called up at night, when, as people generally slept in rooms without fires, he prudently fortified himself against taking cold. [4]

For the record, today a dram is measured as one-eighth of an ounce of a beverage. That is not what the pioneers meant when they used that word over two hundred years ago. At that time it was a rough measurement of the amount one could consume in one swallow. That would usually amount to what today we call a "shot." An even earlier story exists of how the measure of a "shot" came to be. King Edgar of England, in the mid-900s AD, recognized the need to control errant behavior brought on by the excessive consumption of spirits. He not only tried to make it a law to limit the number of establishments that sold liquor in any given Anglo-Saxon village, but he is also responsible for coming up with the idea of measuring the amount of alcohol to be dispensed at any one serving. Knowing from experience the effect a certain quantity of alcohol had on any given individual, the reasoning was that the house serving drinks to the public could set limits on the consumption if they had a baseline measure. Edgar called it a "peg." It was about thirty millimeters of hard liquor, or about an ounce in the US measures of today. And so we learn that King Edgar, over a thousand years ago, defined the volume of what we refer to as a "shot" to this day. The expression to, "take (someone) down a peg or two" comes from this era as being the process of cutting off a belligerent customer, who might have become a bit boisterous, by refusing him any more pegs.

The second and more obvious use of alcohol was as a stress reliever and relaxant. Some things never change. There was plenty of tension on the frontier to warrant the relief that a drink could provide. In colonial days, when people gathered together, alcohol was often involved. It was a social elixir that broke down restraint during conversations with friends and neighbors. Our founding fathers indulged just as much, and by some claims even more than the rest of the population.

If ever there is a situation of high anxiety and tension it has to be during the times of war. Knowing the relief that a belt or two can bring, the armies and militias of this era were well-supplied with liquor. For convenience of transport and to avoid spoilage, barrels of rum and whiskey were sent with the troops to almost every engagement. The "shelf-life" of beer and cider was too short. In most confrontations, each man, each day, would be issued a gill of whichever distilled spirits were available. That measures to about four ounces or four shots per gill. The men definitely looked forward to this ration. It was a priority on the same level as acquiring any of the foodstuffs.

The use of alcohol can be seen through each succeeding set of battles that our country incurred. A metaphorical carrot, in the form of booze, was dangled in front of the first official fighting force of the Revolution, both as a reward and to discipline the men.

> A chaplain of a regiment of the Continental army complained that the men were not punctual at morning prayers. "Oh, I'll fix that," said the colonel, so he issued an order that the liquor ration would hereafter be given out at the close of morning prayers. It worked like a miracle; not a man was missing. [5]

Later, in the course of the Indian wars of the early 1790s, General Anthony Wayne's orderly expressed concern over the lack of whiskey that his troops had on hand, just days after their victory at the Battle of Fallen Timbers. While at Fort Defiance he noted that

> the number of our sick increases daily; provision is nearly exhausted; the whisky has been out for some time, which makes the hours pass heavily to the tune of Roslin Castle [a funeral dirge of the day], when in our present situation they ought to go to the quick step of the merry man down to his grave. Hard duty and scanty allowance will cause an army to be low spirited, particularly the want of a little of the wet. [6]

Six days later, the same orderly gives a further glimpse into the importance of liquor. Supplies of food had arrived, including some two hundred head of cattle and the same number of kegs full of flour. However, he wrote:

> ...we received no liquor by this command, and I fancy we shall not receive any until we get into winter quarters, which will make the fatigues of the campaign appear double, as I am persuaded the troops would much rather live on half rations of beef and bread, provided they could obtain their full rations of whisky. [7]

Unfortunately, the downside of alcohol was on display three weeks later when whiskey finally did make it into Wayne's camp, "and a number of the soldiery became much intoxicated, they having stolen a quantity of liquor from the quartermaster"[8] In a few more days, the troops would arrive at the confluence of the St. Joseph, St. Marys, and Maumee rivers. There they began construction of the fort that would bear Wayne's name. The work was grueling and was carried on through harsh weather. The first course of action was felling trees

and on October 4, 1794,

> every officer, non-commissioned officer[,] and soldier belonging to the square are on fatigue this day, hauling trees on the hind wheels of wagons; the first day we got an extra gill per man, which appears to be all the compensation at this time in the power of the commander-in-chief to make the troops. [9]

Two days later the supplies must have been replenished as,

> the volunteers engaged to work on the garrison, for which they are to receive three gills of whisky per day; their employment is digging the ditch and filling up the parapet. [10]

Even through the War of 1812, the daily gill was almost as important as waking up. General William H. Harrison keenly used it to get much needed ammunition during the sieges on Fort Meigs. He offered an additional gill to any man who risked a run outside the fort to retrieve British cannonballs that had missed their mark.

Another anecdotal story shows the problems too many drinks could cause amongst the troops as well as the lengths to which men would go to have more of it. From the diary of Lt. Colonel George McFeely, who was marching a detachment of two hundred men from the Susquehanna Valley to Fort Niagara in the autumn of 1812, we read:

> October 15th. This morning a number of our men were drunk here. I ordered the company officers to search the men and destroy all the whiskey that might be found amongst them; for the remainder of the march no soldier would be permitted to carry whiskey with him on the march...
>
> October 16th. This night our men had a frolic, a drunken one, and [we] were at a loss to find where or how they got the whiskey because in the morning every man was searched and all the whiskey was emptied out. After some time it was discovered that they had filled their gun barrels with whiskey and had the vent stopped up with a little plug made of hickory wood and a tomkin of cork in the muzzle [11]

It's common practice today for people on a long journey to eventually stop to get food and rest at a place of lodging. Things were no different on the frontier. Anyone traveling along one of the early paths into the lands of the Ohio River Valley and beyond, naturally needed to take regular breaks. Progress was slower back then. After all, their horsepower was, well, one; not the muscle of two hundred horses that power most of today's automobiles. At first the trails could only accommodate a single file of horses, not even wide enough to handle a wagon. Eventually, through a series of improvements, they were broadened. Regardless of the grueling conditions, travellers made their way until they grew too weary or it grew too dark. The earliest of these would-be settlers had to make do with simply stopping, building a fire, eating whatever they had packed, and being vigilant against an attack from any predators; both wild and human. As the 1700s rolled into the next century and more settlements were established, homes were built along the road to function as inns and taverns for the refreshment of travellers.

The first road into the wilderness came to be named as appropriately as it possibly could have been named – the Wilderness Road. It began east of the Cumberland Gap region of Virginia and extended westward through the mountains with branches leading to Boonesboro, Lexington, and Louisville, Kentucky. In the earliest days, the only stops along the Wilderness Road were at what they referred to as stations. These were either homesteads like the one the Whitleys of Crab Orchard lived in, or small settlements like Fort Harrod, Fort Logan, and Boonesboro. As time went on, regular inns and taverns appeared, and they grew in numbers as the settlements multiplied. Along some routes there would be one of these inns every five to twenty miles – the distance one could conceivably walk or cover on horseback in a day's time. They provided a respite where one could water himself and his horse before moving on.

One example of such a hostelry along the Wilderness Road was the Old Stone Tavern in southwestern Virginia. It was built and operated by Frederick Cullop, a prominent citizen of his day, to accommodate travelers who were heading into the new west at the turn of the eighteenth century. It still stands today just outside of Atkins, Virginia. Its longevity likely due to the fact that it was constructed of the nearby limestone. A journal entry from a Mrs. Julia Tevis, who was heading west in 1822, gives us a glimpse of how the taverns of that day operated; as well as a spark of her own personality. She explains that her group had already endured two days of travel in a stagecoach from her home in eastern Virginia, rolling

> over the rough roads; but we were made of sterner stuff than to dread cold or personal inconvenience. We traveled all day, through a violent snowstorm, over frozen ground and ice-bound torrents, stopping only twice to change horses, ere we reached the old stone tavern where we were to tarry for the night. It was near ten o'clock, the family were all in bed; one little tallow candle burned in the window, casting a feeble light upon the pathway that led to the door standing wide open for the expected stage passengers.
>
> The cheerlessness of the room we entered was made visible by the flickering rays of a few expiring embers. In the middle of the apartment was a square table, upon which were heaped in pewter dishes, cold beef, fat pork, cabbage, potatoes, with a large dish of cucumber pickles. A brown jug of milk and a show of teacups and saucers intimated arrangements for tea or coffee. My head ached so violently that I turned from the supper table with disgust, and stepped into an adjoining room in search of fire and some place upon which to rest my weary limbs. I threw myself upon what I supposed to be an empty bed, and in doing so awakened squalling children. Rising hastily, and turning toward another, I saw the, vision of a red flannel nightcap popping from under the bedclothes, which so frightened me that I flew to the other side of the room, and sunk despairingly into an old armchair, where I remained until my companions had supped, after which we were shown upstairs into a cold room. The feather bed, which I immediately appropriated, was made up like a grave, and surmounted by two little pillows, either of which I might have put into my pocket, and both of which I lost somewhere in the recesses of the bed during the night. [12]

An almost whimsical account has been passed down regarding the visit of some very special guests to a tavern along the Wilderness Road in the Shenandoah Valley. Well before he became King, Louis Philippe and his two younger brothers were in voluntary exile from France in order to save their lives during that country's famous Revolution. While they were here, Louis was able to satisfy his curiosity of the wilderness people of this continent by making a five month tour of the frontier. This meant many days and nights were spent in the inns and taverns of 1797 America.

At the beginning of their trek, after a most cordial visit with President Washington in the city bearing his name, the French dignitaries took a respite at a tavern in Winchester, Virginia. It was here that they became keenly aware of the tenacity and strong bonds of fellowship many frontiersmen possessed.

> ... they stopped at the public house of Mr. Bush, a portly old revolutionary soldier, who considered the relations between the traveller and himself as a favor to the former. He was a native of Manheim on the Rhine, and Louis Philippe, thinking he had won his good graces by speaking to him in German about his "fatherland," proposed that the meals of his party should be sent up into their room. Such a proposition had never been heard in the whole valley of the Shenandoah, and least of all in the mansion of our friend, Mr. Bush. The rules of his house, to which the laws of the Medes and Persians were but transitory regulations, had been attacked, and his professional pride wounded; and the recollections of Manheim, and the pleasure of his native language, and the modest conversation of the young strangers, were all thrown to the wind, and the worthy and offended dignitary exclaimed: "If you are too good to eat at the same table with my other guests, you are too good to eat in my house – begone!" And notwithstanding the deprecatory tone which Louis Philippe immediately took, his disavowal of any intention to offend, and his offer to eat wherever it would be agreeable to this governor of hungry appetites to decide, the young men were compelled to leave the house, and to seek refuge elsewhere. [13]

It seems that the swagger of the Frenchmen got them into trouble more than once. At least one other account states that a legendary personality living in the Indian country just north of Zanesville, Ohio, had a problem with the royals as well. In 1797, Charlie Williams, known affectionately by the locals as "King Charlie," had

> rolled up a log house-trading-post-tavern at the forks of the White Woman (the Tuscarawas River) and the Walhonding where they conjoin to form the Muskingum. He virtually ran the settlement of Tuscarawa (Coshocton), was a great hunter, got along fine with the Injuns. Touring about was young Louis. He came up River, entered the tavern, loiterers gazed on him. Louis became a bit flippant. (No place, this, for French flippancy). The House of Tuscarawa glowered at the House of Orleans [Louis's family's home]. They failed to see eye to eye. The loiterers egged the two on – they would make fun – and they did! Polite version has it that Charles the First of Tuscarawa took the Royal One by the scruff of the neck and evicted him. Aiming at Truth we must tell you that sound local tradition insists that Charlie "kicked him out the front door on the seat of his pants" and that he sprawled ingloriously toward the River. [14]

The Old Stone Tavern as it appeared in 2023. Located on the former Wilderness Road, now US Route 11, outside of Atkins, Virginia.

As pioneers moved north of the Ohio River in the late 1790s, one of the first significant paths across the southern region of that future state was cut by a team of men led by Ebenezer Zane and other members of his family. It became known as Zane's Trace. The purpose of its creation was to foster a more accessible route for settlement across Ohio, as well as a means of getting farm goods to the Ohio River for shipment. The trail ran in an arc from Wheeling, in what was still Virginia; to Maysville, which was situated along the south shores of the Ohio River in Kentucky. Of course it wasn't long before this artery was dotted with taverns and inns for the comfort of its travellers.

One of these establishments was run by the McGate family in Manchester, Ohio, nearly across from Maysville. An account from an older gentleman who reminisced about a visit he made to the area one day in 1797 tells of the congenial side of life these taverns often provided.

> There were fifteen to twenty cabins at Manchester, one of which was called a tavern. It was at least a grogshop. There were about a dozen visitors at the tavern, and as the landlord was a heyday, well-met tippler with the rest, they appointed me to assist the landlady in making eggnog. I was inexperienced in the art, but I made out to suit them very well. I put about a dozen eggs in a large bowl, and after beating , or rather stirring the eggs up a little, I added about a pound of sugar and a little milk to

this mass; I then filled the bowl up with whiskey, and set it up on the table; and they sat about the table and sipped it with spoons. Tumblers or glasses of any sort had not then come in fashion. [15]

However, tavern owners had to be a rugged sort. These McGates of Manchester were that type. According to an early historian of the area:

> ... John McGate, an Irishman, who with his good wife Katy were noted characters in the pioneer days of Manchester. The early Court records tell the story of many broils and fisticuffs at McGate's in which the landlord and landlady were participants. One James Dunbar, school-master, seems to have given much time to the "manly art," in and about this resort from the number of "mills" reported to the Court in which he is alleged to have taken a principal part. In fact the grand jury report of the day would be incomplete without the familiar return: "We do present James Dunbar and William Hannah for beating and abusing John McGate and wife." Or, "We do find a bill against Catherine McGate for a breach of the peace on the body of James Dunbar." [16]

About fifteen miles northeast of McGate's Tavern was another operated by John Treber. Ever since it was built in 1798, it was one of the more popular taverns along Zane's Trace. The sign along the road read "Travellers Entertainment," inviting anyone to step inside for a spell. In fact, for years it was a "must stop" for dignitaries and politicians journeying to and fro in the countryside. The acclaimed statesmen Henry Clay and Thomas Benton were known to have visited Treber's. In 1828, on the way to Washington for his inauguration as President, then General Andrew Jackson and his entourage took a respite from the cold winter of Ohio with some food and drink in the tavern.

It seems John Treber's daughter-in-law, Jane, was a key part of the tavern's appeal. It was her charm and cooking that drew them in. One day, some of the guests decided to test her humility.

> "Mother Treber" as she was familiarly known, was very proud of the reputation she had acquired of making the "best coffee" and "finest biscuits" anywhere to be had. On one occasion some noted guests were present at table, and had purposefully refrained from praising the coffee and biscuits to annoy Mother Treber who had bestowed extra care in the preparation of that portion of the meal. After waiting for the accustomed word of praise and not having received it, she ventured to remark

that the meal was not to her liking and offered some apology. A guest more daring than others replied that the meal was very satisfactory with the exception of the coffee and biscuits; whereupon came the impetuous retort "you never tasted finer coffee nor eat better biscuits, for I prepared them myself." [17]

The menu at rest stops like the one run by the Treber's varied day to day, as would be expected in the woodlands. What was caught by local hunters or successfully harvested from the nearby fields was what ended up being served to the customers, especially in the early days. There is an interesting account to this effect experienced by Mother Treber's husband, Jacob Treber, the son of the original owner of the tavern by that name. It seems that

> one morning in winter, after a heavy snowfall, he [John] found the fresh tracks of a full grown bear. They led up to the north of his father's house. He followed them a short distance and returned for an ax and a gun. Then he returned to the trail of the bear. It led to the cabin of a neighbor named Simms, who with ax and gun followed it. They tracked the bear to the mouth of a cavern in a hillside two miles north of the Treber Tavern. Young Treber tried Gen. Putnam's device of smoking the bear out, but it would not answer. Then he determined to follow the bear into the cavern. Simms undertook to dissuade him, but it was useless. Treber made a block of wood and cut a cup or depression in it. This he filled with grease from a small box in the side of the gun-stock where it was carried and used for greasing bullet patches and took part of his shirt to make a wick for his improvised lamp. When his torch was completed, he entered the cavern. He could distinguish the eyes of the bear and fired at them. He then made for the entrance and in the narrow passage, a bear crashed by him and almost squeezed the life out of him. The bear got out first, however, only to meet its death from Simm's gun on the outside. When Treber got out, he felt convinced that the bear Simms killed was the mate of the one he had shot. He entered the cavern a second time and found his bear dead. The problem was to get the bear out, but it was too large and heavy. He tried to roll it over and force it through the passage, but the body got fast in that place with Treber behind it in the cavern. With main strength, he pulled it back and went out to devise a plan. He and Simms cut hickory withes, secured them about the bear's shoulders and pulled it out. Thus Treber and Simms secured two bears for their morning's sport and the guests of Treber's tavern had bear meat for a number of days. [18]

The Treber Inn as it appeared in 2015. Located on the former Zanes Trace, now Ohio Route 41, outside of West Union, Ohio.

Other taverns and hotels of the day lined these two main routes over time, as well as the many other trails that crossed this region. People were also coming into the wilderness by sailing down the Ohio River in ever increasing numbers. Settlements were planted and blossomed; first at Marietta and then Cincinnati as well as at numerous other locations along the riverfront; and inland. As populations grew, so did the number of taverns to accommodate the residents as well as the folks who were just passing through. Many such inns served dual, if not multiple, duties beyond the obvious purpose of providing food, drink, and a place to rest their heads. When not used for such relaxation, many functioned as the town courthouse, post office, library, temporary jail, horse stable with feed, and even a house of worship to the Almighty.

Setters also came up to the shores of the Great Lakes via other paths as well as the river system, which is pervasive across the Ohio country. After William H. Harrison built and defended Fort Meigs during the War of 1812, the northwest corner of the state slowly began to populate, though it was still considered Indian territory until the Treaty of the Maumee Rapids was signed in 1817. This agreement opened the door to more robust settlement where the Maumee River flows into Lake Erie. Amos Spafford, was one of the very first settlers in the area, sent by the government to act as the first postmaster of the region in

1810. In 1823, it was his son Samuel who opened the *Exchange Hotel* which is still standing today in the city of Perrysburg, Ohio.

From one early historian's report, we get a glimpse of some of the antics that alcohol had induced some of the local celebrities to engage in at *"Spafford's Exchange"* which ...

> ...was the most prominent hotel between Buffalo and St. Louis, and the only frame public house between Buffalo and St. Louis... It was here at some public doings that Guy Nearing, a prominent character on the river, and a man of giant frame and herculean strength, in one of his periodical sprees strode upon the whole length of the dining table, kicking all the dishes off as he went. It was here that James Bloom, of Liberty, shortly after his return from South America, and while on his wedding trip, gave a select party, offering bank bills to his guests to light their cigars with. The reputation of the liquors kept at the "Exchange" was better than that of most any other house. [19]

We might be surprised to learn the reason that the best liquors were available in such a remote location of this era.

> The story of the "Queen Mab," as associated with the old "Exchange Hotel," is a familiar one to the people of Perrysburg. Inside the bar was a small trap door in the floor known to but few persons. Beneath was a walled cellar deep and dark which was reached by a step ladder. This unknown vault was once stored full of the highest grades of imported liquors. How they came there, where from and when, outsiders did not know. About that time a fellow named Jack Olney frequented the Maumee a good deal. Jack was a New Yorker, a confirmed cripple, yet a jolly, openhanded sort of a fellow, a favorite with sporting men. Jack owned a little pleasure craft called "Queen Mab." She was ship-rigged in every appointment, painted black, and as handsome as a bird and a good sailer. Jack frequented the river, bay, and lake as far as Detroit and Malden [Ontario], and often indulged his friends in a pleasure ride on the "Queen Mab," treating them with the most generous hospitality. But the report leaked out after the "Queen" had gone, that she was a sly little smuggler, false lined and equipped for the business, yet so carefully as to leave no ground for suspicion. So insignificant a craft of course received no attention from the custom officer who was stationed then at Miami, and the dark-mantled little "Queen" had no trouble in taking on a valuable cargo at Malden [in Canada on the north shore of Lake Erie] in the night and making her way unsuspected to any of the lake or river ports. Whether she ever landed a cargo on the island in the Maumee in front

of Perrysburg, which afterward found its way to the dark cellar, is at best only a surmise... the cellar walls have long since tumbled in, but the impressions of our chronicler are that Jack Olney could tell how that cellar came to be stored with the best imported high grade liquors, and that there never was a gayer smuggler than the little "Queen Mab."[20]

Of course it wasn't just in the taverns that liquor was enjoyed. The consumption of spirits became synonymous with many varied activities. It would be a mainstay in some form at most weddings, funerals, trials, elections, and any other celebration of note. In fact, just as the women of the frontier gathered to create clothing and called it a "sewing bee," the men periodically had to clear a section of land and referred to it as a "logging bee." However, the men's "bee" featured alcohol. These assemblies were similar to the more familiar barn-raisings where the men of the neighborhood gathered to accomplish a complicated feat by working as a team. In this case, it was the rolling of previously felled trees into a pile so the land could be made ready for planting.

These were occasions for rare fun. A keg of whiskey was usually the leading factor in these "bees."

The women of the household prepared large baskets of fried cakes and old-time gingerbread, such as none but Yankee women knew how to make. All the men, boys and ox-teams of the neighborhood were assembled in the logging-field, and divided into "teams."

A logging team consisted of a yoke of oxen, their driver, two "lever men," and two boys to handle the chain and assist with the levers. A first-class logging-bee had two captains, who chose sides, the field was divided and a choice settled by flipping a penny. The captain winning the choice gave the word, and the work began in earnest. The captains selected the points for the log heaps, preferably where several logs could be piled without hauling. The teamster sought the nearest log, and as he turned his team to the proper end, one of the chain-boys carried the end of the chain to the end of the log, where the other boy seized it three or four feet from the end and the two drew it under the log, which had already been raised sufficiently for the purpose by the two lever men. The chain was quickly "hitched," and the team as quickly started for the pile. The lever men had properly placed the "skids" before leaving the pile and by the time the boys had the chain unfastened, the lever men had the log rolling to its position on the pile. The large logs were systematically laid at the bottom, the captains keeping a sharp eye out for every possible advantage. [21]

Often times the lever men were the rougher breed of frontiersmen and the ones who made the rounds of a region to participate in the "bees" as often as they could.

> They filled themselves with whiskey and sometimes a fight was the result, but on the [Western] Reserve there was generally a constable or justice, or both, present at the gatherings and fighting was promptly suppressed. The "bee" usually wound up with such recreation as wrestling, jumping and rifle-shooting. The quantity of logs piled at these bees would appear incredible to any one who had never witnessed the operations. [22]

For some of the pioneers it was this type of occasional over-indulgence that caused a spot of trouble, for others it had become a habitual practice. The vast majority of people frowned on excessive drinking. Everyone had a host of responsibilities which would go unattended if they were chronically incapacitated. Crops had to be raised and meat had to be hunted to feed the families. There were civic duties and businesses to be run. Though a few women imbibed on occasion, most wives were generally opposed to the excessive consumption of liquor by their men. When the husbands over did it, they temporarily became unable to fulfill their obligations to their families, especially the vital physical protection of their kin from a potential attack by man or beast.

From a small village known as Poland, near today's Youngstown, Ohio, we learn of one somewhat humorous approach to curbing the over-indulgence of the spirits.

> One woman of this section, whose husband took too much at stated intervals, when he came home in that condition, obliged him to sit in a straight-back chair till he was sober. If he started to move, she raised a stick of wood as if to strike him, when he immediately resumed his seat. He finally declared that there was no use in drinking if one had to sit still until sober, and he reformed. [23]

By the time the third and fourth decade of life on the frontier unfolded, calls for temperance were beginning to be heard in louder and louder voices. This was by no means limited to the wilderness settlements. As early as the 1790s even President Thomas Jefferson was publicly expressing concern about the abuse of alcohol, in particular amongst government officials. He once noted that the excessive use of alcohol

> has often produced more injury to public service, and more trouble to me, than any other circumstance that has occurred in the internal concerns of the country during my administration. And were I to commence my administration again, with the knowledge that from experience I have acquired, the first question that I would ask with regard to every candidate for office would be, "Is he addicted to the use of ardent spirits?" [24]

The concern of Jefferson was reinforced with a publication authored by the famed physician of the day, Dr. Benjamin Rush. It was titled, *An Inquiry Into the Effects of Ardent Spirits Upon the Human Body and Mind.* This book gained wide acclaim as it pointed out that alcohol was not the cure-all for every ailment as many had been led to believe. In fact, he felt it was a detriment, both physically and ethically. Protestant preachers took up that moral banner. They began sermonizing on the evils of these ardent spirits on the frontier throughout the first three decades of the 1800s, a period that came to be known as the "Second Great Awakening." The message was first met with strong resistance, but as the years went by attitudes changed and people took the pledge of sobriety in increasing numbers.

Consumption of alcohol had even infiltrated the education community of the era. On the campus of Harvard University, no less, was a brewery producing swill for the students and faculty since the days of its founding in the early 1600s. In fact, it came to have three breweries by the next century. However, as the temperance idea took root in the very late 1700s, and a more concerted focus was made on academics, the breweries were abandoned. On the frontier, schools of higher learning were slow to be established, except for Transylvania University near Lexington, Kentucky. This college was holding its first classes in 1780. It was run by the Disciples of Christ, a protestant denomination, so its spiritual leaders did not promote the use of alcohol.

Throughout these decades, alcohol came to be used as an element of currency; something to barter with. As seen in the "logging bees," an expected treat or outright payment for services was often in the form of alcohol. Men who joined in barn raisings and home constructions were often paid for their efforts with bottles of booze which in some cases were distilled on the properties involved.

Spirits were also used as barter in trade negotiations, especially with the Native Americans. The indigenous people were savvy hunters and the pelts they offered to the Americans of this time period were highly coveted. In exchange, the Indians, not being skilled in metal-working, received practical and necessary items like pots and pans, guns, ammunition, blades for their knives, and heads for their tomahawks. In addition, alcohol was very often thrown into the mix.

Treaties were being signed almost annually through this era, expanding the frontier for the Americans. Spirits were used in at least two significant ways during the deliberations. It was offered freely to relax the negotiating team and create a friendly atmosphere for the discussions; and it was usually included in the package of bulk goods which were promised in return for the land being acquired.

It was not that the Native Americans were unfamiliar with any type of hallucinogens, but when they were used, it was predominantly during ceremonial, spiritual affairs; not as a recreational intoxicant. This seems to be a key difference between the two cultures at this time. The Americans had a long history of alcohol use for personal relaxation. Moderate to heavy drinking came to be tolerated and even expected, with most who indulged still being reasonable in their behavior and able to function at their jobs throughout the day. Outright drunkenness was abhorred. It was those who lost all control while intoxicated that were the real targets of the temperance movement. The introduction of the idea of using strong alcoholic beverages for individual recreation was a bit of a jolt to the Indian culture. Some could tolerate it, but many quickly became addicted. Unfortunately, when that happened scenes amongst themselves often became ugly and deadly.

How and why the American negotiators at treaty discussions used alcohol was multi-faceted and complicated. Was it used for leverage to dull the Indians' senses a bit during negotiations? Was it pushed as a subversive measure to slowly eat away at the fabric of the Indian society since it was obvious to all that it caused chaos amongst the tribesmen? Was it strictly business, being a product that was relatively inexpensive to produce that yielded a high return in trade? Based on the abundance of historical accounts, it is likely that all these questions could be answered "yes" in most of the negotiating situations of this era.

There are many a sad stories of deaths due to alcohol among the Indians. Often fellow tribesmen, friends, even relatives had lost all they had because of over-indulgence. Chief Seneca, also known as "Standing Stone," was one Indian of stature who suffered greatly as a result of his decision to partake of ardent spirits. While living in the lands that evolved into Cleveland, Ohio, Seneca was described as

> tall, dignified, and of pleasing address, but in his youth was an ardent lover of "fire water." In one of his drunken frolics of the earlier days he attempted to kill his squaw; but the tomahawk blow intended for her killed his favorite pappoose which was lashed to her back. This mishap so affected the young chief as to make him a temperate drinker during his entire life... [25]

Speaking of "fire-water," one may have assumed that the origin of this term for hard liquor was the scorch that it can give to the back of one's throat. Well, while that makes for a sensible assumption, according to an early twentieth century historian, there is a more reasoned explanation.

> When the Fur Company first began to supply ardent spirits to the Indians in order to help their trade, the liquor was imported from England. It was the cheapest and most poisonous brand manufactured at the time, and for that reason was all the more acceptable to the Indian. When it reached the Hudson Bay territory, or the great region within which the rival fur companies traded, it had to be carried overland to the various posts. For convenience of transportation, barrels of such whisky were divided into kegs. The carriers soon learned that they could make a profit by diluting the liquor with water, when changing it from the barrels into kegs. The Indians, however, missed the powerful effects and suspected that they were being cheated. They learned how to test the liquor before exchanging their peltries for it. They poured a small quantity of the liquor on the fire and if the flame was extinguished it was evident to them that the liquor was watered, and they at once pronounced it "bad." If, on the contrary, the liquor added to the flame, they knew that the alcohol had not been tampered with, and it was accepted as genuine "fire-water." [26]

He goes on to note:

> That the "fire-water" supplied to the Indians of that day was comparable to the villainous stuff of present-day [1900] manufacture is illustrated by the statement of an Indian chief who had experienced its effects, and who had witnessed the sad havoc it had produced among his people. "Fire-water," exclaimed the savage, "can only be distilled from the hearts of wildcats and the tongues of women, it makes my people so fierce and so foolish." [27]

Many years later, at the Columbian Exposition of 1893, also known as the Chicago World's Fair, the distinguished writer and speaker Chief Pokagon of the Potawatomi tribe addressed the visitors and in part expounded on the evils of alcohol.

> ...Now as we have been taught that our first parents ate of the forbidden fruit and fell, so we as fully believe that this fire-water is the hard cider of the whiteman's devil, made from the fruit of that tree that brought death into the world, and all our woes. The arrow, the scalping knife, the tomahawk used on the warpath were merciful compared with it; they were used in our defense, but the accursed drink came like a serpent in the form of a dove. Many of our people partook of it without mistrust, as children pluck the flowers and clutch a scorpion in their grasp; only when they feel the sting, they let the flowers fall. But Nature's children had no such power; for when the viper's fangs they felt, they only hugged the reptile the more closely to their breasts, while friends before them stood pleading with prayers and tears that they would let the deadly serpent drop. But all is vain. Although they promised so to do, yet with laughing grin and steps uncertain like the fool, they still more frequently guzzled down the hellish drug. Finally, conscience ceased to give alarm, and, led by deep despair to life's last brink, and goaded by demons on every side, they cursed themselves, they cursed their friends, they cursed their beggar babes and wives, they cursed their God, and died. [28]

It seems that the attitudes and restrictions regarding alcohol consumption were in a constant flux for all who inhabited the frontier lands from the end of the American Revolution through the War of 1812. Some wanted legal measures taken to stop its use. Others wanted laws to protect the rights of people to make their own choice. Some grew to be against all forms of alcohol, while others saw only hard liquors as a problem; beers, ciders, and wines being deemed acceptable.

As before and after this era, everyone had their own opinions, moral codes, and self-discipline; or lack there-of.

Some historians have cast a wide net to insinuate that most people of this era were drunkards. Others gloss over the influence alcohol may have had on daily life altogether. Opinions are usually based on a pick and choose basis of parts of varied accounts and are then spun to make any point an author intended. The truth is that alcohol had served many purposes. It was a safety net from pollutants and disease in the waters of the day, a medicine when few others existed, a business venture for farmers, an item of trade through the barter system, and of course a simple means of refreshment and relaxation. As at any time in history, people of the frontier had both fun and friction as a result of alcohol consumption. Some indulged a little, some a lot; some too much, and some not at all. There must be a reason that so many intellectuals over the centuries have stated, in one way or another, that moderation is the key to happiness. With regard to alcohol, this would appear to be very sage advice which has proven its worth through the ages. ◆

HMMM...

One Indian's Discernment.

The Rev. Alvan Coe, a very worthy and devout man, at an early day established a school for Indian boys, on the Fire-Lands in the vicinity of Milan, where he sought to instruct them in the mysteries of religion and teach them to read and write. The father of one of the Indian boys came over from the Sandusky river to visit his son, and while lingering in the vicinity wandered into a distillery. As was the custom in those days, the proprietor offered him a cup of whiskey.

The Indian shook his head, and with much dignity said: "My boy tell me Mr. Coe say, Ingin no drink, good man: go up much happy. Ingin drink, bad man: go down burn much." Then looking wistfully at the whiskey he picked it up, and raising it slowly to his lips said: "Maybe Mr. Coe tell d_ _ n lie," and drank it down.

In Henry Howe's, Historical Collections of Ohio, 1907 [29]

IX.
FIGHTIN' AND HANGIN' AROUND THE FIRELANDS.

In 1783, when the American Revolution had ended, the colonies were rebooted and united into states of the newborn country. As colonies, many of them had claims on the lands lying over the Appalachians. Those ownership rights continued through the initial change of the governmental structure, but after just four years, the acreage came under the control of the federal government. Desperately in need of funds, the elected politicians of 1787 legally made what today is referred to as the Midwest national property. Officially, it became known as the Northwest Territory. In order for that transition to have occurred, however; they needed the new states to turn over their deeds to these western lands. Except for Connecticut, every state involved did so.

The Connecticuters reserved the right of ownership to a part of their original claim. They kept a swath that stretched from the eastern border of what would become Ohio to just west of the present-day city of Sandusky; with Lake Erie marking the northern border and the 41st parallel, the current latitude of Akron, marking the southern border. As of this writing it is still generally referred to as the Western Reserve. The far western section of this corridor, the acreage between today's Port Clinton and Vermillion, Ohio, was further designated as the Firelands; exclusively reserved for those who were burned out of their Connecticut homes during the Revolution.

After the signing of the Greenville Treaty in 1795, settlement soared across Ohio lands; including the eastern half of Connecticut's Reserve.

Some even ventured into the western end; but at this point in time the Firelands were still considered Indian territory. In fact, numerous Indians had continued to maintain villages therein, inevitably making settlement by the Americans, well, unsettling.

A few more years passed, and in 1803 the borders of the new state of Ohio were legally defined. Most of the northwest quarter of the state, however, still remained Indian territory. This included the Firelands. Two years into statehood, on the 4th of July, 1805, yet another treaty was signed. This one was made at Fort Industry, a small stockade on the Maumee River in what is now downtown Toledo. As a result of this accord, the western half of the Western Reserve was finally ceded to the United States by the Chippewa, Delaware, Huron, Munsee, Ottawa, Potawatomi and Shawnee tribes. The Firelands were now uncontested property and open to settlement, at least on paper. Some residents of Connecticut began to populate their promised lands, but with only a modicum of assurance for their safety. Inspite of the agreement, many Indians continued to call the Reserve area their home. Only the Maumee Valley to their west was land still set apart as Indian territory within the state.

As the population grew, so did the business dealings between the Americans and the Indians. In fact, the Reserve became a boom market for trade with the Indians. As more and more settlers arrived, among them were numerous entrepreneurs who would set up shops of trade along the shores of Lake Erie. Many friendships evolved out of the exchange of goods between the two cultures. However, these were often tempered relationships with an air of caution hovering over them. Both parties were keenly aware of each other's capabilities and past deceptions.

Zalmon Wildman was a land speculator from Conneticut who owned a significant amount of property in the Firelands. He had acquired it from some of the many people of that state who chose to sell their grants rather than relocate. As early as 1810, Wildman was known to periodically ride on horseback from his home in Danbury, Connecticut to the Lake Erie region so he could directly evaluate his holdings and their development. While back home, he would depend on friends to work on his behalf in the wheeling and dealing in real estate. Charles P. Barnum was one of those friends. With a touch of political musings, Barnum wrote to Wildman in November of 1810 from the Huron River area near Sandusky, Ohio. He observed the early build-up of tensions between the settlers and the Indians.

> For three years past the British have secretly been stirring up the Indians and urging them to war against the U.S. They are at the bottom of the Shawnee Prophet's conduct. He is hired and paid by them, and he receives his instructions how to act from the British agents. For three Summers past, the back Indians, under the influence of Britain, have sent the war belt and hatchet through all the different tribes to join them in a war against the U.S.
>
> The tribes near these parts have buried the hatchet every year until this past Summer. Last year the Ottawas buried it at the Miami of the Lake [Maumee River]; this year all the tribes generally accepted the hatchet and smoked the bloody tobacco, which always accompanied it. The hatchet passed Sandusky last July and was accepted, it is now gone through the Eastern tribes, and will round through Canada; it will get round next Summer it is expected, when, if the Indians strike at all, they will then strike; probably in the green corn time [late July and August].
>
> The information was communicated to Mr. Flammond [Flemmond] by an Indian, his confidential friend, under the greatest injunction of Secrecy. This Indian also informed Mr. F. that he was present at Sandusky when they held their Council, and that he smoked the tobacco that accompanied the hatchet, and that they agreed to make war with the Americans.
>
> What the result will be, time must determine; but it is a fact that the Indians have had many private Councils the past summer, and have been much agitated; they are insolent and saucy, more so than usual, & That the British have a deep aid scheme of villainny on foot, which nothing but a timely intervention of our government can frustrate.
>
> Strange that our government should calmly look on and see the Savages of the Western wild whetting the tomahawk and scalping knife for the destruction of defenceless citizens…
>
> …I intend to get me a good Rifle and ammunition and tarry for a while yet, and see the result of the War talk. [1]

Yes, the British were indeed stirring up the emotions of the Indians. As the unrest became more and more palpable, the citizens and governments of the region began to form military defenses, albeit meager ones. John Baptiste Flemmond, some say his name was Flemming, referred to in this letter, was one of the first French-Canadian traders to settle in the Firelands. In 1805, he set-up a post to trade goods with settlers and the Indians very near the mouth of the Huron River. It became known as Flemmonds Cove. It was here in the fall of 1811 that he organized thirty-two volunteers into a militia company known as the Huron Rangers. By law they were required to report for a muster call at the post on the first Saturday of April in 1812. As it fell that year, it was April 4.

The men were assembling as ordered that afternoon along the east side of the mouth of the Huron River when Sam Pettengill raced in, alone. Pettengill lived at the village known as Ogontz Place, where Chief Ogontz of the Ottawa had been residing for many years. It was just a stone's throw inland from the shores of Lake Erie in today's downtown Sandusky. Two days previous, Pettengill had successfully persuaded two fur trappers named Daniel Buell and Michael Gibbs to join him at this muster of the militia along the Huron River. Pettengill was to pick them up at their cabin on Pipe Creek, just a mile or two away from his home, on the following morning of April 3. The three of them would then make their way along the trail to Huron together. As it happened, when he arrived at their cabin, Pettengill found the two men dead. More precisely, both were murdered, apparently attacked in their sleep.

Pettengill was shaken by his discovery. He doubled back to his home and is believed to have taken a canoe to Huron rather than risk being attacked on the open road that connected the two locations. Once he arrived and divulged his news, the commander of the new militia, Captain Barret, asked for volunteers to track down the murderers. Not one of the rangers refused. Some other residents of the area joined in the hunt as well. They took the land path back to the site, being ever cautious of an ambush. Late that afternoon, their march ended at the crime scene.

Daniel Buell's body was found in the cabin, Michael Gibbs' corpse was outside lying a few feet from the dwelling. Furs and pelts of the trappers were missing; their theft being the apparent reason for the murders. As the moon began its rise the militia divided. Half stayed at the cabin to protect against any further abuse, while the others moved on to the home of Jonas Gibbs who was known to live nearby. Jonas was the brother of the slain Michael Gibbs and it was feared that his family might have suffered a similar fate. Luckily, they had not.

The next morning, this group returned to the trappers' cabin. Buell and Gibbs were buried before a meeting was held to strategize the militia's next move. It was decided that they would again split up. One group would cross the bay and follow the paths heading west along the Lake Erie shore while the other would march inland in the direction of Upper Sandusky. Unless the suspects were successfully caught along the way, both groups would eventually meet up at the rapids of the Maumee River.

It was the lake shore group who happened to meet the trader, John Flemmond, at the mouth of the Portage River, where today's town of Port Clinton was just beginning to develop. Because he had established relationships with the Indians and was well-versed in several of their dialects, Flemmond stepped-up to help in the search for the criminals. He interviewed many of the Indians in the vicinity and managed to glean a few clues as to who might have been responsible for the murders. Though the Indians' allegiance was steadily growing toward the British, it was in their self-interest that they cooperate with the American settlers to a certain extent. At this point in time, the Reserve was part of the new state of Ohio and hence US laws were being applied to the Indians as well as the white citizens. They rightfully feared repercussions if they didn't cooperate.

It was at Locust Point, about ten miles west of their current position on the Portage River, that the militia found one of the men they had learned about through the Indian interviews. He was the son of Old O'Mic, a chief of the Chippewa tribe who lived in the Reserve. The chief was well known to the settlers, but had a somewhat fickle relationship with them. In most historical accounts, his son, who was now in custody, has been referred to by the same name as his father, simply, O'Mic. It seems early reports of that day indiscriminately applied the father's name to the son with no differentiation. Adding a first name of "John" to the young O'Mic is how some made a distinction between the son and his father. A few credible sources state that he was actually named Devil Poc-con, though American reports rarely use that appellation. Evidence that the younger O'Mic had at least some admiration for the Americans comes from a report stating that he had once made a trip to Washington City. So proud was he of the adventure that when he returned to his village he was grandly attired in some amount of US military garb. A few of the settlers apparently teased him afterwards with the nickname, "Tom Jefferson," since Jefferson was then the president.

With John O'Mic under guard, John Flemmond was now called upon to do an interrogation of the prisoner. He succeeded in gaining a full confession. O'Mic explained that two others were involved with him. One was an Indian boy of merely fifteen years whose name is uncertain. The other was an adult Indian known as Semo.

There are hints that the boy may have been acquainted with Semo, who was known to belong to an Ottawa tribe living along the Maumee River. Though present at the crime scene, O'Mic said the boy did not directly participate in the murders or the theft. After his capture and questioning, the young Indian was released due to his age and O'Mic's testimony. There are some who believe that this boy grew to be the Indian known as Negosheck who led two others in a very eerily similar murder of two trappers along the Portage River five years later for which he was executed by hanging in 1819.

The third culprit mixed up in this affair was Semo, an Indian familiar to many in the region. John Garrison was one of those settlers who knew him well. In 1810, Garrison, originally of New York State, came to the burgeoning trading region of the Sandusky Bay and set up a trading post much like Flemmond and others had done before him. He established himself at Ogontz Place, just yards from the chief's main lodge. Garrison was interviewed years later and distinctly remembered Semo. He noted that Semo had befriended him, knew English well, and helped him as an interpreter in his dealings with the other Indians. Once, he even nursed Garrison back to health when he was sick for an extended period of time. But things were not as they seemed. According to Garrison, one day late in the autumn of 1811, Semo came to the trading post in a frantic mood, overly concerned about the war talk between the Americans and the British. Semo pointed out to him that, "You take white man's papers, and know what white man do; me take red man's papers, and know what Injun do. Big war is comin; Injun help the British." [2]

A few days later, apparently further agitated about the reports of impending war, Semo returned to the post and told Garrison that he

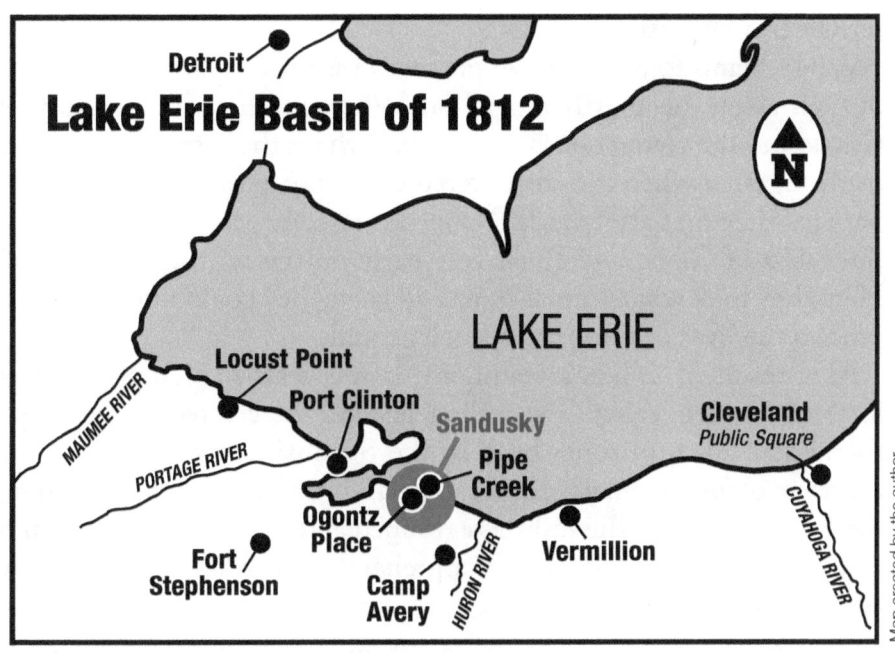

was leaving. He was going to head upriver, probably on the Sandusky, but possibly on the Maumee or Portage Rivers which were in Indian territory. He wanted to have Garrison hide his valuables for safe keeping. He further queried what Garrison was going to do in lieu of the rumors of the approaching hostilities. Garrison volunteered that he was going to wait it out until the spring of 1812, at which time he would re-evaluate the situation. He further explained that if it was then necessary to leave, the lake ice should be thawed and he would head back to Buffalo. Semo then made clear why he wanted Garrison to secure his belongings. "Bad Injun up there; he steal Semo's jewelry. You got much money; put Semo's jewelry with white man's money, and Injun no steal it."[3] Semo then followed Garrison to a chest kept hidden under his bed and watched as he placed the jewelry and other valuables alongside Garrison's own money.

That was the last Garrison had ever seen of Semo, and that was quite fortunate for John Garrison's well-being. Semo returned to the trading post in April of 1812. It was not a social call. Semo had been plotting all along to rob and murder Garrison. Lucky for John, he had already left the area, as many others had, amidst the multiplying reports of serious trouble with the British.

When Semo found that the post was vacant of Garrison and both of their assets, he angrily moved on. When and how he met up with O'Mic and the young boy is unknown. Perhaps the threesome were already together when they discovered Garrison's post to be abandoned, perhaps they met afterwards. None-the-less, they were all together at the cabin of Gibbs and Buell very early on the morning of April 3. Here they took what animal skins and coats they could find and in the process the lives of Gibbs and Buell as well.

As a result of O'Mic's testimony, it was learned that Semo lived in the Maumee Valley. The militia headed there directly. Semo was found and taken prisoner back to the Sandusky area. It wasn't long, however, before he managed to escape and got back to his home along the Maumee River. The militia regrouped and with the cooperation of Indians in the valley, Semo was apprehended once again. Then, as one account goes, Semo

> had been bound, for the purpose of being delivered up to justice. To avoid this, he rolled himself to a tree, against which stood a loaded gun. Though pinioned with his arms behind, he contrived to place the muzzle to his throat, and discharged the piece with his toe. [4]

Thus the sentence for his crime of shooting Michael Gibbs was served by Semo upon himself. Only John O'Mic was left to answer for the death of Daniel Buell whom he had tomahawked.

John O'Mic was only twenty-one years old at the time of the murder. One interesting account of his day shows that his pernicious personality was already in development during his teenage years. One day he had picked the wrong settler's wife to make the object of his taunts.

It was in the summer of 1807 when sixteen year old O'Mic's stomach began to rumble as he walked through the east side of the Cuyahoga River basin. Spotting the opulent garden alongside Lorenzo Carter's home, he dared to begin picking vegetables at will. That was until Mrs. Carter spotted him and ran out to shew him away. A bit brazen for his age, the Indian boy boldly presented a knife and began chasing Lorenzo's wife around the grounds. It wasn't until an unidentified young man happened by, that the delinquent was chased off. The story could have ended there without incident, but Lorenzo Carter was not a man to be messed with.

Being the very first European white man to permanently settle with his family along the Cuyahoga River in 1797 inherently meant that Carter was quite a rugged character. Before and after the official establishment of law in 1803, he took it upon his shoulders to be in charge of the site that would evolve into Cleveland, and he had the personality and strength to do so. He had been referred to by a contemporary as, "a man of uncommon energy." To say he was multi-talented would be a severe understatement as well. He was a builder of homes, warehouses, and stockades; a farmer, a tavern-owner, a constable, a major in the militia, a ship-builder and so much more.

When he came home later that day and learned from his wife about the threat that the young Indian boy posed to her, his blood, as it was known to do, quickly overheated. He set out for an Indian encampment on the west side of the Cuyahoga River; intent on exacting consequences on somebody for daring to terrorize Mrs. Carter. As he entered the Indian village where he guessed the boy lived, he sharply stated the reason for his visit. With a rope in hand that he had brought for the occasion, he swore he would hang the youth for his actions against his wife. Impressed by Carter's boldness, Old O'Mic, who must have been acquainted with the man over the years, came forward apologizing for his son and managed to convince the enraged husband that the boy would not be crossing to the east side of the river again. As far as anyone knows, young O'Mic never did venture to the east banks until five years later on the day he was taken there by authorities for his trial.

In 1812, Pipe Creek, along which the crime had taken place, was in Huron county. However, Cuyahoga county to the east had just recently been created and they had legal jurisdiction over both of the counties. Because this government was operating out of the burgeoning village of Cleveland, O'Mic was taken there. Less than a hundred families lived in the immediate Cleveland area in that year, but more were settling in the outlying areas of the Reserve every day. One thing was certain; all were attracted to the upcoming trial.

It was a Wednesday morning, April 29, when the proceedings began. The weather cooperated, which was important because this was an open-air trial. No courthouse or jail had yet been built in which to carry on legal proceedings nor to house any criminals

The Public Square in Cleveland circa 1833. The courthouse built by Levi Johnson is seen at the far end of the wide road.

facing prosecution. John O'Mic was led out of Lorenzo Carter's home, where he was being held, and escorted to a literal court yard. Yes, because there was no jail in which to house him, when O'Mic had finally re-crossed the Cuyahoga River he was ironically given over to the custody of one Lorenzo Carter. According to the respected lawyer and congressman of the day, Elisha Whittlesey:

> The prisoner was confined in a chamber of Mr. Carter's house. Strong irons were above his ancles, with which was connected a staple that was driven into a joist that supported the floor, so that the prisoner could not go to any window. Probably I should have said with more accuracy, that a chain was attached to the fetters, and a staple was attached to the other end, which was driven into the joist, &c. [5]

Under the shade of a large cherry tree near today's intersection of 10th and Superior streets the trial was conducted in front of more than a hundred excited citizens. It didn't take long for the jury to come to their verdict — guilty. The sentence was death by hanging. A further irony cannot be ignored of how this same sentence was prophetically threatened on O'Mic by Carter just five years earlier for affronting Mrs. Carter. The hanging date was set for June 26, just two months later. This gave Cleveland's Levi Johnson, a member of the jury and a distinguished master builder of structures and ships, time enough to construct a gallows platform for the man he had just voted to convict. It would be the first execution of an Indian by hanging in Ohio's young history.

The punishment was administered in the Public Square, an open courtyard so-named to this day in downtown Cleveland. The gallows was erected in front of a pile of lumber, beams, and other building materials that would soon be transformed into the first courthouse. For now though, some of those materials sufficed as makeshift benches for members of the crowd which had grown even larger than the one that the trial had attracted. They had come long distances from many of the surrounding towns and villages to witness this historic event. Dignitaries mixed with the common settlers. Zalmon Wildman happened to be in the Cleveland area checking on his properties and wrote to his wife the following day that he had witnessed the hanging. Another luminary in attendance was Elisha Whittlesey from whose trusted testimony we get many of the specifics of that day. And, it wasn't just American citizens who assembled on the Public Square. Many of the Indians who lived west of the Cuyahoga River arrived as well. As one might suspect, this caused some anxiety among the citizens who feared a potential uprising to save John O'Mic from his fate. That did not occur.

The much anticipated proceedings of that Friday began with a religious ceremony. It was held on a large, flat, grassy stretch of land below and in front of Lorenzo Carter's hilltop home. Onlookers listened to prayerful intercessions and a sermon by the Reverend Mr. Darrow who had come up from Vienna, in Trumbull county, over fifty miles away. Nearby, John O'Mic heard the preacher's words from where he sat; squirming awkwardly upon his own coffin in a wagon that was specially re-painted for this occasion.

The spiritual solemnity was to be followed by a military display led by Major Jones. The men were to form a simple hollow square around the wagon holding O'Mic and then parade with him thus enclosed to the Public Square. However, the officer's memory failed him at the most inopportune time. He could not remember, no matter how hard he tried, the correct commands to signal the troops into the required formation. Some suspected he had spent a little too much time in Lorenzo's tavern beforehand. Elisha Whittlesey explains:

> Major Jones endeavored to form a hollow square, so that the prisoner

should be guarded on all sides. He rode backwards and forwards with drawn sword, epaulets, and scabbard flying, but he did not know what order to give. The wagon with O'Mic moved ahead and stopped; but as the Sheriff doubted whether he was to be aided by the military, he proceeded onward. Major Jones finally took the suggestion of some one, who told him to ride to the head of the line, and double it round until the front and the rear of the line met. [6]

The parade route stretched about a quarter of a mile from Carter's house to the Public Square. Before O'Mic's wagon, led by Sheriff Baldwin, reached its final destination, the military company had finally caught up and successfully encircled it; to the delight of the crowd walking alongside the route. Soon the entire ensemble came to a stop in the courtyard. The upcoming proceedings would exceed the large crowd's expectations.

The eye-witness account of Elisha Whittlesey gives the most complete description of what transpired next.

> Arriving at the gallows, Mr Carter, the Sheriff and O'Mic ascended to the platform by a ladder. The arms of the prisoner were loosely pinioned. A rope was around his neck with a loop in the end. Another was let down through a hole in the top piece, on which was a hook to attach to the rope on his neck. The rope with the hook was brought over to one of the posts, and fastened to it near the ground.
>
> After some little time Mr. Carter came down, leaving O'Mic and Sheriff Baldwin on the platform. As the Sheriff drew down the cap, O'Mic was the most terrified being, rational or irrational, I ever saw, and seizing the cap with his right hand, which he could reach by bending his head and inclining his neck in that direction, he stepped to one of the posts and put his arm around it. The Sheriff approached him to loose his hold, and for a moment it was doubtful whether O'Mic would not throw him to the ground. Mr. Carter ascended to the platform and a negotiation in regular diplomatic style was had. It was in the native tongue, as I understood at the time. Mr. Carter appealed to O'Mic to display his courage, narrating what he had said about showing pale faces how an Indian could die, but it had no effect. [7]

Weeks earlier, O'Mic had indeed boasted that he would die with dignity. He went so far as to tell Carter and Sheriff Baldwin that they wouldn't even need to secure his arms because he would freely jump off the gallows. However, according to the honorable Judge Frederick

Fowler of Milan, Ohio, O'Mic's true colors were made known when he was first captured by the militia.

> After his confession of the crime to Flemmond, he [O'Mic] wanted to be taken out, and shot by the guard, of which I was one. He could not bear the thought of hanging. When Flemmond told him that could not be done, he, with great earnestness and sincerity, implored the Divine being for mercy for fifteen to twenty minutes. [8]

The discussion continued on the platform between Carter and the skittish O'Mic.

> Finally, O'Mic made a proposition, that if Mr. Carter would give him half a pint of whisky he would consent to die. The whisky was soon on hand, in a large glass tumbler, real old Monongahela [a treasured rye whiskey distilled using waters of the Monongahela River], for which an old settler would almost be willing to be hung, if he could now obtain the like. The glass was given to O'Mic and he drank the whisky, in as little time as he could have turned it out of the glass. Mr. Carter again came down, and the Sheriff again drew down the cap and the same scene was re-enacted, O'Mic expressing the same terror. Mr. Carter again ascended to the platform, and O'Mic gave him the honor of an Indian, in pledge that he would no longer resist the sentence of the court, if he should have another half pint of whisky. Mr. Carter, representing the people of Ohio and the dignity of the laws, thought the terms were reasonable, and the whisky was forthcoming on short order. The tumbler was not given to O'Mic, but was held to his mouth, and as he sucked the whisky out, Sheriff Baldwin drew the rope that pinioned his arms more tight, and the rope was drawn down to prevent the prisoner from going to the post, and to prevent him from pulling off his cap. The platform was immediately cleared of all but O'Mic, who run the ends of his fingers on his right hand, between the rope and his neck. The rope that held up one end of the platform was cut, and the body swung in a straight line towards the lake, as far as the rope permitted and returned, and after swinging back and forth several times, and the weight being about to be suspended perpendicular under the center of the top of the gallows, the body turned in a circle and finally rested still. [9]

One of the onlookers in the crowd was Julianna Long, the young, seventeen year old wife of the town's lone doctor, David Long. She watched alongside her husband and several other doctors who had travelled to Cleveland from nearby counties. Later in life she stated,

"I was in the crowd on the square when O'Mic was to be hung, and I suddenly thought, 'why should I wish to see my old play-fellow die!' I got out of the crowd as quick as possible and went home." [10]

Julianna had known both O'Mics since she had come to the region eight years previous. As she testified, the younger O'Mic was at least a childhood acquaintance if not a friend. They used to play together along the Grand River when she lived at her father's home in what is now Painesville, Ohio just east of Cleveland proper. Though their relationship was cordial in those early days, by 1812 the rumors of war had induced fear of the Indians amongst the settlers and friendships were strained.

Another story told by Julianna testifies to this apprehension that was looming over Cleveland and the whole Reserve itself. It seems that one day, shortly before punishment was about to be dispersed to his son, Old O'Mic paid a curious visit to Mrs. Long's home. Julianna explains:

> I was alone, and my babe, (Mrs. Severence [her later married name]), was sleeping in the cradle. He [Old O'Mic] took up a gun which was in the room, in order to show me how Semo killed himself, after he had been arrested. I thought he was going to kill me or my baby, in revenge for his son. I seized the child and ran up Water street towards Mr. Williamson's screaming pretty hard, I suppose. [Old] O'Mic followed after me, trying to explain what he meant. Mr. Williamson caught the child, and we all went to Mr. Carter's house, which was on the corner of Superior street and Union lane. Major Carter had a short talk with O'Mic, who explained what he meant, and we all had a hearty laugh. [11]

Back at the scene of the hanging, O'Mic's body came to a stop. Whittlesey explains that

> at that time a terrific storm appeared and came up from the north north-west with great rapidity, to avoid which, and it being doubtful whether the neck was broken, and to accomplish so necessary part of a hanging, the rope was drawn down with the design of raising the body, so that, by a sudden relaxing of the rope, the body would fall several feet, and thereby dislocate the neck beyond any doubt, but when the body fell, the rope broke as readily as a tow string [a thin thread of flax] and fell upon the ground. The coffin and grave were near the gallows and the body was picked up, put into the coffin, and the coffin immediately put into the grave. The storm was heavy and all scampered but O'Mic. [12]

And yet, this was not the end of O'Mic's story. It seems that as night

Portrait of Lorenzo Carter, the first permanent settler of Cleveland.

fell, the visiting doctors and Dr. Long, went on an adventure of their own. The physicians saw an opportunity. The men involved in the escapade that followed the hanging included Dr. Allen of Trumbull county, Dr. Coleman of Ashtabula county, Dr. Johnson of Conneaut, and Dr. Hawley of Austintown. According to Mrs. Long, who should know because all these gentlemen were spending the night at her home,

> the Public Square was only partly cleared then, and had many stumps and bushes on it. At night the doctors went for the body, with the tacit consent of the Sheriff. O'Mic was about twenty-one years of age, and was very fat and heavy. Dr. Long did not think one man could carry him, but Dr. Allen, who was very stout, thought he could. He was put upon Dr. Allen's back, who soon fellover a stump and O'Mic on top of him. The doctors dare not laugh aloud, for fear they might be discovered, but some of them were obliged to lie down on the ground and roll around there, before they came to the relief of Dr. Allen. [13]

Perhaps the good doctors had been indulging in a little bit of the same "Old Monongahela" that had tempered the anxiety of O'Mic. None-the-less, they did manage to secure the corpse of this young man from which they would later gain a better understanding of the body's workings. Such cadavers, kept for study, were in extremely short supply for the isolated doctors of the Firelands.

The disturbed grave was discovered the next day. For some time the truth of the matter was unknown to the general public. Though it was obvious that O'Mic was no longer resting where he had been laid, no intense investigation seems to have taken place. That was likely due to the fact that the local authorities had given a mere wink and a nod to the thieving doctors. However, there was a stir caused by some residents who suggested that there had been a resurrection. Due to the frenzied conclusion of the hanging, which left the breaking of the Indian's neck an uncertainty, it seemed plausible to some of the community that O'Mic had managed to claw his way to a new life. This rumor, as most beguiling ones do, spread rapidly across the Firelands.

As we've seen, it was years later that Dr. Long's wife, Julianna, would explain how the theft took place. Likewise, over fifty years later, Dr. Allen's grandson, Dudley, who had also become a doctor, would reveal the excursions that O'Mic had taken in death.

> The skeleton was for a long time in the possession of Dr. Long, but was later in Hudson in the office of Dr. Town. From there, it was supposed, it was carried to Penn, near Pittsburgh, to Dr. Murray, a son-in-law of Dr. Town. The writer [Dr. Dudley Allen] has made every effort to discover its whereabouts [circa 1886] and restore the bones to Cleveland, which should be their proper resting place, but all efforts to this end have proven fruitless. [14]

And so it was that the exhumed body of O'Mic served the medical community of the Western Reserve for at least fifty years and maybe much longer.

Unbeknownst to the crowd who were surrounding the gallows on that twenty-sixth day of June in 1812, war was officially on between the Americans and the British/Indian coalition. Eight days previous, President James Madison, signed the declaration. The fears of the people living in the Reserve had been realized though they would not be conscious of it for a few more days. Any buzz over O'Mic's whereabouts would quickly dissipate.

A few weeks before the war became official, the nation's Revolutionary War hero, and now Governor of the Michigan Territory, William

Hull, took command of the Northwestern Army. Hull was to lead a force of militia, organized by Ohio Governor Return J. Meigs, northward from Cincinnati. He was directed to advance to Fort Detroit for both the protection of that community's residents and to be in position to invade Canada.

Hull followed orders and his 1,500-plus troops were on their way. As it happened, while the settlers were gathered in Cleveland's Public Square on June 26, Hull's troops were camped a hundred miles away at Fort Findlay, the site from which grew today's Findlay, Ohio. They were resting after blazing a trail to that point through the Black Swamp of northwest Ohio. In an account of his experiences as part of Hull's militia, an anonymous volunteer wrote:

> On the 26th instant [June], the day previous to our leaving this place, colonel Dunlap, arrived express from Chillicothe, with dispatches from the secretary at war to general Hull, which, although they were confidential, were supposed to contain official intelligence of the declaration of War. Indeed it was believed by every one, that war had been declared, as the general had ordered all the heavy camp equipage to be left at Fort Findley, and determined to commence a forced march.
>
> Having stationed the balance of capt. Dill's company at Fort Findley, and detached col. Cass' regiment to cut the remainder of the road to the Rapids, the army proceeded on, (but not with more than usual celerity) and in a few days encamped on the bank of the Miami of the Lake [Maumee River], opposite the battle ground of general Wayne [Fallen Timbers], and in view of a little town at the foot of the rapids [Perrysburg, Ohio]. [15]

Even General Hull and the men of his militia had only learned of the official declaration of war after the fact, on the very day O'Mic provided a spectacle in Cleveland.

Hull and the troops proceeded to Detroit and then into Canada. The story of his actions and inactions from that point on are historic; and for them, he was court-martialed two years later. Found guilty of neglect of duty and cowardice, he was sentenced to be shot. Only because of his earlier heroics during the Revolution did President Madison commute his sentence and have him merely discharged from service. What led to such radical actions being taken against General Hull? In an unfairly small nutshell, the following is what transpired.

When the British garrison of Fort Malden, the object of Hull's foray into Canada, was most susceptible to capture, the General retreated to Fort Detroit instead of taking it. Then, with very questionable conduct and little resistance, he surrendered the American fortress at Detroit to the British. On August 16, 1812, the men of his army became prisoners of war.

From the numerous letters received by the real estate icon Zalmon Wildman from associates in the Reserve at this point in time, it is clear that real panic set in when Hull's surrender became common knowledge.

John Patch wrote of Hull from Canfield, Ohio just nine days after the capitulation.

> The object of this letter is to give you a sketch of the news of the day which, I presume, will reach you from me sooner than from any other source.
>
> Gen. Hull has surrendered his whole force to the British. He had retreated back to Detroit where the British attacked him, and it is said he surrendered without any opposition. His Officers and men all blame him very much and accuse him in strong terms of being a Traitor. [16]

A few days later, Wildman received similar sentiments from Jabez Wright who was seventy miles west of Cleveland in Vermillion, Ohio.

> The misfortune of our Country no doubt you will be acquainted with before this reaches you. On the 15th Inst., Old Hull surrendered the Fort of Detroit with his whole army to the British without Firing a Gun, which has put our Country in a very hazardus situation…
>
> … It is said that our Army at Buffalo are dismissed. What is our Govt., about? Are we now to lose our Republican Govt? It appears as tho something was in motion at the head that we do not understand, or why appoint Old Hull to such an important office and why is our army dismissed in Buffalo?…
>
> …I think our country might now hang its head in grief at the gloomy fate that stands prominant on every side ready to force our destruction. But I hope there is virtue sufficient in our Country to harken at the advice of our forefathers in the glorious cause of Liberty and Independence. Tho our atmosphere hangs fraught with dispare and the conduct of our Govt., looks somewhat misterious, yet I think the patriotism of our Country is yet sufficient to stand the trial of these troublesome times and once more establish our rights and domestic peace – but God only knows. [17]

Even Sheriff Baldwin, who led O'Mic to his execution, wrote to Wildman some three weeks after the fact.

> When you were last with me I did not expect to have had the lamentable tale to relate that now I must. You have ere this seen the News of the surrender of Fort Detroit in one of the most awful ways that man could ever be guilty of Surrendering up arms, &c...
> ... This I think is the greatest blow that America ever had. Arnold, Burr, &c. was never half equal to Hull [18]

With the news flooding across the state, residents along the shores of Lake Erie felt the most vulnerable to an attack. The British navy could control shipments across the waters. Shipments of goods and more importantly, of troops. Fort Detroit, now occupied by the British, was just a short sail across the lake. Many in the Western Reserve and the Firelands, if they hadn't already left for safer grounds to the south when they learned that the war had begun, were certainly leaving their homes behind now.

Troops too, like the small militia of Huron Rangers that had formed at the Huron River back in April, were beginning to grow in numbers and more units came from across the state to defend the southern shores of Lake Erie. Intertwined with the commotion of US troop buildup at this time was the unexpected sight of British boats approaching Cleveland and other nearby ports. Part of the terms of Hull's surrender was that the American prisoners of war would be sent home, but the citizenry of the Reserve were not aware of that decision. From a distance all that could be discerned was that uniformed men were coming ashore from British boats. One can feel the immediacy of the tension that their appearance caused by reading the rest of John Patch's letter of August 25 to Wildman.

> An Express arrived here on Saturday last [August 22] giving information that the British and Indians were advancing on our frontiers. The consequence was that Gen. Wadsworth [Commander of the main body of militia based at Old Portage near Akron, Ohio] ordered out a small portion of his men for Cleveland, but before he arrived there another Express met him informing him that the Enemy had arrived as far as Huron. This caused a new order for every other man in the two Brigades to be drafted and march immediately for Cleveland tomorrow morning. The Company of light horse from this town were all drafted and

marched last Sunday...

...6 'clock P.M. [August 25] An express has this moment arrived with orders for the whole division to march immediately. We have not heard the cause of this additional order. We fear the consequences, yet hope for the best. Pray excuse my shortness. I will endeavor to give you further particulars hereafter; the mail is waiting...

...P. S. 500 of our prisoners arrived at Cleaveland yesterday morning. [19]

More insight into the emotions and movements of troops, Indians, and settlers in these days comes by reading further into Sheriff Baldwin's letter, written about twelve days after the one from Patch.

We have seen Col. Cass, McArthur, &c., who, after their surrender, was put on board of boats & vessels and sent to this place [Cleveland]; and on their arrival at Sandusky put the whole People in an uproar. All left the town of Danbury [on the present-day Marblehead peninsula of Sandusky Bay] as fast as possible, escaped to the Bay, many of them, and lay in the woods... All the people move off of the Firelands.

I came only as far as Vermillion River, and returned home on assurance of Troops being sent on to Huron [ten miles further west of Vermillion], which was done last week. Three companies went on, and in a short time a Regiment men is to march. We have 1000 men in this place under arms, and daily expect about 1400 more to meet with 2100 or 3000 that is on the move from the southward, where it is supposed that they will make a stand at Miammus [Maumee River], but is not known. Almost all the families moved from this town [Cleveland] a short distance & returned. [20]

The Sheriff further explained how chaotic things had become. Near his home in Cleveland, he says that

forty waggons & carts was there at one time loaded with women and children not knowing where to go; cattle all drove that could be found, which in all was a sorrowful sight to see. Sick people not able to sit up, drove off in the night, laying in waggons, &c.

I cannot say at present that I feel as if it was necessary to move from this place, but all is confusion. Many a one has come here from River Raisin [thirty miles south of Detroit] who had good living there, who has not a change of clothing, or bread to eat, being plundered of all that Devils & Indians could take from them. The Miamme is strip'd of all inhabitants; some has gone to the South; some down the Lake. [21]

Through August and into September troops continued to establish themselves along the lakeshores of the Reserve. One young man of Ashtabula county, to the east of Cleveland, quickly joined the regiment of General Hayes which was forming in his neighborhood. The sixteen year-old boy was Joshua Giddings and it is from him that we have learned the most reliable details of what became the first foray on Ohio lands between the Americans and their newly declared enemies. This skirmish, generally forgotten in the history books, cost the lives of several brave souls on both sides of the conflict.

In Warren, Ohio, General Wadsworth was a prominent man. He had spent his life organizing local government infrastructures; overseeing the formation of schools, post offices, and even Masonic lodges. Now at the age of sixty-five he headed a force of 3,000 militia formed to protect the north-eastern corner of Ohio. The response to the call for Ohio men to defend their frontier homes was tremendous. As companies of volunteers assembled, Wadsworth actually had to turn away nearly half of their number. He recognized the need for them to provide protection on the premises of their households. There, situated across the interior of the Reserve, were the defenseless women and children who had remained behind. In addition, it was easy for the General to discern that some of these courageous settlers were ill-equipped for military battle. Though disheartened, the men returned to their families.

Soon, Wadsworth put General Simon Perkins, another distinguished civic leader, landowner, and businessman from the Warren area, in command of the newly formed Ohio militia companies. The whole moved westward to the Huron River arriving there on September 6. The same Judge Frederick Fowler, who overheard O'Mic pleading with the Almighty, was at this time a member of one of these companies and explains how Perkins seemed to have become foolishly impulsive as the troops settled in:

> Gen. Perkins immediately commenced building a Fort on the Lake Shore, in the wilderness, about three miles East of Huron River... This was called "Fort Nonsense!" A more injudicious point could not have been selected on the whole lake shore. It was open to attack from both land and water. After being bored for a few days, by his old acquaintances in this section, on account of his skill in engineering, the General concluded to change his position. Accordingly he removed his army to a

Photo Portrait of Joshua R. Giddings circa 1855.

point on the East side of the Huron River, on lands of Ebenezer Merry, in the township of Avery. It took the name of "Camp Avery."[22]

A few weeks went by before circumstances developed which would lead to what has become known as the "Skirmish on the Peninsula." In actuality, two skirmishes were had.

It began when a report of Hull's defeat reached the men who were guarding a small fortress in Lower Sandusky, today's Fremont, Ohio. The news caused the fort to be abandoned by the Americans. Left behind was a supply of foodstuffs originally intended to feed Hull's men as they progressed to the north. On September 24, Major Frazier left Camp Avery with one hundred and fifty men under orders to recover the edibles rather than have them go to waste. Joshua Giddings explained that upon his arrival at Lower Sandusky, Major Frazier

> loaded four small boats with pork and beef, and directed them to be taken to our encampment. The number of men accompanying these boats I am unable to state, but think it was eighteen. They started down the Bay [Sandusky Bay], intending to proceed directly to Huron, but finding the Lake so much agitated by a storm at that time prevailing,

that they thought it prudent to wait until the storm should abate. [23]

The Lake Erie storm, as they are still known to do today, came up quickly and sent the four boats in search of the leeward side of the nearby island for protection. This turned out to be its eastern shore. The island was known by the last name of its owner, Epaphras Bull, a young man from Connecticut who settled there after working as a surveyor a few years previous. As the boats waited out the storm, Bull himself happened to be miles away at Sheriff Baldwin's home in Cleveland, mortally ill after escaping from his island home under horrific circumstances. (Decades later Bull's Island would be purchased by Leonard B. Johnson and to this day bear's his name. It would gain notoriety for being the site of a Confederate POW Depot during the Civil War.)

At dawn the waters had calmed. It was decided that a handful of the men would take one of the boats and scout the peninsula for any sign of the enemy Indians or British who were suspected to be in the vicinity. The remainder of the men and boats waited for their return on the island. The crew of this spy boat came ashore just across from the island's northern edge. Making their way inland they soon passed a log cabin. It was the one that most historians believe had belonged to the earliest settler of this peninsula, Benajah Wolcott. Wolcott was not there, however; he too had already fled with his family for safer grounds. He would eventually make a safe return and a decade later would become the first lighthouse keeper of what is still the oldest continuously operating lighthouse on the Great Lakes, the Marblehead Lighthouse.

Joshua Giddings notes that

> among the spies were one or two of the Ramsdells, who had resided at what then was called "The Two Harbors," on the shore of the Lake, some six or seven miles from Bull's Island. This party proceeded to the former residence of the Ramsdells, with the steady caution which the backwoodsmen of that day knew so well how to practice. They were careful to leave no track, nor to approach by any of the frequented ways leading to or from their former dwelling.
>
> By creeping stealthily through a corn field, they obtained a view of the house, and discovered around it a number of Indians, who appeared to be feasting on roast corn and honey, which they found in abundance on

the premises. They remained here until they supposed they had obtained an accurate knowledge of the number of the enemy, which they reported at forty-seven. They then returned to their comrades, on Bull's Island, and made report of their discoveries. The whole party then moved across to Cedar Point, and dispatched a messenger to Camp Avery (as our encampment was called) with the tidings. [24]

The Indians spotted at the Ramsdell's farm were believed to be Potawatomi, allied with the British. One later report says that their number was even greater than the spies had counted that day, more in the neighborhood of one hundred and thirty warriors who had made a deliberate expedition from the Maumee Valley to the Marblehead peninsula.

The Ramsdell farm was established by Joseph Ramsdell just a year earlier in 1811. He was the second person to settle on Marblehead. Like Benajah Wolcott, he had worked as a surveyor a few years previous, liked what he saw, and established a homestead. His property was also referred to as the "point 'tween the harbors" and today is the site known as East Harbor State Park. But, on Sunday, September 28, 1812, the Indians were there harvesting his crops without permission. It's not certain, however, whether it was Joseph alongside his son, Valentine, or another of his sons, who was in that spy company witnessing the occupation of their farm.

Without the manpower to take any action, the scouting party carefully retraced its steps back to their boat and rowed across the bay to their fellows who were still waiting for them at Bull's Island. As Giddings noted, immediately upon their return, all four boats rowed to East Point, now known as Cedar Point, which was a safe distance from potential trouble. There the men remained, after sending a lone messenger to Camp Avery, alerting the authorities of the Indian presence that they had just discovered.

Giddings was at his post guarding the camp when the courier arrived. It was near five o'clock in the afternoon and within a few hours, the word was out. The cadence of the drums' beating was a call for volunteers. The mission at hand was to head back to Marblehead and confront the Indians. Some sixty-four men answered the call, including Giddings who had just finished six hours of guard duty. After a quick meal, it was near nine o'clock in the evening when the men began their

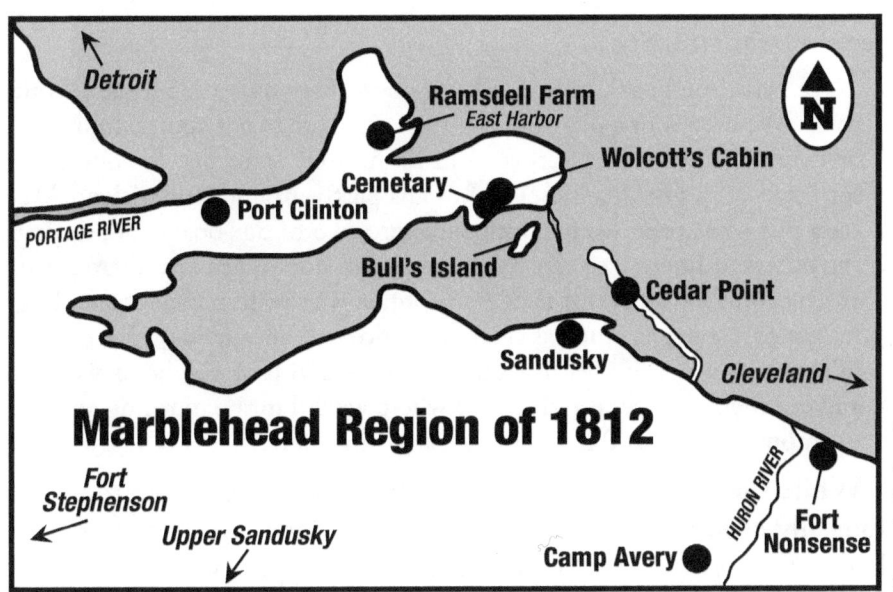

march through the darkness toward Cedar Point. It was a seven hour trek. They arrived just before sunrise. The men who had remained at the ready after discovering the Indians on Ramsdell's farm greeted them heartily. Giddings reported that he and others from Avery

> unloaded the boats and embarked onboard theirs, accompanied by eight of the men who had come from Lower Sandusky with the provisions, and leaving the remainder of that party on the Point. We steered for what was called the "middle orchard," lying on the shore of the bay nearly opposite Bull's Island. Our whole number now amounted to seventy-two. We landed a little after sun rise at the "middle orchard;" here our arrangements were made as follows: Eight men, including a corporal, were detailed as a guard to remain with the boats. They were directed to take them to a thicket of small bullrushes, apparently half way to Bull's Island, and there to await further orders. Two flank guards of twelve men each, were also detailed, one under the command of Acting Sergeant James Root, and the other under command of Acting Sergent Thomas Hamilton.
>
> These guards were to keep at suitable distance on each side of the road, in which the main body under the command of Capt. Cotton was to march. [25]

From a letter to his mother, written just two days later, Giddings recounts the situation:

> We, with the boats, moved off out about fifty rods [275 yards] from shore. We then sent a boat and five men on shore to get apples. In fifteen or twenty minutes they returned in haste; told us to flee for our lives, for there were four [canoes?] of Indians partly around Bull's island. We then put what pack we had on board into two of our boats and, setting the others at liberty, we ran on the opposite side of the island from the enemy and then stood for East Point, when we saw four canoes standing for the east shore as much as six miles above us. We landed on East Point in about twenty minutes. The Indians came and took the boats we left, and cut them in pieces, and landed where we did in the morning and lay in ambush within 100 rods [550 yards] from there. [26]

While the boat guards, like their biblical parents before them, had foolishly been lured by the sight of nearby dangling apples; the main body of troops under Captain Cotton were approaching Ramsdell's farm. They saw before them the remnants of an Indian presence; embers burning in small fires and meat strewn around the grounds, but no Indians. It being his property, Valentine Ramsdell was one to point out that his harvested wheat was ready for the taking near the lakeshore. He wanted it for the men back at Camp Avery. With no Indians in sight, Sergeant Root's party of guards was ordered to quickly gather the grain while the rest of the group returned to the farmhouse. Sometime after ten o'clock in the morning, most of the contingent began to retrace its steps back to where they had landed. Captain Cotton and the bulk of the troops again followed the main road with Sergeant Hamilton's guards flanking his right. Sergeant Root was lagging a little behind because of the time spent bundling the wheat. They began coming up from the lake at an angle, planning to intercept the others about a mile down the road.

All had progressed perhaps three quarters of a mile, when suddenly Root and his party were fired upon by the enemy. His party was led by young Ramsdell [Valentine], who acted as pilot. The ground was open timberland, with grass as high as a man's waist. The Indians rose from the grass directly in front of the party, and fired simultaneously as a platoon of militia would have fired at the word of command. At the instant they fired they raised the war whoop, and disappeared in the grass. Young Ramsdell fell at the first fire pierced by several balls. One other man was also disabled, leaving but nine men beside their commander to return the fire of the enemy, and hold them at bay until they should be supported by their friends under Capt. Cotton. [27]

The Captain heard the shots ringing out. Before he could give an order, several of his men ran in the direction of the sound screeching a war whoop of their own. The men slowed as they neared the action and began firing from behind trees and through the tall grasses. The contest continued for at least fifteen minutes until only random shots were made from either side. The main troops under Captain Cotton slowly retreated some distance while Sergeant Root and his contingent remained, waiting until the Indian gunfire had totally ceased. When that occurred, they moved out and caught up to the rest of the troops. All now resumed their retreat to the "middle orchard" where they had landed. But that was not before they buried the dead. Three men had fallen. They were Valentine Ramsdell, James S. Bills, and Simeon Blackman. They would be buried together as ably as was possible under the hazardous circumstances. Only then did the men move on. Soon a second altercation would be had.

When the main body moving along the road had arrived in sight of the improvement at the middle orchard, there suddenly appeared two Indians, some thirty or forty rods in front of the foremost members of our party. The Indians appeared to have suddenly discovered our men and started to run from them, our men in front made pursuit, while others were more cautious than their comrades, called loudly for them to stop, assuring them there was danger near. Our friends stopped suddenly, and at that instant the whole body of Indians fired upon our line, being at farthest not more than twenty rods distant, entirely concealed behind a ledge of trees that had been prostrated by the wind. It was a most unaccountable circumstance that not a man of our party was injured at this fire. [28]

For about five minutes the firing was sporadic as each man scurried to find a tree for protection. Two or three of the Indians were killed as the skirmish intensified. A group of about twenty men with Captain Cotton precariously shot their way to the nearby log cabin of Benajah Wolcott. There they found protection and a fortress from which they could defend themselves. More men eventually maneuvered their way to the cabin until some forty of them were sheltered inside. From here they were able to provide cover for those men from the back of the lines who were still passing by the log house, struggling to return to the boats which were supposed to be just a short jaunt away. However, when they finally arrived at the landing site, they discovered an inexplicable reality. Two of the boats were gone and two others were found with holes and sunk in the shallow shoreline waters; the tragic result of the earlier apple-picking adventure of the guards.

To return to the cabin was certain death for these men as the Indians were there en masse and continuing to riddle the dwelling with balls from their guns. The only option they saw was to run as far as they could to the eastern shores of the peninsula in hope of somehow getting across the bay. The nearest stretch of land was Cedar Point, where unbeknownst to these fleeing soldiers, the eight guards with their two boats had held up.

The guards on Cedar Point had heard the guns of battle echoing across the open waters. Their senses and fears were naturally heightened. It wasn't long before they decided to reboard the boats and row closer to the peninsula; keeping what they hoped was a safe distance from any attack upon themselves. When they did,

> they rejoiced to see their friends coming down the Point, bringing their wounded, wet with perspiration, many of them stained in blood, and all appearing ready to sink under the fatigues and excitement of nearly twenty-four hours unmitigated effort.
>
> The boats were small, and one of them was loaded at once and crossed to Cedar Point, and returned with the assistance of the other, took in all that remained on the point of the Peninsula and crossed over. [29]

The men recuperated on the beach of Cedar Point before heading east for the Huron River. The two boats at hand were believed to be smaller skows; barge-like flat boats use for transport of men and supplies. One boat took at least eight of the troops back to the base camp and the second had eight oarsmen paddling as best they could to get the six wounded men the medical attention they needed. Giddings was one of the rowers of the injured. The rest of the men returned to camp on foot. Ever present in all their minds was the unknown fate of Captain Cotton and the forty men with him still barricaded in Wolcott's cabin; stranded with no boats or reinforcements available to them should they try to return.

When the first of the battle-worn men landed at Camp Avery from Cedar Point it was very early in the morning of Wednesday, September 30. They described the scene that they had left behind to General Perkins. For various reasons, the General concluded that those men held up in Wolcott's cabin were surely dead or already taken as prisoners. Part of his decision to not send help was further due to the fact that there were so few men available to make such an attempt. The camp had been ravaged by disease and otherwise already spread thin.

A messenger, however, was sent to the forces at Cleveland with details of the occurrence. Early the next morning, this courier stopped on his way to rest at the Black River, about twenty miles to the east. A militia there had been earlier released to their nearby homes, but they were on-call for service should the need arise. The messenger found Captain Quigley who led that militia along with John Reid, one of the earliest settlers in the area and who was as well a reserve militia man. Learning the fate of those left fighting off the savages on the peninsula, Quigley and Reid immediately started off for the Huron River where Giddings says his company commander, Lieutenant Allen, succeeded in rounding up thirty volunteers of his own. The problem for all the would-be rescuers was a lack of boats.

One report states that as Quigley and Reid arrived at the mouth of the river

> they there met with Amos Spafford, Esq., from Maumee, removing his family to Cleveland in two boats. On request of Reed and Quigley, Mr. Spafford at once unloaded his boats on the beach. It was now in the evening, and the lake was smooth. All taking to the boats, they gained the Peninsula in the vicinity of Bull's Island after midnight. Secreting themselves as well as possible, they waited for day light. At dawn of day, they made for the house, where they found, to the joy of their anxious hearts, thirty-seven of our brave men, all alive – though weak from want of food. They had eat nothing for three days. [30]

After several boat trips, all the men were soon rescued and returned to Camp Avery. The wounded were left to the care of a physician at the mouth of the Huron River. One of their number was Joseph Ramsdell, the owner of the farm, who survived his wounds but had suffered the loss of one of his sons. The rest of the survivors were taken upstream to the camp where they gained the comfort of a much needed meal

Monument to the men who did not survive the *Skirmish on the Peninsula* in 1812. Located in Battlefield Park in Marblehead, Ohio on land Joshua Giddings purchased in 1857 to honor them.

and peaceful sleep.

The exact number of Indians slain through these skirmishes is uncertain, but three more Americans were killed in the second attack near the Wolcott house. They were Alexander Mason, Daniel Mingus, and Abraham Simons. In 1858, Joshua Giddings placed a headstone with their names engraved upon it, so that they would be remembered as the ones "who fell near this place in battle with the Indians Sept. 29, 1812." That headstone, and an additional, updated one, is still visitable on the Marblehead Peninsula.

Giddings, who went on to an influential career as a US Congressman for over twenty years, had planned for a fifty-year reunion in 1862 with the other survivors of the "skirmishes on the peninsula," but learned five years previous that none but himself was still of this world.

The fate of one of those killed near the cabin is described by Giddings and sheds light on the fact that it was not just Potawatomi from the west that were united in this assault. At least one of the well-known locals, who had a personal axe to grind, had done so.

They mutilated the body of Simons, who fell during the skirmish. His right hand was cut off and the scalping knife of a chief named O'Mick was left plunged to the hilt in his breast. This Indian had previously resided at a small village on the east bank of the Parmatoony Creek, in the Township of Wayne, in the county of Ashtabula. I had been well-acquainted with him for many years, and so had many others who were engaged in the combat of that day, some of whom declared that they recognized him during the skirmish. It is also supposed that he must have recognized some of his old acquaintances, and left his knife in the body of Simons as a token of triumph. The knife was recognized by some of the soldiers from its peculiar handle of carved ivory. [31]

Just three months after his son had been the morbid, main attraction in the public square of nearby Cleveland; a bit of revenge was seemingly had by Old O'Mic on at least one of the possible onlookers of his son's death. ♦

HMMM...

The Winds of Lake Erie.

Before the starting of the flour mills in the fire-lands, the earliest settlers in some cases took their wheat in boats over the lake to the French mills near Detroit. A touching incident is told of a party of men who started with their year's wheat in a boat and landed near the close of the day on one of the islands and then went inland a short distance to select a place to camp over night. On their return to the shore, lo and behold their boat was nowhere to be seen. A sudden gust of wind had freed it from its mooring and it had floated off with its precious load upon the broad expanse of Lake Erie. What situation could be more deplorable!
They were on a lone island and no way of escape. There were no passing vessels to rescue them. The lake was at that time but a solitude of water. Thoughts of their families, starvation for them and starvation for themselves seemed inevitable. Poor men! they broke down and shed tears and passed a night of woe. Morning came. Heartbroken, they wandered down to the shore and gazed upon the wild waste of waters. Then al at once in a little nook, safe and close to shore, they discovered their boat. A change of wind in the night had floated it back as silently as it had floated away.

In Henry Howe's, Historical Collections of Ohio, 1907 [32]

X.
THE STARS BEHIND THE STAR SPANGLED BANNER.

Bright, crimson-colored reflections glistened on the waves of the Patapsco River before they eerily dissolved into its watery depths. They were lingering remnants of the fiery tails enemy rockets had left behind as they screeched across the night sky. There were bombs as well, exploding in the air above, illuminating the surroundings the way fireworks do on any Fourth of July gala. But this night they marked no celebration. This was war. The place was Fort McHenry at the port of Baltimore. The thirteenth day of September, 1814, was a Tuesday that had begun with a bang; many of them, and there would be even more throughout the entire day and night.

For twenty-five straight hours the British Navy relentlessly shelled the American fortress. It rained through much of the bombing; the thunder and lightning only adding to the theatrics. Just after dawn of the following morning the firing had finally ceased and all nineteen British ships involved in the onslaught were heading out of the Chesapeake Bay. Evidence that the Americans had withstood the attack was that their banner, not the British Union Jack, was waving through the morning mist from the tall pole inside the fort.

Most of us are at least vaguely familiar with the story of this battle and how it inspired the composition of the poem that eventually became our national anthem. The author, of course, was the celebrated Francis Scott Key. He was a lawyer, fairly well-to-do, and friends with men in high social and political positions. His poetry was a hobby, written purely for fun and amusement. His biography is interesting enough, but there are a few questions begging to be answered surrounding his writing of that one particular poem. What was a wealthy American lawyer doing on a ship anchored with the British fleet in the midst of their naval attack upon a US fortress? And, how was he able to see that flag, which he so eloquently had written about, when his ship had to be at least more than a mile away from it through a prolonged, rainy, and foggy day and night? And how did his simple poem rise so quickly in popularity to eventually become our national anthem? The answers to these inquiries come from several lesser known personalities who were, in their own right, stars during the historic autumn of 1814 in and around Baltimore.

The hand written poem that we now know as The Star Spangled Banner, was first published as a handbill or flyer, what was called a broadside in that day. *The Defense of Fort McHenry*, was its original title when it was printed by fourteen year-old Samuel Sands, the youngest employee at the *Baltimore American* newspaper. He was the only one manning the shop that Saturday when a man walked in requesting to have copies made of a handwritten poem. It was just the third day since the tumultuous bombing had ceased. The other employees were still absent, having left to serve in the militia several days before the British had attacked the fort. Young Samuel got right to work setting the type and inking the press. The gentleman customer was Joseph H. Nicholson, a judge and chief justice in Maryland; but of late he was a captain of artillery and second in command at Fort McHenry. He also happened to be married to Rebecca, the sister of Francis Key's wife.

The patriotism of Nicholson was self-evident; especially noticeable by the leadership he displayed in the many positions he held throughout his life in military and government arenas. His own words testify to his fiery genuineness. On the precipice of war in May of 1812, he delivered a speech in Baltimore with the question:

> Is there an American sword that will not leap from its scabbard to avenge the wrongs and contumely treatment under which we have so long suffered? No, my countrymen, it is impossible. Let us act with one heart, and with one hand; let us show to an admiring world, that however we may differ among ourselves about some of our eternal concerns, yet in the great cause of our country, the American people are animated by one soul and by one spirit.... [1]

Portrait of Francis Scott Key by Rembrandt Peale.

Key had met up with Nicholson on the Saturday morning following Tuesday's bombardment of Fort McHenry. He had just finished putting the final touches on his latest composition. As Nicholson read it, he was touched by it and recognized its value. He soon headed off to the nearby newspaper office to have copies made. He wanted to pass them out as inspiration to the thousand-plus soldiers still recuperating in the fortress, as well as to other citizens about the city. The verses on the little six-and-a-half by five-and-a-half inch cards did the trick. The triumphant spirits of the physically exhausted men in the fortress were lifted to an even higher level.

To call Key's verses a poem is a bit misleading, as it was actually written as lyrics. He had composed the verses to match the rhythm of an established drinking song titled, *To Anacreon in Heaven*. He once had written a similar ballad to the same melody in tribute to John Adams. The uniqueness of the rhythm in the composition proves that the melody had to of been in his head as he wrote. When published, a note reading: "Tune – Anacreon in Heaven," preceded the lyrics. This particular ode to the Greek poet Anacreon was originally composed and sung by a young men's music club based in London. In that context, it marked an evening's transition from orchestral music to a looser time of sing-a-longs. Usually after a soloist sang several verses, a chorus would repeat the refrain. The song, and others like it, spilled into American culture as well. These so-called drinking songs had been well-established in European circles, being a part of opera and musical theatrical performances. In the states, it was in the taverns, theaters, and streets themselves that such lively tunes often echoed as they were sung by folks fueled by patriotism and perhaps a few intoxicating spirits.

A light-hearted example of Key's spontaneous creativity is found in this example preserved by his great-grandson. It seems that at a dinner party he once attended, the guests entertained themselves with challenges to create and solve riddles. Francis's puzzle read:

> I made myself, and though no form have I,
> Am fairer than the fairest you can spy;
> The sun I outshine in his mid-day light,
> And yet am darker than the darkest night;
> Hotter I am than fire, than ice more cold,
> Richer than purest gems of finest gold,
> Yet I am never either bought or sold;
> The man that wants me, never yet was seen;
> The poor alone possess me; yet the mean
> And grudging rich oft give me to the poor,
> Who yet are not made richer than before;
> The blindest see me, and the deafest hear;
> Cowards defy me, and the bravest fear:
> If you're a fool, you know me; if you grow
> In knowledge, me you will soon cease to know.
> Get me – and low and poor thy state will be;
> Forget me – and no equal shalt thou see.
> Now catch me if you can – I'm sometimes caught,
> Though never thought worth catching, never sought.
> Am I still hid? then let whoever tries
> To see me, give it up, and shut his eyes. [2]

Due to the tension of the British presence around the Chesapeake Bay during August and September of 1814, Baltimore newspapers had intermittently suspended publication. The first paper to publish the patriotic poem in its pages was the *Baltimore Patriot*. It was in the Tuesday evening edition of September 20, a week to the day after the initial bombardment. The following morning a new edition of another newspaper, the *Baltimore American*, included the *The Defense of Fort McHenry*, just as it appeared on the small broadsides printed earlier in their office by the young Mr. Sands. In another week the *National Intelligencer* of Washington ran the poem; and so it's printing snowballed with more and more newspapers across the country soon following suit. For quite some time, the tune enjoyed immense popularity, though Key's name was rarely attached to it. Seemingly, the author acknowledged its origin, but never required any form of credit. Eventually, the ballad waned just a bit from its initial rise of notoriety, but saw a major resurgence some fifty years after its conception, during the Civil War. At that time, many inherently felt it was already their national anthem, but it took until 1931 for Congress to make it official. Key's name was reattached to the lyrics when sheet music of the mid-1800s was printed.

With a step backward in time we can review some of the events that led up to the attack on Fort McHenry, and in doing so, reveal a little of Key's own involvement in the military before he wrote his poem.

A few months previous to the bombing, citizens in and around the Chesapeake Bay region were on high alert as British ships had blockaded strategic ports and skirmishes with the Americans were increasing. In April of 1814, the Napoleonic War, which had garnered significantly more attention than this squabble with the United States, took a drastic turn. Napoleon was forced to abdicate his throne when Paris had fallen. That event released seasoned British troops from duty in France. They came by the thousands to the American shores with a much more focussed determination to finally end the conflict here as well.

Most of the able-bodied American men in residence had formed into militias. Key himself was one of them. Over a year previous, in July of 1813, he had gotten a very brief taste of service as a private in an artillery militia. With the renewed British threats in June of 1814, he enlisted again; this time promoted to a lieutenant and acting as quartermaster.

The flag Key saw flying over Fort McHenry in 1814
on display in the Boston Navy Yard in 1873.

He was stationed near his home on the shores of Georgetown, across the bay and to the east of the fort. The militias formed at this time were a bit loose. To some degree many men came and went as they pleased. Structure was not what it needed to be. These were common citizens, some of modest means and some well-to-do, but all worried about their nearby families and businesses. Some would briefly leave their units to partake in dinners at their homes or engage in meetings with their business associates and then return to camp. Key acted as the others had, somewhat in and out of service through July and early August. However, when it became obvious that an attack was imminent near Washington, Key was there.

It has become known as the Battle of Bladensburg, a site about eight miles outside of Washington City. Admittedly, Key was as ill-trained for this military action as were many of the men alongside him. What surprised him even more, however, was the number of men who were not even supplied a weapon with which to fight. Key had purchased his own uniform and supplied his own horse and pistols. He had the means to do so. On August 24, 1814, Major General Robert Ross led nearly five thousand seasoned British troops into the town of Bladensburg and readily overpowered the raw, poorly armed, and unorganized Americans trying to defend their homeland. Ross's victory that afternoon gave him and his men an unopposed path into Washington City which they readily took. Once there, Ross himself explained what happened in a letter to his Secretary of State for War:

> Having Halted the Army for a short time I determined to March upon Washington and reached that City at 8. O'Clock that Night. – Judging it of consequence to complete the Destruction of the Public Buildings with the least possible delay so that the Army might retire without Loss of time the following Building(s) were set Fire to and consumed--the Capital including the Senate House and House of Representation, the Arsenal, the Dock Yard, Treasury, War Office, Presidents Palace, Rope Walk and the Great Bridge across the Potowmack, in the Dock Yard a Frigate nearly ready to be Launched and a Sloop of War were consumed. – The two B[r]idges leading to Washington over the Eastern Branch had been destroyed by the Enemy who apprehended an Attack from that Quarter. The Object of the Expedition being accomplished I determined before any greater Force of the Enemy could be assembled to withdraw the Troops and accordingly commenced retiring on the Night of the 25th; on the evening of the 29th. we reached Benedict and re-embarked the following day.[3]

In the minds of many of the enemy this was vengence for the Americans' destruction of their Upper Canadian capital city of York, today's Toronto, a year previous. In less than twenty-four hours the United States had suffered one of its most demoralizing defeats in their history.

Reports vary as to whether Key had helped or unwittingly hindered the battle situation at Bladensburg. He is said to have seen the disarray of the American troops and took it upon himself to ride to several points on the field and advise officers to move their forces into alternate positions. Some witnesses said that he and others caused more confusion than assistance. In his defense, if the Americans hadn't been so blatantly ill-prepared Key would not have had to of acted as independently as he had. Whether one considers Lieutenant Key to have over-stepped his bounds, or appropriately stepped-up to try and save the day, seems irrelevent as the British had, and would have, won the day regardless. This strategic success encouraged and propelled them to continue their assaults. The next target was Baltimore.

Again under the leadership of General Ross, on September 12, British troops established a force of several thousand men on a peninsula east of the fort known as North Point. From there they drove toward Baltimore. At first, the attack was going in their favor, but after regrouping, the American foot soldiers put up a staunch defense; so much so that the British troops decided to retreat. In the action, General Ross had been killed. Grief stricken at the loss of their beloved leader, his fellow British soldiers likely did not complain that the officers in charge "… expended 129 Gallons of Rum to preserve the Corpse of Major General Ross."[4] As was the practice for high level officers in the Royal Navy, Ross's body was thus distilled and soon transported to Halifax, Nova Scotia for burial.

The next phase of the planned offensive commenced as artillery was fired from the ships of the Royal Navy in the direction of Fort McHenry. The bombing of the US fortress began around six o'clock on the morning of September 13. It continued through the entire day and night, finally ceasing at seven o'clock on Wednesday morning. Through it all, three Americans had the aggressor's view of the attack. They were Francis Scott Key, John S. Skinner, and Dr. William Beanes. For a week they shared deck space with British commanders and the crews of several ships. Key and Skinner had come to seek the release of their friend Dr. Beanes who had been taken prisoner a couple weeks earlier. They succeeded in gaining his freedom, however; because in the process they all had become privy to the details of the impending assault on Fort McHenry, they were required to stay with their enemy until it was finished. In was in this dire situation that Key wrote most of his poem.

The only documented comments of any consequence by Key regarding this event came twenty years after the fact. As one on the rostrum of speakers at a grand dinner party for five hundred Democrat supporters of Andrew Jackson, Key addressed the crowd explaining…

> …I saw the flag of my country waving over a city – the strength and pride of my native State – a city devoted to plunder and desolution by its assailants. I witnessed the preparation for its assaults, and I saw the

array of its enemies as they advanced to the attack. I heard the sound of battle; the noise of the conflict fell upon my listening ear, and told me that "the brave and the free" had met the invaders...Then did I remember that there were gathered around that banner, among its defenders, men who had heard and answered the call of their country – from these mountain sides, from this beautiful valley, and from this fair city of my native Country; and though I walked upon a deck surrounded by a hostile fleet, detained as a prisoner, yet was my step firm, and my heart strong, as these recollections came upon me. Through the clouds of war, the stars of that banner still shone in my view, and I saw the discomfited host of its assailants driven back in ignominy to their ships. Then, in that hour of deliverance and joyful triumph, my heart spoke; and "Does not such a country, and such defenders of their country deserve a song?" was its question. With it came an inspiration not to be resisted; and even though it had been a hanging matter to make a song, I must have written it. Let the praise, then, if any be due, be given, not to me, who only did what I could not help doing; not to the writer, but to the inspirers of the song!... [5]

Beyond this speech, little was ever written by Key about those seven days with the British fleet. He seemingly had no aspirations to be seriously recognized in literary or musical circles.

John Skinner, who had accompanied Key, was an officer in the US Navy, commissioned as Purser. Besides keeping the accounts of provisions and providing other services for the United States' Chesapeake Flotilla, he was also acting as an agent for the government who negotiated for exchanges of prisoners of war. In that capacity he was asked by President Madison to join Key in an effort to have the British release Dr. Beanes, who had been abducted from his home on August 25, the night after Washington was burned.

Just a couple weeks previous, it was Purser Skinner who is reported to have spotted the movements of the British Fleet up the Chesapeake Bay and realized that they meant trouble. He mounted his horse and rode some ninety miles to the President's Palace to warn James Madison of their advance toward Washington. Because of his long, overnight ride and daring he has since been dubbed, "Maryland's Paul Revere."

The ship upon which the three men were held during the bombing is confused by some historians. Key and Skinner had sailed into the

Chesapeake Bay under a white flag of truce on a cartel ship; a vessel commissioned during wartime for use in humanitarian efforts like the conveyance of messages between combatants, or, as in this case, the exchange of prisoners. Upon arriving at the enemy's fleet on September 7, they boarded the flagship of British Admiral Cochrane, the *HMS Tonnant*. After a short time, they were transfered to the *HMS Surprise* because the *Tonnan*t was crowded with British sailors. Some say they were on the *Surprise* during the bombing, however; if we trust the words of Skinner himself, they were all back on board the US cartel ship upon which they had sailed into the bay. The name of their ship was likely the *President*, but some argue it was the *Minden*. A historian of that time, Charles Ingersoll, had published a history of the War of 1812 sometime after the war. In an article published in 1849, a rebuttal to some erroneous claims of Ingersoll was made by John Skinner:

> "It was," says your extract, "during the striking concussions of that night that the song of The Star Spangled Banner was composed in the Admiral's ship."
>
> Now, as it is not unworthy of that noble inspiration that its circumstances should be more exactly known. The author of the Star Spangled Banner was never on board the Admiral's ship after we were in sight of Baltimore. We had been invited during our detention to take up our quarters with the Admiral's son, Sir Thomas Cochrane, on board the Surprise frigate, the Admiral expressing regret that his own, the flag ship [HMS Tonnant], was so crowded with officers that he could not accommodate us as he wished; but promised that his son (which he well redeemed) would make us comfortable until after the denouement of the expedition then going forward.
>
> Dining every day with the Admiral and a large party of army and navy officers, his objects and plans were freely spoken of, and thus, when we arrived in sight of the city, the undersigned [Skinner] again demanded an answer to his despatches, to which Sir Alexander [Cochrane] answered smilingly, "Ah, Mr. S., after discussing so freely as we have done in your presence our purposes and plans, you could hardly expect us to let you go onshore now in advance of us. Your despatches are all ready. You will have to remain with us until all is over, when I promise you there shall be no further delay." Seeing no help for it, I demanded that we should then be returned to our own vessel — one of Ferguson's Norfolk packets, under our own "Star-Spangled Banner," during the attack. It was from her

deck, in view of Fort McHenry, that we witnessed through an anxious day and night, "The rocket's red glare, the bombs bursting in air;" and the song, which was written the night after we got back to Baltimore, in the hotel then kept at the corner of Hanover and Market streets, was but a versified and almost literal transcript of our expressed hopes and apprehensions, through that ever memorable period of anxiety to all, but never of despair. Calling on its accomplished author the next morning, he handed it to the undersigned, who passed it to the Baltimore Patriot, and through it to immortality.

Your obedient servant, J. S. S. [J. S. Skinner, Agent for Prisoners.] [6]

Besides explaining which ship the three men were aboard during the attack, this excerpt points out another avenue through which the poem appeared so quickly in print. Only a day apart, two local newspapers were the first to publish it, and apparently two different men delivered it to each press office. As already noted, the *Baltimore American* is where Joseph Nicholson is said to have had the broadsides printed by Samuel Sands on September 17. A curious footnote to this printing was that young Samuel had taken some liberties with the capitalization of several letters which were not written as capitals in Key's original hand-written version. When his newspaper, the *Baltimore American*, resumed publication four days later on September 21, they printed the poem with all the changes Sands had made to it in typesetting the broadside. However, one day sooner, September 20, the *Baltimore Patriot* newspaper published the poem much closer to the way Key had written it. Historians speculate that having spotted the inappropriateness of Sands' capitalizations the editor of the *Patriot* made his own changes but some of Sands' other minor modifications remained. In lieu of these discrepancies, it is certain that Skinner gave the *Patriot's* editor a copy of the broadside rather than the original. It is even theorized by some that Skinner may have been with Nicholson that day at the *American* and then took a copy of the broadside to the *Patriot*.

All of this minutiae simply highlights the fact that both Joseph Nicholson and John Skinner played a significant role in the poem's history by immediately getting it into print and thus circulated through the populace of Baltimore.

But wait, as they say, there's more. Writing in 1927, P. H. Magruder, then secretary of the Naval Academy, and more importantly the great-grandson of Joseph Nicholson, detailed the traditional story of the Nicholson family surrounding the events of 1814. Though oftentimes personal pride can color family testimonials like this one, Magruder was a highly respected figure at the Naval Academy and backs up much of what he states with tangible evidence, such as a photo of the original poem, in Key's handwriting, found in his family's desk. Part of Magruder's testimony states that:

> ...Although, because of his judicial office, he [Joseph Nicholson] was not liable to military duty, he had accepted the command of a volunteer company to assist in the defense of Fort McHenry; and, as second in command, rendered most efficient service during the bombardment. In his interview with his brother-in-law, after they had recounted to each other their thrilling experiences since they last met, Mr. Key showed Judge Nicholson some verses which he told him be had written on the American ship, Minden, the vessel carrying the flag of truce, during the night of the bombardment and early on the next morning after it had ceased, on the back of a letter which he happened to have in his pocket; and the night before in Baltimore he had finally rewritten parts of them into the form in which they then stood. Upon hearing it read, Judge Nicholson expressed his warm admiration of the poem, and declared it must be printed forthwith and circulated unsparingly. Without delay, Judge Nicholson gave it to his wife, Mrs. Rebecca Lloyd Nicholson, who took it to a neighboring printer (although some authors state that Judge Nicholson took it himself—this I [P. H. Magruder] was informed is in error), who willingly agreed to strike off a large number of copies in handbill form, and these were delivered at once to newsboys with directions to sell or give them to all whom they should meet on the street...[7]

So now we can (possibly) add Mrs. Nicholson to the mix of people to thank for getting the poem quickly into the popular culture of that day. Though it is just one person's word, the idea of Mrs. Nicholson taking the poem to the printer has some credibility when you consider that Joseph most certainly was extremely fatigued that first day after the bombing had ceased, and that he was at that moment in full command of the fort because General Armistead had taken ill. Joe had a lot on his plate, so sending his wife to the printer is not wholly unrealistic, though it contradicts the word of Samuel Sands who did the printing.

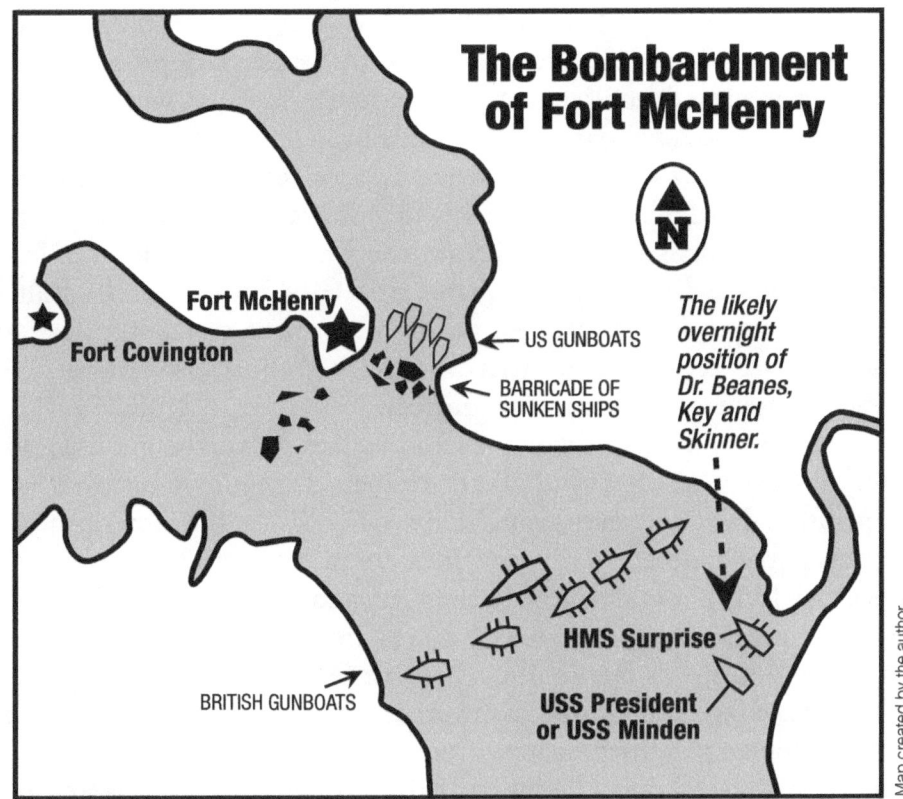

Dr. William Beanes, whom Key and Skinner were sent to rescue, was the primary cause of Key being in his position to view the historic bombing of Fort McHenry. The good doctor was a prominent physician living in Upper Marlborough, Maryland, (today known as Upper Marlboro), a sparse community on the outskirts of Washington City. He was very well liked and respected by all who knew him. Throughout much of the American Revolution he worked at the General Hospital in Philadelphia where he had patched up men who had been wounded at Lexington, Valley Forge, and many other places of battle and hardship. In 1799, at age fifty, his accolades were such that he became one of the founding fathers of the Medical and Chirurgical Faculty of Maryland (MedChi); the state affiliate of today's American Medical Association. (Chirurgical is how "surgical" was pronounced and spelled at that time.)

In 1814, at sixty-five years of age, Dr. Beanes was quite comfortable on his estate in Upper Marlborough. He worked at farming as well as doctoring. He was quite popular in the same circle of successful businessmen and politicians that Key had associated with and was considered the town patriarch. There is little doubt of his patriotism, but it was shrewdly disguised when he received an unexpected visit from British Major General Ross and Admiral George Cockburn on August 23. Unbeknownst to Beanes, these officers were about to lead the assaults at Bladensburg, Washington City, and eventually Baltimore. The troops were camped nearby when Beanes was surprised to be asked to accommodate the distinguished officers overnight. He obliged them with the utmost courtesy.

It seems the British dignitaries had assumed that the good doctor was at least somewhat sympathetic to their cause due to his overt cooperation. It's likely they thought him a Federalist, the American political party opposed to the war. They are said to have lounged in the doctor's lavish garden enjoying the food and drink that was so freely offered to them. All the while, Beanes's mind was surely troubled by the many turns his fate might take. One fear was that certain papers he had concealed might be discovered. There had been general alarm about the region that nearby Annapolis, the capital of Maryland, might be burned down by these British invaders, just as Washington, ironically, soon would be. As a precaution, Beanes had earlier hidden some vital, state government documents in his home. Now, he prayed that his visitors would not come upon them. They did not.

Early in the afternoon of the twenty-fourth of August, Beanes found himself home alone, except for his servants and a couple British guards left behind, while the regular forces began their march to Bladensburg. Within hours, the enemy had scored a decisive victory at Bladensburg and proceeded to the nation's capital of Washington City where they decimated the central government district. It had evolved into a very eventful autumn day.

With their mission accomplished, the following morning Ross and his troops were headed back toward their ships in the bay. They retraced the path that they had taken to get to Washington; first through Bladensburg and then toward Upper Marlborough. Before long, Ross and Cockburn were retrieving the belongings that they had left behind at Beanes's home. At this point, the guards were relieved of their duty and in short order the officers and most of their army left Upper Marlborough. Later that day, some stragglers of the British force arrived in Upper Marlborough and created a bit of a stir. The specifics of what transpired in Beanes's home town that day are confused by varying reports. It is certain, however, that Dr. Beanes was indeed involved in the apprehension of several British combatants. While stopped a few miles out of Upper Marlborough, at the home of Richard West in Woodyard, word came to Ross of Beanes's apparent bad faith. Ross was beside himself with anger at the nerve Beanes showed by arresting and jailing British soldiers. The doctor was apprehended as a prisoner of war by the British that night.

One account says that stragglers from the returning British forces had ransacked several homes around Upper Marlborough. Fellow citizens came to Dr. Beanes for help in the capture of the marauders, to which he willingly responded. Another version is that Dr. Beanes was having a small get-together in his garden when the said enemy soldiers burst onto the property and became obnoxious by boasting of their deeds in Washington. Thus riled up themselves, Beanes and his friends found the means to arrest the uninvited guests. Still other accounts say that it was Dr, Beanes and friends that were celebrating what they had mistakenly thought was an American victory in Washington; and the soldiers in the vicinity took umbrage, became unruly, and so were arrested. Alcohol may have played a factor on both sides in all of these stories.

Roger B. Taney, by marriage to Key's sister, Anne Phoebe Charlton Key, was the second brother-in-law of Francis Key to be directly invested in this event. He had stayed behind to protect Key's family members during the battles. Taney later became famous by presiding as Chief Justice of the Supreme Court over the Dred Scott case. In 1857, he penned a letter introducing a book of poems written by Key. In it he explained his understanding of how events unfolded in the Baltimore region circa 1814 per his earlier conversations with the lyricist. In this citation he shares how Beanes was arrested and how Key was asked to help secure his release:

> On the evening of the day that the enemy disappeared, Mr. Richard West arrived at Mr. Key's and told him that after the British army passed through Upper Marlbro', on their return to their ships, and had

encamped some miles below the town, a detachment was sent back, which entered Dr. Beanes's house about midnight, compelled him to rise from his bed, and hurried him off to the British camp, hardly allowing him time to put his clothes on; that he was treated with great harshness, and closely guarded; and that as soon as his friends were apprized of his situation, they hastened to the head-quarters of the English army to solicit his release, but it was peremptorily refused, and they were not even permitted to see him; and that he had been carried as a prisoner on board the fleet. And finding their own efforts unavailing, and alarmed for his safety, his friends in and about Marlbro' thought it advisable that Mr. West should hasten to Georgetown, and request Mr. Key to obtain the sanction of the government to his going on board the admiral's ship under a flag of truce, and endeavoring to procure the release of Dr. Beanes before the fleet sailed. It was then lying at the mouth of the Potomac, and its destination was not at that time known with certainty... [8]

Two other men were arrested with Beanes, a Dr. Hill and a Mr. Weems, but because they were unknown to Ross they were released. Only Dr. Beanes was taken to the British flagship, the *HMS Tonnant*. Taken is an inappropriate description. He was forced to ride an emaciated old horse over thirty miles to the docked British ships. Even further, one unsubstantiated rumor has it that he was forced to ride backwards so that the "ass" was facing the ass of the horse. The citizenry of Upper Marlborough was furious and enlisted Richard West to take the next step. From a 1914 speech by Caleb Magruder, then president of the Star Spangled Banner Society we learn that

... at this juncture, Richard W. West, of Woodyard, appealed to Francis Scott Key, a then resident of Georgetown. With the consent of President Madison, John S. Skinner, a Prince Georgeian then living in Baltimore, and in charge of the exchange of prisoners, accompanied Key down the Chesapeake Bay under a flag of truce aboard the Minden. Preparations were making for an attack on Baltimore but Key and Skinner were courteously received by Admiral Cochrane. When their mission was made known to General Ross and Admiral Cockburn [they] bitterly opposed the prisoner's release, the latter speaking of him in the harshest and most venomous manner... [9]

Richard West was not only a patient and close friend of Dr. Beanes, but he was the third brother-in-law to Key who was instrumental to this entire situation. He had married Maria Lloyd, the sister of Mary Key. Francis was the perfect person to be called upon to act on this matter. He was already passionate about the arrest because he was a very close friend of the doctor. He also had had great success in his law career because of his persuasive and charming manner of speaking. This all worked in his favor as a negotiator for Beanes's release. After accepting West's appeal, he went to another friend, President Madison, to request official permission to approach the British. Madison approved and solicited Skinner to accompany him. Key soon acknowledged his mission and travel plans in a letter to his mother dated September 2, 1814, saying:

> I am going in the morning to Baltimore, to proceed in a flag vessel to General Ross. Old Dr. Beanes, of Marlboro', is taken prisoner by the enemy, who threaten to carry him off. Some of his friends have urged me to apply for a flag of truce to go and try to procure his release. I hope to return in about eight or ten days, though it is uncertain, as I do not know where to find the fleet. [10]

On September 7, Key and Skinner found the fleet and hitched their cartel boat to the British flagship the *HMS Tonnant*. From Roger Taney's letter we again find that the two arresting officers had an inordinate amount of disgust for Beanes. We also learn of the reason they finally agreed to free their captive.

> He [Key] told me that he found the British fleet at the mouth of the Potomac preparing for the expedition against Baltimore. He was courteously received by Admiral Cochrane, and the officers of the army, as well as the navy. But when he made known his business, his application was received so coldly, that he feared it would fail. General Ross and Admiral Cockburn – who accompanied the expedition to Washington – particularly the latter, spoke of Dr. Beanes, in very harsh terms, and seemed at first, not disposed to release him. It, however, happened, fortunately, that Mr. Skinner carried letters from the wounded British officers left at Bladensburg; and in these letters to their friends on board the fleet, they all spoke of the humanity and kindness with which they had been treated, after they had fallen into our hands. And after a good deal of conversation, and strong representations from Mr. Key, as to the character and standing of Dr. Beanes, and of the deep interest which the community in which he lived, took in his fate, General Ross said that Dr. Beanes deserved much more punishment than he had received;

The Indian Queen Hotel; doing business in Baltimore, Maryland from 1782 through 1832. The possible site where Francis Scott Key finalized his historic poem.

but that he felt himself bound to make a return for the kindness which had been shown to his wounded officers, whom he had been compelled to leave at Bladensburg; and upon that ground, and that only, he would release him…

… Mr. Key had an interview with Dr. Beanes, before General Ross consented to release him. I do not recollect whether he was on board the admiral's ship, or the Surprise, but I believe it was the former. He found him in the forward part of the ship, among the sailors and soldiers; he had not had a change of clothes from the time he was seized; was constantly treated with indignity by those around him, and no officer would speak to him. He was treated as a culprit, and not as a prisoner of war. And this harsh and humiliating treatment continued until he was placed on board the cartel.

Something must have passed, when the officers were quartered at his house, on the march to Washington, which, in the judgment of General Ross, bound him not to take up arms against the English forces, until the troops had re-embarked. It is impossible on any other ground, to account for the manner in which he was spoken of, and treated. But whatever General Ross, and the other officers may have thought, I am quite sure that Dr. Beanes did not think he was in any way pledged to abstain from active hostilities against the public enemy. And when he made prisoners of the stragglers, he did not consider himself as a prisoner on parole, nor suppose himself to be violating any obligation he had incurred. For he was a gentleman of untainted character, and a nice sense of honor, and incapable of doing anything that could have justified such treatment. Mr. Key imputed the ill usage he received to the influence of Admiral Cockburn, who, it is still remembered, while he commanded in the Chesapeake, carried on hostilities in a vindictive temper, assailing and plundering defenceless villages; or countenancing such proceedings by those under his command... [11]

The anger of Ross and Cockburn toward Beanes seemed disproportionate to the offense considering how well they were treated at his home. It has been speculated that the officers had simply been so utterly convinced by Beanes's manner, supposing that he would do nothing to impede their cause, that they felt betrayed and made fools of when he dared to arrest British soldiers.

But Dr. Beanes had indeed treated many of the British wounded who had fought at Bladensburg. Numbers of them had been transported back to Upper Marlborough the day after the battle due a shortage of medical help around Bladensburg. John Skinner was familiar with Dr. Beanes and his reputation. He also learned that Beanes had attended to many of these impaired British soldiers. With this knowledge he cunningly took the liberty of securing letters from those men regarding their care at the hands of the doctor. It was those British words of praise and gratitude for Dr. Beanes's unending, selfless care for them that ultimately saved the doctor's life. And, the calm demeanor and persuasive tenor of Francis Key, while referencing these letters in his negotiations, cannot be ignored.

For nine days Dr. Beanes was held captive on the British ships before Key and Skinner arrived on September 7. Six more days would pass before the British lit the first fuse on one of their cannons. And, it wasn't until the night of September 16, after two and a half weeks of captivity for Beanes, that the three men were back on dry land.

Key had written parts of his poem, along with raw notes to himself about what he was feeling, on the back of a letter he had in his pocket through the bombing. While recuperating at a Baltimore hotel that first night back, he put pen to fresh paper and completed his poetic thoughts. The exact hotel that he had stayed in is yet another historically contested question. The Smithsonian's National Museum of American History, amongst other sources, states that it was the Indian Queen Hotel at the corner of Baltimore and Hanover streets. However, a popular Washington columnist known as "Perley" wrote a tribute to John Skinner in the 1854 issue of *The Plough, the Loom, and the Anvil* (a publication Skinner and the adult Samuel Sands were associated with) and in the article he claims that all three men: Key, Skinner, and Beanes; spent their first night back in the old Fountain Inn hotel on High Street. Regardless which hotel they were in, Key finalized his poem while resting in one of them.

After the War of 1812, Skinner went on to be the postmaster of Baltimore for many years, but more importantly he published several agriculturally based periodicals throughout the rest of his life. The first, and possibly most acclaimed, came out just five years after his adventure with Key and was titled *American Farmer*.

Dr. Beanes lived another fourteen years at his home in Upper Marlborough where he continued his medical practice and tended his gardens and fields. His wife preceded him in death, and because they had no children much of their estate was divided and passed down to their numerous friends and relatives.

For the record, Francis Key continued a practice in law handling numerous high-profile cases involving such personalities as Aaron Burr and Andrew Jackson. He had a contradictory stance on slavery as the subject arose in some of his trials, but did release his own in 1830. Over the last ten years of his life he acted as the district attorney for Washington DC until his passing in 1843.

The oldest weather records of Baltimore only go back to 1893. In all the years since, the average temperature for September has been about eighty degrees. So, it seems a safe bet to assume that it was a typical warm summer day and night as Key watched the bombing of Fort McHenry. It was probably a bit steamy and foggy because it is certain that it rained through much of the twenty-five hour assault. Add to the mix the smoke of rockets and bombs exploding and one can assume that visibility had to be quite poor. As they looked on, some say it was the older Dr. Beanes who kept asking the younger Key and Skinner whether the US flag was still there; ultimately planting the seed for one of Key's verses. The US cartel ship that the three men were on was anchored alongside the British command vessels at least two miles from the fort, perhaps up to three. All these conditions make one question how the three Americans could have seen any flag being flown from so far away. Well, there are two more historic personalities who had something to do with making that possible.

One was Major George Armistead who was in command of Fort McHenry during the bombardment. As a result of his successful defense that day, President Madison almost immediately promoted him to Lieutenant Colonel. Unfortunately, Armistead became ill due to fatigue and exposure during the battle and remained sickly for some time thereafter. It was Armistead's foresight and boldness that had made him as strong and steadfast as he was up to and through this battle. However, the intense physical stress of this event had taken its ultimate toll when he passed away just three years later at the young age of thirty-eight.

Armistead liked to flaunt his patriotism in his enemy's face and was never shy about doing things on a grand scale. As an old saying suggests, Armistead's philosophy seems to have been "go big or stay home." In 1801, at a mere twenty-one years of age, he was assigned to Fort Niagara with the rank of first lieutenant. One of the first things he noticed was that there was no garrison flag waving from the fort's flagpole. That bothered him. Five years previous, in 1796, one of the first versions of the 15-star and 15-stripe design flags was raised over the fortress when the Americans had captured it from the British, but it was now missing. Armistead almost immediately ordered material to have a huge flag sewn, 38 x 48 feet. For reasons unknown it took until for 1809, seven years later, before Armistead's flag arrived at Fort Niagara. When it did, it measured 22 x 36 feet, still a gigantic banner, but significantly smaller than what was ordered. Why it came in smaller is yet another mystery.

Armistead was not at Fort Niagara to see his flag ascend into the breeze. By that time he had been assigned as a captain to serve at Fort McHenry, after first pulling duty for a few years in the Arkansas Territory. In May of 1811, he was trying to have a new flagpole erected at Fort McHenry in place of one damaged years previously by lightning. As well, he wanted a new flag. He wrote to his regimental commander, Col. Henry Burbeck

> ... I have my hands full[;] the Secretary [of] War [Eustis] has consented to have the barracks painted and I am getting up a new Flag staf as it will be among the hands[omest] now standing. I have to solicit

your [aid in] getting a new Flag. In a few days I [will] have the Post in much better order than you have ever seen it... [12]

Armistead remained at Fort McHenry until early in 1813. Then, for just a few months in the spring, he was sent back to Fort Niagara as a Major. It was there that fighting had escalated with the British just across the Niagara River at Fort George. Armistead turned out to be a key player in the Americans' taking of that enemy fortress in late May of 1813. As a reward for his distinguished service, he was chosen to present the captured Union Jack to President Madison in Washington City. Soon after his arrival, Madison assigned him to take full command of Fort McHenry which he began doing in June of 1813. It was then, that he finally had authority to order the flag that Key would write about.

The War of 1812 was expanding on many fronts by the summer of 1813. Battles were breaking out at the US and Canadian border; on the frontier lands of Ohio, Indiana, and Kentucky; and increasingly along the eastern seaboard. British ships appeared in the Chesapeake Bay taunting the Americans into confrontations. Armistead was not intimidated. Fort McHenry was located at a most strategic point for the defense of Baltimore. Upon his return, he became dismayed that there was still not a proper banner flying to identify who was in control of the fortress. Within weeks, in a letter to the commander of the Maryland militia, Major General Samuel Smith, he wrote:

> We, sir, are ready at Fort McHenry to defend Baltimore against invading by the enemy...except that we have no suitable ensign to display over the Star Fort, and it is my desire to have a flag so large that the British will have no difficulty in seeing it from a distance. [13]

And so, in short order, Commodore Joshua Barney, who commanded the Chesapeake Bay Flotilla, and Brigadier General John George Stricker, who led the Third Brigade of the Maryland militia, along with Lieutenant Colonel William McDonald, of the Maryland militia, were all on there way to Mary Pickersgill's home to request the creation of two new flags for their fort. It helped that Mary was related to people in high places. The first two officers just referred to, Joshua Barney and John Stricker, happened to be married to Ann and Martha Young respectively, Mary's cousins. When Armistead requested the flags, Barney and Stricker knew that Mary was the perfect person to call upon.

Photographic Portrait of Mary Scott Pickersgill.

Portrait of George Armistead by Rembrandt Peale.

Mary Pickersgill came from a very patriotic and experienced flag-making family. Her mother was Rebecca Young, from whom she learned the art of sewing. Through the Revolution, Rebecca was a popular flag-maker around Philadelphia. For the most part she made all sorts of "colors" which would fly over Navy ships and Army camps. Rebecca was well connected with prominent citizens and family members. She was friends with the noted physician of that time, Dr. Benjamin Rush who signed the Declaration of Independence and who trained her son Benjamin in the art of medicine. In 1778, when her husband William Young passed away, her daughter, Mary, was but a two-year old toddler. It was Rebecca's brother, Colonel Benjamin Flower, who set her and her five children up in a home where she continued her business. She provided a variety of flags to the military, as well as drum cases, blankets, cap linings, and articles of clothing. Her brother's position of contracting for military supplies likely helped provide her ample work. It was this same Ben Flower who, with his company of men in 1777, is remembered for removing the famed Liberty Bell from Philadelphia to avoid its capture by the British. Sadly, Ben also passed away just a few years after Rebecca's husband had.

Rebecca's grand-daughter, Caroline Pickersgill Purdy, attests to the strong service records of her patriotic family members. In a letter written to General Armistead's daughter, Georgiana Armistead Appleton in 1876, she says

> ... I would like to state, that many of my ancestors were in the Revolution. My grandfather William Young was a captain in the war; my uncle Col. Flower was "Commisary General of Military stores," and Colonel of "Artillery" – these, both lost their lives by camp fever; I had another uncle taken prisoner by the British, and whipped through the fleet for attempting to escape; and my father-in-law, Henry Purdy, served through the war. [14]

Rebecca ran an ad in the *Philadelphia Packet* newspaper in 1781 offering flags for sale. It was a bold move for that day, when few women were involved in their own business ventures. And, luckily for us, the advertisement provides historical evidence of her skills. It was headlined with the words: "ALL KINDS OF COLOURS, For the ARMY and NAVY, Made and Sold on the most reasonable Terms by Rebecca Young."

Rebecca's daughter, Mary, had married John Pickersgill in 1795. Like her mother, she had a short-lived marriage. John passed away after just ten years in 1805. The next year, the widowed Rebecca and Mary, as well as Mary's toddler daughter, Caroline, moved to Baltimore to be closer to other relatives. Sadly, Caroline was destined to spend more than the second half of her eighty-three years as a widow as well.

By June of 1813, the entrepreneurs were flourishing and, at age thirty-seven, Mary was now in charge. The ladies immediately re-established their flag-making business and their reputation grew in the new city. When her cousin's husbands explained that Armistead wanted the flags asap, Mary accepted the challenge. With the help of thirteen year-old Caroline; two teenage nieces, Eliza and Margaret Young; an indentured thirteen year-old African-American girl named Grace Wisher (who was serving an apprenticeship to learn Mary's flag-making craft in exchange for doing housework); and perhaps with a little oversight by her seventy-three year-old ailing mother, Rebecca; Mary pulled off the project in the six or seven week window she was allotted. She likely also solicited the help of additional ladies and teenage girls of the area who were skilled in sewing.

In Caroline's letter to Georgiana Armistead Appleton there are further details surrounding the construction of the flags.

> It was made by my mother, Mrs. Mary Pickersgill, and I assisted her. My grandmother, Rebecca Young made the first flag of the Revolution, (under General Washington's direction) and for this reason my mother was selected by Commo. Barney and [John] George Stricker, (family connections), to make this "Star Spangled Banner" which she did, being an exceedingly patriotic woman.
>
> The flag being so very large, mother was obliged to obtain permission from the proprietors of Claggetts [Brown's] brewery which was in our neighborhood, to spread it out in their malt house; and I remember seeing my mother down on the floor, placing the stars: after the completion of the flag, she superintended the topping of it, having it fastened in the most secure manner to prevent its being torn away by (cannon) balls: the wisdom of her precaution was shown during the engagement: many shots piercing it, but it still remained firm to the staff. Your father (Col. Armistead) declared that no one but the maker of the flag should mend it, and requested that the rents [tears] should merely be bound around.
>
> The flag contained, I think, four hundred yards of bunting, and my mother worked many nights until 12 o'clock to complete it in the given time.[15]

Mary's home was simply not large enough to create such prodigious flags. Specifically, the larger banner was to be 30 x 42 feet. And there was a smaller storm flag requested that measured 17 x 25 feet. For comparison, the standard size for flags flown over today's US military bases are 20 x 36 feet for a main garrison flag, and 4 feet 2 inches x 8 feet for a storm flag. Mary was lucky to get George Brown, the owner of Brown's Brewery just a block away, to let her use one of his malt houses to assemble her flags. Some sources refer to it as Claggett's Brewery, but it was not sold to Eli Claggett until 1818. In fact, the brewery which had been in operation for thirty years by the time Mary used it, suffered a disastrous fire that burned down the key brewing buildings just eight months beforehand. It was immediately rebuilt and put up for auction. In July of 1813, while Mary was already in production of the flags, George Brown purchased the establishment. It would seem that the timing was fortuitous as the 30 x 100 foot malt house was not in use at that moment and was twice the length of the garrison flag under construction.

In August of 1813, Mary invoiced Major Armistead $405.90 for the larger flag and $168.54 for the smaller one. That was a substantial sum in those days but it had to of included material costs and was likely divided between all involved. Being a widow and seeing her mother raise her and her siblings without a husband likely influenced Mary deeply. She spent her life striving to help other women who were in need to find work. She served for forty years as president of the Impartial Female Humane Society which served that purpose. Late in life she further established the Aged Women's Home which grew into today's Pickersgill Retirement Community in Baltimore.

It is likely that the flags Mary created were flown regularly once received in 1813; the storm flag replacing the large one during bad weather as its name implies. That practice continued through the attack on Fort McHenry in September the following year. It is assumed that the larger banner was raised on the morning of the thirteenth just before or after the bombing had begun. By early afternoon the rains began and so the smaller flag was raised. The downpours continued on-and-off through the rest of the day and night. Most of the firing ceased from both sides around four o'clock in the morning of the fourteenth. Only occasional shots were launched by the British thereafter. With the obvious successful defense of the fort, and the rains subsiding, the large banner was run up the ninety-foot flagpole in view of Mr. Key and his two fellow Americans.

Key uses the word "spangled" in his description of the banner. That term usually referred to any sort of glittering objects affixed to a material as ornamentation. Key used it to describe the fifteen stars which were also notably tilted in alternating rows to the left or the right. This is in contrast to all the stars being pointed upward in today's flag.

Major Armistead's own words tell of how they miraculously withstood the bombardment.

> On Tuesday morning about sunrise, the enemy commenced the attack from his five bomb vessels, at the distance about two miles, when finding that his shells reached us, he anchored and kept an incessant and well directed bombardment. We immediately opened our batteries, and kept a brisk fire from our guns and mortars, but unfortunately our shot and shells all fell considerably short of him. This was to me a most distressing circumstance, as it left us exposed to constant and tremendous shower of shells, without the remote possibility of our doing him the slightest injury. It affords me the highest gratification to state,

that although we were left exposed, and thus inactive, not a man shrunk from the conflict.

About 2 o'clock, P.M. one of the 24 pounders on the south west bastion, under the immediate command of Capt. Nicholson, was dismounted by a shell, the explosion of which killed his second Lieut. and wounded several of his men; the bustle necessarily produced in removing the wounded and remounting the gun probably induced the enemy to suspect that we were in a state of confusion, as he brought three of the bomb ships to what I believed to be a good striking distance. I immediately ordered a fire to be opened, which was obeyed with alacrity through the whole garrison, and in a half an hour those intruders again sheltered themselves by withdrawing beyond our reach. - We gave three cheers, and again ceased firing. The enemy continued throwing shells, with one or two slight intermissions, till one o'clock in the morning of Wednesday; when it was discovered that he had availed himself of the darkness of the night and had thrown a considerable force above to our right; they had approached very near to Fort Covington, when they began to throw rockets; intended I presume, to give them an opportunity of examining the shores - as I have since understood, they had detached 1250 picket men with scaling ladders, for the purpose of storming this Fort. We once more had an opportunity of opening our batteries, and kept a continued blaze for nearly two hours which had the effect again to drive them off.

In justice to Lieut. Newcomb, of the United States Navy, who commanded Fort Covington, with a detachment of sailors, and Lieut. Webster, of the flotilla, who commanded the Six Gun Battery, near the Fort, I ought to state, that during this time, they kept an animated, and I believe very destructive fire, to which I am persuaded, we are much indebted in repulsing the enemy. One of his sunken barges has since been found with two dead men in it - others have been seen floating in the river. The only means we had of directing our guns, was by the blaze of their rockets and the flashes of their guns. Had they ventured to the same situation in the day time, not a man would have escaped.

The bombardment continued on the part of the enemy until 7 o'clock on Wednesday morning, when it ceased; and about nine, their ships got under weigh and stood down the river. During the bombardment which lasted 25 hours (with two slight intermissions) from the best calculations I can make, from fifteen to eighteen hundred shells were thrown by the enemy. A few of these fell short. A large proportion burst over us, throwing their fragments among us, and threatening destruction. Many passed over, and about four hundred fell within the works. Two of the public buildings are materially injured - the others but slightly. I am happy to inform you (wonderful as it may appear) that our loss amounts to only four men killed, and 24 wounded. The latter will all recover. [16]

Perhaps a backhanded "thank you" for our descriptive anthem is due to be given to two Britishers as well. Henry Shrapnel developed a special type of bomb which is forever associated with his name. The British military began using it in earnest just a few years prior to the assault on Baltimore. It was Shrapnel's hollowed out mortar shells, some weighing as much as two hundred pounds and filled with all types of sharp metal pieces and balls, that were seen by Key bursting in the air over the fortress. A wooden fuse was screwed into the ball, its length determining the time before it exploded and showered all below with its deadly fragments. Likewise, it was William Congreve who re-engineered the centuries-old Chinese fireworks rocket into an incendiary weapon of war. His iron cylinders were topped with a warhead of flammable material intended to ignite the wooden enemy ship or fort at which it was aimed. These projectiles required their own launching platform which is why the HMS Erebus was designed exclusively as a rocket firing vessel and was on-duty shooting thirty-two pound versions at Fort McHenry. It is likely that it was their fading, orange-red, burnt powder streaks that Key had witnessed.

The actual Star Spangled Banner is now on display at the Smithsonian's National Museum of American History. The storm flag has never been recovered. The lyrics, written by Francis Scott Key, live on as our national anthem as of this writing. From its earliest reading, and singing, Americans have loved it, and we have many ordinary and extra-ordinary people of his day to thank for Mr. Francis Scott Key being where he was, for his ability to see the subject of his poem, and for its immediate rise in popularity.

In case it's been bothersome, the answer to Key's dinner-party riddle is "nothing!" You're welcome. ♦

HMMM…

Tarhe, or the Crane, the Patriotic Wyandot Chief.

At the commencement of the War of 1812 a council was called by the British officer commanding at Malden, in upper Canada. It was held at Brownstown in the State of Michigan, and its object was to induce the Wyandots to take sides with the British in the war which was inevitable. Several speeches were first delivered, and great promises made by the British agent about what their Great Father, King George, would do for them if the nation would fight the Americans; and he closed by presenting Tarhe with a likeness of King George.

Holding it in his hand, the head chief arose and said: "We have no confidence in King George. He is always quarreling with his white children in this country. He sends his armies over the great water, in their big canoes, and then he gets his Indian friends here to join with him to conquer his children, and promises if they will fight for him, he will do great things for them. So he promised if we would fight Wayne, and if he whipped us, he would open the gates of his fort on the Maumee and let us in, and open his big guns on our enemies; but when we were whipped, and the flower of our nation were killed, we fled to this place, but instead of opening the gates, and letting us in, you shut yourselves up in your ground-hog hole, and kept out of sight, while my warriors were killed at your gates. We have no confidence in any promise you make. When the Americans scratch your backs with their war clubs, you jump into your big canoes and run home, and leave the poor Indians to fight it out, or make peace with them, the best they may."

He took the likeness of General Washington from his bosom and said: "This is our Great Father, and for him we will fight." Then taking the likeness of King George in his left hand he drew his tomahawk and with the edge struck the likeness, and added, "And so we will serve your Great Father."

This so excited the British officer that it is said he turned black in the face. He replied that he would make the chief repent that act. "This is my land and country," said Tarhe; "go home to your own land, and tell your countrymen that Tarhe and his warriors are ready and that they are the friends of the Americans."

Thus broke up the council. Tarhe returned to his home at Upper Sandusky and with his warriors aided the Americans, with all their force, till the battle of the Thames; numbers of his Wyandots were in the army of General Harrison at the time he fought the last battle with the British and Indians.

In Norman B. Wood's, Lives of Famous Indian Chiefs, 1906 [17]

NOTES TO THE SKETCHES.

SKETCH I. From Where to Eternity.
1. Jean Marzollo, *In 1492*, (Scholastic, 1991).
2. Allen P. Slickpoo Sr., written in 1973, in *National Park Service Cultural Landscapes Inventory*, (Seattle, WA, East Kamiah/Heart of the Monster Nez Perce National Historical Park, 1994 - revised 2002), http://npshistory.com/publications/nepe/cli-heart-of-the-monster.pdf, pgs 16-18.
3. Lakota Creation Story, Aka Lakota Museum Cultural Center, http://aktalakota.stjo.org/site.
4. Huron Creation Myth, *A Wyandot (Huron) Legend*, https://www.firstpeople.us.
5. Angie Drake, *The Origin of the Canari*, (Not Your Average American, January 9, 2019), https://notyouraverageamerican.com/canari-origin-myth/.
6. Francis L. Hawks, *Narrative of the Expedition of an American Squadron to the China Seas and Japan, Performed in the Years 1852, 1853, and 1854, Under the Command of Commodore M. C. Perry, United States Navy, by Order of the Government of the United States*, (New York, D. Appleton and Co., 1857), pgs. 578-9.
7. Andrew J. Blackbird, *History of the Ottawa and Chippewa Indians*, (Ypsilanti, MI, The Ypsilantian Job Printing House, 1887), pgs. 103-5.

SKETCH II. Temper, Temper, Mr. McGary.
1. Draper notes from Mrs. Robert Shanklin. Draper 11CC219.
2. Mary Powell Hammersmith, *Hugh McGary, Senior Pioneer of Virginia, North Carolina, Kentucky and Indiana*, (Wheaton, IL, Nodus Press, 2000), pgs. 126-8.
3. Ibid. pgs. 128-9
4. Letter – Col. John Taylor Griffin Flauntleroy to Draper, January 13, 1845. Draper 12C24-5.
5. Draper notes from Mr. Jacob Stevens. Draper 12CC136.
6. Ibid.
7. Marshall Humphrey, *History of Kentucky*, (Frankfort, KY, Henry Gore, 1812), pg. 164.
8. Clark, Thomas D., *The Voice of the Frontier - John Bradford's Notes on Kentucky*, (Lexington, KY, University Press of Kentucky, 1993), pg. 56. (Originally published in the *Kentucky Gazette*, 1826-1829 - Sources cited for quote are obscure.)
9. Draper 6S152-3.
10. Letter of Peter Houston to Lyman Draper, *Narrative of Daniel Boone*, Nov. 14, 1889, Draper 20C84-32.
11. Draper notes from Mr. Jacob Stevens. Draper 12CC134.
12. Letter — Andrew Steele to Governor Benjamin Harrison, August 26, 1782, in *Calendar of Virginia State Papers*, Vol. III, 1883. pgs. 269-70.
13. Letter — Col. Daniel Boone to Governor Benjamin Harrison, August 30, 1782, in *Calendar of Virginia State Papers*, Vol. III, 1883. pg. 275.

14. Letter — Col. Benjamin Logan to Governor Benjamin Harrison, August 31, 1782, in *Calendar of Virginia State Papers*, Vol. III, 1883. pgs. 282-3.
15. Letter — Col. Levi Todd to Captain Robert Todd, August 26, 1782, in *Calendar of Virginia State Papers*, Vol. III, 1883. pgs. 333-4.
16. Letter — Col. Arthur Campbell to Col, William Davies, October 3, 1782, in *Calendar of Virginia State Papers*, Vol. III, 1883. pg. 337.
17. Letter — Hugh McGary to Col. Benjamin Logan, in James A. James, *George Rogers Clark Papers 1771-1784*, Vol. 19, (Springfield, IL, Schnepp & Barnes Printers, 1924), pg. 92.
18. Ibid.
19. Letter — Rebecca Boone Grant to Lyman Draper, August 23, 1895, Draper 22C35-1-2.
20. Letter – Grandson of Peter Houston to Lyman Draper, November 14, 1889, Draper 20C84-30.
21. Ibid. pgs. 33-4.
22. Letter — Simon Girty to Captain Alexander McKee, October 11, 1786, in *Michigan Pioneer and Historical Society*, Vol. 24, (Lansing, MI, Robert Smith & Co., 1895), pg. 34.
23. Draper Notes of Henry Hall, April 1844 in Draper MSS, in Ohio History Journal, *Logan's Campaign - 1786*, October 1913, Volume 22, No. 4, pgs 520-1.
24. Quote — of William Lytle in Stephen Kelley, *Logan's Gap*, in *Ohio Southland, 1993*, Issue #4, pgs. 35-6.
25. Hammersmith, *Hugh McGary, Senior Pioneer of Virginia, North Carolina, Kentucky and Indiana*, pg. 147.
26. Proceedings of General Court Martial, March 21, 1787, *Calendar of Virginia State Papers*, Vol. IV, 1884. pgs. 258-60.
27. Hammersmith, *Hugh McGary, Senior Pioneer of Virginia, North Carolina, Kentucky and Indiana*, pgs. 147-8.
28. Henry Wilson Pension Statement, Draper 9J1-79-80.
29. A. Wright, May 27, 1827, Statement in Hammersmith, *Hugh McGary, Senior Pioneer of Virginia, North Carolina, Kentucky and Indiana*, pg. 171.
30. Henry Wilson Pension Statement, Draper 9J1-47.
31. John A. Raynor, *The First Century of Piqua, Ohio*, (Piqua, Ohio, The Magee Bros. Publishing Co., 1916), pgs. 26-7.

SKETCH III. Watchdogs of the Wilderness.

1. Lewis Collins, *Collins' Historical Sketches of Kentucky, History of Kentucky*, (Covington, Kentucky, Collins & Co., 1878), pg 760.
2. Ibid., pgs 417-8.
3. Whitley Papers, Vol. 9, Draper Manuscripts, Kentucky Papers, in *Register, Kentucky State Historical Society*, Vol. 36, July, 1938, No. 116, pg. 190.
4. Ibid., pg. 191.
5. Ibid., pg. *192*.
6. Ibid.

7. Robert L. Kincaid, *The Wilderness Road*, (Middlesboro, Kentucky, Arcata Graphics, 1992), pgs. 140-1.
8. Advertisement, *Kenntucky Gazette*, December 26,1789.
9. Dale Payne, *Narratives of Pioneer Life and Border Warfare*, (Kansas City, Kansas, Dale Payne, 2004), pg. 125.
10. Solomon Clark, Letter to Draper, June 1842, *Whitley Papers*, Draper 9CC6-7.
11. Ibid., Draper 9CC7-8.
12. Drake and McFarland, Sept, 1793, Draper 9CC8-9.
13. McFarland, 1793, Draper 9CC9.
14. Clark, Draper 9CC2.
15. Will M. Dunn II, *The Romance of a True Hero – The Life and Achievement of Col. William Whitley*, Copy in the Kentucky Historical Society, Whitley Files.
16. Clark, Draper 9CC11-12.
17. Esther Whitley Burch, *Whitley of Old Lincoln*, Speech to DAR Logan-Whitley Chapter, Stanford, KY, January, 1943. Copy in the Kentucky Historical Society, Whitley Files.
18. Ibid., Draper 9CC10.
19. Statement by R. I. Spurr of *Events of the Battle of the Thames 1813*, October 2, 1895, Courtesy of the William Whitley State Historic Site.
20. Theodore Roosevelt, *The Winning of the West*, (New York, The Current Literature Publishing Co., 1906), Part IV, pgs. 84-5.

SKETCH IV. The Winds of Change.

1. Letter -- George Washington to John Washington, *George Washington Papers*, Library of Congress, Series 2, Letterbooks 1754-1799: Letterbook 1, Aug. 11, 1754 - Dec. 25, 1755.
2. Jared Sparks, *The Life of George Washington*, (Boston, MA, Ferdinand Andrews, 1839), pg. 66.
3. Jared Sparks footnote No. 45 in *George Washington Papers*, Library of Congress, Series 2, Letterbooks 1754-1799: Letterbook 1, Aug. 11, 1754-Dec. 25, 1755.
4. Edna Kenton, *Simon Kenton, His Life and Period 1755-1836*, (Garden City, NY, The Country Life Press, 1930), pgs. 104-5.
5. Ibid., pgs. 108-110.
6. Ibid., pg. 110.
7. Ibid., pg. 118. Footnote of *Narrative of Reverand Asal Owen*, in Draper MSS – 7BB63, pgs. 33-4.
8. Ibid., pg. 132.
9. Ibid., pg. 144.
10. Draper interview with John and Sarah Kenton McCord, Draper 5S145, in John Mack Faragher, *Daniel Boone, The Life and Legend of an American Pioneer*, (New York, Henry Holt and Company, 1992), pg. 149.
11. George W. Ranck, *Boonesborough - Its Founding, Pioneer Struggles, Indian Experiences, Transylvania Days, and Revolutionary Annals*, (Louisville, Kentucky, John P. Morton & Co., 1901), pg. 88.

12. Ibid., pg. 89.
13. Daniel Trabue, *Westward Into Kentucky*, (Lexington, Kentucky, The University Press of Kentucky, 1981), pg. 59.
14. Ranck, *Boonesborough - Its Founding, Pioneer Struggles, Indian Experiences, Transylvania Days, and Revolutionary Annals*, pgs. 100-1.
15. Letter — Joseph Ficklin to Lyman Draper, Draper 13C74, June 26, 1845, in Virginia Webb Howard, *Bryan Station Heroes and Heroines*, (Lexington, Kentucky, Press of the Commercial Printing Co., 1932), pg. 160.
16. Letter — Rev. William Gordon to Samuel Wilcon, in *Proceedings of the Massachusetts Historical Society*, Vol. 60, 1926-7, pgs 362-3.
17. Ibid., pg. 363.
18. Ibid., pg. 364.
19. Thomas Sullivan, in *From Redcoat to Rebel: the Thomas Sullivan Journal*, Joseph L. Boyle, ed., (Bowie, Maryland, Heritage Books, 1997), pg. 34.
20. Letter — Major-General William Howe to Earl of Dartmouth, in *Documents of the American Revolution 1770-1783*, (London and Truro, Netherton & Worth, 1976), Vol. XII, pg. 82.
21. Philip Vickers Fithian, *Philip Vickers Fithian, Journal*, 1775-1776, (Princeton, NJ, Princeton University Press, 1934), pg. 220.
22. Diary of Rev. Mr. Shewkirk, August 28-29, 1776, in Henry P. Johnston, *The Campaign of 1776 Around New York and Brooklyn*, (Brooklyn, NY, Long Island Historical Society, S. W. Green, 1878), Part II, pgs. 114-5.
23. Letter — Lieut. Tench Tilghman to his father, September 3, 1776, in Henry P. Johnston, *The Campaign of 1776 Around New York and Brooklyn*, (Brooklyn, NY, Long Island Historical Society, S. W. Green, 1878), Part II, pg. 85.
24. Memoir — Memoir of Col. Benjamin Tallmadge, 1858, in Henry P. Johnston, *The Campaign of 1776 Around New York and Brooklyn*, (Brooklyn, NY, Long Island Historical Society, S. W. Green, 1878), Part II, pgs. 77-8.
25. Ibid., pgs. 78-9.
26. Ibid., pg. 79.
27. Letter — Anonymous from New York, in Thomas W. Field, *The Battle of Long Island, with Connected Preceding Events, and the Subsequent American Retreat*, (Brooklyn, NY, Long Island Historical Society, 1869), Vol. II, pgs. 522-3.
28. Alexander Graydon, *Memoirs of His Own Time: With Reminiscences of the Men and Events of the Revolution*, (Philadelphia, PA, Lindsay & Blakiston, 1846), pgs. 168-9.
29. Letter — Anonymous officer to Joseph Reed, in William B. Reed, *Life and Correspondance of Joseph Reed*, (Philadelphia, PA, Lindsay & Blakiston, 1847), pg. 276.
30. Letter — Major General Nathanael Greene to General James Ewing, Cited on *Washington Crossing Historic Park* Website: https://www.washingtoncrossingpark.org/where-washington-get-durham-boats/.
31. John Greenwood, *The Revolutionary Services of John Greenwood of Boston and New York*, 1775-1783, (New York, The De Vinne Press, 1922), pgs. 38-9.

32. Ensign Henry Hamilton's testimony, in Don Loprieno, T*he Enterprise in Contemplation: the Midnight Assault of Stony Point*, (Westminster, MD: Heritage Books, 2009), pg. 141.
33. Letter -- Sir Henry Clinton to Lord Germaine, July 25, 1779, in Henry P. Johnston, A. M., *The Storming of Stony Point on the Hudson*, (New York, James T. White, 1900), pg. 124.
34. Ibid., pg. 125.
35. Letter -- Lieutenant-General Cornwallis to Lord Germaine, March 17, 1781, in Ian Saberton, *The Cornwallis Papers*, (Uckfield, East Sussex, England, The Naval & Military Press, 2010), Vol. IV, Part Seven, pg. 13.
36. Ibid.
37. Ibid.
38. Ibid., pg. 14.
39. Letter -- Major General Nathanael Greene to George Washington, February, 25, 1781, Cited on Website: http://oldhalifax.com/Crossing/CrossingPage3.htm.
40. Letter -- Lieutenant-General Cornwallis to Major General Phillips, April 10, 1781, in Ian Saberton, *The Cornwallis Papers*, (Uckfield, East Sussex, England, The Naval & Military Press, 2010), Vol. IV, Part Seven, pg. 114-5.
41. John B. Moreau, *The Operations of the French Fleet under the Count De Grasse in 1781-2*, (New York, The Bradford Club, 1864), pg. 154.
42. Letter -- Lieutenant-General Cornwallis to Lieutenant General Sir Henry Clinton, October 20, 1781, in Ian Saberton, *The Cornwallis Papers*, (Uckfield, East Sussex, England, The Naval & Military Press, 2010), Vol. VI, Part Twelve, pg. 125.
43. Ibid., pg. 127.
44. Crisfield Johnson, *History of Cuyahoga County, Ohio*, (Cleveland, OH, D. W. Ensign & Co., 1879), Part Second, Chapter XI, pg. 61.
45. Ibid.
46. Ibid., pgs. 61-2.
47. Alexander Mackenzie, *The Life of Commodore Oliver Hazard Perry*, (Bedford, MA, Applewood Books, 2009), (Originally printed in New York, Harper Brothers, 1843), Vol. I, pgs. 236-7.
48. Ibid., pgs. 244-5.
49. Ibid., pg. 250.
50. Ibid., pgs. 274-5.
51. Ibid., pgs. 250-1.
52. Robert B. McAfee, *History of the Late War in the Western Country*, (Originally published in 1816), (Bowling Green, OH, Ohio Historical Publications Co. C.C. Van Tassel, 1919), pg. 387.
53. Mackenzie, The Life of Commodore Oliver Hazard Perry, pg. 251.
54. Ibid., pg. 252.
55. Ibid., pg. 253.

56. Letter -- Oliver Perry to William Jones, September 10, 1813, Cited on Website: https://www.navyhistory.org/battle-of-lake-erie-building-the-fleet-in-the-wilderness/.
57. McAfee, *History of the Late War in the Western Country*, pg. 414.
58. George Monro Grant, *Picturesque Canada*, (Toronto, James Clarke, Publisher, 1882), pgs. 533-4.
17. Esther Whitley Burch, *Whitley of Old Lincoln*, Speech to DAR Logan-Whitley Chapter, Stanford, KY, January, 1943. Copy in the Kentucky Historical Society, Whitley Files.
18. Ibid., Draper 9CC10.
19. Statement by R. I. Spurr of *Events of the Battle of the Thames 1813*, October 2, 1895, Courtesy of the William Whitley State Historic Site.
20. Theodore Roosevelt, *The Winning of the West*, (New York, The Current Literature Publishing Co., 1906), Part IV, pgs. 84-5.

SKETCH V. No More Squabbling.

1. Jesuit Relations, Vol. 43, pg. 153, in *Journal of the Washington Academy of Sciences*, Vol. 33, No. 10, October 15, 1943, pg 289.
2. John James Audubon, *Ornithological Biography. Birds of the United States of America. The Birds of America*, (Edinburgh, Adam Black, 1831), Vol. 1, pgs. 320-1.
3. Simon Pokagon, *The Wild Pigeon of North America*, in The Chautauquan, Theodore L. Flood, Vol. XXII – New Series, Vol. XIII, (Meadville, PA, The T. L. Flood Publishing House, September 1895 to March 1896), pg. 202.
4. James Fenimore Cooper, *The Chainbearer*, (London, Richard Bentley, 1845), Vol. 1, pgs. 103-5.
5. Audubon, *Ornithological Biography. Birds of the United States of America. The Birds of America*, pg. 320.
6. G. W. Featherstonhaugh, *Excursion Through the Slave States*, (New York, Harper and Brothers, 1844), pg. 88.
7. Alexander Wilson, in John French, *The Passenger Pigeon in Pennsylvania*, (Altoona, Pennsylvania, Altoona Tribune Company, 1919), pgs. 34-5.
8. S. G. Goodrich, *Personal Recollections of Poets, Philosophers and Statesmen*, (New York, The Arundel Print, 1856), pg. 101.
9. Simon Pokagon, *The Wild Pigeon of North America*, in *The Chautauquan*, Theodore L. Flood, Vol. XXII – New Series, Vol. XIII, (Meadville, PA, The T. L. Flood Publishing House, September, 1895 to March, 1896), pg. 205.
10. William Faux Journal in Emily Foster, *The Ohio Frontier*, (Kentucky, The University Press of Kentucky, 1996), pg 157.
11. George H. Harris, *The Life of Horatio Jones*, (Cornell University Library New York State Historical monographs collection, Digital copyright 1994, Original copyright 1903), pgs. 450-1.
12. Charles Whittlesey, *Early History of Cleveland*, (Cleveland, Ohio, Fairbanks, Benedict & Co., 1867), pgs. 265-6.

13. James Freeman Clarke, *Memorial and Biographical Sketches*, (Boston, Massachusetts, Houghton, Osgood and Co., 1878), pg. 266-78.
14. James McBride, *Pioneer Biography*, (Cincinnati, Robert Clarke & Co., 1869), Vol. I, pgs. 36-8.

SKETCH VI. I Spy...

1. Letter – Governor Arthur St. Clair to President George Washington, October 1, 1790 in *Josiah Harmar Papers, 1681-1937*, in collection of University of Michigan William L. Clements Library.
2. George Washington's Presidential Speech to Congress, December 8, 1790, in *The Writings of George Washington*, (New York and London, The Knickerbocker Press, 1891), Vol. XII, 1790-1794, on website: https://oll.libertyfund.org.
3. Letter – General St. Clair to Secretary Knox, November 1, 1791, in William H. Smith, *The St. Clair Papers*, (Cincinnati, Robert Clarke and Co., 1882), Vol. II, pg. 249.
4. Ibid., pg. 250.
5. Entry – Winthrop Sargent's Diary While with General Arthur St. Clair's Expedition Against the Indians, October 28, 1791, in *Ohio History Journal*, Volume 33, Number 2, April 1924, pg. 249.
6. Entry – *Diary of Major Ebeneezer Denny*, October 29,1791, in William H. Smith, *The St. Clair Papers*, (Cincinnati, Robert Clarke and Co., 1882), Vol. II, pg. 256.
7. Ibid., Entry – November 4, 1791, pgs. 259-61.
8. Entry – *Diary of Col. Winthrop Sargent*, November 11, 1791, (Wormsloe, 1851), pg. 27.
9. Smith, The St. Clair Papers, Entry – November 7, 1791, pg 262.
10. John B. Dillon, *A History of Indiana*, (Indianapolis, Bingham & Doughty, 1859), pg. 283.
11. *Minutes of Debates in Council on the Banks of the Ottawa River*, November 1791, (Philadelphia, PA, William Young, 1792), pgs. 18-9.
12. Ibid., pgs. 20-1.
13. Statement – Henry Knox to Congress, December 26, 1791, in *American State Papers*, (Washington, Gales and Beaton, 1832), Vol. IV, pgs. 198-9.
14. Speech of Henry Knox, Secretary of War, to the Indians, April 4, 1792, in *Michigan Pioneer and Historical Society*, (Lansing, MI, Robert Smith & Co., 1895), Vol. XXIV, pg. 394.
15. *Peter Pond and William Steedman's Communications to the Secretary of War, 1792*, in *Guidebook to Manuscripts*, 1969, Gilcrease Museum website: https://collections.gilcrease.org.
16. *Instructions to Captain Peter Pond and William Steedman*, January 9, 1792, in Henry R. Wagner, *Peter Pond - Fur Trader and Explorer*, (Yale University Library, 1955), pgs. 97-9.
17. Letter – Wilkinson to Armstrong, April 10, 1792, in John B.Dillon, *A History of Indiana*, (Indianapolis, Bingham & Doughty, 1859), pgs. 289-90.

18. Calvin M. Young, *Little Turtle*, (Mt. Vernon, IN, Windmill Publications, Inc., 1917), pg. 180.
19. Letter – Jacob White to Lyman Draper, in Draper 11E74.
20. James McBride, *Pioneer Biography*, (Cincinnati, Robert Clarke and Co., 1871), pgs. 18-9.
21. Henry Howe, *Historical Collections of Ohio*, (Cincinnati, Derby, Bradley & Co., 1848), pgs. 324-5.
22. Ibid., pg. 325.
23. Ibid., pg. 326.
24. John Brickell, *John Brickell's Narrative*, in John S. Williams, *The American Pioneer*, (Cincinnati, Ohio, R. P. Brooks, 1842), Vol. I, pg. 52.
25. Henry Howe, *Historical Collections of Ohio*, (Cincinnati, Ohio, C. J. Krehbiel & Co., 1907), Vol. II, pg. 155.

SKETCH VII. The Lore of Loramie Creek.

1. *Treaty Held By Commissioners, Members of the Council of the Province of Pennsylvania, at the Town of Lancaster...*, in *Indiana Treaties printed by Benjam Franklin, 1736-1762*, The Historical Society of Pennsylvania, 1938, pg. 122 (10).
2. Celeron Plate cited on the Virginia Museum of History and Culture website. https://virginiahistory.org/learn/celeron-plate.
3. Joseph Pierre de Bonnecamps, in his Diary, in C. B. Galbreath, *Expedition of Celeron to the Ohio Country in 1749*, (Columbus, Ohio, The F. J. Heer Printing Co., 1921), pg. 90.
4. Celeron, Entry of September 12, 1749 in *Celeron's Journal*, in C. B. Galbreath, *Expedition of Celeron to the Ohio Country in 1749*, pg. 51.
5. Ibid.
6. Ibid., pg. 52.
7. Ibid., pg. 53.
8. Ibid., pg. 54.
9. Ibid.
10. Ibid., pg. 56.
11. Captain William Trent, *Journal of Captain William Trent From Logstown to Pickawillany, A.D. 1752*, (Cincinnati, Ohio, Robert Clarke & Co., 1871), pg. 43.
12. George Croghan, *Report of Croghan in Colonial Records of PA.*, V. 522.523, in Francis Parkman, *Montcalm and Wolfe*, (Boston, Little, Brown, and Company, 1885), Vol. I, pg. 57.
13. Ibid.
14. Letter –– Captain Charles DeRaymond to Baron de Longueuil in Parkman, *Montcalm and Wolfe*, pg. 82.
15. Consul Willshire Butterfield, in Shelby County, *Destruction of Pickawillany by the French and Indians in 1752*, in Henry Howe, *Historical Collections of Ohio*, (Cincinnati, Ohio, C. J. Krehbiel & Co., 1907), Vol. II, pgs. 599-600.

16. Letter -- Miamis to the Governor of Pennsylvania, in William Trent, *Journal of Captain William Trent From Logstown to Pickawillany*, pgs. 48-9.
17. Linda Clark Nash, *The Journals of Pierre-Louis de Lorimier*, (Montreal, Quebec, Baraka Books of Montreal, 2012), pgs. 7.
18. Ibid., pgs. 77-8.
19. Ibid., pgs. 76-7.
20. Letter -- Clark to Benjamin Harrison, Nov. 27, 1782 in James A. James, *George Rogers Clark Papers 1781-1784*, (Springfield, IL, Illinois State Historical Library, 1926), Virginia Series, Vol. IV, pg. 157.
21. Howe, Historical Collections of Ohio, pg. 594.
22. Treaty of Greeneville, Ohio History Connection – Ohio History Central, Website. https://ohiohistorycentral.org/w/Treaty_of_Greeneville_(1795)_ (Transcript).
23. Letter -- Eustis to Harrison, July 1, 1812, in John A. Rayner, *The First Century of Piqua, Ohio*, (Piqua, Ohio, The Magee Bros. Publishing Co., 1916), pgs. 23-4.
24. Letter -- Johnston to Buchanan, July 18, 1812, in Rayner, *The First Century of Piqua, Ohio*, pg. 24.
25. Letter -- Harrison to Meigs, September 2, 1812, in Logan Esarey, *Messages and Letters of William Henry Harrison*, (Indianapolis, IN, Indiana Historical Commission, 1922), Volume II, pgs. 106-7, in *Indiana Historical Collections*, Vol. IX.
26. Order of Harrison via Meigs, September 5, 1812, in Esarey, *Messages and Letters of William Henry Harrison*, pg. 116, in *Indiana Historical Collections*, Vol. IX.
27. John Johnston in Leonard U. Hill, *John Johnston and the Indians*, (Piqua, Ohio, Stoneman Press, 1957), pgs. 182-3.

SKETCH VIII. One for the Road.

1. *Hymn to Ninkasi*, on University of Massachusetts-Amherst, website: https://people.umass.edu/mrenaud/kas/poem.htm, originally at Oriental Institute, University of Chicago.
2. George Washington notebook as a Virginia colonel (1757), The New York Public Library, Manuscripts and Archives Division, MssCol 23122, http://archives.nypl.org/mss/23122, on website: *George Washington's Mount Vernon*, www.mountvernon.org.
3. Harriet Taylor Upton, *History of the Western Reserve*, (Chicago - New York, The Lewis Publishing Co., 1910), Vol. 1, pg. 190.
4. Henry Howe, *Historical Collections of Ohio*, (Cincinnati, Ohio, C. J. Krehbiel & Co., 1907), Vol. 2, pg. 827.
5. Ibid.
6. Entry of September 4, 1794 in *General Wayne's Orderly Book*, in *Michigan Pioneer and Historical Society*, (Lansing, Michigan, Wynkoop Hallenbeck Crawford Co., 1905), Vol 34, pg 552.
7. Ibid.

8. Ibid., pg 557.
9. Ibid., pg. 558.
10. Ibid.
11. Entry in George McFeely: Diary, in Donald R. Hickey, *The War of 1812*, (New York, NY, Literary Classics of the United States, Inc., 2013), pgs. 158-9.
12. Julia Tevis citation in Goodridge Wilson, *Smyth County History and Traditions*, (Kingsport, Tennessee, Kingsport Press, 1932), pgs. 206-7.
13. Ben: Perley Poore, *The Rise and Fall of Louis Philippe, ex-King of the French*, (Boston, Massachusetts, William D. Ticknor and Co., 1848), pgs. 85-6.
14. Rhea Mansfield Knittle, *The Ohio Frontier Series*, (Ashland, Ohio, 1937), No. 1, pgs. 18-9.
15. George Sample citation in Nelson W. Evans and Emmons B. Stivers, *A History of Adams County, Ohio*, (West Union, Ohio, E. B. Stivers, 1900), pg. 124.
16. Ibid., pgs. 124-5.
17. Ibid., pg. 127.
18. Nelson W. Evans and Emmons B. Stivers, *A History of Adams County, Ohio*, (West Union, Ohio, H. B. Stivers, 1900), pgs. 480-1.
19. *Commemorative Historical and Biographical Record of Wood County, Ohio*, (Chicago, J. H. Beers & Co., 1897), pg. 368.
20. Ibid., pg. 185.
21. Howe, *Historical Collections of Ohio*, Vol. 2, pgs. 207-8.
22. Ibid. pg. 208.
23. Upton, *History of the Western Reserve*, Vol. 1, pg. 23.
24. Quote of Thomas Jefferson, in Paul Aaron and David Musto, *Temperance and Prohibition in America: A Historical Overview*, on website of The National Center for Biotechnology, NIH, National Library of Medicine, (Originally in John Kobler, *Ardent Spirits: The Rise and Fall of Prohibition*, New York: Putnam, 1973), pg. 33.
25. Harriet Taylor Upton, *History of the Western Reserve*, (Chicago/New York, Lewis Publishing Co., 1910) Vol. 1, pg. 345.
26. Norman B. Wood, *Lives of Famous Indian Chiefs*, (Aurora, Illinois, American Indian Historical Publishing Co., 1906), pgs. 674-5.
27. Ibid., pg. 675.
28. Bernd C. Peyer, *American Indian Nonfiction, An Anthology of Writings, 1760s – 1930s*, (Norman, Oklahoma, University of Oklahoma Press, 2007), pg. 235.
29. Henry Howe, *Historical Collections of Ohio*, (Cincinnati, Ohio, C. J. Krehbiel & Co., 1907), Vol. I, pg. 582.

SKETCH IX. Fightin' and Hangin' Around the Firelands.

1. Letter – Chas. P. Barnum to Zalmon Wildman, November 13, 1810, in Ohio History Connection Archives and Library.
2. John Garrison, *An Aged Pioneer*, originally published in the *Sandusky Register*, June, 1862; in *The Firelands Pioneer*, (Norwalk, OH, Fire Lands Historical Society, 1862) Vol. 3, pg. 77.

3. Ibid.
4. Charles Whittlesey, *Sketch of the Location, Settlement, and Progress of the City of Cleveland*, originally in *American Pioneer*, Vol. II, No. 1, January, 1843, in Fugitive Essays, (Hudson, OH, Sawyer Ingersoll and Co., 1852), pg. 222.
5. Hon. E. Whittlesey, *Execution of O'Mic*, June 24th, 1812, in Col. Chas. Whittlesey, *Early History of Cleveland, Ohio*, (Cleveland, OH: Fairbanks, Benedict, and Co., 1867), pg. 438.
6. Ibid., pg. 439.
7. Ibid., pgs. 439-40.
8. F. W. Fowler, *Reminiscences*, originally published in the *Sandusky Register*, March, 1859; in *The Firelands Pioneer*, (Norwalk, OH, Fire Lands Historical Society, 1862) Vol. 3, pg. 3.
9. Hon. E. Whittlesey, *Execution of O'Mic*, June 24th, 1812, in Col. Chas. Whittlesey, *Early History of Cleveland, Ohio*, (Cleveland, OH: Fairbanks, Benedict, and Co., 1867), pg. 440-1.
10. Julianna Long, *Statement of Mrs. Julianna Long*, June 14th, 1866, in Col. Chas. Whittlesey, *Early History of Cleveland, Ohio*, (Cleveland, OH: Fairbanks, Benedict, and Co., 1867), pg. 446.
11. Ibid., pgs. 448-9.
12. Hon. E. Whittlesey, *Execution of O'Mic*, June 24th, 1812, in Col. Chas. Whittlesey, *Early History of Cleveland, Ohio*, (Cleveland, OH: Fairbanks, Benedict, and Co., 1867), pg. 441.
13. Julianna Long, *Statement of Mrs. Julianna Long*, June 14th, 1866, in Col. Chas. Whittlesey, *Early History of Cleveland, Ohio*, (Cleveland, OH: Fairbanks, Benedict, and Co., 1867), pgs. 449-50.
14. Dudley P. Allen, *Pioneer Medicine on the Western Reserve*, 1886, in George E. Condon, *Cleveland - The Best Kept Secret*, (Cleveland, OH: J. T. Zubal & P.D. Dole, 1981), pg. 32.
15. An Ohio Volunteer (Anonymous), *The Capitulation or a History of the Expedition Conducted by William Hull, Brigadier-General of the Northwestern Army*, (Chillicothe, James Barnes, 1812), pg. 20.
16. Letter – Jno. H. Patch to Zalmon Wildman, August 25, 1812, in Ohio History Connection Archives and Library.
17. Letter – Jabez Wright to Zalmon Wildman, August 30, 1812, in Ohio History Connection Archives and Library.
18. Letter – Samuel S. Baldwin to Zalmon Wildman, September 6, 1812, in Ohio History Connection Archives and Library.
19. Letter – Jno. H. Patch to Zalmon Wildman, August 25, 1812, in Ohio History Connection Archives and Library.
20. Letter – Samuel S. Baldwin to Zalmon Wildman, September 6, 1812, in Ohio History Connection Archives and Library.
21. Ibid.
22. F. W. Fowler, *Reminiscences*, Sandusky, March, 1859, in *The Firelands Pioneer*, (Norwalk, OH, The Firelands Historical Society, 1862) pg. 5.

23. Hon. J. R. Giddings, *Remembrances*, Sandusky, May, 1859, in *The Firelands Pioneer*, (Norwalk, OH, Fire Lands Historical Society, 1862) Vol. 1, pg. 38.
24. Ibid.
25. Ibid., pg. 39.
26. Letter, Joshua R. Giddings, October 1, 1812, in *History of the Western Reserve*, (Chicago/New York, Harriet Taylor Upton, Lewis Publishing Co., 1910) Vol. 1, pg. 100.
27. Hon. J. R. Giddings, *Remembrances*, Sandusky, May, 1859, in *The Firelands Pioneer*, (Norwalk, OH, Fire Lands Historical Society, 1862) Vol. 1, pg. 40.
28. Ibid., pgs. 41-2.
29. Ibid., pg. 42.
30. F. W. Fowler, *Reminiscences*, Sandusky, March, 1859, in *The Firelands Pioneer*, (Norwalk, OH, The Firelands Historical Society, 1862) pg. 6.
31. Hon. J. R. Giddings, *Remembrances*, Sandusky, May, 1859, in *The Firelands Pioneer*, (Norwalk, OH, Fire Lands Historical Society, 1862) Vol. 1, pgs. 43-4.
32. Henry Howe, *Historical Collections of Ohio*, (Cincinnati, Ohio, C. J. Krehbiel & Co., 1907), Vol. I, pg. 565.

SKETCH X. The Stars Behind the Star Spangled Banner.

1. Joseph Hopper Nicholson in a speech delivered at Baltimore's Fountain Inn, May 6, 1812, Courtesy of the *Maryland Historical Society and the Baltimore City Archives*. On site, https://www.theamazingmendes.com.
2. Francis S. Key, *A Riddle*, in F. S. Key-Smith, *Francis Scott Key - Author of the Star Spangled Banner - What Else He Was and Who*, (National Capital Press, Inc., Washington D. C., 1911) pg. 103.
3. Letter – Major General Robert Ross to Earl Bathurst, August 30, 1814, in *Naval History and Heritage Command*, On site: https://www.history.navy.mil/research/library.
4. Joseph Pearce, Esq., in *A Log of the Proceedings of H.M. Ship Royal Oak, Joseph Pearce, Esq. Captain between the 6th September 1814 and 6th March 1815*. (ADM 51/2760, Captains Log, HMS Royal Oak, Public Records Office, The National Archives). On site: https://maryland1812.com/category/his-majestys-forces/.
5. *Francis Scott Key: Life and Times*, Edward S. Delaplaine, *Francis Scott Key: Life and Times*, (New York: Biography Press, 1937), pgs. 379-380; *Baltimore Patriot*, August 15, 1834.
6. Incidents of the War of 1812, *Maryland Historical Magazine*, Vol. XXXII. March, 1937. No. 1, pgs. 346-7.
7. P. H. Magruder, *The Original Manuscript of the Final Text of the "Star-Spangled Banner"*, United States Naval Institute Proceedings, June, 1927, Vol. 53/6/292.
8. Roger B. Taney, *Poems of the Late Francis S. Key, Esq., Author of "The Star Spangled Banner,"* (New York, Robert Carter & Brothers, No. 530 Broadway, 1857), pgs. 16-7.

9. Caleb Clarke Magruder, *Dr. William Beanes, the Incidental Cause of the Authorship of the Star-Spangled Banner*, (Records of the Columbus Historical Society, Washington, D.C., 1919), Vol. 22 (1919), pgs. 217-8.
10. Letter – Francis S. Key to Ann Phoebe Penn (Charlton) Key, September 2, 1814, in George H. Preble, *History of the Flag of the United States of America*, (Boston and New York, Houghton, Mifflin and Company, 1894), pg. 722.
11. Taney, *Poems of the Late Francis S. Key, Esq., Author of "The Star Spangled Banner,"* pgs. 20-3.
12. Letter, Armistead to Col. Henry Burbeck, May 3, 1811, Auctioned through Alexander Historical Auctions, September 9, 2014. On site, https://www.alexautographs.com/auction-lot/the-defender-of-fort-mchenry-erects-the-flagstaff_2D5A170D88.
13. Cate Lineberry, *The Story Behind the Star Spangled Banner*, in *Smithsonian Magazine*, March 1, 2007. On site, https://www.smithsonianmag.com/history/the-story-behind-the-star-spangled-banner-149220970/.
14. Letter – Caroline Pickersgill Purdy to Georgiana Armistead Appleton, Baltimore, 1876, National Museum of American History. On site, https://amhistory.si.edu/starspangledbanner/pdf/Caroline%20Purdy%20Letter%20transcript.pdf.
15. Ibid.
16. Letter – Lieut. Colonel Armistead to Hon. James Monroe, Secretary of War, Fort McHenry, Sept. 24th, 1814, National Museum of American History. On site: https://amhistory.si.edu/starspangledbanner/pdf/.
17. Norman B. Wood, *Lives of Famous Indian Chiefs*, (Aurora, IL, American Indian Historical Publishing Co., 1906), pgs. 706-7.

INDEX.

Adams, John, 327
Adams, John Quincy, 56
Adena, 15, 17
Africa, 1, 2, 24
Aged Women's Home, 350
Aix la Chapelle, 237
Akron, Ohio, 293, 311
Alabama, 25, 44
Alabama River, 25
Alaska, 19
Allegheny River, 96, 236
Allen, Dr., 307, 308
Allen, Dudley, 308
Alliance of Friendship, 235
American Farmer, 344
American Medical Association, 337
American Revolution, 31, 33, 43, 44, 48, 85, 95, 96, 99, 100, 113, 116, 137, 145, 150, 187, 189, 195, 212, 252, 253, 254, 256, 268, 274, 276, 279, 291, 293, 309, 337, 347 348, 349
Amherstburg, Ontario, 153
Anacreon, 327
Annapolis, Maryland, 338
Ancient Mariner, 181
Anglican Church, 64
Appalachian Mountains, 31, 48, 63, 96, 293 116, 188, 233, 243, 268
Appleseed, Johnny, 271
Appleton, Georgiana (Armistead), 348
Ariel (Ship), 153
Arkansas Territory, 345
Armistead, George, 336, 345, 346, 347, 348, 349, 350
Arnold, Benedict, 311
Ashley, Mrs., 30
Ashtabula County, 307
Asia (Asian), 1, 2, 20
Assunpink Creek, 133
Astor, John Jacob, 219

Ataorupagui, 14
Atkins, Virginia, 278
Atlantic Ocean (coast), 1, 19, 23, 24, 27, 116, 144, 148, 164, 187, 268, 274
Audubon, John James, 164, 165, 167, 176
Auglaize River, 210, 235
Augusta County, 27
Austintown, 307
Avery (Camp), 314, 316, 317, 318, 321
Aztec, 18
Babuan Islands, 21
Bahama Islands, 1
Baldwin, Sheriff, 304, 305, 311, 312, 315
Baltimore American, 326, 329, 335
Baltimore, Maryland, 325, 326, 328, 332, 334, 335, 336, 338, 340, 341, 343, 344, 346, 348, 350, 352
Baltimore Patriot, 329, 335
Baltimore Street, 343
Barclay, General Robert, 91, 153
Barney, Ann, 346
Barney, Commodore Joshua, 346, 349
Barnum, Charles, P., 294, 295
Barrel, The (Le Baril), 238, 239, 240, 241, 242
Barret, Captain, 296
Battle of Bladensburg, 330
Battle of Cowpens, 137, 138, 139, 140, 142, 143
Battle of Fallen Timbers, 85, 90, 223, 230, 276, 309
Battle of Lake Erie, 151, 152
Battle of Long Island, 121, 126
Battle of the Monongahela, 96, 99
Battle of Point Pleasant, 202, 252
Battle of the Thames, 92, 159, 353
Battlefield Park, 322
Beale, Philip, 24

Beanes, Dr. William, 332, 333, 337, 338, 339, 340, 341, 342, 343, 344
Belgium, 167
Bellefontaine, Ohio, 49, 104
Belt (ship), 1578
Benton, Thomas, 282
Benzie County, Michigan, 172
Beriga, 19, 20
Bering Sea, 20
Bering Strait, 25
Bentinck Isles, 22
Beaubien, Charles, 253
Bible, 95, 187
Bills, James S., 319
Black River, 321
Black Swamp, 309
Blackfeet, 8
Blackfish, Chief, 80, 81, 101, 107, 108, 109, 110, 113, 253
Blackman, Simeon, 319
Bladensburg, 331, 338, 342, 343
Bloom. James, 285
Blue Jacket, 50, 85, 207, 225
Blue Licks, 37, 38, 40, 41, 44, 47, 50, 51, 52, 81, 110, 116, 254
Bolivia, 19
Bombay, 22
Boone, Daniel, 27, 28, 35, 37, 38, 39, 40, 41, 43, 46, 47, 64, 67, 68, 74, 87, 93, 100, 102, 107, 108, 109, 111, 113, 114, 253
Boone, Jemima, 68
Boone, Squire, 111
Boone, William, 46
Boonesborough (Boonesboro), 29, 31, 35, 36, 37, 46, 67, 68, 74, 80, 101, 107, 109, 110, 111, 112, 113, 114, 160, 253, 278
Booth, John Wilkes, 182
Booth, Junius B., 179, 180, 181, 182
Boston, Massachusetts, 116, 117, 120, 121
Boston Massacre, 117
Bougainville, Charlotte Pemanpieh, 255, 256
Bowling Green, Kentucky, 58
Bowman, John, 35, 80, 81

Boyd's Ferry, 142, 143
Boyle, Captain, 221
Braddock's Defeat, 96
Braddock, Edward, 96, 97, 98
Brant, Joseph, 200
Broad River, 138, 139, 140
Brown, George, 349
Bristol. 129
Britain (England), 24, 32, 68, 87, 90, 96, 110, 188, 190, 232, 233, 234, 250, 261, 275, 295
British Union Jack, 325
Brodhead, Kentucky, 29, 74
Brooklyn (Heights), 121, 122, 123, 125
Brown Bear, 7
Brownstown, Michigan, 353
Bryan's Station, 36, 37, 41, 46, 114, 115
Buell, Daniel, 296, 297, 300
Buffalo, New York, 176, 285, 299, 310
Bull, Epaphras, 315
Bull's Island, 315, 316, 317, 318, 321
Bunker Hill, 116
Burbeck, Colonel Henry, 345
Buren, Martin Van, 90
Burke, 255
Burney, Thomas, 247
Burr, Aaron, 61, 311, 344
Bush, Mr., 280
Butler, General, 206, 207
Cahokia, 15, 16, 35, 72
Caldwell, William, 36
Caledonia (Ship), 157
Callaway, Captain, 112
Callaway (Sisters), 68
Cambridge, 116, 117, 118
Campbell, Arthur, 42, 43, 44
Canad, 3
Canada, 91, 150, 159, 167, 177, 213, 214, 233, 234, 236, 244, 246, 248, 249, 255, 256, 285, 295, 309, 310, 353
Canari, 13, 14

INDEX 369

Canfield, Ohio, 310
Capa (beaver), 9
Cape Girardeau, Missouri, 256
Caribbean Islands, 1
Carpenter, John, 72
Carter, Lorenzo, 300, 301, 302, 303, 304, 305, 306, 307
Carter, Mrs., 300, 301, 302
Carthage, 23, 24
Cass, Colonel, 309, 312
Castle William, 120
Catawba River, 140, 141, 142
Catholic Church, 249
Cayuse, 8
Cedar Creek, 68, 72, 75, 81
Cedar Point, 316, 317, 320, 321
Celeron de Bienville, 236, 237
Celilio Falls, Oregon, 5
Celtics, 25
Central America, 3, 18
Chainbearer, The, 166
Chaplin, Captain Abraham, 33
Chapman, Walter, 271, 272
Charlotte, North Carolina, 138
Chatham, Ontario, 91
Cherokee, 25, 29, 66, 85, 88, 202
Chesapeake Bay, 144, 145, 146, 147, 148, 325, 328, 329, 333, 334, 340, 343, 346
Chesapeake Flotilla, 333
Chicago, Illinois, 262
Chicago World's Fair, 291
Chickamauga, 85
Chickasaw, 15, 202, 203, 208
Chillicothe, Ohio, 80, 101, 103, 107, 108, 309
China, 20, 22
Chippewa, 26, 48, 177, 294, 297
Choctaw, 163
Christ, Jesus, 2, 272
Christian, Colonel, 43
CIA, The, 190
Cincinnati, Ohio, 48, 175, 176, 184, 189, 236, 256, 263, 284, 309
Civil War, 87, 315, 329

Claggetts (Brown's) Brewery, 349
Claggett, Eli, 349
Clark, George, 65, 66, 67
Clark, George Rogers, 33, 35, 43, 44, 46, 47, 49. 64, 72, 73, 80, 81, 87, 100, 101, 102, 254, 255, 256
Clark, Solomon, 81
Clarke, James, 179, 180, 181, 182
Clay, Henry, 282
Clayton, Mr., 184
Cleaveland, Moses, 150
Cleveland (Cleaveland), 150, 151, 290, 301, 302, 303, 305, 306, 310, 311, 312, 313, 315, 321, 323
Clinton, Sir Henry, 137, 149
Cochrane, Admiral Alexander, 334, 341
Cochrane, Thomas, 334, 340
Cockburn, Admiral George, 338, 340, 341, 343
Coe, Rev. Alvin, 292
Columbia (Ohio), 185
Columbus, Christopher, 1, 2, 4. 18, 23, 24, 25
Coeur d'Arlene, 8
Colbert, George, 203, 208
Colbert, William, 203, 208
Cold Foot, 242, 245
Coleman, Dr., 307
Coleman, Mrs. Mary, 184, 85
Coleridge, Samuel Taylor, 182
Columbian Exposition, 291
Com-sing-moon, 22
Conewango River, 236
Confederate POW Depot, 315
Congress, 211,
Congreve, William, 352
Conneaut, 307
Conneticut, 293, 294, 315
Continental (Confederation) Congress, 29, 196
Cooper, James Fennimore, 68, 166, 176
Cornplanter, 198
Cornstalk, 35, 49, 52
Cornwallis, 127, 128, 133, 138, 139, 140, 141, 142, 143, 144, 146, 147, 148, 149

Cotton, Captain, 317, 318, 319, 320
Coyote, 5, 6, 7
Crab Orchard, 68, 74, 79, 83, 88, 278
Craig, Captain, 44
Craik, James, 98, 99
Crawford, Colonel, 202
Creator, 63
Creeks, 25, 202
Croghan, George, 234, 235, 243
Cuba, 1
Cullop, Frederick, 278
Cumberland Gap, 67, 79, 81, 278
Curtis, Parke, 99
Cusicayo, 14
Custer's Last Stand, 207
Cuyahoga River, 150, 151, 152, 300, 301, 303
Dan River, 140, 142, 143
Danbury, Connecticut, 294, 312
Darrow, Rev. Mr., 303
Davies, Colonel William, 42
Davies, James, 82
Davies, Mrs. Samuel, 82
Davies, Polly, 82
Davies, Rev. Samuel, 99
Davies, Samuel, 81, 82
Dayton, Ohio, 262, 263
Deer Creek, 184, 185
Defence of Fort McHenry. 326
Defiance, Ohio, 210, 264
Denton, Mrs., 30
Delaware, 48, 202, 259
Delaware River, 127, 128, 129, 131
Delmonico's, 178
DeBarras, Count, 147, 148
DeBellestre, Sieur, 244, 245
DeBienville, Celeron 236, 237, 238, 239, 240, 241, 242, 243, 244
DeBonnecamps, Joseph Pierre, 238
Declaration of Independence, 347
DeCourtemanche, M., 239
DeContrecoeur, M., 239
Defense of Fort McHenry, The, 329
DeGrasse, Admiral, 144, 145, 146, 148

De La Rivière, Claude-Nicolas de Lorimier, 249, 250
Delaware, 235, 243, 294
DeLongueuil, Baron, 245
Denny, Major Ebenezer, 204, 205, 207, 208
DeQuindre, 110, 112, 253
DeRaymond, Charles, 242, 245
Detroit (Fort), 41, 71, 100, 106, 110, 150, 153, 185, 194, 200, 208, 213, 214, 234, 243, 244, 245, 246, 262, 309, 310, 311, 312, 323
Detroit, (ship), 153, 154, 158, 159
Devil, 61, 312
Devil Poc-con, 297
Di'Caprio, Leonardo, 220
Dick, Captain, 66
Dickens, Charles, 178
Dill, Captain, 309
Disciples of Christ, 288
Dix (Dick's) River, 29, 65, 66, 68
Dobbins, Daniel, 150, 151
Dominican Republic, 24
Donkey-Kong, 117
Dorchester Heights, 116, 117, 118, 119, 120, 121, 160
Drake, Mr. and Mrs., 83
Drake, Betsy, 83
Draper, Lyman, 34
Dred Scott Case, 339
Drouillard, Peter, 106, 107, 113
Dunbar, James, 282
Dunlap, Colonel, 309
Dunsmore, Lord, 29
East Indies, 2
East Harbor State Park, 316
East Point, 316, 318
East River, 121, 122, 125
Easter Sunday, 265
Eel River, 199
Egypt, 16
Elliot, Jesse, 153, 154, 156, 157
Eliot, Captain, 50
Empire Strikes Back, The, 220

Equador, 13
Erie, Pennsylvania, 150, 151, 153, 178, 236, 248
Erikson, Leif, 24, 25
Euclid, Ohio, 152
Euphrates River, 268
Europe, 1, 2, 231
Episcopalian, 258
Estill, James, 35, 36
Eustis, William, 260, 345
Evacuation Day, 121
Ewing, General James, 130
Exchange Hotel, 285
Faux, 174
Fayette County, 53, 54
Featherstonhaugh, George, 168
Federalist, 338
Ferguson, 334
Ficklin, Joseph, 115
Findlay, Ohio, 309
Firelands, 293, 294, 296, 308, 311, 312
Flatbush, 121, 123
Flatheads, 8
Flemmond (Flammond), John Baptiste, 295, 297, 298, 305
Flemmond's Cove, 296
Flower, Colonel Benjamin, 347, 348
Fontaine, John, 193
Fort Adams, 257
Fort Ancient. 16, 17
Fort Covington, 351
Fort Cumberland, 98
Fort Dearborn, 262
Fort Defiance, 223, 224, 257, 276
Fort Duquesne, 96, 247, 248
Fort Findlay, 309
Fort Finney, 48, 49, 50
Fort George, 346
Fort Hamilton, 215, 220
Fort Huntington, 151, 152
Fort Industry, 294
Fort Jefferson, 207
Fort Lafayette, 135
Fort La Presentation, 249
Fort Lawrence, 257
Fort Lexington, 36
Fort Loramie, 257
Fort Malden, 91, 150, 152, 285, 309, 353
Fort McHenry, 325, 326, 327, 329, 330, 332, 335, 336, 337, 344, 345, 346, 350, 352
Fort McIntosh, 48, 189
Fort Meigs, 90, 91, 152, 277, 284
Fort Miamis, 224, 225, 231, 234, 239, 241, 242, 245, 246, 258
Fort Michilimackinac, 234, 246, 262
Fort Niagara, 277, 345, 346
Fort Nonsense, 313
Fort Pitt, 33
Fort Piqua, 257, 258
Fort Randolph, 35
Fort Recovery, 257, 261
Fort Stephenson, 91
Fort Ticonderoga, 117
Fort Washington, 184, 185, 189, 190, 191, 193, 194, 197, 199, 203, 207, 215, 219, 256
Fort Wayne, 61, 191, 230, 257, 258, 259, 262, 263
Fountain Inn Hotel, 344
Fowler, Judge Frederick, 304, 305, 313
France, 28, 96, 149, 232, 233, 237, 279
Frankland (Franklin), 44
Franklin, Pennsylvania, 236
Frazier, Major, 314
Fremont, Ohio, 91, 314
French and Indian War, 27, 29, 63, 72, 96, 99, 248, 249, 252, 268, 273
French Creek, 236
Furrow, James, 257
Gallissoniere, Marquis de la, 237
Garrison, John, 298, 299, 300
Genesee River, 176
Georgetown, 330, 340
Georgia, 44
Germain, Lord George, 137, 140
Gibbs, Jonas, 296
Gibbs, Michael, 296, 297, 300

Gibralter, Straits of, 24
Giddings, Joshua, 313, 314, 315, 316, 317, 320, 321, 322
Gilmore's Lick, 81
Girty, James, 254
Girty, Simon, 36, 49, 50, 81, 105, 107, 114, 115, 254
Girty's Town, 254
Gist, Christopher, 243
Glass, Hugh, 220
Glouchester, 149
God, (Great Spirit, Creator), 9, 10, 26, 63, 95, 96, 99, 101, 106, 107, 150, 160, 161, 167, 179, 182, 284, 310, 313
Goodrich, Samuel, 171
Gordon, Rev. William, 118, 119
Grand Glaize, 210, 212, 224
Grand River, 306
Grant, Rebecca Boone, 46
Graves, Admiral, 146, 147, 149
Great Miami River, (Rock River), 49, 230, 234, 235, 236, 238, 240, 242, 254, 256, 257, 258, 259, 262, 264
Great Pyramid, 16
Greene, General Nathanael, 130, 141, 142, 143, 144
Greensboro, North Carolina, 141
Greenville, Ohio (Fort), 220, 222, 257, 261
Greenville Treaty, 226, 257, 293
Grizzly Bear, 7
Guayacamayas, 14
Guilford Courthouse, 141, 142, 143, 144
Gulf of Mexico, 233
Halifax, Nova Scotia, 332
Hall, Henry, 50, 51
Hamilton, Colonel Henry, 71, 72, 74, 253
Hamilton County, 220
Hamilton, Sergeant Thomas, 317, 318
Hammersmith, Mary Powell, 53
Hanover (street), 335, 343
Hardin, Colonel John, 192, 193, 194, 215
Hardin's Defeat, 193
Hardinsburg, Kentucky, 164

Harlan, (Harlin) Major Silas, 41, 43, 46, 47
Harmar, Josiah, 189, 190, 191, 192, 193, 194, 195, 196, 197, 198, 199, 205, 208, 224, 256
Harmar's Defeat, 192, 193
Harmon, J.B., 273
Harrison, Benjamin, 39, 41, 42, 254
Harrison, Burr, 70, 71
Harrison, William H., 61, 90, 91, 93, 159, 160, 262, 263, 265, 277, 284, 353
Harrod, James, 29, 34, 44, 64, 68, 74, 87, 93
Harrod, Mrs., 30
Harrod's Town (Harrodsburg), 29, 31, 33, 34, 36, 37, 58, 68, 72, 73, 278
Harvard University, 288
Haverstraw Bay, 137
Hawaiin Islands, 20
Hawley, Dr., 307
Hawley, Rev. Doctor, 265
Hayes, General, 313
Hayward, Susan, 56
Heart of the Monster, 5
Henderson, Kentucky, 58, 164
Henderson, Richard, 29, 44, 67
Hessians, 127, 128, 130, 131, 132, 160
Heston, Charlton, 56
Heyerdahl, Thor, 23
High Street, 344
Hill, Dr., 340
Hillsborough, North Carolina, 143
History of Kentucky, 38, 42, 47
HMS Erebus, 352
HMS Surprise, 334
HMS Tonnant, 334, 340, 341
Hogan, Mrs., 30
Holston River (Valley), 66, 71, 73
Hood, Admiral, 146, 147
Hopewell, 15, 16, 17
Hopi, 13
Houston, Peter, 46
Howe, General, 118, 119, 120, 121, 122, 127, 128

INDEX 373

Howe, Henry, 255
House of Orleans, 280
House of Tuscarawa, 280
Howell, Mary Ann Jones, 59
Hudson, Ohio, 308
Hudson River, 133, 134, 137
Hueston, Matthew, 220
Hull, General, 150, 262, 308, 309, 310, 311, 314
Huntington, Samuel, 151
Huron, 10, 12, 294, 296, 311, 312, 314
Huron County, 301
Huron Rangers, 296, 311
Huron River, 295, 296, 311, 313, 314, 320, 321
Illinois, 35, 59, 72
Impartial Female Humane Society, 350
Inca, 18, 19
India, 1
Indian Agency, 259, 263
Indian Ocean, 1
Indian Queen Hotel, 342, 343
Indiana (Territory), 59, 96, 106, 190, 346
Ingersoll, Charles, 334
Into, 19
Iraq, 267
Ireland, 27
Iroquis, 28, 163, 198, 200, 234, 235, 239
Irving, Washington, 219
Israel, 190
Jackson, Andrew, 51, 56, 57, 58, 178, 263, 282, 332, 344
Jackson, Rachel, 56, 57, 58
Jamieson, Captain, 22
Japan, 20, 21
Jefferson, Thomas, 288, 298
Jessup, Major, 152
Jesuit Missionaries, 163, 249, 250
Job, 95
Johnson, Colonel Richard M., 90, 91, 92
Johnson, Dr., 307
Johnson, Leonard B., 315
Johnson, Levi, 302

Jones, Horatio, 176
Jones, Major, 303, 304
Jones, William, 159
Johnston, John, 258, 259, 260, 261, 262, 263, 264, 265
Kamiah, Idaho, 5
Kanawa River, 236, 237
Kanehsatake, 249, 250
Kangi, (the crow), 9
Kaskaskia, 35, 72
Kekionga, 191, 192, 193, 194, 195, 196, 199, 200, 210, 230, 231, 233, 234, 235, 240, 243, 245, 248, 258, 259, 264
Kenton, Edna, 101
Kenton, Simon, 100, 101, 102, 103, 104, 105, 106, 107, 108, 113
Kentucky, 28, 29, 30, 31, 32, 33, 38, 44, 60, 65, 74, 75, 76, 79, 85, 86, 88, 89, 90, 94, 96, 106, 185, 202, 253, 268, 346
Kentucky County, 32, 33
Kentucky Gazette, 74
Kentucky River, 35, 65, 111, 112, 170
Keya (turtle), 9
Kenyon College, 263
Key, Francis Scott, 325, 327, 328, 329, 330, 331, 332, 333, 335, 336, 337, 338, 339, 340, 341, 342, 343, 344, 350, 352
Kibbe, Epraim, 218
Kickapoo, 203
King Edgar, 275
King George II, 232
King George III, 28, 29, 61, 187, 248, 353
King George III Proclamation, 28, 251
King George's War, 231
King Leopold II, 167
King Louis XV, 232, 237, 238
King's Ferry, 134
Kingsbury, Eunice, 177, 178
Kingsbury, Judge James, 177, 178
Knox, Henry, 116, 117, 201, 211, 212, 213, 214, 215
Kon-Tiki, 23
La Chine, 236, 249, 250

La Demoiselle, 234, 238, 239, 242, 247
Lady Provost, Prevost (ship), 152, 153, 158
Lake Erie, 91, 150, 152, 213, 229, 233, 236, 248, 257, 284, 285, 293, 294, 296, 297, 311, 315, 323
Lake Huron, 246
Lake of Two Mountains, 249
Lake Ontario, 91, 159, 177, 236
Lake Titicaca, 19
Lakota, 9
Lancaster, Pennsylvania, 235
L'Anguille, 200
L'Anse aux Meadows, 24
La Jonquiere, 244
Langlade, Charles, 246, 247
Largeau, Louis, 250, 253
Last of the Mohicans, 68
La-te-tel-wit (human beings), 6, 9
Lawrence, James, 153
Lawrence (ship), 153, 154, 156, 157, 158
Lenape, 259
Lexington, Kentucky, 37, 88, 220, 278, 288
Lexington, Massachusetts, 252, 337
Liberty Bell, 347
Liberty, (Ohio), 285
Licking River, 35, 37, 42, 46, 80, 253
Light, Jacob, 184, 185
Lima, Ohio, 209
Lincoln County, 88
Lindsay, 43
Little Miami River, 49, 58, 59
Little Turtle, 85, 207, 217, 224, 225, 259
Littlepage, Mordaunt, 166
Locust Point, Ohio, 297
Logan, Benjamin, 37, 41, 43, 44, 45, 46, 47, 49, 51, 52, 53, 54, 55, 64, 68, 71, 72, 74, 80, 87, 93, 105, 254, 255
Logan, Chief, 106
Logan, Mrs., 70
Logan's Fort (St. Asaph), 31, 36, 68, 69, 71, 72, 73, 81, 278
London, 328

Long Island, 121, 123, 124
Long, Dr. David, 305, 307
Long, Julianna, 305, 306, 307, 308
Long Woods, 161
Loramie Creek, 229, 230, 248, 249, 256, 264
Loramie, Peter, (Pierre-Louis de Lorimier), 249, 250, 251, 252, 253, 254, 255, 256, 257
Loramie's Station, 250, 253, 254, 255, 256, 257
Louisiana (Territory), 202, 203
Louisvile, Kentucky, 74, 164, 165, 179, 217, 278
Lower Piqua, 259
Lower Sandusky, 314, 317
Loyal Company, 232
Lytle, William, 51, 53
M16, 190
Macacheek (Maycockey) Towns, 49, 50, 51, 53
Mackinaw City, Michigan, 234
Mad River, 49
Madden, Sergeant, 130
Madison, James, 259, 260, 308, 309, 333, 340, 341, 345, 346
Madison, Major, 45
Madoc, 25
Magruder, P.H., 335, 336, 340
Malaysia, 1
Manchester, Ohio, 281, 282
Manhattan (Island), 121, 122, 123, 124
Manheim, 280
Manor, Paul, 227
Marblehead Lighthouse, 315
Marblehead, Ohio, 312, 316, 317, 322
Market (street), 335
Marietta, Ohio, 236, 284
Marshall, Humphrey, 38, 39, 42, 47
Martha (Passenger Pigeon), 183
Maryland, 126, 326, 346
Maryland's Paul Revere, 333
Mason, Alexander, 322

Masonic Lodge, 313
Massachusetts Bay Colony, 252
Maumee, (Miami) Ohio, 200, 276, 285, 321
Maumee River, (Miami), 61, 90, 190, 200, 210, 217, 218, 223, 224, 225, 227, 231, 246, 284, 285, 294, 295, 297, 298, 299, 300, 309, 312, 353
Maumee River Valley, 85, 195, 197, 198, 210, 215, 217, 218, 227, 230, 294, 300, 316
May, William, 215, 216, 219, 224
Maya, 18
Maysville, Kentucky, 281
McAfee, Robert, 159
McArthur, Colonel, 312
McBride, James, 220
McBryer, Andrew, 247
McClellan, Robert, 219, 220, 221, 222, 223, 224
McClure, Mr., 82, 83
McClure, Mrs., 82, 83
McDonald, Colonel William, 346
McFeely, George, 277
McGary, Edward, 27
McGary, Hugh, 27, 28, 29, 30, 32, 33, 34, 35, 36, 37, 38, 39, 41, 42, 43, 44, 45, 46, 47, 50, 51, 52, 53, 54, 55, 56, 57, 58, 59, 60, 67, 93
McGary, Mrs. Caty Yokum, 35, 59
McGary, Mrs. Mary, 30, 34, 35
McGate, John, 281, 282
McGate, Katy, 281, 282
McGate's Tavern, 282
McGunnigle, John, 92, 93
McKee, Alexander, 36, 49, 254
McKonkey's Ferry, 129, 130, 131
Meadowlark, 5, 6
Medes, 280
Medical and Chirurgical Faculty of Maryland, 337
Mediterranian Sea, 23, 24
Meigs, Return J., 151, 259, 309

Memeskia (Meemeehsihkia), 234, 235, 238, 239, 241, 242, 243, 244, 245, 248, 249, 251, 257
Mercer County, 53, 55, 56
Merril, John, 94
Merril, Mrs., 94
Merry, Ebenezer, 314
Mesopotamia, 267
Metis, 256
Mexico, 3
Miami-Erie Canal, 263, 264
Miami University, 263
Miamis, 210, 224, 230, 231, 235, 238, 239, 240, 242, 244, 245, 246, 247, 248, 251, 262, 264
Michigan (Territory), 96, 308
Milan, Ohio, 305
Miller, 61
Miller, Chris, 219, 221, 222, 224, 225
Miller, Henry, 219, 220, 221, 222
Minden (ship), 334, 336, 340
Mingo, 247
Mingus, Daniel, 322
Minutemen, 252
Mississippi, 56, 202, 203
Mississippi River, 15, 16, 31, 48, 188, 231, 233, 256, 261, 264
Mississippians, 15, 16, 17
Missouri (Horse), 169
Mohawk, 200
Moluntha, 49, 50, 51, 52, 53, 54, 55
Monk's Mound, 16
Monongahela, Old, 305, 307
Monongahela River, 96, 305
Monroe, Michigan, 90
Monster, 5, 6, 7, 8, 9
Montgomery, Alexander, 101, 102
Montgomery, John, 85
Montreal, 236, 249
Morgan, General Daniel, 138, 139, 140, 141, 142
Mossad, 190
Mountain Leader Trace, 203
Munsee, 294

Murrey, Dr., 308
Muskingum River, 236, 257, 280
Muskrat, 8
Nanticoke, 235
Napoleanic Wars, 90, 329
Nashville, Tennessee, 56, 85
Natchez Trace, 56, 57, 203
National Intelligencer, 329
Naval Academy (US), 335, 336
Navajo, 13
Near East, 23
Nearing, Guy, 285
Negosheck, 298
Netherland, Major, 43
New England, 167
New France, 164, 233, 237, 244, 245, 246, 249, 250
New Guinea, 1
New Hampshire, 177
New Jersey, 127
New Orleans, Louisiana, 56, 58
New River Company, 233
New York, 121, 125, 126, 127, 133, 144, 145, 149, 163, 176, 232, 298
New York City, 146, 147, 148
Newcomb, Lieutenent, 351
Newfoundland, 24
Newport, Rhode Island, 147
Nez Perce (Nimiipuu/ Tsoop-nit-pa-lu), 4, 5, 9
Niagara Falls, 166, 213, 214
Niagara River, 346
Niagara (ship), 153, 154, 156, 157, 158
Nickajack Expedition, 85, 86, 87
Nicholas, 233, 234
Nicholson, Joseph H., 326, 327, 335, 336, 351
Nicholson, Rebecca, 326, 336
Ninkasi, 267
Norfolk, 334
North America, 3, 4, 14, 15, 16, 18, 19, 20, 24, 25, 163, 165, 166, 182, 232, 233
North Carolina, 28, 29, 140, 143
North Point, 332

Northwest Territory, 188, 189, 259, 293
Northwestern Army, 159, 309
Nova Scotia, 232
O'Mic, John, 297, 298, 300, 301, 302, 303, 304, 305, 306, 307, 308, 311, 313
O'Mic (O'Mick), Old, 297, 301, 323
Ogdensburg, New York, 249
Ogontz, Chief, 296
Ogontz Place, 296, 298
Ohio, 49, 58, 85, 96, 185, 189, 190, 229, 235, 257, 258, 259, 260, 263, 264, 268, 274, 281, 282, 293, 294, 297, 303, 309, 346
Ohio Canal Commission, 263
Ohio Company, 232, 243
Ohio River, 15, 28, 31, 35, 47, 48, 54, 58, 59, 74, 80, 96, 101, 103, 107, 164, 184, 188, 189, 190, 196, 197, 198, 229, 236, 237, 238, 244, 252, 254, 264, 281, 284
Ohio (ship), 151
Ohio Valley, 48, 49, 189, 195, 199, 203, 231, 232, 233, 236, 238, 242, 245, 246, 248, 249, 250, 252, 256, 260, 264, 277
Ojibwe, 163, 246
Old Briton, 234, 246, 247, 248
Old Emperor, 93
Old Portage, 311
Old Stone Tavern, 278
Olney, Jack, 285, 286
Onondaga Lake, 163
Orontony, 233
Osage, 15
Ottawa, 26, 48, 209, 227, 243, 244, 246, 294, 295, 296, 298
Ottawa River, 209
Ouiatanonas, 199
Overton, John, 57
Owen, Asal, 104
Pachamama, 13
Pacific Fur Company, 219

Pacific Ocean, 19, 20, 21
Paris, 329
Parmatoony Creek, 323
Patch, John, 310, 311, 312
Painesville, Ohio, 306
Patapsco River, 325
Patterson, Colonel Robert, 53, 54
Pennsylvania, 33, 96, 126, 127, 128, 232, 244, 258
Peoria, 15
Perkins, Simon, 313, 321
Perley, 343
Perry Blockhouse, 261
Perry, Commodore Oliver, 21, 91, 150, 152, 153, 154, 156, 157, 158, 159, 160
Perry, Commodore Matthew, 21, 22
Perrysburg, Ohio, 285, 286, 309
Persians, 280
Peru, 19, 23
Petoskey, Michigan, 175
Pettengill, Sam, 296
Philadelphia Packet, 348
Philadelphia, Pennsylvania, 198, 337, 347
Phillipines, 1, 21
Philippe, (King) Louis, 279, 280
Phoenicians, 23, 24
Piamingo, 202, 203, 204, 207, 208
Piankashaw, 234, 248
Pickawillany (Fort), 235, 242, 243, 244, 245, 246, 247, 248, 249, 250, 251, 256, 257, 258, 259, 264
Pickersgill, Caroline, 348
Pickersgill, John, 348
Pickersgill, Mary Scott, 346, 347, 348, 349, 350
Pickersgill Retirement Community, 350
Pipe Creek, 296, 301
Piqua, Ohio, 230, 235, 258, 259, 260, 261, 262, 263
Pittsburgh, Pennsylvania, 33, 48, 96, 217, 236, 248, 308
Platt River, 172

Plough, the Loom, and the Anvil, The, 344
Point Pleasant, West Virginia, 35, 236
Pokagon, Chief Simon, 165, 172, 173, 174, 291
Poland, Ohio, 287
Polynesia, 20, 21, 23
Pond, Peter, 213, 214
Pope Clement XIV, 250
Port Clinton, Ohio 159, 293, 297
Portage River, 159, 297, 298, 299
Portsmouth, Ohio, 236
Potawatomi, 165, 290, 294, 316, 322
Potomac River, (Potowmack), 331, 340, 341
Presbyterian, 64
President (Ship) 334
President's Palace, 333
Presque Isle, 153
Princeton, Indiana, 59, 60, 133
Proctor, Colonel Henry, 90, 91, 151, 159
Prophet, The, 295
Prophetstown, 199
Ptan (otter), 9
Public Square, The, 302, 303, 304, 309
Pukeshinwa, 202
Purdy, Caroline Pickersgill, 347
Purdy, Henry, 348
Putnam, General, 283
Quaker, 258
Queen Elizabeth II, 167
Queen Charlotte, (ship), 152, 153, 154, 158, 159
Queen Mab, 181, 285, 286
Quigley, Captain, 321
Raisin River, 90, 312
Rall, Colonel, 131, 132
Ramsdell's (Farm), 315, 316, 317, 318
Ramsdell, Joseph, 316, 321
Ramsdell, Valentine, 316, 318, 319
Ramsoure's Mill, 140
Ranck, George W., 113
Rattlesnke, 7

Ray, James, 34
Ray, Mary Buntin, 28
Ray, William, 34
Red Banks, Kentucky, 58, 59
Reid, John, 321
Revenant, The, 220
Rhine River, 280
Richmond, Kentucky, 35
Robards, Lewis, 55, 56
Robards, Rachel Donelson. 56
Rochambeau, Comte, 145, 146, 147
Roche de Bouef, 224, 227
Rogue's March, 61
Rome, 23
Roosevelt, Theodore, 94
Root, Sergeant James, 317, 318, 319
Roslin Castle, 276
Ross, Hugh, 80
Ross, General Robert, 331, 332, 338, 339, 340, 341, 342, 343
Royal Navy, 145, 232, 332
Ruddell, Isaac, 71
Rush, Dr. Benjamin, 288
Russia, 20
Ryswick, 237
Salisbury, 141, 142
Sands, Samuel, 326, 329, 335, 336, 344
Sandusky Bay, 298, 312, 314
Sandusky (Ohio), 105, 233, 293, 295, 296
Sandusky River, 215, 292
Santo Domingo, 24
Sargent, Winthrop, 203, 207
Scioto River, 235, 236
Scots-Irish, 64, 65
Scott, General Charles, 199, 200
Second Great Awakening, 288
Semo, 298, 299, 300
Seneca, 198, 259
Seneca, Chief, 290
Seneca Lake, 176, 177
Serpent Mound, 16, 17, 18
Se-sak-khey-mekhs (Seven Devil's Mountain), 6

Severence, Mrs., 306
Shawnee, 17, 35, 47, 48, 49, 50, 52, 80, 91, 101, 107, 202, 207, 221, 225, 235, 241, 243, 247, 251, 252, 253, 254, 255, 256, 294
Shawnee Run, 58
Shawnee Springs, Kentucky, 34
Shelby, Isaac, 64, 85, 87
Shenandoah Valley, 65, 279
Shrapnel, Henry, 352
Siberia, 19, 20
Sillibaboo, 21, 22
Simms, 283
Simons, Abraham, 322, 323
Sioux, 9
Skaggs, 65, 74
Skaggs Creek, 66
Skinner, John S., 332, 333, 334, 335, 337, 340, 341, 343, 344
Skirmish on the Peninsula, 314
Skywalker, Luke, 220
Smith, General Samuel, 346
Smithsonian Institution, 175, 343, 352
Solo, Hans, 220
South America, 3, 4, 14, 15, 18, 19, 20, 23, 25, 285
Southhampton, 21, 22
Spain, Spaniards, 1, 2, 18, 20
Spafford, Amos, 321
Spafford's Exchange, 285
Sparks, Captain Richard, 202, 203, 204
Spencer, Oliver, 184, 185
Sportsman's Hill, 86, 87, 88
Spurr, Richard, 92
St. Clair, Arthur, 189, 191, 195, 198, 199, 201, 202, 204, 205, 206, 207, 209, 210, 212, 214, 217, 224, 256
St. Clair River, 246
St. John's Church, 265
St. Joseph River, 231, 276
St. Lawrence River, 236
St. Louis, Missouri, 16, 285

St. Mary's, Ohio, 254
St. Mary's River, 216, 222, 231, 234, 235, 246, 276
St. Patrick's Day, 121
Stanford, Kentucky, 68, 69
Star Spangled Banner, 326, 330, 334, 340, 349, 352
Staten Island, 121
Ste. Genevieve, 256
Steedman, William, 213
Stevens, Jacob, 34, 39
Stirling, General, 137
Stone, Irving, 56
Stony Point, 133, 134, 135, 136, 137
Stricker, General John George, 346, 349
Stricker, Martha Young, 346
Suchraquery, 235
Suffolk County, 121
Sullivan, Thomas, 120
Sumeria, 267, 268
Susquehanna Valley, 277
Swan Creek, 224
Sweet Breeze, 217
Syracuse, New York, 163
Tallmadge, Major Benjamin, 125, 126
Taney, Robert B., 339, 341
Taney, Anne Phoebe Charlton (Key), 339
Tarhe, (The Crane), 353
Tarleton, General Banastre, 138, 139
Tawis-karong, 11, 13
Ta-ya-mekhs (Cottonwood Butte), 6
Tecumseh, 90, 91, 92, 93, 152, 159, 199, 202, 203
Tennessee, 28, 29, 44, 85, 203
Tennessee Valley, 25
Tevis, Mrs. Julia, 278
Thames River, 91, 92, 159, 160, 161
Thomas, General, 118
To Anacreon in Heaven, 327
Tigris River, 268
Tijuskaha., 11, 12, 13
Tippecanoe, 262
Todd, Levi, 42, 43, 44, 45, 47

Todd, John, 37, 39, 40, 41, 42,
Todd, Robert, 42
Toledo, Ohio, 200, 224, 294
Toronto, 331
Town, Dr., 308
Trabue, Daniel, 111
Transylvania, 29, 44
Transylvania University, 288
Treaty of Fort Stanwix, 28, 188
Treaty of Paris, 150
Treber, Jacob, 283
Treber, John, 282, 283
Treber, Mother, 282, 283
Treber's Inn, 282, 283, 284
Trenton, 127, 128, 129, 131, 132, 133, 160
Trueman, Alexander, 215
Trigg, Stephen, 37, 39, 40, 41, 42, 43, 44
Trippe, 157
Trotter, Colonel James, 53, 54, 192
Trumbull County, 303, 307
Tuhm-lo-yeets-mekhs (Pilot Knob), 6
Turkey Creek, 138, 139
Tunisia, 24
Tuscarawa (Coshocton), 280
Tuscarawas River, 257, 280
Twightwee, 235, 247
Two Harbors, The, 315
Ulster, Ireland, 64
Union Jack, 346
United States, 21, 48, 95, 149, 159, 160, 188, 190, 197, 202, 210, 211, 212, 213, 226, 257, 259, 260, 294, 331
United States Army, 198, 226
United States Navy, 333, 351
Upper Marlborough (Marlboro), 337, 338, 339, 340, 341, 343, 344
Upper Piqua, 61, 258, 259, 262, 263, 265
Upper Sandusky, Ohio, 49, 50, 105, 297, 353
Utrecht, 237
Valley Forge, 337

VanCleve, 261
Verplank's Point, 134, 135, 136, 137
Vermillion, Ohio, 293, 310, 312
Vermillion River, 312
Vienna, Ohio, 303
Vincennes, Indiana, 35, 72, 73, 217, 234, 256
Vincennes, Monsieur de, 240, 241
Viracocha, 19
Virginia, 27, 28, 29, 31, 32, 33, 34, 43, 44, 53, 65, 66, 72, 75, 105, 142, 144, 145, 146, 147, 149, 190, 232, 244, 278, 279
Virginia General Assembly, 31
Virginia Museum of History and Culture, 236
Virginia Reel, 84
Wabash-Erie Canal, 264
Wabash River, 49, 190, 197, 199, 215, 234, 240
Wadsworth, General, 311, 313
Wakaynan, 14
Wakitumikie Town, 50
Wales, 25
Walhonding River, 280
Walnut Flat, 68, 72
Wappaatomika, (Ohio), 104, 105
War of 1812, 87, 150, 202, 259, 277, 284, 291, 334, 344, 346, 353
War of Austrian Succession, 231, 233
Warren, Ohio, 313
Washington Crossing, 129, 131
Washington, George, 97, 98, 99, 116, 117, 122, 123, 125, 126, 127, 128, 129, 130, 131, 132, 133, 135, 136, 137, 143, 145, 146, 147, 149, 160, 185, 187, 189, 190, 197, 198, 203, 204, 208, 210, 211, 212, 248, 273, 279, 349, 353
Washington (City/D.C.), 265, 297, 329, 330, 331, 333, 337, 338, 339, 341, 342, 344, 346
Washington, John, 98
Washington, Martha, 175
Washington's Indian War, 190, 191, 201, 203, 226, 258, 276

Waterville, Ohio, 224
Wayne, Anthony, 85, 90, 135, 212, 217, 218, 220, 222, 223, 224, 225, 226, 230, 256, 257, 258, 276, 309, 353
Wea, 199
Webster, Lieutenent, 351
Weems, Mr., 340
Wells, William, 217, 218, 219, 220, 221, 222, 223, 224, 269
West Indies (Caribbean), 144, 145, 274
West Point, 133, 134, 263
West, Maria Llyod (Key), 341
West, Richard, 339, 340, 341
West Virginia, 96
Western Reserve, 273, 287, 293, 294, 297, 301, 306, 308, 310, 311
Wheeling Creek, 236
Wheeling, West Virginia, 236, 281
Whig Party, 263
White, Captain Jacob, 219
White River, 238, 256
White's Station, 219
Whitley, Elizabeth, 67, 73
Whitley, Elizabeth (Senior), 73
Whitley, Esther (Fullen), 64, 65, 68, 69, 70, 72, 73, 76, 77, 78, 79, 80, 83, 86, 87, 88, 89, 93, 278
Whitley, Isabella, 67
Whitley, Levissa, 69
Whitley, Solomon, 73
Whitley, Solomon (Senior), 73
Whitley Station (House), 67, 72, 73, 74, 76, 77, 78, 81, 89
Whitley, William, 64, 65, 66, 67, 68, 69, 70, 71, 72, 73, 74, 75, 76, 77, 78, 79, 80, 81, 82, 83, 84, 85, 86, 87, 88, 89, 91, 92, 93, 278
Whittlesey, Elisha, 302, 303, 304, 306
Wilderness Road, 29, 74, 79, 81, 82, 83, 84, 85, 89, 278, 279
Wildman, Zalmon, 294, 295, 303, 310, 311
Wilkes County, 28

Wilkinson, General James, 199, 200, 215
Williams, Daniel, 193
Williams, Otto, 142, 143
Williamsburg, 73
Wilmington, North Carolina, 144
Wilson, Alexander, 170
Winchester, Virginia, 142, 279
Windsor, Ontario, 150
Wisher, Grace, 348
Wolcott, Benajah, 315, 316, 319, 320, 321, 322
World War II, 167
Wright, Jabez, 310
Wyandot, 10, 13, 48, 202, 233, 243, 251, 259, 353
Yadkin River, 28, 142
Yakima, 8
York, 331
York River, 149
Yorktown, Virginia, 139, 144, 146, 147, 148
Young, Benjamin, 347
Young, Eliza, 348
Young, Margaret, 348
Young, Rebecca, 347, 348, 349
Young, William, 347, 348
Youngstown, Ohio, 287
Zane, Ebenezer, 281
Zane's Trace, 281, 282, 284
Zanesville, Ohio, 174, 280

www.ingramcontent.com/pod-product-compliance
Lightning Source LLC
LaVergne TN
LVHW041654060526
838201LV00043B/433